Still Voices—Still Heard

Still Voices—Still Heard

Sermons, Addresses, Letters, and Reports
The Presbyterian College, Montreal, 1865–2015

J. S. S. Armour, Judith Kashul, William Klempa,
Lucille Marr, and Dan Shute, editors

FOREWORD BY
Professor Stephen C. Farris

WIPF & STOCK · Eugene, Oregon

STILL VOICES—STILL HEARD
Sermons, Addresses, Letters, and Reports
The Presbyterian College, Montreal, 1865–2015

Copyright © 2015 Wipf and Stock Publishers. All rights reserved. Except for brief quotations in critical publications or reviews, no part of this book may be reproduced in any manner without prior written permission from the publisher. Write: Permissions, Wipf and Stock Publishers, 199 W. 8th Ave., Suite 3, Eugene, OR 97401.

Wipf & Stock
An Imprint of Wipf and Stock Publishers
199 W. 8th Ave., Suite 3
Eugene, OR 97401

www.wipfandstock.com

ISBN 13: 978-1-4982-0831-4

Manufactured in the U.S.A.   09/17/2015

Legal deposit – Bibliothèque et Archives nationales du Québec, 2015
Legal deposit – Library and Archives Canada, 2015

New Revised Standard Version Bible, copyright 1989, Division of Christian Education of the National Council of the Churches of Christ in the United States of America. Used by permission. All rights reserved.

"Athletics and Religion" by James Naismith is reprinted with permission of The William L. Clements Library, University of Michigan.

Every effort has been made to trace the publisher of *The Indwelling Christ* for permission to reprint Pidgeon's sermon "The Word of the Cross;" if you have information regarding who to apply to for permission, please contact Wipf & Stock.

Contents

List of Illustrations | vii

Foreword by Professor Stephen C. Farris | ix

Preface by Principal Dale S. Woods | xv

Early Years

1. The College and the University: John William Dawson | 3
   By Harry Kuntz

2. The College and the Church: Donald Harvey MacVicar | 24
   By John P. Vaudry

3. The College and Missions: Jane Drummond Redpath | 44
   By Lucille Marr

4. The College and French Work: A. Daniel Coussirat | 63
   By Richard Lougheed

Middle Years

5. The College and the North: Andrew S. Grant | 81
   By William J. Klempa

6. The College and Athletics: James Naismith | 100
   By David S. Mulder

7. The College and Ecumenism: George C. Pidgeon | 117
   By Joseph C. McLelland

8. The College and Politics: W. G. Brown | 136
   By Dan Shute

Later Years

9   The College and the Nation: Cairine R. Mackay Wilson | 159
    By Andrew J. R. Johnston

10 The College and Chaplaincy: John W. Foote | 178
    By Thomas J. Hamilton

11 The College and the Pastor: C. Ritchie Bell | 198
    By Malcolm Campbell

12 The College and Women in Ministry: Alison Stewart-Patterson | 215
    By David Stewart-Patterson

13 The College and Missional Leadership: R. Sheldon MacKenzie | 228
    By Richard R. Topping

Lists: Our Graduates / Honorary Degrees / Faculty / Founders /
       War Memorials / Benefactors / Buildings / Governance /
       Staff / Student Societies / Lectureships | 251–297

Acknowledgments and Credits | 299

List of Illustrations

1 Sir William Dawson, CMG, FRS, FRSC (1820–1899), principal of McGill University, 1855–1893 | 3

2 Donald Harvey MacVicar, DD, LLD (1831–1902), principal of The Presbyterian College, Montreal, 1865–1902 | 24

3 Jane Drummond Redpath (1815–1907) | 44

4 The Reverend Professor A. Daniel Coussirat, DD (1841–1907) | 63

5 The Reverend Andrew Shaw Grant (1860–1935) | 81

6 The Reverend Dr. James Naismith, MD, MPE, DD (1861–1939) | 100

7 The Very Reverend George C. Pidgeon, DD, LLD (1872–1971) | 117

8 The Reverend Walter George Brown, MP (1875–1940) | 136

9 Senator Cairine Reay Wilson, née Mackay (1885–1962) | 159

10 Lieutenant Colonel the Reverend John W. Foote, VC, CD, DD (1904–1988) | 178

11 The Very Reverend Professor C. Ritchie Bell, DD, DCL (1905–1982) | 198

12 The Reverend Lady Alison Stewart-Patterson, LRAM, BTh, STM, DMin (1931–1992) | 215

13 The Reverend Professor R. Sheldon MacKenzie, PhD, DD (1930–2012) | 228

Foreword

It is an honour to be invited to write a foreword to this collection of essays gathered both as a celebration of and a theological reflection upon the one hundred fifty years of service to the church and world of Presbyterian College, Montreal. I sense that honour particularly strongly since I have passed much of my teaching career at the "Other Place," namely the friendly rival of "PC," Knox College, Toronto. I do not know whether it is the secondhand righteousness of fathering a son who is a graduate of Presbyterian College or the fact that I am serving, at the time of writing, as Moderator of the 140th General Assembly, which has elicited this signal honour. In case it is the latter, it is my pleasant duty to congratulate on behalf of the national church the editors of and the contributors to this fine collection for their excellent efforts. More importantly, it is both my duty and my strong inclination to give thanks to God on behalf of the church for the work of ministers and other leaders of the church who have been shaped for service by Presbyterian College during those one hundred fifty years. Where would we be without PC?

Some of the more notable of those ministers and leaders are the subjects of the thirteen biographical essays contained in this volume. Any theological college, let alone one so notable as Presbyterian College, is more than its graduates. A college consists also of its teachers and administrators, of its supporters and benefactors and also of those who are shaped by its influence in wider society. The subjects of these essays include examples of all these different kinds of members of the college community.

Some of the subjects are well known to the wider world, most notably James Naismith, the originator of basketball. Others have fallen into undeserved obscurity but all deserve our interest. A particularly valuable feature of the book may be that most chapters include a sermon, address or report composed by the subject plus a useful commentary on those compositions. In this way the cleverness of the title of the collection becomes manifest. All the voices are "still," that is, all the subjects have died. But through these sermons and addresses included in this volume, those still voices are also "still heard."

As the reader will note, the essays are gathered into broad groupings according to chronology. The first such grouping covers the early years of Presbyterian College. Though always a small college in a large city, Presbyterian College was not a small-minded or closed, sectarian institution and its influence was greater than enrollment numbers might suggest. It was founded by people who were key members of the English-speaking community of Montreal and thus of Canada as a whole. Younger readers may not know, and older readers may have forgotten, that for much of the period covered in this book, Montreal, not upstart Toronto, was the largest and certainly the most cosmopolitan city in Canada. (Many will claim that it remains the latter!) Presbyterian College was shaped by people who helped shape the city and thus also the wider society of Canada. Perhaps the most notable of the founding circle was Sir John William Dawson, noted geologist, Fellow of the Royal Society, and for four decades principal of McGill. Dawson made a college whose precincts were a cow pasture when he arrived into a first-class university of world standard. Such a scholar would have no interest in founding an institution which would shut itself off from the intellectual currents around it. The book then turns to Donald MacVicar, who taught the first classes at PC and who soon became its principal. MacVicar shaped the early life of the college more than any other individual. There follows a valuable chapter on the life of benefactor Jane Drummond Redpath, who involved herself deeply in the support not only of the college but of Christian ministry and mission in general. She took the path of service available to women of her time and station in life, that is, the active support of good causes. A comparison of this chapter with the study of Rev. Alison Stewart-Patterson, who lived in an era when ordination had become open to women, would be instructive. Given the ardent commitment evidenced in and the clarity of thought and expression of the reports authored by Mrs. Redpath, one might be justified in wondering whether she would have sought ordination had that possibility been available in her time. It certainly appears that she would have been an effective preacher. One emphasis of the period that emerges in several of the essays is a marked interest in mission to the French population of Quebec. In our more ecumenically minded days such an emphasis would be suspect, but in those times of confrontation between an aggressive and confident Protestantism and a very conservative or "ultramontane" form of Roman Catholicism, the emphasis is more easily understood. The final chapter in this grouping, on French Protestant preacher Daniel Coussirat, explores this matter thoroughly.

The next grouping covers the middle years of the college's existence. Here Presbyterian College nurtures the leaders for a growing and expanding Protestant society in Canada and indeed in North America. The section begins with the work in the North of Andrew S. Grant. The author of this chapter does valuable service in bringing to light the life of one whose contributions have been allowed to slip into undeserved obscurity. Obscurity is scarcely the word to apply to the work of the subject of the next chapter, James Naismith, the inventor of basketball. It happens that this foreword is being written during "March Madness" when millions across North America obsess over the quest to become champion of American university basketball. It also happens that Kansas, the university where Naismith became the first basketball coach, lost in a marked upset as these words were written. Naismith would probably take the loss with greater equanimity than rabid present-day fans, not only because he would be the only coach of hoops at powerhouse Kansas with a career losing record, but because he viewed all sports, including the one he created, primarily as instruments in the development of Christian character.

If, with Naismith, we move beyond the boundaries of the nation, with the next subject, George Pidgeon, we move beyond the limits of the Presbyterian Church. Pidgeon was chair of the Union committee that helped bring to birth the United Church of Canada and served as that denomination's first moderator. The primary audience for this collection will be Presbyterian, of course, but this essay will also be of particular interest to members of the United Church who wish to trace the origins of their denomination. We then are introduced to a staunch anti-Unionist, W. G. Brown, one of the leaders of the resistance to Church Union who ensured that there would be a continuing Presbyterian Church. More will be written of Brown shortly.

The final grouping brings us into the latter years of the college's existence. This section reminds us that Cairine Wilson, first female senator of Canada and advocate for the needs of refugees, though not a graduate of Presbyterian College, was a benefactor of the college and, more significantly, an outstanding example of the kind of person nurtured by its teaching and witness. Possibly the second most famous graduate of the college, John Foote, is the subject of the next essay. Foote was well known as the recipient of the Victoria Cross, then the highest award for heroism available to Canadians, for his valour during the catastrophic Dieppe Raid of 1942. Paradoxically, he is also perhaps the least known of the subjects of the book, for he left very little in writing. There follows a study of the ministry of Ritchie Bell, professor and acting principal, who helped develop a pastor's heart in so many of the graduates of his era. If PC graduates of Bell's time had a reputation for being caring pastors, and they did, it may have been primarily due to Ritchie Bell. We then turn to an essay on the life and ministry of a woman graduate of the college, Rev. Alison Stewart-Patterson, mentioned earlier in this foreword. By contrast to Jane Drummond Redpath, we need not speculate on her path to ordination and her skills as a preacher are manifest in one of her sermons included in this chapter. The final chapter in the book discusses the work of Sheldon MacKenzie, a graduate of the college and a long-serving professor of New Testament in several settings. A college should not simply turn out caring pastors; it should produce scholars. John Knox is reputed to have said, "Every scholar is something added to the treasure of the commonwealth." Presbyterian College helped Sheldon MacKenzie become "something added."

When I received the manuscript of this book, I noted in the table of contents the name of one person to whom I had a personal connection, though he died before I was born and I had no direct knowledge of him whatever. This was W. G. Brown, minister of St. Andrew's Church, Saskatoon, and also, late in his life, member of Parliament. Brown had an immense influence on many people in his city, from many walks of life, among them students at the University of Saskatchewan, some of whom were led to prepare for the ministry. One of those students was my late father, Allan Farris. (Many years later that same Allan Farris would be awarded the DD *honoris causa* by Presbyterian College, an honour he valued highly. But that is an aside.) The relationship between the young theological student and the veteran preacher was significant enough that at some point after Brown's sudden and untimely death, my father came into possession of the preaching gown presented to Brown on the occasion of his election as moderator of the General Assembly. My father did not wear the gown himself, however, since Brown was a larger man than my six-foot-one-inch-tall father. There arose an occasion many years later, however, when I myself needed a preaching gown as a theological student. Since I was considerably taller and more heavily built than my father, finding one that would fit was a difficult task and the finances of my student days certainly did not permit me to order a custom-made garment. Brown's gown fit well, however, and was loaned to me by my father to wear during a student-in-ministry year in a coal-mining town in West Virginia. I did so with a sense of pride.

I returned the gown to my father's possession when I was presented with new vestments as a gift marking my own graduation from seminary. Consequently, I do not know what has become of that gown. As I recall, it was not among my father's effects when we went through them after his own death shortly thereafter. Perhaps he passed it on to another student, which would have been fitting. It may be, however, that this little tale (or not so little considering the size of the garment in question) may remind us of a larger and more enduring truth. In the church we always wear borrowed garments, garments of tradition, practices and modes of thinking passed down to us by those we may not know. But whether we know them or not, we are their debtors. I am grateful that this volume serves to raise our knowledge of thirteen of the most notable of those forebears, all of them part of the heritage of Presbyterian College, Montreal.

Let their names be held in honour and *Soli Deo Gloria, to God alone be the Glory.*

Stephen Farris

Dean, St. Andrew's Hall, Vancouver School of Theology
Moderator, 140th General Assembly
Presbyterian Church in Canada
Vancouver, Spring 2015

Preface

In the fall of 2013 a committee of faculty and friends of the college met to discuss the 150th anniversary of the Presbyterian College, Montreal, to be celebrated in 2015. Various ideas were discussed and it was agreed that the college could be celebrated in four interrelated ways. The first would be "telling our story," communicating the long and rich history of the college. The second would be "celebrating our story," with a number of special and significant events over the calendar year of 2015. The third would be "continuing the story," highlighting the new strategic plan of the college and the financial campaign that would help build the foundations of a new direction to serve the church and the world. The fourth would be "connecting the story," focusing on maintaining and strengthening relationships with the alumni and friends of the college.

A committee dedicated to the story of the Presbyterian College was formed and tasked and soon became known as the Book Editorial Committee. The committee discussed various ways we might tell our story. The college already had a short history written by Professor H. Keith Markell entitled *History of the Presbyterian College, Montreal 1865–1986*. It was first suggested that this period of history be researched more thoroughly and that the years from 1986 to 2015 be added to create a new and updated history of the college. As discussion continued, it became clear that a chronological history of the college was only one way to tell the story of the college. Another and perhaps more dynamic way to tell the story would be to try to capture the spirit and passion of those who helped shape the life of the college and those who graduated from the college and helped shape the life of the church and the world, and to let them speak in their own words. By doing so it was hoped that those who read the book would find their own spirits and passions rekindled. Thus the title of the book evolved to be *Still Voices—Still Heard*.

In reviewing the many friends, faculty, and graduates of the college over a century and a half, difficult choices were made to reduce the book to only a few people who would illustrate the quality, commitment and character of those who helped build Presbyterian College and those who graduated from the college and committed themselves to serve God in the church and in the world, sometimes at great cost to themselves.

In the Acts of the Apostles, Paul, in one of his speeches to the crowds, summarizes King David's life in these words: "For David, after he had served the purpose of God in his own generation, died."[1] Paul's words are true of all of us. We are part of a particular generation and it is in that generation that we are called to serve God. We both contribute to the generation in which we live and are influenced by it. In many cases the contributions made by the men and women in this book far exceeded their own generation. In order to deal with the historical context and the contributions that went beyond that context, the committee decided on thirteen themed chapters that chronologically tell the history of the Presbyterian College through the voices of the past that are still relevant today. Each chapter begins with a carefully researched biographical summary that places each person within his or her own generation. This is followed by a sermon, letter, report or address written by the historical figure that expresses something of the beliefs and passion that undergirded their sense of commitment and their particular contribution. Each chapter concludes with a brief reflection from the perspective of the biographer on the words of the "still voice" and our own day and time, and what these voices still have to say to us today.

By choosing to tell our story in this way we hope that our readership will discover the significant contributions made through Presbyterian College as well as something of the spirit that has been part of the life of the college in the continuum from its very beginning through its one hundred and fifty years. As anyone who has worked in the church knows, one of the great challenges is how to understand the role of tradition. It is possible to use tradition as an anchor that holds us in one place once and for all. But it is also possible to use the best of our tradition as a rudder that guides us into a new future. As the stories in this book indicate, one of the best traditions of the Presbyterian Church in Canada is the Reformation understanding that the calling of the church is in the world. Throughout the book there are numerous examples of those who committed themselves to making the world a better place for all, whether through education, sports, or concern for the needy in many different settings across Canada and beyond. Their desire was not simply an attempt to make a difference in the world; their stories demonstrate their longing to be connected to the difference they believed God was making and desired to make in the world.

1. Acts 13:36 NRSV.

I believe this sense of being missional is built into the DNA of the Presbyterian Church in Canada. True, we may have let the flames of mission dampen somewhat, but these stories remind us that we have a rich history of laity and clergy who took risks, pioneered new forms of ministry and demonstrated the desire for collaboration with others for the sake of the world and the Gospel. The scope of this book, therefore, is not simply historical. It directs us to the future in which we are invited to recapture this spirit of mission, risk-taking, pioneering and collaboration. It invites us to live our own lives with a deep passion for the Gospel, committing ourselves to our congregations, communities and the wider world.

We envisioned a broad readership in compiling this work. The sermons will be of special interest to those who preach or study preaching. The historical background provides valuable research for those interested in church history. Members and adherents of the Presbyterian Church in Canada will find it a rich resource in understanding the broader contribution that Presbyterians have made in the church and in the world. Those interested in the mission of God will find numerous examples of God using different kinds of people with a variety of gifts to bless the world. And those who wonder what the future holds for the church in North America will find encouragement in the various stories of perseverance, faith, courage and imagination.

Readers will note the depth, breadth and variety in the sermons reproduced here. They are a study in themselves. The sermons show the evolution of the sermon from a rather formal oration of one hour in length to the final one which is almost poetic in its narration, style and content. A study of the evolution of sermons over the history of the college is embedded in this book. This is a historically valuable resource on the sermons of still voices.

When D. H. MacVicar agreed to be the first principal of the Presbyterian College in 1865, he was reluctant to undertake the challenge because he had reservations regarding the viability of the institution. He could hardly have imagined the impact the college would make over the next one hundred and fifty years with one thousand graduates and 273 honorary Doctors of Divinity, as well as the numerous laypeople who took courses through the college. This book highlights thirteen voices of graduates, benefactors and friends of the college. Their contributions do not eclipse the contribution of those who went on to serve congregations of all sizes and in various locations across Canada and around the world, or those who chose vocations in chaplaincy, teaching and international ministries outside of the pastorate. Thus the book concludes with an exhaustive list of alumni, faculty and staff who are also integral to the story of Presbyterian College.

I wish to acknowledge the people who committed their time and energy to bring this book to completion. The writers include faculty, clergy and laity. All gave their time freely over and above their regular work. The college is indebted to them for their generosity and commitment to this project. In particular I would like to thank Judith Kashul, James Armour, Lucille Marr, Dan Shute and William Klempa, whose dedication made this book a reality.

As the college looks to the future, its one desire is to reignite the sense of mission that undergirds the stories in this book with the hope that it may also be said of us: "They served the purpose of God in their own generation."

Dale Woods, Principal

The Presbyterian College, Montreal

April 2015

Early Years

CHAPTER 1

The College and the University
John William Dawson

By Harry Kuntz

Sir William Dawson, CMG, FRS, FRSC (1820–1899), principal of McGill University, 1855–1893. Picture taken in the 1880s by William Notman, credit McGill University Archives PR009076.

"THE REAL CREDIT FOR founding the institution would rightly seem to belong to one of Canada's most distinguished sons, that far-seeing educationist, Sir William Dawson."[1] So wrote J. H. MacVicar in the biography of his father. Dawson gave substance to the possibility of a theological college in Montreal for Presbyterians. In a December 1863 letter, Dawson told John Redpath, one of the prominent lay leaders of the Free Church movement in 1844, about the possible constitution of the college and the increased influence Montreal would have in the missionary effort in Lower Canada. Then he added, "The University here would be more useful to the Presbyterian Church, and on the other hand would be strengthened by such usefulness. If the institute were affiliated to the University its principal would have a seat in the corporation, and its students would have such privileges as would enable them to take the degree in Arts without interference with their theological studies."[2]

In his 1855 inaugural address as principal of McGill University, Dawson twice alluded to the possibility of affiliated theological colleges: "The department of Theology cannot be introduced into McGill College, but the advantages of the institution are available for all the preliminary training of a secular character that may be required; and by the provisions of its statutes for the affiliation of other institutions, it offers its assistance to any theological seminaries that may be erected in the vicinity."[3] The provision of the 1854 statutes of the Corporation of McGill permitting the affiliation of other institutions with McGill University proved beneficial to the nascent theological colleges. A meeting was held in Redpath's home in January 1864 attended by Revs. D. H. MacVicar and A. F. Kemp and seven laymen, Principal J. W. Dawson, John Redpath, Joseph Mackay, Laird Paton, George Rogers, Warden King and John Sterling. There Dawson was named head of a committee to prepare a preliminary proposal for a theological college. At a meeting in February 1864 at the home of John Becket, Dawson reported that "McGill in its Arts course was prepared to give as cordial recognition to students of affiliated Theological Colleges" as students in the other professional faculties "throwing open to them its library, museum, scholarships, medals and class rooms. An advanced training in the so-called 'Humanities' could thus be secured without depriving candidates for the ministry of the advantage of wholesome contact with young men looking toward other professions, and without imposing on the Church a load of financial obligation for secular education which it would not be disposed to assume."[4]

1. MacVicar, *Life and Work*, 75.
2. Ibid., 75–76.
3. Dawson, *Collegiate Education*, 23.
4. MacVicar, *Life and Work*, 65.

In 1864 the Congregational College moved from Toronto to Montreal and affiliated with McGill in 1865. The Presbyterian College obtained a charter in 1865, began teaching in 1867, and affiliated with McGill in 1868. The Wesleyan College began teaching in 1873 and affiliated with McGill in 1879. The Montreal Diocesan College established in 1873 was affiliated with McGill in 1880.[5]

In a June 1891 memorandum on the question of free tuition in arts, Dawson wrote, "As to the Theological Colleges, we are only giving a privilege which every other University gives, and on terms on which any University would be glad to take from us all our students of this class, because it is well known that a connection of this kind is a principal means of bringing students not to Arts only but to all Faculties. The connection of these Colleges to the University has been effected largely by my own exertions, and I consider it a main stay of the prosperity of the Faculty of Arts."[6]

In a "Memo on Theological Free Tuitions Prepared for Peter Redpath, May 1892," Dawson wrote, "The matter is one vital to the prosperity of the Faculty of Arts, which now depends on the support of the Theological Colleges and the bodies they represent, more than any other influence for its success as regards Ontario competition." He added that "no educational function can be higher or more honourable than that of providing a highly educated Christian ministry for this province in which the Protestant religion, owing to its being the faith of a scattered minority, is exposed to so many difficulties. Yet McGill has been doing no more in this direction than the Universities of Ontario, and less than many of those in the United States."[7]

John William Dawson (usually William) was born October 13, 1820, in Pictou, Nova Scotia, the elder son of James Dawson (1789–1861) and his wife Mary Rankin (d. 1854), both born in Scotland. William's brother, James, was born in 1824 and died in 1837. William married Margaret Ann Mercer Young (c. 1828–1913) March 19, 1847, in Edinburgh Scotland. They had six children: four sons born in Pictou and two daughters born in Montreal.

Religion was a constant in the Dawson family life. James and his brother Robert were the founders of the Pictou Sabbath School movement. William credits his father as an active "worker in Bible Society, Missionary, Sunday School, and Temperance enterprises." And, he "ever retained a warm sympathy with movements in favour of Christian union, peace, free trade, and the abolition of slavery. . . . [He] became active in the face of

---

5. McGill Archives Index: R.G. 90: Affiliated Educational Institutions.
6. Dawson, *Memoranda and Statements*, 2.
7. Ibid., 5–7.

much opposition, in establishing a temperance society."[8] James was an elder in Harbour Church (later Prince Street Church) Pictou.

William said that the death of his younger brother aroused his religious feelings. Religion was a constant in his life. It has been suggested that as an only son his religious sense of duty to help repay his father's debts prevented him from entering the ministry.[9] His addresses to the Pictou Total Abstinence Society, published in 1848 were reissued in a third edition in 1898.[10] Because of his abstinence William was known as a "water-man" in Montreal. He taught large Sunday school classes and prepared Sunday school class literature. Frank Dawson Adams referred to William, a steadfast evangelical, as "a Presbyterian of the old school."[11] William's autobiographical notes are prefaced with Psalm 71:17, "O God, thou hast taught me from my youth, and hitherto have I declared thy wondrous works."[12]

William attributed his interest in natural history to his home life. "My early home had much in it to foster studies of nature, and both my parents encouraged such pursuits. . . . Nothing pleased my father more than to take an early morning hour, or rare holiday, and wander through such places with his boys, studying and collecting their treasures."[13] He related natural history to his religious belief using the words of Psalm 104:24: "O Lord, how manifold are Thy works; All of them in wisdom thou hast made!"[14] At an early age he began collecting shells (mollusks), fossils, insects, rare birds and native plants. William also strolled with his family. His daughter Anna wrote that he "frequently took short excursions on Saturday to places of interest, geologically or botanically and my brother & I used to go also—when we would be set to hunt for some rare violet to be found in that locality, or to search for small shells on a hillside or trilobites in the rocks or leda[?] shells in the blue clay."[15]

William remarked on his father's "strong zeal for education." He stated, "At a time when he was in straitened circumstances, my father contributed liberally in aid of educational institutions, then being established in Pictou,

---

8. Dawson, *Fifty Years*, 12.
9. Eakins and Eakins, "Dawson."
10. Dawson, *Testimony of the Holy Scriptures*.
11. Adams, *Memoir*, 557.
12. All Scripture references in the chapter are KJV.
13. Dawson, *Fifty Years*, 21.
14. These words were inscribed on the Peter Redpath Museum at McGill and appear to be paraphrases from the KJV.
15. Michel, "Anna Dawson Harrington's Memoir," 182, bracketed question mark in the original.

with a view to securing their benefits for his sons."[16] William went to the Grammar School and Pictou Academy, which under the Rev. Thomas McCulloch offered a liberal education and had a library, museum and instruments for the illustration of physical sciences. McCulloch encouraged his collecting and study of geology and McCulloch's son taught him to prepare specimens of birds, butterflies and insects. William studied geological and mineralogical works by Lyell, de la Beche, Phillips, and Moh, and took longer excursions in Nova Scotia. He became known for his geological and mineralogical collections and exchanged specimens with other collectors.

After working with his father in the printing business, William went to Edinburgh in 1840–41 to study natural history. On his return he was introduced to Sir Charles Lyell and spent a month with him on geological exploration. Recognizing the accuracy of Dawson's observations, Lyell encouraged him to publish his findings. In 1846 William returned to Edinburgh to study chemistry to help with his explorations on behalf of various mining enterprises. In March 1847 he married Margaret Mercer, whom he had met in 1840–41. After returning to Pictou, he lectured on natural history at the Pictou Academy, the Pictou Literary and Scientific Society, and Dalhousie College and published a handbook on the geography and natural history of Nova Scotia.[17] Among other mining assessments, William evaluated the prospects for coal in southern Cape Breton for the government of Nova Scotia.

In early 1850 William Young and Joseph Howe offered William the position of superintendent of education for Nova Scotia established under the Act for the Encouragement of Education. In preparation for the task William visited schools and normal schools in New England and the state of New York. He developed a vision of education that centred on a normal school for the training of teachers, a standard curriculum and an assessment basis of taxation for schooling. He recognized the value of young women in elementary education and believed that a normal school would make teaching more accessible to them and when they married would provide wives and mothers with a superior education. Travelling in Nova Scotia William was able to combine his interest in geology with his visits to schools and school districts. In his 1850 Preliminary Report William wrote, "The nature of the duties of my office and its limited powers, as well as the state of the schools, have required me to act rather as an educational missionary than in a merely official capacity. . . I have been obliged . . . to prepare the public

---

16. Dawson, *Fifty Years*, 19.

17. Dawson, *Geography and Natural History*. A sixth edition was published in 1863. He had the map of Nova Scotia lithographed for the book while in Edinburgh.

mind for a new and improved educational system."[18] He held institutes for training and encouraging teachers, fostered the formation of teacher associations, and advocated the introduction in the schools of lessons on agriculture, and to that end, published a textbook.[19]

While superintendent of education, William published several reports and founded the *Journal of Education* for Nova Scotia. By the end of 1851 he "had visited more than 500 schools, given 113 lectures on education, held 56 public meetings" and organized eight teacher institutes.[20] By late 1853 William Dawson had established the need and public support for a normal school (opened in 1855), and collected statistics on schools that permitted an intelligent approach to management of education.

In September 1852 when Lyell visited Nova Scotia, Dawson met him in Halifax, where Lyell introduced him to Sir Edmund Head, then lieutenant governor of New Brunswick, later governor general of the Canadas. Lyell and Dawson proceeded to South Joggins, where they discovered an ancient reptile (*Dendrerepton acadianum*) and a small early land snail (*Pupa vetusta*). They went to Hillsborough, New Brunswick, to examine the area of the Albert Mine.

The encounter with Sir Edmund Head proved decisive for William's future. He was invited to be a member of the Ryerson Commission of Inquiry on King's College, Fredericton, New Brunswick, which resulted in its reorganization as the nondenominational provincial University of New Brunswick. The final report of the commission called for a highly integrated educational system. William wrote in support of it,

> The unity of plan and operation which will be secured by adopting the system proposed will remedy many of the most serious evils affecting the Schools and the College.... The Schools will be provided with better instructed teachers, and the course of instruction in them will be rendered more thorough, while the pupils will have a greater tendency than at present to press forward into higher institutions and will be better prepared for entering them. The sphere of each institution from the Parish School to the College, will be better defined, and the work of all therefore better done.[21]

18. Cited Frost, *McGill University*, 181.

19. Dawson, *Scientific Contributions*. There was a second edition, *Contributions and Practical Hints*. The addition of material on livestock was made at the request of Nova Scotia's lieutenant governor Sir Gaspard Le Marchand.

20. Sheets-Pyenson, *Dawson*, 30.

21. Cited Frost, *McGill University*, 195.

After becoming governor general of the Canadas, Head brought William Dawson's name to the governors of McGill College who were seeking a principal.

Lyell urged William to apply for the professorship at the University of Edinburgh. He had arranged for the publication of his *Acadian Geology* and he planned to attend the Glasgow meeting of the British Association for the Advancement of Science. On the eve of departure, Dawson learned the post had been filled and by coincidence, he received the offer of the principalship of McGill.[22] At the bidding of the McGill governors he sought and was granted an MA from the University of Edinburgh.

William Dawson moved his family to Montreal where they found a college with buildings almost in ruins and grounds that were strewn with debris and hardly accessible from the city. But he also found a group of governors who saw McGill as "the nucleus of the educational interests of the English-speaking people of Lower Canada ... [and who desired] that no aspect of denominationalism should be given to the university."[23] Dawson worked to establish his vision of an integrated public education system.[24] In November 1855 Principal Dawson's inaugural address outlined the liberal and practical education, which he envisioned for McGill with affiliated theological colleges as foreseen in the 1852 charter.[25]

In September 1856 the board of governors set up a committee to establish a normal school. An agreement was reached with the Anglican bishop of Montreal regarding the Bonaventure Normal School, founded by the Church and School Society. McGill took over its staff and model school. The McGill Normal School opened March 3, 1857, in the Belmont Building, the former home of the High School of Montreal, which was a department of the university from 1852 to 1869.[26] Dawson saw it as a college devoted largely to women, saying, "It is one of the chief merits of the Normal School, that it gives to young women an honourable walk of professional usefulness; and that it gives to our schools teachers, who, from their kind and loving treatment of the children, and their devotion to the work, are really superior, at least for the work of elementary education, to teachers of the male sex."[27]

22. Dawson, *Thirty-Eight Years of McGill*, 5: "The story forms a striking illustration of the way in which Providence shapes our ends."

23. Dawson, *Fifty Years*, 95–97.

24. Ibid., 283, "my ideal of a complete and symmetrical university suited to this country."

25. Dawson, *Collegiate Education*, 14 and 23.

26. The Belmont Building, which had housed the high school on the main floor and college classes on the second floor had been damaged by fire in 1856 and rebuilt.

27. *Quebec Journal of Education for 1857* (Excerpt preserved in material on McGill Normal School).

In 1858 Dawson proposed that McGill establish examinations for students from academies and higher schools entitling them to the appellation of associate in arts. In early years most were from the High School of Montreal, but subsequent developments saw the use of these examinations in numerous schools throughout Canada.[28] The first of the affiliated colleges joined that year, St. Francis College, Richmond. Later, Morrin College, Quebec, and Stanstead College were also affiliated with McGill.[29]

In 1870 Dawson and his wife set up the Ladies Educational Association for the higher education of women. Two subsequent appointments enabled Dawson to further the unity of the Protestant school system throughout Quebec. In 1869 the increased revenues of the Protestant School Board of Montreal enabled support for the High School of Montreal ceded by McGill in 1870. In 1872 Dawson was named school commissioner. At school board meetings he urged that a normal school certificate be required to teach in Montreal Protestant schools.[30] In 1874 Dawson moved that a committee be appointed to arrange for a High School for Girls. The committee composed of Dawson, W. Lunn, and D. H. MacVicar arranged for rooms; certified staff were hired and the school commenced. The examination for associate in arts was opened to women in 1877 and separate university classes for women began in 1884.

In 1876 Dawson was appointed to the Protestant Committee of the Council of Public Instruction. There he had the support of some members of the McGill Board: the Honourable Messrs. Day, Dunkin, and Ferrier; and Vice-Principal Leach. The first resolution passed by the Protestant Committee dealt with the superior schools, "High schools and Academies receiving aid from the Superior Education Fund will in future be required to satisfy the inspector that such instruction is being given as will enable pupils who may so desire to matriculate at a university and that the Ladies' schools will be aided when the teaching is such as to qualify for an Academy diploma."[31] Because of this, Dawson declined an offer from Princeton University stating, "The inducements were strong, both in my own interests and in those of my family, but I disliked the idea of leaving my own country and allegiance, and of abandoning a work which seemed so necessary in Canada, and especially in Quebec." Dawson resigned from the Protestant Committee in 1883 for his sabbatical in Europe, Egypt and Palestine.

28. McGill Archives Index: R.G. 90: Affiliated Educational Institutions.

29. Ibid. Vancouver College and Victoria College in British Columbia and Alberta College in Edmonton were affiliated in the early twentieth century until they attained university status. The affiliated theological colleges are noted in the third section.

30. See Macleod and Poutanen, *Meeting of the People*, 132.

31. Percival, *Across the Years*, 147–49.

After spending the winter of 1892 recuperating from pneumonia, Dawson returned to McGill and suffered a stroke. At the end of 1893 he announced his retirement. He could look back on tremendous growth in physical facilities, professional faculty members and student population, and establishing a tradition of growing financial philanthropic support for the university. McGill's academic offerings were highly regarded, science was integral to the curriculum, and the university enjoyed great renown.[32]

Besides being an educator, Dawson was a working scientist and a promoter of science. His research on the Carboniferous fossils and plants and the Devonian era was highly regarded. He was active in the Montreal Natural History Society and accepted the invitation and proceedings of the American Association for the Advancement of Science 1857 and 1882 meetings in Montreal and the 1884 British Association for the Advancement of Science. Dawson concentrated on the Pliocene deposits of the Saint Lawrence Valley and their fossils, which the Geological Survey of Canada had left untouched.

In 1870 Dawson was invited to give the Royal Society of London prize Bakerian Lecture. He took many specimens with him to illustrate and to give to various societies and collectors.[33] A committee of readers judged his paper unsuitable for publication for various reasons. He felt humiliated and reacted by turning to publication of popular versions of science and its relationship to Scripture. In effect, he became an apologist for his Christian faith.

When Dawson came to McGill in 1855 he had completed a manuscript, *Archaia; or, Studies on the Cosmogony and Natural History of the Hebrew Scriptures*, which he published in 1860. That year, Dawson's review of Charles Darwin's *On the Origin of Species, by Natural Selection; or, The Preservation of Favoured Races in the Struggle for Life* was critical of its flawed reasoning and lack of evidence[34] and was severely critical of Darwin's followers, T. H. Huxley and Herbert Spencer. Dawson reworked *Archaia* into a popular form published in 1877 as *The Origin of the World, according to Revelation and Science*,[35] a title that some saw as an allusion to Darwin.

Dawson authored more than four hundred articles and books. Much of his work on paleobotany, the delimitation of the various geological strata

32. Dawson recounts the changes in *Thirty-eight Years*.

33. "On the pre-Carboniferous Floras of Northeastern America, with special reference to the Erian (Devonian) Period." Sheets-Pyenson, *Dawson*, 112, suggests that it was too long (150 pages) and that the fourth section, "Bearing of Erian Botany on Questions as to the Introduction and Extinction of Species," was too controversial.

34. Dawson, review of *On the Origin of Species*, 100–121.

35. Dawson, *Archaia*. It had reached its 6th ed. in 1893.

in Canada, and anthropology have stood the test of time.[36] Throughout his life, Dawson received honorary degrees, fellowships, presidencies, medals and awards.

Dawson was a member of the Presbyterian College board and senate until his failing health. At his death in 1899 the college board recorded his support: "Sir William Dawson was the first to suggest the establishment of the Presbyterian College in affiliation with McGill University."[37]

Science, the Ally of Religion

The Substance of an Address at the Jubilee Conference of the Evangelical Alliance

Mildmay Park, London, July 1, 1896

If revelation is the thought, and nature the work of the same Almighty and All-wise Creator, we may be sure that they are in harmony, and that when we find students of the Bible and students of science ranged in opposition to each other there must be a mistake somewhere. Believing the Nature and the Bible are one in origin, I propose to notice a few points in which they are unnecessarily placed in antagonism to each other.

The sciences that relate to the natural history of animals, plants, and minerals, and to the structure and changes of the earth itself, are, in their simplest or most elementary forms, concerned with facts relating to material things or phenomena, with their proximate and secondary causes, and with the grouping of such facts and causes under general expressions which we term natural laws. In all this, while they may have much to do with mental culture, and or with material interests and prosperity, they have no direct relation to our religious beliefs or hopes. There is, however, a tendency in connexion with the present division of every science into specialties, and with the efforts to teach the rudiments of certain sciences to young people, to descend to a low materialistic level, which, while making science itself less attractive, may make it, at least, a deterrent from faith in higher things, in the same way that an exclusive devotion to any other worldly pursuit tends in this direction.

Yet those who enter with enthusiasm on the study of nature cannot be content always to remain on this low ground. They find rising before them

---

36. Falcon-Lang and Calder, "Sir William Dawson," and Trigger, "Faithful Anthropologist."

37. Minutes November 24, 1899, cited Markell, *History*, 8–9.

ultimate questions which they cannot solve—questions relating to the nature of causation itself, and of the natural laws to which it is subject—questions as to the origin and import of the properties of material objects, and to the correlations and combinations of these in the great cosmos or orderly system of nature with all its adjustments and uses. The attempt to answer these questions from a merely physical point of view and without faith in the unseen and spiritual must certainly be abortive.

There is, however, no need of this, for so soon as the student of nature arrives at this point, he can scarcely fail to conceive that, in addition to the world of the seen or phenomenal with which he is occupied, there must be another world of the unseen or spiritual, inviting his consideration. It then becomes an object of the highest importance that his entrance into this new field of thought and feeling should be facilitated rather than hindered. I fear, however, that there is much in the current modes of thought and expression in the religious world which tends to bar his entrance. Of these, one of the most important has been the mis-use of the term "supernatural," as distinguished from the natural.

The word does not occur in the Bible, nor is the idea which it represents one that is sanctioned by the spirit of God. In the Bible, God, who alone is supernatural, is at once over and in all His works; and the distinction between those that we can refer in some degree to secondary or proximate causes in natural laws, and those we cannot so understand, is one purely subjective or human, and in no way expressive of the Divine action. It is, in short, an idea dependent on our imperfect knowledge; and hence, if we make such a distinction we shall find that as knowledge increases, the domain of the so-called supernatural appears to diminish as if about to vanish away. The true distinction which the Bible adheres to throughout is that between the natural as embodied in matter and energy, and the spiritual as denoting the domain of intelligence and will.

When in this lower world we seek for ultimate causes, we find only one—the human will—which cannot be referred to material power, nor brought under the dominion of the laws of matter and force; yet we do not regard reason and will as supernatural, though, like the Creator Himself, they belong to the unseen and spiritual. The First Cause, or Creator, whose existence we must, even independently of revelation, assume, in order to avoid the absurdity of mere chance and causelessness, must also be spiritual, and His modes of action, though inconceivably greater, must have some analogy to those of the will of which we are conscious in ourselves. Hence arise two different but not contradictory modes of expressing ourselves respecting material nature. The first is that which relates to secondary causes and natural laws; the second that which relates to the First Cause as present in all phenomena. In all elementary science we are occupied with the first aspect of the matter. In more philosophical science, and in religious beliefs, we rise to the consideration of the latter. So far as we can understand, not only the whole material universe, but even the spiritual world, must be within the domain of Divine law; but in any case we may be sure that God is over all and in all, and this is the appropriate view of Holy Scripture, which speaks of all things as originating in God, and does not, except on rare occasions, concern itself with secondary causes.

Let us not then present to our scientific friends the partial and inaccurate distinction of the natural and the supernatural, but the true and Scriptural one of the Natural and the Spiritual. We shall thus find the real meeting-place of Science and Religion, excluding atheism and agnosticism, and leading easily and naturally to the Almighty Creator and loving Father and Saviour presented to us by Divine revelation.

Nor should we forget here that revelation sanctions this union of the natural and the spiritual by claiming for God the creation and the constant care of all things in heaven and in earth, and by it appeals to nature as evidence of His being, power, wisdom and love. Christ Himself, though the great Revealer, and asserting that only through Him can we know the Father, does not disdain to call upon the sparrows, the ravens, and the flowers of the field to bear witness with Him. Paul assures the heathen people of Lystra that God has not left Himself without a witness in that He "did good and sent them rain from heaven and fruitful seasons, filling their hearts with food and gladness."[38] In the noble introduction to his Epistle to the Romans, he defines more clearly than any other writer precisely what we can know of God from his works, when he says: "The invisible things of Him since the creation of the world are clearly seen, being perceived through the things that are made, even His eternal power and divinity."[39]

These two things all men may perceive in nature—power beyond our conception and contrivance beyond our comprehension; and the whole eternal, and so far above us that they must be held to be divine. Paul goes even further than this, and proceeds to argue that those who fail to glorify this Almighty Architect of man and nature, and to give thanks to Him for His goodness are "without excuse." But he has the authority of the Gospel to add to this the proclamation that even for those who have neglected and despised the manifestation of God in nature and have turned it into the basest uses, a loving Father offers mercy and salvation through Jesus Christ.

---

38. Acts 14:17.
39. Rom 1:20.

Another point on which there seems to be much misunderstanding between writers of popular science and Christians, is that which relates to the nature of faith as distinguished from credulity and superstition, and its place as one of the springs of human action. It has even been said, on no mean authority, that the progress of science has made faith "a cardinal sin," while on the opposite side we often hear the demands of science for material evidence denounced as hostile to faith. Physical science, no doubt, has to insist on proof of its facts and laws, either by observation, experiment, or mathematical demonstration. Yet it cannot dispense with faith in its own perceptions and intuitions, and in the testimony of others with reference to facts and processes. Still more are we dependent on faith in the domain of the spiritual. In a question of how much weight a beam will sustain, we may apply a mechanical test, and after this a mathematical calculation, but who can test or calculate the trust of a child in a parent, or of one friend in another? Yet this might be quite as sure and reasonable as the other, though perhaps not reasoned out at all, but based on affection or experience. In this domain a glance, a gesture, or a word, may be as trustworthy as a demonstration in matters physical; and without this assured faith the world could not go on for a day. All this applies still more clearly to our relations to God. He is willing to give us physical proofs of material matters; but, in regard to our higher spiritual interests, He declines to give us a physical "sign from heaven," but he presents to us the testimony of a Divine Saviour, full of goodness, love, truth, and self-sacrifice, and invites us to trust in Him, as willing and able to save to the uttermost. Our faith in such a person as the Christ of the Gospels is our own willing trust; yet it is also the gift of God, who has given us the evidence of it, and the capacity to entertain it and to live by it. Between such reasonable faith and anything deserving the name of science there can be no conflict; but we must beware not to limit the grace of God by any narrowness of our own.

It is often said that students of Nature are, as a whole, hostile to religion. Unfortunately those who are so have often put themselves very much in evidence in their writings and so have given occasion to the enemy. In so far, however, as my experience extends, I have reason to believe that as large a proportion of the votaries of science are pious men as of any other class. It is not to be denied, however, that they have been so under some disadvantages, both on account of the constant effort of infidels and popular agitators to wrest science to their own uses, and of the intolerance, errors in matters of fact, and unwise concessions of Christian teachers, who should practice in such matters the same wise reticence that appears in Christ Himself.

Much stress has been laid on the alleged retreat of religion before the advance of science, and of the persecutions said to have been suffered by scientific innovators. This depends partly on the error already referred to of supposing that the reference of effects to natural causes withdraws them from the domain of the Creator. It also results from misapprehension of historical facts....

The Bible itself, while so explicit as to the Divine creation of and immanence in nature, is perfectly non-committal as to secondary causes and theoretical explanations; and this rightly, because it is revelation and not science. It is the nature of science to be ever advancing. Its goal today is its starting point tomorrow. Revelation, on the other hand, like the great natural laws which regulate the universe, is unchanging from age to age, yet capable of endless new applications to the wants and conditions of men in every age. Its old truths can never pass away. Its new applications will ever appear till all is fulfilled.

Commentary on "Science, the Ally of Religion"

In 1896, Sir William Dawson and his wife went to England to attend the June wedding of his son Rankine and Gloranna Coats. He also gave the keynote address at the conference celebrating the fiftieth anniversary of the founding of the Evangelical Alliance and attended meetings of the Royal Society, the Geological Society, and the British Association, returning to Montreal in October 1896.[40]

Dawson began the address with his core belief that Scripture (the word of God) and nature (the work of God) are harmonious. This belief was the result of his religious upbringing, his educational background, and the religious reverence of his approach to nature. The Bible was for him literally the revealed Word of God given through inspired persons. Interpreted correctly its words were unerring in their witness to God's activity in the world. For a period of more than fifty years he sought to demonstrate the congruence of Scripture and natural history.[41]

Dawson then outlined the nature of science in Baconian fashion. Each of the sciences is involved with the collection of facts that are basic to its field, whether zoology and animals, botany and plants, mineralogy and

40. Dawson, *Fifty Years*, 283–84.

41. In the 1840s Dawson wrestled with the issue of the congruence of his scientific interests and his religious commitment. In 1855 he had submitted a manuscript to the Scottish competition for the Burnett Prize for the best essay: "In proof of the existence of a supreme Creator, upon grounds both of reason and revelation." Sheets-Pyenson, *Dawson*, 119–21. This essay appears to have been an early version of *Archaia*, which was published in Montreal in 1860. It was revised and reissued in 1877 as *Origin of the World*. A similar effort at harmonization was issued earlier in 1873 as *Earth and Man*.

minerals, or geology and the structure and changes of the earth, and so on. The empirical observations that are made and then classified are related to each other by induction through a study of similarities and differences. The facts and secondary causes of change and effect are then expressed in natural laws. Dawson stated that such methods and operations have no direct connection to religious faith but suggested that the enthusiast of science would not be content to remain on this material level. His references to the teaching of science to young people "at a low materialistic level, which, while making science itself less attractive, may make it, at least, a deterrent from faith in higher things" and the exclusion of "atheism and agnosticism" appear to be a reference to men who sought to professionalize science by liberating it from theological control.[42]

He approached science with a Baconian need to amass observable facts amenable to inductive reasoning, and a Paleyite-like belief in design and purpose in nature.[43] His education at the Pictou Academy was reinforced by the Bridgewater Treatises, in particular, William Buckland,[44] Thomas Chalmers,[45] and Charles Bell.[46] In addition, Dawson was strongly influenced by the works of Hugh Miller.[47] Therefore, he found a divine design and purpose in nature that when rightly understood revealed God's power and divinity and that endowed the study of natural history with dignity.[48]

Dawson was convinced that the adept of science would want to go beyond the material view of the phenomena of science to ultimate questions of causation and origins. He expressed a fear that the religious use of the expression "supernatural" would hinder such an approach. Here he resorted to definition to obviate the difficulty. The same type of concern for definition from the side of science appears in his book *Some Salient Points in the Science of the Earth*.

42. See David N. Livingstone's account of John Tyndall's speech to the BAAS in Belfast in 1874, *Dealing*, 67–68.

43. William Paley (1743–1805) was known for his argument from design. Using the analogy that from a watch found in a field one could infer a watchmaker, given the evidence of design in nature one could infer the existence of God. His *Natural Theology; or, Evidence of the Existence and Attributes of the Deity* (1802) went through many editions. Sheets-Pyenson, *John William Dawson*, 21, notes that there were fifteen copies of his works in the Pictou Academy library.

44. Buckland, *Geology and Mineralogy*.

45. Chalmers, *Adaptation of External Nature*.

46. Bell, *The Hand*.

47. Miller, *Old Red Sandstone, Footprint of the Creator*, and *Testimony of the Rocks*.

48. Dawson, *Salient Points*, 6; "The Supreme Intelligence reveals to us in nature His power and divinity, and it is this, and this alone, that gives attraction and dignity to natural science."

Dawson preferred the use of the contrast between what is "natural" and the "spiritual" rather than the contrast of "natural" and the "supernatural." The spiritual, which he claimed was the more scriptural distinction, related to intelligence and will, which permits one to find God's design and purpose in nature rather than leaving one with "the absurdity of mere chance and causelessness." Thus nature provides evidence of "His being, power, wisdom and love."

His reminder that revelation claims "for God the creation and the constant care of all things in heaven and in earth" moved beyond Paley's Deism to a providential immanence of God in nature. Dawson elaborated, "Creation, as maintained against such materialistic evolution, whether by theology, philosophy, or Holy Scripture, is necessarily a continuous, nay, an eternal, influence, not an intervention of disconnected acts. It is the true continuity, which includes and binds together all other continuity."[49]

He continued, "It is here that natural science meets with theology, not as an antagonist, but as a friend and ally in its time of greatest need; and I must here record my belief that neither men of science nor theologians have a right to separate what God in Holy Scripture has joined together, or to build up a wall between nature and religion, and write upon it, 'no thoroughfare.' The science that does this must be impotent to explain nature, and without hold on the higher sentiments of man. The theology that does this must sink into mere superstition."[50]

Dawson's second concern was with the "nature of faith as distinguished from credulity and superstition, and its place as one of the springs of human action." For example, this arises in his writings where he argued against agnosticism: "As a matter of faith, we must hold fast to the proposition 'I exist' as the only standpoint for science, philosophy, or common life. If we are asked for evidence of this faith, we can appeal only to our consciousness of effects which imply the existence of the ego, which we thus have to admit or suppose before we can begin to prove even its existence."[51]

He illustrated the need for faith in science, stating:

> Our attempts to form rational conceptions of atoms resolve themselves into complex conjectures as to vortices of ethers and the like, of which no one pretends to have any distinct mental picture; yet on this basis of the incomprehensible rests all our

---

49. Ibid., 193–94. Moore, *Post-Darwinian Controversies*, 212, reads Dawson's writings as "an elaborate attempt to show how the geological and biblical records 'exhibit the progressive nature of creation'" . . . "not a mere spontaneous evolution, but a progressive plan carried on by great variety of causes."

50. Ibid.

51. Dawson, *Facts and Fancies*, 23.

physical science, the first truths in which are really matters of pure faith in the existence of that which we cannot understand. Yet all men would scoff at the agnostic who on this account should express unbelief in physical science.

Let us observe here, further, that since the mysterious and inscrutable "I" is surrounded with an equally mysterious and inscrutable universe, and since the ego and the external world are linked together by indissoluble relations, we are introduced to certain alternatives as to origins. Either the universe or "nature" is a mere phantom conjured up by the ego, or the ego is a product of the universe, or both are the result of some equally mysterious power beyond us and the material world.[52]

Dawson decried the idea that the progress of science had eliminated the need for faith in a Creator, whereas the demand that science provide material evidence to support its thesis was "denounced as hostile to faith." He averred that physical science had to supply "proof of its facts and laws, either by observation, experiment, or mathematical demonstration." Scientific work implied that the scientist had faith in his own perceptions and intuitions and those of others. He argued that "agnosticism postulates primary force or forces self-existent and including potentially all that is subsequently evolved from them. The only way in which it approximates to theism is in its extreme monistic form, where the one force or power supposed to underlie all existence is a sort of God shorn of personality, will, and reason."[53]

Dawson inverted the dictum of the monist zoologist Ernst Haeckel, "Where faith begins, science ends,"[54] to read, "Where science ends, faith begins," and continued:

> It is only by faith that we know of any force, or even of the atoms of matter themselves, and in like manner it is "by faith we know that the creative ages have been constituted by the word of God." The only difference is that the monist has faith in the potency of nothing to produce something, or of something material to exist for ever and to acquire at some point of time the power spontaneously to enter on the process of development; while the theist has faith in a primary intelligent Will as the Author of all things.[55]

---

52. Ibid., 25.
53. Ibid., 43–44.
54. Ibid.
55. Ibid.

He disputed the notion that scientists "as a whole" were hostile to religion. It also was a mistake to think that referring effects to secondary causes left less room for Divine action. Indeed, "the Bible itself . . . is perfectly non-committal as to secondary causes and theoretical explanations; and this rightly, because it is revelation and not science."

Dawson's attempt to harmonize science and Scripture, particularly Genesis and geology by means of a concordance between the "days" of Genesis and the periods delineated by geology, must be seen and evaluated in its historical context. Rupke traced the "cognitive dissonance" between the scientific studies and the biblical cosmogony of the early chapters of Genesis outlining several schemes that attempted to reconcile the differences. He claims that such efforts allowed the scientists to freely pursue the investigation of the material world.[56] This freedom led to the specialization of the sciences and the disintegration of the study of natural history. References to creation and the role of God in nature gradually disappeared from science. Ironically, Dawson' work on the relation of science and religion detracted from his scientific reputation and became the literature of present-day Christian fundamentalism.

Dawson's literalist interpretation of the early chapters of Genesis was disputed. Scientific methods applied to Scripture indicated that the book of Genesis was a compilation of several sources and oral traditions. S. R. Driver wrote: "If, then, at least provisionally, day be interpreted [figuratively] as equivalent to period, two questions at once arise: Do the days of Genesis correspond with well-defined geological periods? And does the order in which different living things are stated to have been created agree with the facts of geology? To both these questions candour compels the answer, No."[57]

Driver continued: "Read without prejudice or bias, the narrative of Genesis 1 creates an impression at variance with the facts revealed by science: the efforts of reconciliation . . . are different modes of obliterating its characteristic features, and of reading into it a view which it does not express."[58] . . . "The cosmogony of Genesis is not meant to be an authoritative exposition of the past history of the earth, but that it subserves a different purpose altogether. Its purpose is to teach *religious* truth, not scientific truth."[59]

Driver was more severe in his review of Dawson's *Modern Science in Bible Lands*: "Sir J. Dawson is eminent as a geologist: he is not equally distinguished as a Biblical critic or as a theologian. And thus, when he touches

56. Rupke, *Christianity*, 164–80; see Bowler, *Christianity*, 569–81.
57. Driver, "Cosmogony," 24.
58. Ibid., 37.
59. Ibid., 41, my emphasis (H.K.).

upon Biblical subjects, he falls readily into misstatements and mistakes. His first chapter is an attempt, by the use of violent means to force the cosmogony of Genesis into harmony with the teachings of modern science."[60]

> The endeavour to reconcile the [two] narratives of Genesis with each other and with science is prompted by laudable motives; but if it does not succeed by the use of honest and legitimate motives, it must be abandoned; and unlearned readers should not be told that Hebrew words mean what they do not mean. Sir J. Dawson's allusions to Biblical criticism . . . show that he views it entirely from the outside, and that he is unacquainted equally with the grounds upon which it rests and with the results that have been obtained, and accepted universally . . . by those engaged in it.[61]

Dawson replied: "I think it right to express with the utmost decision my strong conviction, arrived at by original work, that such processes as those to which the reviewer refers, as establishing 'the composite structure of the Pentateuch,' in the sense in which he uses the expression, and the conclusion that the second chapter of Genesis is 'contradictory' to the first, are unscientific and unreliable."[62]

William Dawson continued to uphold the Mosaic authorship of the Pentateuch and the literal interpretation of the account of creation as well as its compatibility with science.

The Author

A graduate of Presbyterian College in 1960, Harry Kuntz did postgraduate work at McGill Faculty of Religious Studies while serving as assistant to the minister of Knox Crescent and Kensington Church, Montreal. After ordination in 1962 he served at Greenbrier Church, Brantford and St. Columba by-the-Lake, Pointe Claire. After several years teaching high school English and history, he was successively coordinator responsible for moral and religious education in the Protestant Schools of Quebec and then secretary of the Protestant Committee of the Quebec Superior Council of Education. He earned the PhD in humanities at Concordia University with a thesis on "Science Culture in English-Speaking Montreal, 1815–1842." His interests include the history of education, of literary and scientific institutions, and

---

60. Driver, *Bible Lands*, 399.
61. Ibid., 402.
62. Dawson, *Genesis*, 901.

of the Presbyterian Church. He has led a number of studies on hymns and religious music, and on books of the Old and New Testament at Briarwood Church, Beaconsfield.

Bibliography

Adams, Frank Dawson. "Memoir of Sir J. William Dawson." *Bulletin of the Geological Society of America* 11 (1899) 550–57.

Ami, Henry M. "A Brief Biographical Sketch of Sir John William Dawson." *American Geologist* 26 (1900) 1–49.

Berger, Carl. *Science, God, and Nature in Victorian Canada*. Toronto: University of Toronto Press, 1983.

Bowler, Peter J. "Christianity and the Sciences." In *The Cambridge History of Christianity*, vol. 9, *World Christianities c. 1914–c. 2000*, edited by Hugh McLeod, 569–81. Cambridge: Cambridge University Press, 2008.

Collard, Edgar A. "Lyell and Dawson: A Centenary." *Dalhousie Review* 22 (1942) 133–44.

Dawson, J. W. "Annual Address of the President [Memoir of Lyell]." *Canadian Naturalist and Geologist*, n.s., 8 (1875) 8–16.

———. *Archaia: or, Studies of the Cosmogony and Natural History of the Hebrew Scriptures*. Montreal: Dawson, 1860.

———. *Facts and Fancies of Modern Science: Studies of the Relations of Science to Prevalent Speculations and Religious Belief*. Philadelphia: American Baptist, 1882.

———. "Genesis and Some of Its Critics." *Contemporary Review* 55 (1889) 900–909.

———. "Memoranda and Statements Relating to Benefactors' Exemptions and Free Tuitions to Theological Students in McGill University." 1892. CIHM_03671.

———. *On the Course of Collegiate Education Adapted to the Circumstances of British America*. Montreal: Ramsay, 1855.

———. *The Origin of the World according to Revelation and Science*. Montreal: Dawson, 1877.

———. "Recent Discussions of the First Chapter of Genesis." *Expositor*, 3rd ser., 16 (1885) 284–301.

———. Review of *The Testimony of the Rocks*, by Hugh Miller. *Canadian Naturalist and Geologist* 2 (1857) 81–92.

———. Review of *On the Origin of Species by Means of Natural Selection*, by Charles Darwin. *Canadian Naturalist and Geologist* 5 (1860) 100–120.

———. *Science, the Ally of Religion. The Substance of an Address at the Jubilee Conference of the Evangelical Alliance, Mildmay Park, London, July 1, 1896*. CIHM_06870.

———. *Some Salient Points in the Science of the Earth*. Montreal: Drysdale, 1893.

———. *The Story of Earth and Man*. Toronto: Copp Clark, 1873.

———. *The Testimony of the Holy Scriptures respecting wine and strong drink . . .* Montreal: Grafton, 1898.

———. "Thirty-Eight Years of McGill: Being the Annual University Lecture of McGill University, Montreal for the Session 1893–94." Reprint from *Montreal Medical Journal*, January 1894, 3–23.

Dawson, Rankine, ed. *Fifty Years of Work in Canada, Scientific and Educational.* London: Ballantyne, Hanson, 1901.

Driver, S. R. "The Cosmogony of Genesis." *Expositor*, 3rd ser., 13 (1886) 23–45.

———. Review of *Modern Science in Bible Lands*, by William Dawson. *Contemporary Review* 55 (1889) 399–402.

Eakins, Peter R., and Jean Sinnamon Eakins. "Dawson, Sir John William." In *Dictionary of Canadian Biography*, vol. 12. University of Toronto / Université Laval, 2003. http://www.biographi.ca/en/bio/dawson_john_william_12E.html.

FA6000 Presbyterian College Records. http://www.presbyterianarchives.ca/FA6000-Presbyterian%20College.pdf.

Falcon-Lang, Howard J., and John H. Calder. "Sir William Dawson (1820–1899): A Very Modern Paleobotanist." *Atlantic Geology* 41 (2005) 103–12.

Frost, Stanley B. *McGill University for the Advancement of Learning 1: 1801–95.* Montreal & Kingston: McGill–Queens University Press, 1980.

Livingstone, David N. *Dealing with Darwin: Place, Politics and Rhetoric in Religious Engagements with Evolution: The Gifford Lectures 2014.* Baltimore: John Hopkins University, 2014.

Macleod, Roderick, and Mary Ann Poutanen. *A Meeting of the People.* Montreal & Kingston: McGill–Queens University Press, 2004.

MacVicar, J. H. *Life and Work of Donald Harvey MacVicar, D.D., LL.D.* Toronto: Westminster, 1904.

Markell, H. Keith. *History of the Presbyterian College, Montreal, 1865–1986.* Montreal: Presbyterian College, 1987.

McGill Archives Index: R.G. 90: Affiliated Educational Institutions.

Michel, Robert H. "Anna Dawson Harrington's Memoir of Her Father Sir William Dawson, 1900." *Fontanus* 11 (2003) 174–84.

O'Brien, Charles F. *Sir William Dawson: A Life in Science and Religion.* Philadelphia: American Philosophical Society, 1971.

Percival, W. P. *Across the Years.* Montreal: Gazette, 1946.

Rupke, Nicolas A. "Christianity and the Sciences." In *The Cambridge History of Christianity*, vol. 8, *World Christianities c. 1815–c. 1914*, edited by Sheridan Gilley and Brian Stanley, 164–80. Cambridge: Cambridge University Press, 2006.

Sheets-Pyenson, Susan. *John William Dawson: Faith, Hope and Science.* Montreal & Kingston: McGill-Queen's University Press, 1996.

———. "Sir William Dawson: The Nova Scotia Roots of a Geologist's Worldview." In *Profiles of Science and Society in the Maritimes prior to 1914*, edited by Paul A. Bogaard, 82–99. Sackville, New Brunswick: Acadiensis, 1990.

Trigger, Bruce. "Sir John William Dawson: A Faithful Anthropologist." *Anthropologia* 8 (1966) 351–59.

Wood, B. Anne. "Thomas McCulloch's Use of Science in Promoting a Liberal Education." *Acadiensis* 17 (1987) 57–73.

CHAPTER 2

The College and the Church
Donald Harvey MacVicar

By John P. Vaudry

Donald Harvey MacVicar, DD, LLD, (1831–1902), first and longest-serving principal of The Presbyterian College, Montreal (1865–1902). Image of a 1902 portrait by Robert Harris, CMG, RCA, unveiled at Convocation 1903 in David Morrice Hall, a gift from the alumni. With credit to the Presbyterian College, Owen Egan photography, and Eric Klinkhoff.

IF PRINCIPAL SIR WILLIAM DAWSON can be called "the man who made McGill," Principal Donald Harvey MacVicar might well be described as "the man who made Presbyterian College." MacVicar's life has been well documented. It will be sufficient here to give the briefest outline of his significant life, highlighting his key role in the making of Presbyterian College.[1]

I

Born in Argyleshire, Scotland, in 1831, Donald immigrated to Canada with his parents, John MacVicar and Janet McTavish, when he was four years old. He grew up near Chatham, Ontario. His father was known for his kindness to the poor and to slaves who had escaped from plantations in the American South. His mother was intelligent and energetic, with a streak of pawky humour. Donald was the seventh of twelve children. Educated at Toronto Academy and the University of Toronto, Donald prepared for the ministry at Knox College, Toronto. In 1859, he accepted a call to Knox Church, Guelph, a declining congregation whose membership doubled under his ministry. While in Guelph he married Eleanor Goulding, and they became parents eventually to three sons and two daughters. His one-year pastorate ended when he responded to a call to Montreal to minister to the prestigious Coté Street Free Church, the leadership of which included such wealthy merchants as John Redpath and Joseph Mackay. At Coté Street, MacVicar established a reputation as a highly dedicated and able preacher.[2]

In the winter of 1864, MacVicar was one of the seven laymen and two ministers who met to discuss the possibility of a theological college located in Montreal. Despite MacVicar's vocal opposition, the college was organized and received its charter in 1865; although no classes were offered until 1867.[3] The synod had decided that a theological college located in Montreal could serve Quebec and the eastern part of Ontario better than Knox College in Toronto. A major raison d'etre for the college was the need for a solid base in Quebec where missionaries could be trained to do evangelistic work among French Canadians, most of whom had no access to the Bible and were under the sway of ultramontane Roman Catholicism. In the opinion of evangelical Protestants, French Quebecers had no idea of salvation by grace

---

1. I am indebted to J. H. MacVicar, *Life*; Markell, *History*; Moir, "MacVicar"; and Johnston, "Donald Harvey MacVicar."

2. The Free Church had been formed in 1844 in sympathy with the Scottish Disruption of 1843. In 1861, the Free Church joined the United Presbyterians to form the Canada Presbyterian Church.

3. J. H. MacVicar, *Life*, 67.

through faith in Jesus Christ; thus they believed it was imperative to share the Gospel with them.[4]

MacVicar was not the synod's first choice as professor of divinity. In his account of the beginnings of Presbyterian College in the basement of old Erskine Church (then situated at the corner of St. Catherine and Peel Streets), Keith Markell has discussed the several unsuccessful attempts to secure the appointment of a well-known theologian from either Scotland or the United States.[5] When MacVicar was nominated for the post, some of his colleagues in the Presbytery of Montreal were firmly opposed to his candidacy, feeling that he was not sufficiently qualified academically to be a professor of theology. In the end, he overcame his personal hesitations and was inducted as professor on October 7, 1868.[6]

At first, MacVicar was virtually alone in teaching the students of the college, with the single exception of the Rev. J. Monro Gibson of Erskine Church who gave some assistance by lecturing on exegetics. Having never lost sight of the strategic importance of the college in the evangelization of Quebec, the following year MacVicar invited the Rev. Daniel Coussirat, a native of France who had been teaching at the Institute at Pointe-aux-Trembles, to lecture in theology. In 1873, MacVicar brought in the Rev. John Campbell, a somewhat eccentric scholar who also was fluent in French, to teach church history and apologetics. That same year, the General Assembly of the Canada Presbyterian Church appointed MacVicar principal of the Presbyterian College, Montreal. Eight years later, his leadership in college and church was recognized when he was elected moderator of the General Assembly.

II

A major issue for Donald MacVicar in taking on the responsibilities inherent in becoming sole professor of theology at the college was his "serious reservations concerning the viability of the institution to which he was committing himself."[7] The college was still housed in "makeshift quarters," as Markell has put it, and it was only in 1871 that, under MacVicar's leadership, plans were made to purchase or erect a proper building. Property was purchased on McTavish Street adjoining the McGill University campus. Finally, after an

---

4. Johnston, "Donald Harvey MacVicar," 60; Pidgeon, "Principal MacVicar," 150–51.

5. Markell, *History*, 11–12.

6. One of MacVicar's opponents was the Rev. Dr. William Taylor, a prominent minister in the city, who a few years later became one of his strongest supporters. Ibid., 13.

7. Markell, *History*, 12.

ordeal of four years in the musty Erskine cellar, the new building was dedicated in October 1873. The cost was approximately $52,000—considerably more than had been anticipated. The Presbytery of Montreal raised most of this amount, with Coté Street Church providing a significant portion of the total. MacVicar's connections with his former congregation no doubt played an important part when it came to financing this major building project.[8] The college would soon outgrow the building, but one of MacVicar's admirers, board member David Morrice, a wealthy Montreal textile manufacturer and trustee of Crescent Street Church (the successor to Coté Street) saved the day. In the early 1880s, he donated $60,000 for a new building which would contain a convocation hall, a dining hall, and a library—an edifice that served Presbyterian College well until the 1960s when the present facilities were built on the corner of University and Milton Streets.

In 1874, the college adopted a seal and coat of arms. The coat of arms had a burning bush—the traditional symbol of Presbyterianism, an open Bible—representing the truth and accessibility of the Word of God, and a dove—a familiar image of the Holy Spirit. Underneath was a scroll with the college motto from Philippians 2:16: *Sermonem vitae praetendentes*— "Holding forth the Word of Life." Whether or not MacVicar chose these symbols and the text of Scripture, they certainly reflect beliefs and ideals that he and many others in the Canada Presbyterian Church (soon to become the Presbyterian Church in Canada) cherished at that time.

Donald MacVicar's life and ministry were practically synonymous with Presbyterian College. He served on the faculty for thirty-three years; for twenty-eight he was principal. He accepted a position at the college when it had no building of its own, few students, and no other faculty. In the face of such formidable odds, he was determined to work hard and to do his best to strengthen the institution; by all accounts, he succeeded. MacVicar's successor John Scrimger's eulogy was no exaggeration: "Whatever credit must be given to others for the college's present prominent position, its existence and prosperity are due to him more than to anyone else."[9]

III

Donald MacVicar exerted influence on the college and the church in many ways, not least through his strong personality and Christian character. It is well worth exploring, then, what sort of man he was. An evangelical

---

8. In today's economy, $52,000 would be approximately one and a half million dollars.

9. J. H. MacVicar, *Life*, 349.

believer, his faith centred on Jesus Christ as Saviour. His was an unswerving belief in the divine inspiration and authority of the Bible. There can be little question that, like Charles Hodge, A. A. Hodge, and B. B. Warfield of Princeton Seminary, MacVicar adhered to a belief in the infallibility or inerrancy of Scripture.[10] Indeed, there was an affinity between Princeton and Montreal.[11] Similar to William Caven and William MacLaren of Knox College, and the Princeton theologians who were orthodox in doctrine and fervent in piety, MacVicar was a Calvinist.[12] One of the last of a generation of conservative Presbyterian leaders, he helped to shape the faith and thinking of a significant number in the church, and did much to prevent the complete erosion of conservative theology in the Presbyterian Church for at least a generation.[13]

MacVicar was also characterized by a warm piety and Reformed spirituality. Many years after the event, George C. Pidgeon, one of MacVicar's students and admirers, recalled the moving prayer that the principal had uttered at his ordination to the ministry.[14] MacVicar deplored formalism and spiritual deadness. He once wrote: "I have many faults to find with you Presbyterians. Your coldness I often cannot endure."[15] He affirmed that the Church's greatest need was the reviving of the Holy Spirit. Thus, on one occasion he declared: "The Church may temporarily sink into a state of spiritual decline and vainly imagine that what is needed to right the wrongs of humanity is novelty, departure from old paths, improvement in externalities, more machinery, and not the quickening power of the truth and Spirit of God. This is lamentable and utter folly."[16]

MacVicar was, of course, a theologian, a man of wide reading and sound scholarship, who kept abreast of current philosophical and theological trends. He was able to instruct in mathematics, Latin, Greek, logic, moral

10. See Markell, *History*, 19.

11. At one point, Princeton tried to recruit Sir William Dawson.

12. Connor stated that the professor depicted as God's instrument in spiritual revival in *The Man from Glengarry* was MacVicar. See 209–13; J. H. MacVicar, *Life*, 53–54.

13. John Scrimger, who succeeded him as principal, moved to a more liberal theological position, and later principals such as D. J. Fraser and F. Scott MacKenzie were equally or more liberal. In *History*, Markell, who taught at Presbyterian College from 1947–1980, called MacVicar "rigid," as did Moir, in "MacVicar."

14. Pidgeon became the first moderator of the United Church of Canada in 1925. In "Principal MacVicar," 158, he described his former teacher as "one of the greatest prophets God has given to our age."

15. J. H. MacVicar, *Life*, 27.

16. Quoted in Markell, *History*, 20.

philosophy, systematic theology, and apologetics.[17] Markell has commented that this workload "would have taxed the most accomplished polymath."[18] One has only to read his lecture on "Recent Aspects of Materialism" delivered at the opening of the 1871–72 academic session to see his familiarity with the writings of such thinkers as David Hume, J. S. Mill, Herbert Spencer, T. H. Huxley, and Alexander Bain. The metaphysical and biblical arguments he marshalled in answer to materialism's denial of God and the soul are impressive.[19] MacVicar's defence of orthodox Calvinism may have been dogmatic, but it owed nothing to ignorance; instead, he was persuaded that Reformed Christianity was true and had nothing to fear from its opponents.

MacVicar was an outstanding teacher and preacher. His lectures and articles were well organized, clear, logical expressions of Reformed orthodoxy, sometimes containing memorable illustrations, as well as bits of humour. His preaching was eloquent. Congregations were impressed with his "powerful presence, his incisive style, his sonorous voice," and "his positive accent of conviction." Even when "he read every word," his sermons left a deep impression.[20] His fame spread, and there were efforts by American churches to lure him away. One church in San Francisco offered him a stipend of $10,000 a year, but from a sense of duty he chose to remain in Montreal, despite his paltry salary of $2,000.

MacVicar's motivation for staying in Montreal had much to do with his vision of building a strong Protestant culture in the city and province. He worked tirelessly to promote Protestant education, and was convenor of the church's Committee on French Evangelization for many years. He was a supporter of converted priest Charles Chiniquy, even writing an introduction to Chiniquy's *Forty Years in the Church of Christ*.[21] The day MacVicar died, he had just returned from a meeting of the French committee. Like his friend Sir William Dawson, MacVicar felt his duty lay in aiding the evangelical minority in a time of intense anti-Protestant hostility.

MacVicar possessed a genuine humanity and graciousness. This is illustrated by the tension he felt between duty and friendship in the case of Professor John Campbell. The professor gave a convocation address at Queen's University in 1893 in which he confronted his hearers with a choice

---

17. We know that he spoke Gaelic. It may be wondered, in view of his zeal for evangelism in Quebec, whether he knew French. He seems to have at least been able to read it. In a paper on *Roman Catholicism in Canada*, he referred to an article in the *Revue de Théologie Pratique* of Paris.

18. Markell, *History*, 12.

19. MacVicar, "Recent Aspects."

20. J. H. MacVicar, *Life*, 83.

21. MacVicar, introduction to *Forty Years*.

between "the Perfect Book or the Perfect Father," indicating that one cannot hold to both an infallible Bible and the goodness of God. Despite opposing his colleague's unorthodox views at his heresy trial, and even though the Presbytery of Montreal found Campbell guilty of teaching doctrines contrary to the Confession of Faith, MacVicar made a determined effort to ensure that they remained friends.[22]

According to Markell, MacVicar was "little given to displays of emotion," something that probably was true of many Scots Presbyterians of that time. He was no doubt serious and reserved, but was he "a rather cold, austere individual" (as Markell says) or is this merely a stereotype of the nineteenth-century Presbyterian minister? Any man who could give himself a middle name ("Harvey") simply because he wanted to please his future wife, who admired a character of that name in a novel, does not seem cold or austere![23] Anyone who took pleasure in introducing another serious-minded minister—Benjamin Morgan Palmer of New Orleans—to the thrill of tobogganing on Mount Royal must have had a sense of fun.[24] He enjoyed the writings of Mark Twain, loved to sing Scottish songs, was a good *raconteur* and mimic, and liked to swim. "He knew how to laugh, and how to make others laugh."[25]

MacVicar could deliver stinging denunciations of sin from the pulpit, yet he could also be tender. His son has told of a young woman who had lived a life of "vice." She went to Coté Street Church and sat at the back of the gallery, drawn by MacVicar's preaching. She "apparently discerned" that beneath the "stern exterior of the frowning preacher," there lay "a heart that beat in real sympathy with those who are down." When critically ill she sent for MacVicar, who spoke gently of Christ's promises to the penitent.[26]

He was also a man of catholic sympathies. Long before the word "ecumenical" came into vogue, MacVicar felt a kinship with believers of many denominations and moved among people of a wide variety of cultural backgrounds. His brother Malcolm was a Baptist minister who became chancellor of McMaster College, and the brothers enjoyed warm Christian fellowship (while agreeing to disagree on the subjects and mode of baptism). He sometimes commended the more demonstrative Christianity of Methodists and Baptists. He was active in the Evangelical Alliance, the Bible Society, and other inter-church organizations, and was a friend of Canon

22. Markell, *History*, 23.
23. J. H. MacVicar, *Life*, 25.
24. Ibid., 119.
25. See J. H. MacVicar, *Life*, ch. 18.
26. Ibid., 50.

Charles Bancroft, one of the leading ministers of the Church of England in Montreal.[27] Moreover, when MacVicar died in 1902, he was mourned not only by his fellow Protestants, but also by Roman Catholics and Jews.

Convinced Presbyterian that he was, MacVicar deplored ecclesiastical rivalries and quarrels that diverted energy and resources from the task of evangelizing the nation and the world. He therefore sought to encourage unity and cooperation between denominations. Thus, the unionists of the early twentieth century might well have looked back to him for inspiration as they worked to form The United Church of Canada, while the confessionalist element among the anti-unionists might also have claimed to be continuing his legacy.

Presbyterian College was blessed in having such a gifted and godly man as Donald Harvey MacVicar as its first principal. We owe much to this outstanding leader whom D. C. Masters has called "a fine teacher, an able administrator, and a man of great courage."[28] His faith and determination took a fledgling institution and transformed it into a seminary of great influence. Presbyterians in Canada today have largely forgotten him, and some would probably distance themselves from his outlook. Even the congregation named in his memory has gone out of existence.[29] But Principal MacVicar, a faithful servant of Christ and the church, deserves to be remembered for his work in establishing Presbyterian College as a centre of theological training not only for ministers, but also for the laity.

The Office and Work of Elders[30]

The elders therefore among you I exhort, who am a fellow-elder (Greek-sumpresbuteros), and a witness of the sufferings of Christ, who am also a partaker of the glory that shall be revealed.[31]

—1 Peter 5:1.

---

27. He acted as a pallbearer at Bancroft's funeral in Christ Church Cathedral. Ibid., 129.

28. *Protestant Church Colleges*, 119.

29. MacVicar Memorial Presbyterian Church, Outremont. The building is now used by the Chinese Presbyterian Church.

30. MacVicar's address was delivered in Crescent Street Presbyterian Church, Montreal, on "Sabbath morning," December 2, 1894, "on the occasion of the Ordination of Elders." It was published later that month.

31. The Bible translation for this text is the American Revised Version (ARV). MacVicar usually quoted the Authorized King James Version, but sometimes the ARV.

In defining his own status in the Church of God Peter says, I am an elder, I am a witness of the sufferings of Christ, I am a partaker of the glory that shall be revealed; but he does not say I am the Supreme Pontiff set over all the rest of the apostles—the infallible head of the church universal. No. That was a distinction which he never claimed and never enjoyed, but which was ascribed to him by the superstition of a later age.

He was content to take rank as an elder and a witness of the sufferings which he saw the Son of God pass through in his earthly career, in Gethsemane and on Calvary, when he put away sin by offering himself a sacrifice once for all, "and made reconciliation for the sins of the people."[32]

Peter was content to testify to these redemptive sufferings, and to be a partaker, along with the humblest of God's people, of the glory that shall be revealed when Christ shall appear to be glorified in his saints, and to be admired in all them that believe. Is not this enough, and infinitely better than all the pomp and honours falsely claimed by his pretended successors?

But my wish is to turn your attention specially to the first title claimed by Peter, that of an elder. We are met this morning to ordain additional elders in this church, and it is fitting that we should think about their office and work.

In the New Testament Church, as organized by Christ and His apostles, there were two permanent orders of office-bearers, Deacons and Elders. I do not forget that in subsequent days sundry other orders were added, an imposing hierarchy was set up by mere human authority, with Cardinals, Arch-bishops, and so forth. These were all post-apostolic, and are now acknowledged by candid and scholarly men to be destitute of Scriptural warrant. They no more belong to the simplicity of the apostolic church than the adoration of saints and angels.

With respect to Deacons, we read of the institution of the office in the sixth chapter of the Acts, when "seven men of good report, full of the Spirit and of wisdom,"[33] were elected and ordained to serve in this capacity. They are not called Deacons in the record, but their character, qualifications and work correspond with what was afterwards set forth as belonging to Deacons. And that the office became universal in the apostolic church, and was designed to be permanent, seems clear from Paul's directions to Timothy touching the worth of persons to be chosen as Deacons. They "must be grave, not double-tongued, not given to much wine, not greedy of filthy lucre; holding the mystery of the faith in a pure conscience."[34]

---

32. Heb 2:17.
33. Acts 6:3.
34. 1 Tim 3:8–9.

We are concerned, however, just now with Elders, and regarding them we may note the following points:—

I.—*They are called of God's Spirit to this office.* No man should take this honour to himself unless so called. Hence elders are persons separated and distinctly consecrated to the Lord by their high and sacred vocation. Good men, of course, but more than this as we shall presently see—men of superior intelligence, possessed in some measure of the qualifications which Christ requires of those whom He counts Elders. Every good man who leads a quiet inoffensive life, doing nothing very distinctively Christian or unchristian, is not on this account necessarily qualified for the proper discharge of the duties of the eldership. The fact that a man is singularly good-natured and tolerant, and prone to reconcile contradictories in theology and practical conduct, does not point him out as fit for the office. Mere negative attributes are not enough. Positive qualities and the vigor of character which they impart are demanded. The elder, above all things, must be a man of God—the significant designation by which Old Testament prophets were known. He should be fully persuaded in his own mind and able, by consistent godly living, to convince those who have spiritual discernment that he is a temple of the Holy Ghost; for "if any man have not the Spirit of Christ, he is none of his,"[35] and therefore not fit to be an elder.

More than this, he should feel himself moved by an inward divine impulse constraining him to undertake this work. This divine call is in reality his primary and highest title to office. He receives and holds his patent direct from the Court of Heaven. God the Holy Spirit first makes elders and ministers, and the church merely selects, trains, and installs in office those who are thus divinely fitted for it. When she does otherwise she does wrong, and brings upon herself weakness and deadness.

But can the Church, and can a man himself discern that he is fitted for a certain office? Why not? Has not Christ given her the promise of the presence of his Spirit and the providential guidance of his own hand in such matters? And are not good men consciously moved by the truth and the Spirit of God to consecrate themselves to the special service of the Redeemer? There is no need of wrapping this matter in impenetrable mystery. When God calls a man to office he reveals it to him in his own consciousness, and after intelligent and calm consideration, and by listening to the counsel of those competent to give him wise advice, he is finally persuaded that he possesses in some degree—I do not say in full measure—the qualifications

---

35. Rom 8:9.

of head and heart necessary to the discharge of the duties he is constrained to undertake.

II.—*Elders are called to office by the voice of the people.* There is first the call of God's Spirit addressed to the heart, and then the outward call of the Saints. How do we know that this is the order? By the word of truth which is the only rule we can accept in settling all things pertaining to the house of God. They are not to be determined by custom, however venerable, by the decrees of the church, or the enactments of the State, but only by the word of the Lord and the practice of his inspired apostles.

You recollect how the first deacons were chosen. Even the apostles, although inspired and invested with special authority, did not claim the right to select deacons. On the contrary they said to the people, "Wherefore, brethren, look ye out among you seven men of honest report full of the Holy Ghost and wisdom, whom we may appoint over this business."[36] The brethren did so, and it is added, "Whom they set before the apostles; and when they had prayed they laid their hands on them."[37] That is to say, the people selected the deacons and the apostles ordained them.

The same order was uniformly followed with elders. There was first election by the act of the members of the Church, and then ordination to office. Indeed the Greek word used in the New Testament to describe the transaction conveys the idea that the election was by an open unbiased vote, probably by the uplifting of the hand, or by casting the *sephos* or pebble, the method followed in the Jewish Sanhedrim. And it is not difficult to perceive the propriety, safety and wisdom of this divine order in the choice of the office-bearers of the Church. Here is manifest propriety in it, for surely it is seemly and right that every member of the Church should prayerfully and wisely judge who are to be rulers and teachers therein. There is also safety in this course, for suppose that weak and conceited enthusiasts should appear in a congregation claiming to be called of God and pre-eminently qualified to teach and to rule, this election by the people is an effectual check upon their folly. The whole Church cannot be supposed to be beside herself, and although these pragmatical visionaries may be in this state, the Lord will restrain them by the hand of his flock in declining to elect them to office. And the divine wisdom of this order is conspicuously obvious. The Lord knows that it is most useful for a congregation to make the effort to find among themselves suitable persons to become elders. It will compel them to know one another better than is usual, and this is good. It will reveal to the people

---

36. Acts 6:3 ARV.
37. Acts 6:6.

how poor or how rich they are in spiritual gifts, and this too is most desirable. If they can hardly find any one to serve the Lord in this capacity, then they are poor indeed, and need to seek earnestly more spiritual life and power from on high. If on the other hand they can readily find a dozen men, as is the case in this Church, eminently fitted to the office and willing to undertake its duties, then they are rich, and should give God thanks and take courage.

But this is not all. See God's wisdom in asking you to make choice of elders in the fact that you thereby become responsible to them and responsible for them. You place them over yourselves voluntarily, and hence should find it natural and easy to obey them that have the rule over you in the Lord. You have deliberately given them this place, and you must not contradict your own action by disregarding them.

Nay, more. You are responsible for them. They are your elders, and if without due thought and prayer you have appointed them, and if they are not such as they should be you are to blame in calling them to office. And therefore instead of finding fault, and bewailing the shortcomings of your fellow-Christians and counting this a pious exercise, let us confess our faults one to another, and pray one for another, and be incessant and wise in our efforts to second the Christian endeavours of those charged with special service, that their labours may be crowned with abundant success.

III.—*Elders thus called of God and elected by his flock are ordained to office.* What is ordination, and by whom is it performed? Many vague and superstitious notions are entertained about this matter. We may say in a word that ordination is an act of the Church through her proper officers, presbyters, by which, in the name of the Lord Jesus Christ, she invests a man with sacred office and sets him apart for the discharge of its duties. This act is in no sense sacramental. There are only two sacraments, baptism and the Lord's Supper; and these are signs and seals of the provisions of the eternal covenant of redemption—that covenant between God the Father and God the Son by which we are delivered from sin in its penalty, pollution and power. The Sacraments are seals of this covenant and means of grace to believers, but in no way connected with ordination.

Still more. Ordination is not a charm or talisman by which grace is conferred, and supernatural gifts are imparted to men; and yet it is more than a mere form which may or may not be observed, which may with impunity be treated with neglect or contempt. It is a solemn appointment of the Saviour. "He ordained twelve, that they should be with him, and that he might send them forth to preach" (Mark iii. 14). His apostles also committed the things they had received to faithful men who should be able to teach others; and He gave certain promises to the elders who rule well and labour in word and doctrine, which promises if pleaded in faith at the time of ordination, and are afterwards trusted in, are sure to be fulfilled.

As to the mode of ordination it embraces two acts—prayer, sometimes accompanied by fasting, and the imposition of the hands of presbyters. This was the order followed in the case of the first deacons. The seven men "were set before the Apostles; and when they had prayed, they laid their hands on them" (Acts 6:6). Timothy's authority to "give attendance to reading, to exhortation, to doctrine" was given him "by prophecy, with the laying on of the hands of the presbytery" (1 Tim 4:13, 14). And so at the ordination of Barnabas and Saul to a special mission among the Gentiles, by the Presbytery of Antioch, "when they had fasted and prayed, and laid their hands on them, they sent them away" (Acts 3:3).

It is proper to add that the Presbyterian Church has never regarded the form of ordination as a matter of grave importance. Hence the laying on of hands in ordaining ministers and ruling elders was dispensed with in the First Book of Discipline adopted by the Church of Scotland in 1560, and the ceremony was again enjoined in the case of ministers in the Second Book of Discipline adopted in 1578. The present practice is to ordain ministers in this manner but to omit the imposition of hands in the case of ruling elders. The essential thing is that the Church should carefully guard the right of the people to elect, and should solemnly recognize in an orderly way and in the name of the Lord Jesus Christ the call by the Holy Spirit of such persons to their sacred office.

And now comes the practical question, what are the functions of persons thus called, elected and ordained? I answer:—

IV.—*That they are chiefly to rule, to teach, and to administer the Sacraments.* Their power in these respects is derived from Jesus Christ, the Head of the Church, who is the sole fountain of all ecclesiastical authority. The Church in electing and ordaining elders can clothe them only with such power as she receives from her Head. They are thus constituted bishops or elders, overseers of the flock of God; for elders and bishops in the New Testament are the same, as is now admitted by competent and unbiased interpreters. That this was the opinion of the revisers of the English translation of the Bible in 1881–84 seems evident from a much needed correction which they made in the twentieth chapter of the Acts of the Apostles, substituting the word bishops for overseers. At the seventeenth verse it is stated that Paul "sent from Miletus to Ephesus and called the Elders of the Church." I ask you to notice particularly that in delivering his charge to those elders the apostle said, "Take heed therefore unto yourselves and to all the flock over which the Holy Ghost hath made you bishops, to feed the

Church of God which he purchased with his own blood" (Acts 20:28). The Ephesian elders are thus pronounced bishops by apostolic authority, showing that the two names are used interchangeably, and showing, too, that a plurality of bishops, several bishops existed in one church, instead of what grew up in post-apostolic days when one bishop was set over a number of churches in a whole diocese. The primitive practice was to ordain elders or bishops, as many as might be thought desirable, in every church; and any attentive reader of the New Testament can see plainly that the same qualifications, privileges, responsibilities, and duties belonged to elders and bishops. According to Paul they were "to feed the flock of God" (Acts 14:23). The Greek word is *poimainein*, literally to tend as shepherds do their flocks. And Peter says, "Tend"—using the same Greek word as Paul—"the flock of God which is among you exercising the oversight"—the bishopric—"not of constraint, but willingly, according unto God; nor yet for filthy lucre but of a ready mind; neither as lording it over the charge allotted to you, but making yourselves ensamples to the flock" (1 Pet 2, 3).

In defining the qualifications of elders or bishops we might content ourselves with the analysis of a single passage—that in which Paul directs Titus when left in Crete "to ordain elders in every city."[38] He is told what sort of men to set apart for the office. The negative and positive attributes of their character as well as their official functions are enumerated in detail. "The bishop must be blameless, as the steward of God."[39] "Not self-willed." He must sink his own will in that of Christ, feeling that He is his Master. "Not soon angry"—capable of governing his temper even under sharp provocation. "No brawler," literally not quarrelsome over wine—one whose moral and spiritual nature is not impaired by being given to much wine. "No striker"—free from violence whether of temper or outward conduct. "Not greedy of filthy lucre"—above being biased and controlled by desires of sordid gain.

These five negations express a great deal, and make the elder a very remarkable man even if nothing more could be said of him. But here are positive qualities by which he is characterized. He must be "given to hospitality," prone to entertain strangers without reward, or with generous liberality. "A lover of good"—wherever he finds it in any section of the Church of God—having his delights not with the ungodly and riotous, but with the saints, the excellent of the earth. "Sober," in feeling, in thought, in action. "Just," in his business, in his opinions, and judgments of all things, and therefore both fit to rule and to teach—a man "whose eye though turned on

---

38. Titus 1:5.

39. The passage discussed is Titus 1:7–9.

empty space beams keen with honour."[40] "Holy"—God-like and Christ-like, for the divine nature revealed in Christ is the standard and pattern of human holiness. "Temperate"—free from mental and physical extravagances, well balanced in mind, and therefore showing a calm, even, and consistent career in life. "Holding to the faithful work which is according to the teaching"—having a firm and strong grasp of God's truth as a whole—not weak and uncertain in his convictions as to the Gospel, but clear and decided as the result of diligent personal study of the Word, as well as by showing due deference to the prelections of others. An elder is not simply a person who can pass a creditable examination in some easy theological primer, but rather one who has a goodly mastery of the contents of the whole bible. Hence he is to "be able to exhort in the sound doctrine, and to convict the gainsayers." His strength as a teacher is to be laid out not upon theory or speculation or brilliant oratory or skilful adaption of his lessons to the opinions of others, but upon exhortation in the sound doctrine that he may thus convict the gainsayers.

These, brethren, are the qualifications and functions of the bishop or elder. But who is sufficient for these things?[41] Is it not too much to expect all these qualities in full measure in any man? I answer, the standard must be correct and perfect, and we must do our best to come as near to it as we can, and seek help from God that we may daily rise to a higher plane of spiritual life and service.

It may be too much to lay upon the rank and file of the elders all the duties just described, and as matter of fact our church discriminates in this respect, and divides elders into two classes, those called to rule and those called to teach. Of the ruling elder such teaching power as implied in the passages cited has not been demanded. The divine gift of public teaching in a pre-eminent degree is not very widely distributed. It is certain that many elders justly shrink from delivering public discourses. They are not required to do so, and have not been trained and may not be naturally fitted to render such service. For the sake of doing "all things decently and in order,"[42] the Apostle Paul enjoins, it is well that some should be specially designated to the work of preaching the Gospel, while at the same time exercising the right to rule along with the rest. But if we accept a wide-spread consensus of opinion to the effect that New Testament bishops and elders are identical, we cannot avoid the conclusion that they are all to be "apt to teach."[43] We

---

40. From Robert Burns' poem "The Vision."
41. Allusion to 2 Cor 2:16.
42. 1 Cor 14:40.
43. 1 Tim 3:2.

must, of course, grant them the utmost freedom as to the circumstances under which they perform the task. It may be in the household or office, in small or great classes. Some may excel among the young, and others among the aged, some among the sick and fainting, others among the strong and forward. By a principle of both natural and spiritual selection they will readily find their proper spheres, so that the teaching force of a congregation may thoroughly cover all its needs. And there can be no doubt that with the comprehensive scriptural knowledge proper to elders, many of them who never preach sermons can deal successfully in private with "unruly men, and vain talkers and deceivers, whose mouths must be stopped."[44] And it may be laid down as a general principle that the larger the number of truly devout and able teachers of the Word in any church, the better for its spiritual growth and power. In so far as the thousands of elders belonging to our section of the Holy Catholic Church in Canada are men of the stamp and character that Paul directed Titus to ordain, they constitute an enormous intellectual, moral and spiritual force, for which we cannot be too thankful. It is, let me assure you, a matter of the highest moment for a church to have a wise and strong Congregational Presbytery as a court of primary resort in discipline, composed of a body of men given to prayer and good works, to whom members can look up with reverence and affection; for we are enjoined of God to "count the elders who rule well worthy of double honour, especially those who labour in the word and in teaching."[45] Their services are very precious to the flock, and to be specially sought in seasons of trouble. Hence it is written: "is any sick among you"[46] let him call for the elders of the church; and let them pray over him, anointing him with oil in the name of the Lord; and the prayer of faith shall save the sick, and the Lord shall raise him up, and if he have committed sins they shall be forgiven him."

Observe the divine order to be followed in the matter. The sick one is not to wait until the elders find out that he is sick. Much less is he to assume that teaching or ruling elders are endowed with omniscience to see who are sick and who are not in a large parish. He is to "call for the elders"—for any of them, not necessarily always for the one who statedly occupies the pulpit.

Observe, too, the blessed results which follow the ministry of the elders. They are to pray over the sick one, not merely to talk to him, and to advise and instruct him, but to plead in his behalf with Him who holds the issues of life and death in His hand, at the same time using approved means

---

44. Tit 1: 7–11.
45. 1 Tim 5:17 (ASV, altered).
46. The passage discussed is Jas 5:14.

for his recovery, "and the prayer of faith shall save the sick, and the Lord shall raise him up."

Time fails me to speak fully of the innumerable benefits which these men of God are capable of conferring upon His Church in many ways.

And now it may occur to you that I have so far made no reference to the functions of elders in relation to the two sacraments of the New Covenant. It may be sufficient to say that the practice of our church in this respect is wise and Scriptural. In the case of baptism the preaching elder alone officiates. It belongs to his commission from the Saviour to preach and to baptize. In the case of the Lord's Supper the elders act unitedly or jointly, and there is nothing sacerdotal in the part taken by the presiding elder in this solemn service. It is held by some, and they carefully act upon this belief, that the minister and the minister alone should be permitted to place the elements of the Eucharistic feast in the hands or lips of communicants. With us there is no such restriction. The sacred service is conducted by all the elders. They reverently pass through the church distributing the bread and the wine and placing them in the hands of the members. This is a silent but effectual protest against sacerdotalism. For what is the root and core of this growing error? It is ascribing to one man, known as the priest, or by any other name you please, the exclusive right of transacting with God in spiritual matters in behalf of others.

We seek to guard against this evil chiefly by clinging to Jesus Christ as our only great High Priest before God, and also by denying to every elder, the preaching elder included, as we are fully authorized by Scripture, the right to the name and the functions of a priest, except in the sense in which the whole body of believers are a royal priesthood. And let me remind you, as my final word, that it is only as we all habitually come boldly to the throne of grace, in the name of Christ, in the exercise of our royal priesthood and in concert with those we have chosen to teach and to rule, that we shall bring down the power of God the Spirit into this church to quicken the dead, and to comfort, purify and establish those who believe. Amen.

Commentary on "The Office and Work of Elders"

The sermon begins with a text from 1 Peter 5:1 with some explanation. The text serves to establish the point that Peter viewed himself simply as a "fellow-elder" and disclaimed any special clerical status. The sermon is topical, expounding the nature and role of the eldership in Presbyterianism. Thoroughly biblical, it draws on passages from the Gospels, Acts and Epistles (particularly the Pastorals) to support its assertions.

The sermon is well organized, with four "heads" (as the Scots would say) that develop the subject in logical progression. Elders derive their office from the call of the Holy Spirit; this call is discerned and confirmed by "the voice of the people"; elders thus called and elected by the congregation are ordained to office; ordained elders rule, teach and administer the Sacraments. Dividing the subject into points is typical of MacVicar. In all his writings and addresses he makes these divisions into points and sub-points, usually numbering them. Though out of fashion today, it could be argued that such divisions aid the listener in retaining the message.

It is a scholarly, theological, didactic sermon, closely reasoned in places, filled with references to Scripture (not always identified, as in the discussion of James 5:14-15 towards the close). There are explanations of Greek words (though some of these more technical details are relegated to an appendix, which I have not included due to limitations of space), and historical references, for example, the First and Second Books of Discipline of the sixteenth century in Scotland.

Those who heard this sermon preached were expected to pay careful attention for over forty minutes, and to use their minds. No relief was given by means of humour or anecdotes as they listened to what might almost have been a lecture given to students at the college.[47] At the same time, it is not merely academic. It is a *sermon*. The diction is relatively simple, much of the language resembling that of the Authorized Version of the Bible. The preacher is not aspiring to be literary or to produce any "purple patches." Instead, he seems to be aiming at communicating with the thoughtful layperson. Needless to say, this sermon dates from the late nineteenth century and the language reflects the fact that there were no women elders at that time.

One of the marks of a good sermon is *application*, and MacVicar does seek to apply the Word of God to his hearers. He seeks to encourage the congregation, to exhort the elders to come as near the high standards of the New Testament as possible, and to "seek help from God that we may daily rise to a higher plane of spiritual life and service."

Indirectly, the suggestion is made several times that elders ought to have a "comprehensive scriptural knowledge," and ought to be able to teach others in some capacity, though not necessarily by preaching publicly. Everything is related to Christ and hearers are urged to cling "to Jesus Christ as our only great High Priest before God." The sermon ends with a call to pray "habitually" in order "to bring down the power of God's Spirit into this church."

---

47. This sermon appears to be a reworking of a lecture delivered at the opening of the college session in 1882. In the lecture MacVicar pleaded for younger elders, coming close to suggesting some form of term eldership.

Donald MacVicar believed strongly in the creed and polity of the Presbyterian Church,[48] a fact that comes through clearly in this sermon on the eldership. There is even a reference to the traditional Calvinistic doctrine of the "covenant of redemption," the agreement between the Father and the Son in eternity to save the elect.

One is struck by the high view of the eldership espoused here. One of the controversies in Presbyterian history has been over the nature of the eldership. Are there three distinct offices—minister, elder and deacon; or two offices—elder and deacon (with a distinction between "teaching" and "ruling" elders)? MacVicar leans towards the "two-office" view, championed in the southern United States by such theologians as J. H. Thornwell and Robert Breckinridge.[49] He is at pains to avoid any sacerdotal notion of the ministry, and to stress the truth that all Christians constitute a "royal priesthood." His thinly veiled polemics against Roman Catholicism would have been considered especially relevant in Quebec.

No one hearing this sermon (or reading some of MacVicar's other writings on Presbyterianism) could go away thinking that the eldership is merely an honorific position. The message is clear that elders are to possess solid spiritual and moral qualities, and that they are called to be active in church government, pastoral care and worship. A deeply committed eldership, MacVicar affirms, will be "an enormous intellectual, moral and spiritual force."

The Author

John P. Vaudry is minister of First Presbyterian Church, Pembroke, Ontario. Born in Montreal in 1953, he was raised in Lennoxville, Quebec, and educated at Bishop's University, McGill University, and Presbyterian College. Ordained in 1977, he has ministered in Cape Breton, Nova Scotia, Ontario, and Quebec. His interests include music, old movies and history. He serves on the board of the Pregnancy Resource Centre in Pembroke and is moderator of the Presbytery of Lanark and Renfrew. John and his wife Wendy have three grown children and two grandchildren.

---

48. See his contribution to the "Symposium" on the *Westminster Confession of Faith* in the *Presbyterian College Journal*, 1890–91, and *Hindrances and Helps to the Spread of Presbyterianism*.

49. Palmer, *Life and Letters*, 260. MacVicar and Palmer were friends; it is interesting to see the Canadian's apparent affinities with Southern Presbyterians as well as with Princeton theologians.

Bibliography

Connor, Ralph. *The Man from Glengarry.* Toronto: McClelland & Stewart, 1993.

Johnston, John A. "Donald Harvey MacVicar." In *Called to Witness,* edited by W. Stanford Reid, 2:57–64. Toronto: The Presbyterian Church in Canada, 1980.

MacVicar, D. H. *Helps and Hindrances to the Spread of Presbyterianism.* Toronto: Robinson, 1879.

———. Introduction to *Forty Years in the Church of Christ,* by Charles Chiniquy. Chicago: Revell, 1899.

———. *The Office and Work of Elders.* Montreal: Drysdale, 1864.

———. *Recent Aspects of Materialism.* Montreal: Beckett, 1871.

———. *Roman Catholicism in Canada.* Montreal: Drysdale, 1889.

———. "Symposium on the *Westminster Confession of Faith.*" *Journal of Presbyterian College* (1890–91) 5–16.

MacVicar, J. H. *Life and Work of Donald Harvey MacVicar, D.D., LL.D.* Toronto: Westminster, 1904.

Markell, H. Keith. *History of the Presbyterian College, Montreal 1865–1986.* Montreal: Presbyterian College, 1987.

Masters, D. C. *Protestant Church Colleges in Canada.* Toronto: University of Toronto Press, 1966.

———. *A Short History of Canada.* Princeton: Van Nostrand, 1958.

Moir, John S. "MacVicar, Donald Harvey." In *DCB* 13:1901–10.

Palmer, B. M. *The Life and Letters of James Henley Thornwell.* Edinburgh: Banner of Truth, 1974.

Pidgeon, George C. "Principal MacVicar—A Leader in French Evangelization." In *Missionary Pathfinders,* 1907, 158.

CHAPTER 3

The College and Missions
Jane Drummond Redpath

By Lucille Marr

Jane Drummond Redpath (1815–1907), second wife of John Redpath. Image from a painting by Antoine Plamondon, 1836, with credit to the McCord Museum M994.35.2.

"REDPATH—On January 30, 1907, at Terrace Bank, Jane Drummond, widow of the late John Redpath, aged 91. Funeral private."[1]

THIS TERSE DEATH NOTICE stands in stark contrast to the flowery obituaries published at the time of John Redpath's passing thirty-eight years earlier. His described the large, elaborate funeral celebration with "a good number of our best known citizens amongst the mercantile and professional community," and a large number of clergy in attendance. Superlatives included many examples of the contributions he had made to the community during his "long career of usefulness." Just as an observant reader might search the papers in vain for any reference to Jane Drummond Redpath's presence in her husband's life, her own death notice provides no hint of her remarkable life and her zeal for the cause of missions.

This is surprising. When even though, as one historian has explained, "women's lives, their activities or their work were rarely chronicled in the public press," and few women took "the time to keep a journal or maintain extensive correspondence," their obituaries tended to be detailed and informative.[2] Jane Redpath was well known in Montreal. Although few knew that Drummond Street was named for her, Redpath Street was in the Square Mile where the Canadian wealthy elite lived. Jane was *the* Mrs. Redpath, often qualified by "of Terrace Bank." Better known was Grace Woods Redpath, widow of Peter who was responsible for McGill University's renowned library. But when it was announced in 1907 that "Mrs. Redpath had died," few would have doubted which one. There may have been some confusion: Grace and Jane were the same age and both hoped to outlive the other. Strangely, both died the same day.

Even at a time of extravagant obituaries and lengthy tributes in the minutes of church organizations, why can we find few words about this woman who played such a significant role in the life of the Presbyterian College and the cause of missions both in Montreal and beyond? Was she a submissive wife and mother, a wealthy, well-meaning matron, who widowed at age fifty-four, preferred to live in his shadow? Was she a recluse, as her obituary suggests, only the "widow of the late John Redpath," or was she, perhaps, actually a woman of stature and substance who deserves a place celebrating significant voices in the history of the Presbyterian College, Montreal?

---

1. "Jane Drumond Redpath—notice of death," *Montreal Daily Star*, February 2, 1907. Her burial at Mount Royal Cemetery, Montreal is documented. No obituary or biography is included on the site. http://www.findagrave.com.

2. Errington, *Wives and Mothers*, xi, xiv–xv.

Among historians of women circulates the adage, "anonymous is a woman." In an age when few women wrote, and rarely were the journals or letters of those who did preserved, it requires careful research to learn about a well-known matron like Jane Redpath and her influence on the course of the nineteenth-century evangelical culture of Montreal.[3] Historians have found that "persistent curiosity" is required "to uncover" what often turns out to be worthwhile "significant roles" that women have played.[4] Hints in studies referencing Jane Redpath suggest the importance of hearing again her "still voice."[5] By recalling her place in the development of the evangelical culture and her sense of mission that gave rise to the Presbyterian College, Montreal, we hear a whisper in the chorus of significant "still voices" of the time.[6]

Jane Drummond Redpath made essential contributions to Montreal's evangelical culture in her role as mistress of the Redpath home and to the mission of the Presbyterian College, Montreal, through her leadership in the French Canadian Missionary Society and later the Presbyterian Church in Canada Ladies' French Evangelization Society. It was nearly a century before women were given the opportunity to pursue theological education at Presbyterian College. History also shows that Jane Redpath shared in the early vision of women's education. She gave direction to the Montreal Ladies' Educational Association established in 1871 with strong support by Presbyterian academics including McGill Principal William Dawson and Presbyterian College Principal D. H. MacVicar.

---

3. See Great Unsolved Mysteries in Canadian History (GUMICH) project for hints to the mystery that still surround Jane Redpath's family. We know that at the time of her death, Jane had outlived all her stepchildren and all but three of her own children. See Feltoe's family genealogy, in *Gentleman of Substance*, 124–28. He noted that "the home had been maintained for Jane by the executors of the estate," 210. Census records confirm that she lived at Terrace Bank with only several servants helping to maintain the vast home. Jane Redpath, *1901 Census of Canada*.

4. See for instance Epp, *Mennonite Women in Canada*, 3–4.

5. Feltoe does a wonderful service in weaving together John Redpath's business and philanthropic enterprises with his complicated family life. On Jane Drummond Redpath, please see *Gentleman of Substance*, esp. 69, 118. For glimpses of Jane Redpath's contributions to Montreal benevolent work, see Klempa and Doran, *Certain Women*; Gillett, *We Walked*, 52, 61; and Armour, *Saints*, 125.

6. Scholars have argued that nineteenth-century middle-class and elite women helped to form culture. See, for instance, Theriot, *Mothers*, 4–5; and Kleinberg, *Women in the United States*, 8. In the words of the latter, whatever the phenomena shaping American culture, "women shared it and shaped it, but from a perspective infused with cultural beliefs about appropriate female roles."

Birth

Born in 1815 in Edinburgh to Margaret Pringle and George Drummond, Jane was raised with several siblings in a Presbyterian home of influence.[7] George Drummond, an expert in stone masonry and successful in his contracting building business, was also a political presence on the Edinburgh city council.[8] Among his apprentices were his brother Robert and John Redpath. Orphaned as a child, John went from his half-sister Elspeth Redpath Fairbairn's care to the Drummond home to be taught the trade of stonemasonry.[9] During his apprenticeship, he learned stonemason skills and took on the strong work ethic that guided him for life.[10]

In 1815 when Jane was still an infant, the Drummond household gained a permanent link with Britain's North American colonies. A time of great unrest in the British Isles, tens of thousands of soldiers were returning to seek employment after the Napoleonic Wars. Several of George Drummond's apprentices used the British government's emigration scheme. Jane's future was destined to be intimately connected to the colonies. In 1816, George's brother, Robert Drummond, siblings John and Robert with their nephew Peter Redpath, all skilled and qualified stone masons, set forth on the journey to the Canadas, with Robert settling in Kingston, and John in Montreal.[11]

Marriage

In the summer of 1834, John Redpath's wife Janet McPhee Redpath and his friend Robert Drummond died from the dread cholera that took 7,500 lives in the Canadas. This fate reconnected the Kingston Drummonds and the Montreal Redpaths.[12]

In 1832, sixteen-year-old Jane had come out from Edinburgh on an extended visit with her uncle Robert and his wife Margaret.[13] Not surprisingly,

---

7. With women's lives having been largely confined to the domestic sphere, historians of women have proposed a life cycle approach. See Strong-Boag, *Girls and Women*.

8. Jane Redpath, "1871 Census of Canada," *Ancestry.com*; George Drummond, "1851 Scotland Census," *Ancestry.com*.

9. Although genealogical records are sketchy for the late eighteenth and early nineteenth centuries, the Pringle family connection of John's mother Elizabeth and George's wife Margaret seems likely. See Feltoe, *Gentleman of Substance*, 19.

10. Feltoe, *Gentleman of Substance*, 8.

11. Ibid., 11–12.

12. Ibid., 36–41, 125.

13. Errington, *Wives and Mothers*, 6; Feltoe, *Gentleman of Substance*, 39.

even in the time of mourning, the beautiful young Jane captured the heart of John Redpath, a thirty-nine-year-old widower and father of six. It was wives, not sisters, who provided the "important social and moral symbols . . . representing one of the essential components of the new society" that was being established.[14] John Redpath needed a spouse who would reestablish and manage his household.[15] He had gained a reputation for his work on the Rideau Canal, his successful contracting business as a stone mason and engineer and a gentleman of social status and community influence. Such a position required a worthy wife. During his time of mourning, he recognized Jane Drummond's capacity for helping him to raise his family, and her potential to support his burgeoning career. He saw the companion he would need if he were to further establish his place as a solid Presbyterian in the mercantile culture shaping Montreal.[16]

Jane Drummond would have been schooled for marriage. Nineteenth-century women and men expected to live in distinct worlds and were apprenticed for their respective roles. Just as John had been taught stonemasonry by her father, Jane would have learned what it meant to be a woman from her mother and other relatives. She would have learned the "intimacy and relational meaning" that women of the era shared "with their women friends and in their mothering";[17] and she would have been schooled properly in household management. She would have learned the skills essential to wed a man of stature.

Why did Jane Drummond agree to marry John Redpath, a man nearly twice her age? We can only speculate. We know that for women of that era, marriage was "a rite of passage." and that although women generally had the right of choice, parents held sway. Equal to the importance of affection was the status that marriage gave women in their roles of wife and mother. "Marriage robbed a woman of personal power," but it gained her a strong role where there was plenty of scope for leadership in the household, and in moulding the minds and souls of children.[18] As John Redpath's wife, Jane gained the status to be a force for good in the community. Her acceptance

14. Errington, *Wives and Mothers*, xii–xiii; Kleinberg, *Women in the United States*, 16–17.

15. Feltoe insists that they respected the obligatory year of mourning, dictated by nineteenth-century society. See Feltoe, *Gentleman of Substance*, 40–43.

16. Ibid., 37; Errington, *Wives and Mothers*, 82.

17. Theriot, *Mothers and daughters*, 37; see also 32, 63, and Kleinberg, *Women in the United States*, 14.

18. Theriot, *Mothers and daughters*, 24, 34. See also Errington, *Wives and Mothers*, 7, 28–29, 31; Errington asserts that scholars estimate that 90 percent of women in Upper Canada married.

of John Redpath's offer of marriage gave her opportunities yet to be grasped. Jane would enjoy the status of matron of a ready-made family, the financial ability to sustain an elite lifestyle, and the ability to manage her own household. As well, Jane Drummond chose the potential for adventure and for mission in a city considered a tinderbox of religious and racial tension.

Their wedding on September 11, 1835, compelled Jane to confront the dangers of cholera and civic unrest. This volatile situation forced John to move his family to Jones Falls, a small village on the Rideau Canal, north of Kingston. While still a teenager, Jane had the considerable challenge of being mother to Elizabeth, Peter, Mary, Helen, Jane Margaret, and John James, ranging from age fifteen years to twenty months. Did Montreal's French population (numbering 35,000), present a menacing majority or a promising field for Christian mission?[19]

Motherhood

Jane Drummond Redpath's 1836 portrait by Antoine Plamondon soon after their marriage gives a glimpse: cultured, in the elaborate apparel of the day, and bejewelled, but appropriately dressed in black. Her visage shows strength of character and suggests the virtues valued in the good woman: "kindness, simplicity of manners, Christian commitment, intelligence, industry, frugality, goodness, and generosity."[20] John's letter to a friend soon after their marriage suggests that life with Jane had proven to be good and hints that he had found the "tender wife," "affectionate parent," and most importantly, the potential as a "steady and sincere friend," attributes greatly valued in nineteenth-century colonies.[21]

By the arrival of their first child, Margaret Pringle, born October 26, 1836, John Redpath's distinction as merchant of Montreal marked his acceptance in Montreal Society.[22] Redpath's position was confirmed with the family's move to the 235-acre property of Terrace Bank, located high on Mount Royal. Mountain property was purchased by the wealthy because it was above the smoke, the pollution and the smells of squalidness typical

19. Feltoe, *Gentleman of Substance*, 36–43, 124–26; their mutual decision to marry suggests "the mutual confidence, affection, and respect" idealized in English Canada. See Errington, *Wives and Mothers*, 33.

20. Antoine Plamondon, Portrait; Errington, *Wives and Mothers*, xii.

21. Errington, *Wives and Mothers*, xii; Feltoe, *Gentleman of Substance*, 50. See also Theriot, *Mothers and daughters*, 35, on the important role that the home took for men such as John Redpath.

22. St. Paul's Church Registers, 1994.4012.7.5, The Church of St. Andrew and St. Paul, Montreal Church Archives cited in Feltoe, *Gentleman of Substance*, 48–49.

of an industrial Victorian city. Their new three-story house was one that bespoke stature with its grand hallway, drawing room, parlour, and library. The dozen bedrooms, three inside toilets and central heating were important symbols of the Redpaths' affluence.[23] As mistress of Terrace Bank, Jane "had to hire staff, a cook, a maid, a governess, and perhaps a butler, determine the work, and ensure that it was performed to her satisfaction."[24]

There were plenty of responsibilities for women of the era, but motherhood was their most important role. Servants did the cooking and cleaning, but as mother, Jane was to bear, to nurse, and to ensure that her large and rapidly growing blended family was fed and clothed. Through twenty-two years of childbearing, Jane learned first-hand, through the births of her ten children, of the physical and emotional challenges implicit in motherhood.[25] To show the complexity of her situation, it is noted that Jane became a mother-in-law in 1840 while having her children in 1839, 1841, 1844, 1846, 1848, 1850, 1853, 1854, and 1858, all the while punctuated by weddings and births in John's first family. Perhaps the most challenging was Peter's marriage to Grace Woods, a woman Jane's own age with what must have been at times the formidable challenges of being mother-in-law to a peer.[26]

The family's first loss was the death of ten-month-old Williamina in the summer of 1842. This may well have taught Jane the lesson of "complete self-surrender" which advice writers of the time defined as the meaning of motherhood. Perhaps through this death and the subsequent deaths of Isabella, Charles, and Harriet, Jane was learning the "calm endurance of trials and pain and constant suffering without complaint" that "were . . . essential characteristics of good mothering." It would seem to this writer that she found an outlet in mission.[27] Believing that she was responsible for passing on the essential matters of "religion, morality, and child rearing," Jane endeavoured to create the right environment essential in raising responsible adults.[28] Jane's contributions to the French Canadian Missionary Society

23. Feltoe, *Gentleman of Substance*, 49, 51, 55, 126–27.

24. Errington, *Wives and Mothers*, 134. Two years after John's passing, with only four children still at home, Jane had a laundrywoman, a cook and a parlour maid. Jane Redpath, 1871 Census of Canada. See also Errington, *Wives and Mothers*, 141.

25. Errington, *Wives and Mothers*, 20–21.

26. Feltoe, *Gentleman of Substance*, 69, 120, 127–28.

27. Theriot, *Mothers and Daughters*, 4–5, 22; Errington, *Wives and Mothers*, 72.

28. Theriot, *Mothers and Daughters*, 35; Kleinberg, *Women in the United States*, 60. This was a job she carried off well if the success of at least some of the Redpath progeny is any indication. Feltoe lays out both the complexities of the Redpath-Drummond connections, and something of the heritage that Jane Drummond and John Redpath spawned and nourished. Please see *Gentleman of Substance*, 117–20, 126–27. See also *Wikipedia.org*, s.v. "Peter Redpath"; Lorraine McMullen, "Dougall, Lily," http://www.

(FCMS) must have given her solace and meaning. This involvement set Jane on a path she would follow for the next forty years. Her innate strength and deep spirituality played a significant part in helping shape the evangelical culture of Montreal. These resulted in theological education and eventually giving women access to higher education.

Montreal's Matron in Mission

In the spring of 1839, James Thompson of the Montreal Auxiliary of the British and Foreign Bible Society assembled a group of like-minded Protestant ministers and laymen to discuss how best to evangelize French-speaking Catholics. The patriot rebellions of 1837–38 opened the way for change.[29] In their wake, Lord Durham had recommended assimilation but Protestant leaders believed the answer was conversion. Only by rejecting Catholicism and embracing the evangelical faith could French Canadians be liberated to the peace and prosperity of the colonial life envisioned by evangelicals.[30] John Redpath and his fellow congregants of Côté Street Free Church founded in 1844 proved to be its strongest and most generous backers.[31]

There were suggestions that John was following the lead of his wife. His naming of Drummond Street when he ceded the property to the city in May 1842 confirms his respect for her and hints at her close association in his work.[32] Jane was undoubtedly an evangelical. Was she more evangelical than John? Scholars of this era speculate that men "deferred to women in matters of religion, morality, and child rearing."[33] We know that Jane's missionary zeal matched or surpassed John's. The 1844 report of the Ladies' Auxiliary of the FCMS founded in 1841 shows the sense of mission that allowed her to exert strong influence in women's rights and education.[34] We hear her voice in their own affirmation of their work: it "almost renders it superfluous for your Committee to say that this Auxiliary is one of the main pillars upon which your society rests."[35]

The Society's goal was civic peace. Earlier the FCMS had appealed to imprisoned *patriotes* that acceptance of evangelical faith would lead to the

---

biographi.ca/en/bio/dougall_lily_15E.html, for instance.
29. Scorgie, "French-Canadian Missionary Society," 84, 89–90, 97.
30. Ibid., 86, 94, 98; Lougheed, "Clashes in Worldview," 101–2.
31. Feltoe, 70–72; Moir, *Enduring Witness*, 103, 105; Tulchinsky, "John Redpath."
32. Feltoe, *Gentleman of Substance*, 68–69.
33. Theriot, *Mothers and Daughters*, 35; Kleinberg, *Women in the United States*, 60.
34. Feltoe, *Gentleman of Substance*, 118.
35. FCMS Annual Report I (1844), 22.

security they sought. It would have made sense to Jane Redpath that this was the ideal way to transform the new world into a safer one, with some semblance of the old.[36] The rebellion had forced the Redpaths to flee. In the spirit of nineteenth-century upper-class women, Jane seized the opportunity to engage in missions that held the hope of transforming Montreal and the whole of Lower Canada.[37] As a woman she could not preach the Gospel message, but she could join with other women in supporting mission to French Canadians, confident in the Society's belief, that "the improvement and conversion of the French Canadians . . . a work equally interesting and imperative," would redeem their world.[38]

The Free Church supported the FCMS long after other denominations founded their own, and when they united with the Scottish secessionists in 1861 to form the Canada Presbyterian Church, their allegiance continued and deepened.[39] John and Jane Redpath assumed leadership roles in the FCMS: he as vice-president, then president, until his death in 1869; and she as committee member and president of the ladies' work, until her resignation in 1873. Jane's donations continued until the mission was incorporated into the French ministries of the Presbyterian Church in Canada. Her annual gift of $30, the cost of educating a child for a year, stood large among the more common contributions of $2.[40]

Central to Presbyterianism is the belief that the pulpit is the primary source of religious instruction. It was mandatory to educate good missionary preachers.[41] In January 1864, John and Jane Redpath held "that little meeting at Terrace Bank" for Côté Street friends including McGill's Principal William Dawson and the Reverend D. H. MacVicar, for what came to be called "that little meeting at Terrace Bank."[42] Their home was therefore the birthplace of the Presbyterian College—a seminary in connection with McGill—with the mission to train converts to carry the Gospel to the people of Quebec in French.

36. Scorgie, "French-Canadian Missionary Society," 84, 89–90, 93, 97.

37. Kleinberg, *Women in the United States*, 35; Errington, *Wives and Mothers*, 21, 170, 161; Lougheed, "Clashes in World View," 101–2; Feltoe, *Gentleman of Substance*, 69.

38. Ladies' FCMS (1841), 28. See also Scorgie, "French-Canadian Missionary Society," 79, 85, 95.

39. Lalonde, "French Protestant Missionary Activity," 163–65; Lougheed, "Clashes in Worldview," 105.

40. FCMS (1844–1869).

41. Gauvreau, *Evangelical Century*, 32.

42. Campbell, *History of the Scotch Presbyterian Church*, 394; Markell, *History of the Presbyterian College*, 8–9; Lalonde, "French Protestant Missionary Activity," 165.

It was a vision that Jane Redpath shared as much as anyone in her home that night. She may not have been physically present but her influence was surely felt. The nurturing of those called to the ministry was important to her. The cause of the Presbyterian College was as close to her heart as it was to her husband's.[43] The year he died, 1869, classes were being held in the basement of Erskine Church. Viability, visibility, proper faculty and curriculum had barely begun. There was criticism within the church about the necessity of another theological college. No one doubted that this was a cause that John Redpath had determined would succeed.

Widowhood

On March 8, 1869, Jane Redpath received hundreds of mourners who paid their respects to her late husband John. The funeral procession used a route well travelled during their thirty-five-year marriage through old Montreal to the Côté Street Church. Jane was not mentioned in the Reverend D. H. MacVicar's eulogy. John Redpath would rest in the family cemetery on their property for the next fifteen years until moved to the huge Redpath plot in the new Mount Royal Cemetery where she would eventually join him.[44]

Her encouragement for the fledgling Presbyterian College, whose principal was her minister and friend, continued unabated. Principal MacVicar likely visited Terrace Bank many times. Jane Redpath was a woman who liked to be informed, but not by hearsay. Financial statements and mission statements were equally important to her. Jane established the John Redpath scholarship and the John Redpath chair at the Presbyterian College.[45] There are numerous references to bursaries for needy and deserving students marked "Mrs. Redpath of Terrace Bank."

Her resignation from the executive of the women's branch of the FCMS was not an end, but the beginning of an even wider leadership of Montreal women in the new Presbyterian Church in Canada formed in 1875 and its French work that included the Maritimes and the ever-expanding Northwest Territories. There was great pride that the founding president of the Presbyterian Ladies' French Evangelization Society of Montreal (that was later to evolve into the Women's Missionary Society), was the redoubtable Jane Redpath. Not many years later the WMS reported to the General

---

43. Theriot, *Mothers and Daughters*, 35; Feltoe, *Gentleman of Substance*, 110.

44. *Montreal Witness*, 5 March 1869, cited in Richard Feltoe, *Gentleman of Substance*, 112; See also MacVicar, *In memoriam*.

45. *Presbyterian College Journal*, November 1881, 14; Markell, *History of the Presbyterian College*, 10–11; Campbell, *History of the Scotch Presbyterian Church*, 394.

Assembly both the extensive activities of its French department, and its care for new immigrants, its hospitals, missions and the schools in the West, all staffed and administered by women.

Eventually the WMS in its two divisions sent its own missionaries to India, Africa, and Asia and became a "church within a church" that survived the divisions of 1925. Unlike ministers and professors, the WMS leadership was overwhelmingly Presbyterian in sympathy. It continues its worldwide missions today, though greatly diminished. Perhaps the authors had Jane Redpath, its founder, in mind when they entitled their history of the WMS *Certain Women Amazed Us*.[46]

In the same year Jane Redpath presided over the Montreal Ladies' Educational Association established in 1871 by McGill Principal William Dawson. Her leadership pushed the latter until women were admitted to McGill in 1885. It could be said that her life was her sermon. The following are excerpts from reports of the three organizations that benefited most from Jane Redpath: The Ladies' Auxiliary of the French Canadian Missionary Society; the Ladies' French Evangelization Society; and the Montreal Ladies' Educational Association. Jane Redpath's voice, though long silent, can be still heard.

Twenty-Fifth Annual Report of the Ladies' Auxiliary French Canadian Missionary Society 1867[47]

On this, the twenty-fifth Anniversary of your Society's organization it is peculiarly a duty to review its past history, and describe its present position and prospects.

From year to year, an account of the Girls' Mission School at Pointe-aux-Trembles, has been recorded. The high and holy object for which it was founded, has never been lost sight of: all who seek admission, know that its distinguishing feature is, its evangelical teaching and Christian influence. During these years of experience, it has been found difficult to train to mental effort those whose childhood had been surrounded by ignorance, but now a change is taking place. Side by side with older pupils from the most isolated parts of Canada, who have had no opportunity of intellectual development, are the bright, intelligent faces of those whose parents studied in the same class rooms.

---

46. For a complete and engaging history of the WMS, see Klempa and Doran, *Certain Women*, esp. 13; *Acts and Proceedings*, 1876–77.

47. FCMS I, 3–6.

While calling to mind the great number who have enjoyed the advantages of the Girls' Institution during the past twenty-five years, the sessions of active diligent study and seasons of anxious, earnest religious intent, that have been witnessed there; your Committee also recalls with grateful pleasure, the names of the self-denying Christian women, who have been taken from earth to heaven, while zealously engaged in the School, and of the Missionaries, who at different times, temporarily assumed its charge, and in later years, of those who abandoned friends, home and country, to devote themselves to this most interesting work.

...

Recently a young girl during a fatal illness, urged her parents to send for her former Bible teacher, that she might again hear about a loving Saviour's gracious promises and Divine love, but they refused, and she died while reproaching them for not complying with her wishes....

Two special donations per your President, Mrs. Redpath, one of $200 from a friend, the other of $12.50 from a Society of little Girls in Labrador, taught by Miss McFarlane, a lady who had devoted herself to Missionary labor, in that inhospitable climate. These little girls desiring to show their gratitude for the religious instruction they are permitted to receive, went out on the dreary, desolate hills and picked berries which Miss McFarlane kindly preserved and sold to the strangers that visited the coast during the summer, and remitting to this Society one-half of the proceeds.

President—Mrs. Redpath

Vice-President—Mrs. Bonar

Ladies' French Evangelization Society[48]

The Society... proposes largely to extend its sphere of benevolent exertion; and as its members are unable of themselves to provide the means necessary for its enlarged operations, they call upon all who have at heart the temporal and spiritual interests of the many converts under the care of the Church, to aid them in this good work. The Society has already engaged a house in a central locality, which is to be known as the "French Presbyterian Mission House." A suitable matron and a guardian are about to be engaged, who, together with a bible-woman, will live on the premises and receive all applications for aid in cases of poverty or sickness, and furnish all necessary information in regard to churches, schools, etc. They will also keep a register of persons in need of employment, and recommend the employment of the

---

48. *Presbyterian Record*, September 1876, 232–33.

premises where practicable, of deserving applicants. The Mission House will be visited by the members of the Society in rotation, who will personally inquire into the circumstances of every applicant, and superintend the distribution of articles of food, fuel and clothing. Others will take change of bible classes, and sewing meetings, or whatever other means may be desired, for benefiting those among whom the Society labours. It is hoped that the "Reading Room" may be opened, and a Circulating Library of instructive and religious French books be established in connection with the Mission.

The necessity for such a work has been made abundantly plain during the past winter, when but for timely relief many families would have been left entirely destitute, or have been driven to make their peace with Rome. While among the converts, there are many whose Christianity will compare favorable with that of our English-speaking Church members; there are also very many whose creed is largely negative, consisting in a conviction of the errors of the Popish system, and whom it is most desirable to attract by all legimate [sic] means to the circle of genuine religious influence. A great deal of want arising from the social position of some of the converts, and also from the impossibility of their obtaining work from French employers, on account of their religion,—still continues to exist, and may be expected to continue. The Mission Churches are not able to take care of their poor; nor can the pastors of these churches, with their utmost exertions overtake a tithe of the cases that are presented to them.

In view of these circumstances, the Ladies' French Evangelization Society invites the co-operation of similar associations in the localities of the Missionary and Dorcas Societies of the Presbyterian Church throughout the Dominion, and of all who are interested in the great work of evangelization now in progress in the city of Montreal and its vicinity. Money is needed to defray the expenses of the Mission House and its employees,—to purchase fuel, provisions, and material, to be made up by women in want of employment in the Industrial rooms, or at their homes, as well as medicine for the sick, and other necessaries. Contributions of clothing, boots and shoes, blankets, quilts, bedding, pieces of cotton or stuff, thread, needles, and other working materials, will be acceptable. From friends residing in or near Montreal, donations of fuel, flour, bread, vegetable, meat, with other provisions, and medical comforts, are earnestly desired. An appeal is also made for French books and papers for the Library and Reading Room. Finally, any aid that may be given in furnishing the Mission House will be gratefully acknowledged.

Mrs. Redpath, *President*

Montreal Ladies' Educational Association Annual Report 1877–78[49]

The Association has again the satisfaction of seeing the names of 55 students enrolled, a list which, although it does not equal that of the Session 1876–7, is greater than that of preceding years. Of these students, 31 passed one or more examinations, 60 certificates being given (viz: First Class, 29; Second Class, 20; and Third Class, 11).... The Association has also been able to give certificates for a three years' course to two ladies, and trusts that the number entitled to such certificates may increase.

Many who continue to have a warm interest in the welfare of the Association, have for a time been obliged to withdraw from an active share. It has been suggested that by making some slight difference in the scale of fees, and especially in the Members' Ticket, some of the difficulties which have arisen may be obviated ... Our receipts have been: —From Members' Subscriptions, $972; from Students' Tickets, Interest, &c., $160.32; the expenditure, $1,249.31; leaving a deficit which had to be converted by a further loan from the reserve fund and by the voluntary subscriptions of the Members of the General Committee. We must still hope that more prosperous times for the whole community will soon dawn, and that some share will fall to our struggling Association. Last session when we were compelled to reduce the number of Lectures to 40, we hoped that we should shortly be in a position to again arrange for two long and two short courses, sixty lectures in all, and with this in view, we are still working, feeling often very much hampered by consideration of ways and means, and compelled to be content with doing the best that circumstances will permit for the Association. The programme for 1878–79 contains an entirely new feature, and opens what is in Canada new field in Education, although only following what is already almost a beaten track in the old country. Every speaker at our Annual Meetings, and many of those gentlemen who kindly undertook to give the inaugural lectures, reminded us that, no matter to what extent "Woman's Higher Education" might be carried, it would remain very deficient in its most necessary knowledge, if domestic economy did not form a part of serious study. As a first step towards this, it has been arranged that "Lectures on Theoretical and Practical Cookery" should form part of the Course.... The Committee was desirous of making the course as perfect as possible by preceding it by Lectures on the "Chemistry of Food," but was unable to do so. It has, however, been fortunate in arranging for an equally important subject in connection with it, the "Physiology of Nutrition," which Dr. Osler

---

49. Montreal Ladies' Educational Association (1877–78), 10–13.

has consented to take, and will commence the Session on October 3rd, with lectures to be given twice a week. . . . After Christmas, the usual days and order will be resumed, the Rev. Principal MacVicar taking a branch of Moral Philosophy, "Social Duties." . . .

Though unable, in arranging this programme, to follow out all the suggestions of the committee in our last year's Report, the subjects not touched upon will be kept in view for a succeeding session, viz.: Astronomy, Physical geography, Heat, &c.; in the decision, the Executive being, as heretofore, guided by circumstances.

In closing the year's Report, we can, even with a diminished subscribers' list speak of the good influence of the Lectures. The attendance continues large, showing that all those now connected with the Association are actively interested in it. . . . We have more than doubled the time that most people thought such an Association likely to last, and although still only depending on annual subscribers, sufficient interest is evidently felt in Education by the ladies of Montreal, to enable us to be almost entirely supported by those actually attending the lectures, while we find from one of the late numbers of the "Journal of the Women's Education Union," which formerly honoured us with mention and encouragement, that many useful and important works at home[50] will have to be discontinued, if the general public does not answer to the appeal for assistance. Yet we need scarcely say that although proud of our independence, we should be glad to see some fund established to secure us from the fluctuations to which our position in a business community renders us peculiarly liable.

(Signed) Jane Redpath, *President*,

Mary A. N. Mercer, *Honorary Secretary*

Commentary on the Three Reports of Jane Redpath

These reports underscore Jane Drummond Redpath's strong leadership in mission and women's education, allowing readers to hear her voice in the concerns highlighted. A French speaker herself, and a woman of means and influence, she invested in educational efforts that she and others in the French Canadian Missionary Society believed would benefit the French Catholic population, and by extension themselves.[51] This ministry set the stage for her leadership role in denominational ministry to French Canadians and for higher education for elite and middle-class women.

50. Scotland.
51. Jane Redpath, "1901 Census of Canada."

The report alludes to the "numerous churches, preaching stations, schools and workers," including the Belle-Rivière Institution at Pointe-aux-Trembles, down river from Montreal, boasted by the society at the peak of its work. Initially established as a school for boys, we can hear Jane Redpath's voice in the decision to establish a companion school for girls. Designed to provide a solid liberal education, it was also strongly evangelistic and practical.[52] The organization was run on a shoestring budget. As noted in the preceding biography, in a strategy familiar to women of the time, Jane and others raised major support through their annual bazaar held at Montreal's Place d'Armes. Indeed this money paid the second installment of the farm.[53]

By the last quarter of the century, the support of this mission and other women's French work was incorporated and expanded to include new ministries under MacVicar's leadership in establishing a Presbyterian French Missionary Society that would support the mission of Presbyterian College.[54] Under Jane Redpath's leadership as founding president of the Ladies' French Evangelization Society, to further their goal in evangelizing francophone women, a house leased on downtown Montreal's de la Gauchetière Street "became a centre for mother's meetings, religious instructions, Bible study, and sewing classes."[55] This included a Bible woman, who worked, essentially, as a deaconess before that order was established in 1908, fulfilling an evangelizing mission in visiting the poor.[56]

Meanwhile, the educating mission took the form of looking for an entrance into the halls of higher learning for young women of their own class, ultimately preparing the way decades later for female acceptance into theological education.[57] Jane Redpath played an essential role, to cite Feltoe, "in persuading the ruling authorities at McGill University to break their 'Men Only' rule," finally, in 1885.[58] As early as 1870, her son-in-law, John Dougall, himself a graduate of McGill promoted girls' education at McGill in his liberal paper, *The Witness*. That same year during a visit to the British Isles, Principal Dawson and his wife Margaret felt compelled to gather

---

52. Scorgie, "French-Canadian Missionary Society," 96.

53. FCMS Annual Report (1844), I, 32–33; Lalonde, "French Protestant Missionary Activity," 165; Errington, *Wives and Mothers*, 181.

54. Moir, *Enduring Witness*, 155; Lalonde, "French Protestant Missionary Activity," 167–69; Klempa and Doran, *Certain Women*, 7, 12–13; Klempa, Foreword, 2–3.

55. Klempa and Doran, *Certain Women*, 13.

56. Brouwer, *New Women for God*, 64.

57. Kleinberg, *Women in the United States*, 62.

58. Feltoe, *Gentleman of Substance*, 118.

information in the mother country, and on their return prepared a proposal for a society modeling the Ladies' Educational Association of Edinburgh.

The Montreal Ladies' Educational Association (MLEA) immediately attracted one hundred and sixty-seven members, "a veritable 'who's who' of middle- and upper-class English-speaking Montrealers."[59] Taking full charge of program planning, as well as finances, these women resisted the pressure to make domesticity the major emphasis in lectures, preferring Dawson's mineralogy, and MacVicar's "Applied Logic."[60] And yet, these professors and others such as "McGill's famous Sir William Osler,"[61] "well respected, often kindly men" in Gillett's words, put up some of "most difficult obstacles" to women's education.[62] As the report illustrates, Jane and her peers did comply with outside pressures, but for the association's fourteen years of existence insisted on maintaining an emphasis on intellectual enquiry. In Gillett's words, the MLEA's survival for fourteen years, "in the face of financial difficulties and the possibility, ever present in voluntary organizations, of factionalism and personality conflict, bears testimony to the strength and dedication of the women who began it."[63]

By the time women were accepted into McGill University in 1885, Jane Redpath was seventy years old. Her decade plus as president of the society culminated a lifetime of educational mission. As a woman of her time, the responsibility would have fallen to her to educate her children and stepchildren in spiritual and moral values. In this responsibility, she heard a call to mission to the world where she lived for over seventy years of her long life, serving faithfully by taking leadership in the shaping of the Protestant evangelical culture of Montreal. We can hear Jane Drummond Redpath, perhaps without a pulpit, but with the enthusiasm, intelligence, and vision that would allow this "still voice" to be "still heard" by the generations of women who have benefitted from higher education. Although the idea of the need for French evangelization, and Presbyterian College's ministry to French Protestants faded over time, Jane Drummond Redpath's commitment to her chosen city and significant role in creating the evangelical culture that included education for women makes hers a significant voice worthy of being "still heard."

---

59. Gillett, *We Walked Very Warily*, 51, 53–54.
60. Ibid., 58; MLEA Reports (1871–72, 1872–73, 1875–76).
61. Ibid., 282.
62. Ibid., 412.
63. Ibid., 61.

The Author

Lucille Marr, PhD, is adjunct professor at McGill University's Faculty of Religious Studies and course lecturer in church history there. Having previously served as pastor at Mennonite Fellowship of Montreal, currently she holds the post of chaplain at the Presbyterian College, Montreal. Publications include *Transforming Power of a Century: The Evolution of Mennonite Central Committee in Ontario* (Pandora, 2003), along with numerous articles pertaining to the history of gender and church institutions.

Bibliography

Armour, J. S. S. *Saints, Sinners, and Scots: A History of the Church of St. Andrew and St. Paul, Montreal, 1803–2003.* Montreal: Church of St. Andrew and St. Paul, 2003.

Brouwer, Ruth Compton. *New Women for God: Canadian Presbyterian Women and India Missions, 1876–1914.* Toronto: University of Toronto Press, 1990.

Campbell, Robert. *A History of the Scotch Presbyterian Church, St Gabriel Street, Montreal.* Microform. Montreal: Drysdale, 1887. https://archive.org/details/cihm_00397.

Drummond, George. Ancestry.com. http://interactive.ancestry.ca.

Epp, Marlene. *Mennonite Women in Canada: A History.* Winnipeg: University of Manitoba Press, 2008.

Errington, Elizabeth Jane. *Wives and Mothers, School Mistresses and Scullery Maids Working Women in Upper Canada 1790–1840.* Montreal & Kingston: McGill-Queen's University Press, 1995.

Feltoe, Richard. *A Gentleman of Substance: The Life and Legacy of John Redpath (1796–1869).* Toronto: Redpath Sugars, 2004.

French Canadian Missionary Society. Twenty-Fifth Annual Report of the Ladies' Auxiliary. Montreal: Becket, 1867.

Gillett, Margaret. *We Walked Very Warily: A History of Women at McGill.* Montreal: Eden, 2005.

The Great Unsolved Mysteries in Canadian History (GUMICH) project. http://www.canadianmysteries.ca/en/index.php.

Jane Redpath. "1871 Census of Canada" and "1901 Census of Canada." *Ancestry.com.* http://search.ancestry.ca.

Kleinberg, S. J. *Women in the United States, 1830–1945.* New Brunswick, NJ: Rutgers University Press, 1999.

Klempa, Lois, and Rosemary Doran. *Certain Women Amazed Us: The Women's Missionary Society, Their Story, 1864–2002.* Toronto: Women's Missionary Society, 2002.

Klempa, William. Foreword to *History of the Presbyterian College, Montreal, 1865–1986,* by Keith Markell, 1–6. Montreal: Presbyterian College, 1987.

Lalonde, Jean-Louis. "French Protestant Missionary Activity in Quebec from the 1850s to the 1950s." In *French-Speaking Protestants in Canada: Historical Essays,* edited by Jason Zuidema, 163–90. Leiden: Brill, 2011.

Lougheed, Richard. "Clashes in Worldview: French Protestants and Roman Catholics in the 19th Century." In *French-Speaking Protestants in Canada: Historical Essays*, edited by Jason Zuidema, 99–117. Leiden: Brill, 2011.

MacVicar, D. H. *In memoriam; a sermon, preached in the Canada Presbyterian Church, Côté Street, Montreal, on Sabbath, March 14th, 1869, on the occasion of the death of John Redpath, esq., Terrace Bank* (Montreal, 1869). CIHM/ICMH microfiche series, no. 09626.

Markell, H. Keith. *History of the Presbyterian College, Montreal, 1865–1986*. Montreal: Presbyterian College, 1987.

Moir, John S. *Enduring Witness: A History of the Presbyterian Church in Canada*. Burlington, ON: Eagle, 2004.

Montreal Ladies' Educational Association. Montreal: The Association, 1872–1885. CIHM/ICMH microfiches series, no. A01074.

Plamondon, Antoine. Portrait of Jane Drummond 2nd wife of John Redpath 1815–1907, 1836, M994.35.2, McCord Museum.

Scorgie, Glen G. "The French-Canadian Missionary Society: A Study in Evangelistic Zeal and Civic Ambition." In *French-Speaking Protestants in Canada: Historical Essays*, edited by Jason Zuidema, 79–98. Leiden: Brill, 2011.

Strong-Boag, Veronica. *The New Day Recalled: Lives of Girls and Women in English Canada, 1919–1939*. Toronto: Copp Clark Pitman and Penguin, 1988.

Theriot, Nancy M. *Mothers and Daughters in Nineteenth-Century America: The Biosocial Construction of Femininity*. Rev. ed. Lexington: University Press of Kentucky, c. 1996.

Tulchinsky, Gerald. "Redpath, John" In *Dictionary of Canadian Biography*, vol. 9, University of Toronto / Université Laval, 2003. http://www.biographi.ca/en/bio/redpath_john_9E.html.

CHAPTER 4

The College and French Work
Adrien Daniel Coussirat

By Richard Lougheed

The Reverend Professor A. Daniel Coussirat, DD, (1841–1907). This photograph from the 1905 composite graduation picture shows him wearing the OIP (Officier de l'Instruction Publique, received from the French Republic in 1898) medal of which he was most proud. With credit to the Presbyterian College Library.

DANIEL COUSSIRAT WAS A Protestant of Protestants. He was neither an anglicized Quebecer nor a recent convert to Protestantism. He came from a Huguenot family of the longtime Huguenot area of Salies-de-Béarn that dated from the sixteenth century. This was close to the birthplace of Henry IV, as well as to Orthez, where he later served. For the Coussirats, their Huguenot heritage was a constant source of pride. When in Canada, Daniel often referred to his roots and his contacts with prominent Protestant families.

Adrien Daniel Coussirat was born in 1841 to Pierre Coussirat (Méneault)[1] in Nérac, Lot et Garonne. We do not know Pierre Coussirat's occupation. We do know that he had died before Daniel's marriage in 1868. In his obituary, Daniel's close friend J. L. Morin wrote that Daniel's mother had died while he was young and left him with a religious aunt, who adopted him as her son.[2] Thus we are not sure whether Anne Nobilé, the mother mentioned at the time of his marriage, was his birth mother or his mother by adoption. There was no mention of siblings.

Daniel's elementary and secondary education was in Nérac. After completing his BA in Toulouse in 1859, he felt called to the pastorate. His account mentions that romanticism and idealism were so strong in those days that he and his friends sought the most useful rather than the most lucrative employment.[3] As a theological student at the Reformed Protestant seminary in Montauban, in the Pyrenees region, he began with two years of philosophy, ancient and modern languages, archaeology, history of religions, and Patristics. He then did three years of historical, dogmatic, and practical theology, as well as exegesis, natural science, and homiletics.[4] This solid base of biblical languages and Reformed theology prepared him for preaching, teaching, and Bible translation. He graduated in 1864 with a BTh; his thesis was on Paul's doctrine of election in Romans 9–11.[5] Morin has suggested that the thesis, inspired by the Swiss Free Church leader Alexandre Vinet and the German philosopher Immanuel Kant, anticipated most of his later theology wherein the conscience is our cornerstone around which freedom, responsibility, order, the good, and God are integrated.[6]

On December 8, 1864, Daniel was ordained by L'Église Réformée de France. In 1863 he was named assistant pastor in Bellocq by the local

---

1. Mentioned in his marriage certificate. For more details see Hamelin, "Daniel Coussirat," 5.
2. Morin, "Le professeur D. Coussirat," 1.
3. Hamelin, "Daniel Coussirat," 6.
4. Encrevé, *Protestants français*, cited in Hamelin, "Daniel Coussirat," 6.
5. Hamelin, "Daniel Coussirat," 5.
6. Morin, *Le professeur D. Coussirat*, 2.

Orthez Presbytery. Although calm in his approach, Coussirat was firmly committed to opposing liberal theology in his denomination. However, his heart lay elsewhere, and he ultimately did not stay long in this congregation.

From childhood Coussirat had a dream of going to the New World. While still in France, he had been advised that an American experience would be useful both for his intellectual development and for his long-term ministry. So it is unsurprising that, by April 1865, he was already applying for a post as pastor of a French Reformed congregation in Philadelphia.

On acceptance, he crossed the Atlantic in October 1865. Although Coussirat had not yet mastered English he found the United States to be fascinating. It was during this period that he began what would become a life time practice of having subscriptions to many French journals to keep abreast of political, social, and theological trends there. For years he interpreted the American and Canadian scenes to French journals, and the European scene to North Americans.[7]

In one typical comparative comment he deplored the lack of response of French immigrants to the widespread American evangelical revival. In his church Coussirat reported that he used expository sermons according to 'the rule of faith'.

During the two years he was there, he demonstrated his leadership skills as he tried to calm a church division that led to the establishment of a French Methodist congregation nearby. Among his other ambitious projects was fundraising for the erection of a church building and for a French school designed for immigrants and Americans wanting to broaden their children's cultural experience.

Clearly he was ambitious to see progress where he was, but others suggested new goals that would better use his gifts. Accordingly, when the term he had committed for expired in 1867, he prepared to return to France.[8]

At this time in Canada, the young French Protestant missions had to send their workers to Switzerland, and the need for local French theological teaching quickly became evident while possible French teachers were rare. It had become necessary not only to reduce expenses, but also to avoid students dropping out with culture shock. In Canada's Confederation year, Coussirat was recruited by a Quebecer in New York to teach at the Pointe-aux-Trembles French Protestant school. Clearly the young pastor possessed the intellectual and pastoral gifts needed to teach theology and Bible to students. Moving from the pastorate just two years after his

---

7. "Mort du Rev. Coussirat." He had been correspondent for the *Revue théologique* of Montauban and the *Revue chrétienne* of Paris.

8. Ibid.

arrival in Philadelphia, he began in April 1867 to work for the French Canadian Missionary Society (FCMS). Thus started his long teaching career. At Pointe-aux-Trembles, he taught the wide curriculum of French, Latin, Greek, philosophy, apologetics, and theology.[9] Coussirat quickly raised the courses from high school to university level. Students also had practical placements as colporteurs in the summer.

The small inter-denominational FCMS school on the end of Montreal Island was residential and close-knit. His time with the family of the Swiss missionary Jean-Antoine Moret, who had come to Quebec in 1840 both to administer the farm and also to teach at the school, resulted in a courtship with the Morets' daughter Sarah. On September 1, 1868, less than a year after his arrival, Daniel and Sarah married in l'Église presbytérienne de la rue Craig. Between 1872 and 1877, the couple would have three children: Jeanne Eva, Henri A. D., and Ada. Although their children were educated in English schools, Daniel always insisted that they use French at home. Like many from France he insisted on good French grammar and pronunciation. So when the first two children married they seem to have resisted the common French Protestant pattern of being anglicized. If his own marriage had settled Daniel, family life also brought new financial responsibilities that would require more than a minimum salary.

Meanwhile, Donald MacVicar and James Court were recruiting for the new Presbyterian College, established in 1865. One of the college's aims was to evangelize Catholic Québec. Happily, by 1868 the college was able to secure Coussirat's services as a part-time lecturer in its French department. Coussirat continued to serve both institutions until 1870 when the Presbyterian Church switched its sizable contributions from the FCMS to its own French work. In 1870, then, Presbyterian College hired Coussirat as a full-time lecturer, and the college benefitted when most of his students followed him to his new post.[10] Finally, Coussirat was settled with a well-funded opportunity for university teaching.

Previous to his full-time appointment at the college, Coussirat had been active in the controversial *Institut Canadien* whose aim was to encourage freedom of conscience and freedom of religion for French Quebecers.[11] His wife Sarah was known as a model of missionary commitment and interest in theological matters. At the same time, she was committed to protecting her husband from nonacademic matters so that he would have the time needed for his teaching responsibilities. In return, Daniel supported wom-

---

9. See Hamelin, "Daniel Coussirat," 14, for the details on courses.
10. Hamelin, "Daniel Coussirat," 16.
11. Cousson, "L'Institut Canadien de Montréal," 172.

en's suffrage and even women's leadership in church. As one student stated, his professor from France worked for true liberty, equality, and fraternity.[12]

Despite Sarah's best efforts, Courssirat was much in demand in the Montreal Presbytery. In addition to regular supply preaching, he served as elder, first at l'Église presbytérienne de la rue Craig and later at l'Église Saint-Jean. He also wrote. A stream of articles appeared in the French Protestant paper *L'Aurore*, where he simultaneously reported on developments in Europe and commented on theological and ecclesiastical matters. For short periods, he edited the monthly *Messager des Familles* and *L'Ami des Marins*, both which required the ability to communicate at a popular level.

In 1875, his mother's passing brought the Coussirat family back to France. It must have been a comfort to be back on home turf, and it seems that he was needed there. Before long, he had accepted a position as pastor of the Reformed Church in Orthez, where he became known for his solid preaching and evangelical work. Also continuing to hone his scholarly vocation, he translated Ecclesiastes and Daniel for Ostervald's French Bible.

When the Orthez Presbytery named Coussirat moderator, the Montreal presbytery took note. MacVicar pleaded with him to return to Presbyterian College, with the promise of a position as full professor of the French Department. Coussirat was hardly able to refuse an offer like this one, and returned with his family in 1880. As before, he instructed the college's francophones in apologetics, history, philosophy, and homiletics. In addition, he was named professor of Hebrew and Oriental literature at McGill University.[13]

Coussirat aimed to have both an evangelical and a wide theological perspective in his teaching. At the same time, he strongly resisted the rising liberal tide in Europe, whose thinking was influencing theological schools. Each holiday he would dedicate himself to reading the current thought that would allow him to keep his apologetics current. For over twenty-five years, he would serve as chair of the French department of Presbyterian College, while teaching over sixty francophone and several dozen Anglophone students.[14]

His dedication to teaching can be illustrated by Daniel and Sarah Coussirat's custom of regularly inviting students to their home in groups of

---

12. Hamelin, "Daniel Coussirat," 17–18; Editorial, *Presbyterian College Journal* 26:3 (Feb 1907) 158.

13. *Presbyterian College Journal* 1:3 (March 1881) 21–22; *Annual Calendar of the Presbyterian College, Montreal, session 1872–73*, 13–14.

14. Vogt-Raguy, "Les communautés protestantes francophones au Québec," 789. In 1904 and 1905, he also taught French language and literature in the McGill summer school.

three or four. The qualities that particularly impressed students were his vast knowledge, his polite manner, and the willingness to explain in terms they could understand. Many of his former students would demonstrate their deep appreciation of him as he lay on his deathbed, returning to his home in sorrow to bid him a final adieu.[15] Joseph Morin, for instance, stated in his unpublished obituary notice that Coussirat instilled a passion for truth and reflection, stressing that he was not satisfied with intellectual assent, but wanted spiritual fruit from his students.[16] In his lectures, writings, and sermons, Coussirat insisted on the need for both revival and serious doctrine. He often claimed that he wanted to become superfluous as his students matured. Another student, Edmond Brandt, recalled how he had learned duty, hard work, and the centrality of conscience from his professor.[17]

Teaching was his strong suit. As a preacher, Coussirat was deemed "less effective than as a lecturer." As the editorialist of the *Presbyterian College Journal* noted, he avoided the fervour and imagination that marked good preaching, rather settling for solid, stimulating content. Those who wanted meat instead of milk in their sermons received it from this college professor, for Coussirat, even when quite busy, always agreed to do supply preaching.[18]

In social settings, even Roman Catholic ones, Coussirat was sought after for his polite, widely informed, witty conversation. Apparently apologetics was his favourite subject, and he brought all of his knowledge to bear on convincing any who would listen of the truth of the Christian faith and the Bible. In particular he felt the need to refute "Romanism" and sceptical "free-thinkers." He argued often, but listened well, and admitted weaknesses in his view. He eschewed personal attacks, but targeted Catholic and agnostic principles.[19] Coussirat did not shy away from controversy, even acting as spokesman for the former Catholic priest turned Protestant evangelist, Charles Chiniquy.[20]

In addition to his church interests, Coussirat was active in literary and musical societies. As member of the editorial board of *L'Aurore*, he gave the voice of North American French Protestants crucial credibility and depth.

---

15. Editorial, *Presbyterian College Journal* 26:3 (Feb 1907) 115, 153.

16. Morin, "Le professeur D. Coussirat."

17. Editorial, *Presbyterian College Journal* 26:3 (Feb 1907) 158.

18. Ibid., 116.

19. For a thorough examination of his teaching, his sermons, and his writing consult Hamelin, "Daniel Coussirat."

20. Ibid., 40, includes a quotation of a very pro-Chiniquy paragraph.

In addition to his many articles and letters, he published a short pamphlet on the necessity of baptism.[21]

His contributions as preacher, professor and scholar were acknowledged by several awards from the government of France, an honorary doctorate from Queen's University in 1893, and the gift of a bronze bust of Admiral Coligny from l'Église Saint-Jean.[22] As his obituary in Montreal's *La Patrie* described, he was remembered by the Protestant elite of Montreal, and even the Consul Général of France, who were prominent among the large numbers of mourners that gathered to mark his peaceful passing in 1907.[23] *The Presbyterian College Journal* put it well: "His memory will long be cherished by a wide circle in Canada and his place will be hard to fill."[24]

Over one hundred years later it must be said that although most have never heard of him, recently there has been a burst of articles about Coussirat. His many articles in *L'Aurore* testify that no one since has replaced him in French Protestant North America for his combination of intellectual depth and evangelical fervour.

Saint Paul à Athènes[25]

Actes 17:16–34

À l'époque où nous reporte ce récit du livre des Actes, la ville d'Athènes conservait le prestige des anciens jours. Elle avait bien perdu son indépendance. . . . Elle n'en restait pas moins au sein de son humiliation, la capitale intellectuelle de l'empire. Là revenaient se former les poètes, les artistes, les orateurs les plus accomplis. Rome, elle-même qui l'avait subjuguée, conquise à son tour rendait hommage à son génie.

C'est vers cette illustre cité, que dans le cours de son second voyage missionnaire, au milieu du premier siècle, l'apôtre Paul dirige ses pas. Pour la première fois le Christianisme rencontre le paganisme chez le peuple le

---

21. Du baptême chrétien–réponse à deux questions.

22. He became Officier de l'Académie in 1898 and Officier de l'Instruction Publique in 1898. See Hamelin, "Daniel Coussirat," 36.

23. "Mort du Rev. Coussirat."

24. Editorial, *Presbyterian College Journal* 26:3 (Feb 1907) 117.

25. This sermon was preached four times. In interest of space, approximately two hundred words have been cut and several words are illegible. In "Daniel Coussirat," 2, Hamelin has noted that nearly one hundred of Coussirat's handwritten sermons have been preserved in a box named "French Work" held at the Archives Nationales du Québec (section de l'Église Unie du Canada). This one is in that collection.

plus éclairé de l'univers. Quel accueil y reçoit-il? Quelle est l'impression que s'y produit la première prédication publique de l'Évangile?

Voilà le point spécial sur lequel je désire attirer votre attention, au milieu des inépuisables richesses contenus dans ce récit. En changeant les noms, en magnifiant certains détails vous pouvez lire une page d'histoire contemporaine . . . , vous reconnaîtrez votre propre expérience; vous tirerez de salutaires leçons.

Mais il n'est pas possible de bien comprendre l'accueil fait alors à l'Évangile sans rappeler brièvement le caractère des Athéniens.

Au reste, l'auteur des Actes prend soin lui-même de nous l'indiquer. Pendant que Paul, dit-il, attendait à Athènes Silas et Timothée, son cœur s'indignait de voir cette ville adonnée à l'idolâtrie–où toute pleine d'idoles (v. 8b). C'étaient en effet des gens forts dévots que les Athéniens. Partout des statues de dieux, des déesses, des héros qui rappelaient des vies très peu édifiantes, pour dire le moins. Ils avaient divinisé toutes les formes connus de la nature et toutes les personnes humaines. Ils pouvaient ainsi justifier tous les erreurs et tous les vices par des exemples divins. Nous ne saurions donc être surpris que leur religion servait peu à leur moralité. Pour être si dévots, ils n'en étaient meilleurs.

Comme St-Paul allait tous les jours sur la place publique cherchant et faisant naître l'occasion d'annoncer l'Évangile "quelques épicuriens et des stoïciens conférèrent avec lui" (v. 18). À côté des superstitions se trouvait aussi à Athènes, des hommes plus éclairés, dédaignant les grossières croyances de la foule, tout en leur rendant extérieurement hommage. C'étaient les épicuriens et stoïciens. Puisque le récit sacré les nomme, il ne nous est pas défendu d'en parler . . . les premiers réduisaient la religion à l'athéisme et la morale au plaisir. Jouis, disaient-ils, à leurs adeptes, car la vie s'éteint avec le corps dont elle est le produit; le présent seul t'appartient, il n'y a point pour toi d'avenir. Les autres, aux aspirations plus hautes et plus nobles professaient la croyance en une sorte d'issu du monde s'ignorant elle-même, étrangère aux besoins et aux souffrances de l'homme et engageaient leurs partisans à ne compter que sur eux-mêmes pour le combat de la vie. Le trait commun aux uns et aux autres, on le voit c'était d'ignorer le Dieu personnel vivant et aimant.

Cependant l'esprit de superstitions et l'esprit de système chez les Athéniens cédaient peut-être le pas à la curiosité. "Ce peuple passait son temps à dire ou à écouter des nouvelles" dit St Luc (v. 21). . . . Convenons en toute fois cette extrême curiosité supposait des besoins vivement sentis et non satisfaits. La religion populaire et les vies à la mode ne les contentaient pas absolument; ils attendaient sans bien se rendre compte, quelque chose de mieux. Ce qui plaisait à leur imagination et employait leur intelligence ne répondait pas aux besoins de leur cœur. Ils sentaient vaguement qu'ils pouvaient ne pas connaître une divinité importante, la plus grande de toute, peut-être et cet instinct les avait poussés [sic] à dresser un autel "au dieu inconnu." Il faut voir là une pierre d'attente de l'Évangile dont St-Paul sait admirable faire la base de sa prédication. Cette inquiète curiosité offrait un autre avantage dont St-Paul sait aussi profiter. Elle permettait aux Athéniens d'écouter des docteurs étrangers, des barbares et d'accueillir des doctrines et même des religions nouvelles. Ils n'étouffaient pas l'esprit de recherche. Ils sollicitaient l'exposé et proclamation publique des idées qu'ils ne connaissaient pas et provoquaient la discussion. Ainsi, dit St-Luc, ils prirent Paul et le menèrent à l'Aréopage disant "pourrions-nous savoir quelle est cette nouvelle doctrine que tu prêches?" (v. 19).

Enfin arrêtons-nous un instant et faisons un retour sur nous-mêmes. Si l'apôtre revenait parmi nous en Europe, en Asie, en Amérique, partout où il a exercé son activité d'écoute et au milieu du peuple qui depuis se sont formés, ne retrouverait-il nulle part le caractère d'Athénien? Son cœur n'arriverait-il pas à la vue de nos cités et de nos campagnes adonnées à l'idolâtrie? Ne retrouverait-il pas des statues qu'on adore où qu'on révère, des images qui opèrent des prodiges et préservent de malheur? Ne se croirait-il pas au sein de la chrétienté en plein paganisme? Ne reconnaîtrait-il pas aussi, chez la plupart de ceux qui dédaignaient cette superstitieuse ignorance les héritiers directs, quoique sous d'autres noms de ces philosophies épicuriens et stoïciens qui excluent de la direction matérielle et morale du monde le Dieu vivant et aimant et qui ramènent toutes choses soit à la matière, soit à une force inconsciente et aveugle? Nous aussi, disons-le à notre honneur, ne retrouverait-il pas dans notre société troublée, cette vague inquiétude, indice d'un secret malaise, cet esprit de recherche qui conduit irrésistiblement bien des âmes sincères à l'Évangile qu'il prêchait? Seulement, pas plus que les Athéniens d'autrefois, elle ne connaît le véritable Évangile, et si St-Paul paraissait de nouveau, elle serait obligée de dire: "pourrions-nous savoir quelle est cette nouvelle doctrine que tu prêches?"

St-Paul ne résiste pas aux désirs des Athéniens, heureux qu'il est toujours de rendre témoignage à son Maître. Il parle avec hardiesse et prudence tout ensemble. Il est conciliant dans la forme, ne heurte brusquement aucun préjugé, et bien qu'il ne craigne pas de mesurer la doctrine chrétienne aux superstitions et aux systèmes de ses auditeurs, il se borne à exposer clairement, directement le conseil du Dieu vivant et bon à l'égard de l'homme pécheur et perdu.

Quel est l'effet que produit son discours? Comment accueille-t-on les vérités qu'il annonce? Après dix-huit siècles d'expérience, nous pourrions le deviner. . . .

Les uns se moquèrent dit St-Luc (v. 32). Paul avait parlé du Dieu créateur du monde et de tout ce qu'il contient; il avait parlé de Dieu esprit que l'homme ne sauraient renfermer dans un temple comme un statue ou une image, de Dieu qui a une volonté, un cœur, une conscience pour ainsi dire car nous ne pouvons parler des choses célestes qu'en langage humain, de Dieu qui ayant pitié pour notre misère s'est révélé à nous en Jésus-Christ, pour nous convier au repentir et nous annoncer le jugement final . . . jusqu'à là on l'avait écouter. Un Dieu unique, esprit, créateur, révélateur, amour, ces idées bien que nouvelles et étranges pour eux, leur paraissaient mériter quelque attention. Ils étaient prêts à les discuter comme les autres enseignements qui retentissaient tous les jours sur la place publique mais dès que St-Paul ajoute "en foi de quoi Dieu a ressuscité Jésus des morts" (v. 31) c.-à-d. que Dieu pour donner à tous une éclatante preuve de la vérité du Christianisme, a ressuscité Jésus des morts, par une intervention spéciale. Ils ne se contiennent plus, ils se moquent ouvertement. Comme si Dieu qui nous donne la vie et qui nous l'ôte à son gré, ne pourrait aussi nous le rendre quand il lui plaît; . . . comme si l'insecte qui de son *cocoon* fait son tombeau, ne ressuscitait pas comme un brillant papillon; comme si ce que Dieu fait pour la plante et l'insecte, êtres d'une espèce inférieure, il ne peut pas le faire, à plus forte raison, pour l'homme crée à son image! Ou raillez aussi l'idée d'un Dieu créateur et conservateur des choses, ou cessez de vous moquez de la résurrection des morts. Oh oui, il est facile de se moquer. C'est la ressource des esprits toute à la fois superficiels et prétentieux. Se moquer des croyances sérieuses qu'on a conquise péniblement par le travail de l'intelligence ou qu'on a arraché avec effort dû aux douleurs et aux tentations de la vie; se moquer d'un fait attesté par un témoin aussi sincère et aussi compétent que St-Paul; se moquer d'un fait que la raison avoue, que le cœur réclame, que la conscience exige, sur lequel la volonté s'appuie—c'est là autre chose que du courage et de l'indépendance.

Et qu'avait-il donc à substituer à ce qu'ils raillaient, ces spirituels Athéniens? Nous favoriser avec des fables absurdes ou immorales, des systèmes qui font provenir tout de rien.

Il fut un temps—c'était hier—une raillerie grossière tranchait chez nous les questions les plus graves. Grâce à Dieu ce temps n'est plus. Je ne veux pas dire que le grand cœur du siècle dernier n'ait point d'imitateurs, mais il est certain aujourd'hui que c'est généralement avec sérieux qu'on aborde des questions sérieuses. On a vu tous plus fin, des expériences plus nuancées, on discute avec plus de modération dans les formes et au besoin on sait louer ceux même qu'on attaque. Mais que ce soit par des grossières railleries ou avec un sourire de pitié, on rejette l'Évangile de Jésus-Christ précisément à cause du surnaturel qu'on ne peut s'en séparer et surtout à cause de la résurrection de Jésus-Christ qu'était pour les Grecs une folie. Ce trait nous est commun avec les Athéniens d'autrefois.

Ainsi les uns se moquaient, les autres disent: "nous t'entendrons là-dessus une autre fois" (v. 33). En voilà assez. Ce n'est plus le dédain railleur, c'est l'ennui, l'indifférence. C'est peut-être aussi un peu de frayeur. L'enseignement de St-Paul était trop grave pour ces esprits frivoles. Ils préfèrent leurs dieux complaisants, leurs bonnes déesses, ces brillantes fêtes qui séduisent l'imagination et rompent avec la monotonie des travaux journaliers.

Et puis, ce nouveau Dieu du missionnaire juif avait des exigences incompatibles avec leur vie facile et leurs mœurs libres. Il fallait rendre un culte trop sévère à ce Dieu esprit; il fallait se repentir, changer de conduite et des sentiments. C'était trop demander à une population si légère.

Savez-vous pourquoi mes chers frères, certains pays au 16e siècle repoussèrent le pur Évangile, celui que St-Paul prêchaient aux Athéniens? C'est principalement pour la même raison. C'est parce que l'Évangile exigeait une transformation de vie en même temps qu'il opérait un changement de doctrine. Notre peuple le trouvait trop grave pour sa frivolité, trop austère pour ces penchants naturels. Et c'est pour cela que de nos jours encore, il s'en tient éloigné. Il en a même une frayeur si grande qu'il se refuse à l'étudier. Le Japon, les chemins de fer, la constitution, la liberté de l'enseignement supérieur, tout l'intéresse, tout l'occupe; il trouve le temps de tout connaître suffisamment pour former une opinion personnelle mais quant à St-Paul et à son Évangile, il dit: "nous t'entendrions là-dessus une autre fois."

L'Évangile ne trouva-t-il point d'accueil à Athènes? La Parole de Dieu fut-elle annoncé en vain? Non mon frère. Écoutez encore St-Luc: 'Toutefois quelques personnes s'étant attaché à lui, embrassèrent la foi, savoir Denys l'Aéropogite, une femme nommée Damaris et d'autres avec eux" (v. 34). Il y avait dans cet auditoire, ... quelques âmes affamées et altérées de justice. Quand la Bonne Nouvelle fut annoncée, elles l'acceptèrent, comme elles l'entendaient par toutes leurs aspirations élevées, elles s'empressèrent de le recevoir. C'étaient des terrains bien préparés n'eut qu'à y être répandus, elle y germe tout aussitôt.

Disons le très haut à la gloire de Dieu. La puissance de l'Évangile ne s'est point affaiblie depuis le séjour de St-Paul à Athènes. Elle a éclaté il y a trois siècles, lorsqu'elle créa un monde et un droit nouveau du sein de ce chaos d'alors séculaires qui semblaient indestructible. Elle éclate tous les jours parmi nous. À côté des railleurs et des insouciants, il y a les Denys et les Damaris qui pieusement lui ouvrent leurs cœurs. ...

C'est aussi une époque sombre et triste à bien des égards la nôtre. Les brillantes découvertes qui feront sa gloire, le progrès de l'industrie et du commerce, le développement des sciences, l'accroissement de la richesse publique; toutes ces merveilles ne peuvent faire oublier aux esprits réfléchis, les effroyables dangers qui la menacent. Cette prodigieuse civilisation ressemble au colosse de l'Écriture: elle a des pieds d'argile, elle ne repose pas sur le Rocher des siècles, seule base qui puisse l'affermir contre les tempêtes qui vont se déchaîner. Les caractères sont précisément les mêmes que ceux qu'a signalé le récit des Actes chez les Athéniens à une époque de décadence. Il y a là des sujets de crainte pour les âmes les plus confiants dans l'avenir de la société contemporaine.

Mais ce menu récit nous rassure encore plus qu'il nous trouble. Il nous montre l'Évangile prise avec les mêmes préjugés, les mêmes erreurs qu'aujourd'hui. D'où si l'Évangile est sorti triomphant de toutes ces luttes et a conquis depuis une partie du monde, il remportera de nouvelles victoires jusqu'à ce que la connaissance du Dieu de Jésus-Christ couvre la terre comme les eaux couvrent le fond des mers. . . . Les attaques dirigés contre le surnaturel chrétien, en particulier contre la résurrection du notre Seigneur Jésus-Christ, . . . ces attaques sont aussi vieilles que l'Évangile lui-même. La crise qui traverse notre église n'est pas non plus sans exemples: en l'Amérique du Nord une crise semblable éclata au commencement de ce siècle et elle s'achève aujourd'hui dans la triomphe que prêchait St-Paul. Il n'en sera pas autrement de la nôtre, soyez-en surs, puisque l'Évangile est toujours de Dieu en salut à tout croyant. Courage donc et fidélité. Amen.

Commentary on "Saint Paul à Athènes"

In his handwritten manuscripts, Professor Coussirat recorded the date and place of delivery of most of his sermons. Some of his sermons have the date and time repeated, indicating that he reused at least some of them, though, as the manuscripts indicate, he made minor changes to the originals. This particular sermon was chosen primarily because it is the one which he preached more often than any other in Quebec (four times according to the manuscript). Coussirat preached it first in 1882 in l'Église Saint-Jean on St. Catherine Street. Two other occasions that his detailed notes indicate he preached it were in 1886 in Le Oratoire French Baptist Church and in 1904 back in l'Église Saint-Jean. The fourth occasion is less clear.

This sermon demonstrates the importance of apologetics in the various ministries of Professor Coussirat. His exposition of Paul's visit to Athens in Acts 17:16–34 also shows the exegetical and philosophical prowess of Coussirat and his concern for practical relevance to his own era. According to Coussirat, as Paul moved out of the Jewish/Christian milieu, he had to find new ways of presenting the Gospel since he was interacting with the pagan intellectual culture of the time. Given that this was the primary debate of Paul in Gentile culture, it was easy for Coussirat to make this his favourite biblical text for apologetics. Coussirat himself was confronted in France by what he perceived to be a pagan intellectual culture by the Catholic Church on one side and liberal Protestant or anticlerical thought on the other. While in Quebec, he did not enter so much into contesting liberal theology, but did constantly confront "Romanism" and, though a minority phenomenon in Quebec, rationalism. This sermon targeted both for their concessions to fashion and worldly reason rather than to the revelation of God in Scripture.

In his apologetics, Coussirat followed the model that he saw in Paul. "[Paul] speaks with both audacity and prudence at the same time. Not arousing any prejudice and without compromising any Christian doctrine, he is conciliatory in form; he uses great skill in the face of their superstition and systems of logic to clearly expose the council of the living God concerning sinful and lost humanity."

In this apologetic there was an evangelical Reformed theology not differing much in substance from that of Principal MacVicar, who twice recruited him. Coussirat's theology did not seem to have been altered by Darwin or higher critical thought. Coussirat remained within the French evangelical revival of Vinet, and even of Chiniquy.

There are no explicit references to any current authors or contemporary events, whether sociopolitical or denominational. For Coussirat the pulpit was not the place to lecture about theologians or to express political leanings. Yet work needed to be done to establish a bridge from first-century Athens to nineteenth-century Quebec, and Coussirat was eager to oblige. As Coussirat saw it, Paul addressed Athenian intellectuals whose notion of the divine went beyond idolatry. But in Athens there were also idols and idolaters. Coussirat identified that idolatry with the Roman Catholic ritualism that was willing to at least permit superstition. Although in his writings he often compared the Catholic approach to that of the Pharisees, the Pharisees were not the focus of this text and so he compared Catholics and Pharisees only in passing.

Paul arrived for his first encounter and debate with Greek philosophy at the pinnacle of intellectual development in the Roman Empire. Even if Athens had seen better days, it, the Areopagus, remained the centre for philosophical ideas. Coussirat followed this encounter with enthusiasm. The Athenians, like other pagans, were known for their idolatry, but here the statues were used to justify moral poverty. Paul and Coussirat were unimpressed. The professor, well versed in philosophy, briefly described the hedonist Epicureans and the more serious Stoics. But at heart both were ignorant of the living God and preferred it so. Only their curiosity for the latest fad led them to listen for a while to Paul's new ideas.

Coussirat assumed that Paul would have found Montreal quite similar to Athens. Montreal had, on the one side, the superstitions of Catholicism, and on the other, those who mocked ritualism but indulged in the latest trends of freethinkers. Neither group wanted to be guided in their morals or their beliefs by the true living God. Both saw biblical doctrine as a bizarre, new, and eventually offensive idea. For a time, the rationalists might have been attracted to it by curiosity, but Coussirat believed that they would soon see its potentially invasive implications for their morality.

Coussirat was inspired by the renewed interest in the Gospel that the sixteenth-century Reformations brought, and he again detected progress towards serious talk of religion in his own day in late nineteenth-century Quebec. He felt that there was less mockery and more moderate discussion of theology. Part of the progress that he saw was at Presbyterian College, where his own French department raised the bar for theological training. In his mind, concrete evidence was manifested by the fifty-four French Presbyterian congregations and forty-three mission posts that had been established by the turn of the century.[26] Like many, Coussirat thought that success in French mission would continue to rise, and he was optimistic about the Church Union in 1925 between the Presbyterians and Methodists as a spur to evangelism.[27] He was quickly proven wrong, however; nor were his related aspirations of contesting Catholicism, while encouraging evangelism in Quebec, manifested by the continuing Presbyterians after Union.[28]

In summary, Coussirat saw himself in the line of the Apostle Paul combating the materialism of both ritualists and rationalists. Both wished to exclude the Almighty from material and moral direction of their world by substituting an impersonal force easily manipulated by their own will. Paul waded into the battle to explain patiently the Gospel, to establish some links between philosophy and Gospel, but also to present the stumbling blocks to

26. The number declined after 1900. See the annual statistics compiled by the author held in the Societé historique protestante française de Québec archives. See also Lalonde, *Des loups dans la bergerie*, 175.

27. In reality, Church Union inadvertently caused the disappearance of Presbyterian French work and university-level theology in French. While all the French Presbyterian congregations joined the new United Church, Presbyterian College, including its French Department, was assigned to the continuing Presbyterian Church. The irony was that the United Church had no French college while the Presbyterians had no French students.

28. Although they were revived later by the French Presbyterian work of Allan Reid and Jacques Smith in the mid-twentieth century. See Lalonde, *French Protestant Missionary Activity in Quebec*, and Reid, *Quebec Problem*.

the Gospel. What was the reaction? As is most common throughout history, evangelism and the presentation of Jesus are responded to by many with mockery and insult. Greeks saw the resurrection as folly. They wanted to get back to their more amusing holidays and their malleable gods. Repentance was out of the question for them.

But that is not the end of the story. Some, if only a few, responded. The writer of Acts mentioned two more notable names and a larger group. Coussirat reminded his hearers that God prepared the ground for Paul's message and so the church began in Athens. In Montreal, western industrial and intellectual progress was impressive but rested on fragile clay feet rather than on the solid rock of the Gospel; the future remained precarious. The French professor had confidence in the Gospel to shake up the most homogenous anti-Christian society.

As we look back on the turn of the twentieth century, it appears to us to have been a very Christian period and to have had within it a strong Presbyterian presence and influence. As a French Protestant, Coussirat saw a more precarious and marginal existence. He used the great resources of the Presbyterian Church and Presbyterian College to equip French pastors. But they were like a David against Goliath or a Daniel in the lion's den. Self-confidence was rarely an option in French work. No doubt this kept Coussirat grounded in the need for the supernatural: the divinely revealed Word, the divine intervention in evangelism, and the resurrection and miracles of Jesus. By keeping the priority of his heavenly citizenship, seeking to build bridges, and explaining the Gospel, the French professor negotiated three worlds: English Canada, French Canada, and France. Coussirat dedicated his life to advancing the Word through teaching, preaching, and writing. His final call in the sermon to his hearers was to show courage and faithfulness.

The Author

Richard Lougheed is married to a pediatrician; they have four children. Presently he is librarian and church history professor at the Mennonite Brethren and Christian and Missionary Alliance college L'École de Théologie Évangélique du Québec. He has taught since 1993 as a specialist on French Protestantism, with published books on the ex-priest Charles Chiniquy (a close friend of Coussirat) and the 1970s evangelical revival in Quebec. Presently part of the leadership of a French Mennonite church plant in Montreal, he served earlier as pastor in the United Church. He believes that creative methods and inter-denominational ventures are vital to the future of French Protestantism. Part of his appreciation for Presbyterian College came from computerizing the catalogue of the college and part from the role it played in fostering French Protestantism prior to 1925.

Bibliography

Chareyre, Philippe. "Daniel Coussirat, le 'Jean Calvin du protestantisme québécois'". In *Marie-Claude Rocher et al., Huguenots et protestants francophones au Québec: Fragments d'histoire,* 165-6. Montréal: Novalis, 2014.

Coussirat, Daniel. *Du baptême chrétien—réponse à deux questions.* Montreal: Drysdale, 1895.

Cousson, Clairee. "L'Institut canadien de Montréal et l'intelligentsia protestante." In *Huguenots et protestants francophones au Québec: Fragments d'histoire,* edited by Marie Claude Rocher et al., 161–82. Montreal: Novalis, 2014.

Editorial. "The Late Dr. Coussirat." *Presbyterian College Journal* 26:3 (Feb 1907), 113–17, 152–60.

Encrevé, André. *Protestants français au milieu du XIXe siècle: les Réformés de 1848 à 1870.* Geneva: Labor et Fides, 1986.

Hamelin, Charles. "Daniel Coussirat (1841–1907): La vie et l'œuvre d'un intellectuel franco-protestant." MA thesis, University of Montreal, 2001.

Lalonde, Jean-Louis. *Des loups dans la bergerie: les protestants de langue française au Québec 1534–2000.* Montreal: Fides, 2002.

———. "French Protestant Missionary Activity in Quebec from the 1850s to the 1950s." In *French-Speaking Protestants,* edited by J. Zuidema, 163–90. Leiden: Brill, 2011.

Lougheed, Richard. "Éducation théologique au Canada français 1836–1997." *Le Vigneron* (janvier et mars 1998), 1–2.

Morin, Joseph L. "Le professeur D. Coussirat (1841–1907)." Unpublished manuscript, ca. 1900.

"Mort du Rev. Coussirat." *La Patrie,* 8 January 1907, 12.

Reid, Allan. *The Quebec Problem.* Toronto: Presbyterian French Mission, 1946.

Shute, Dan. "Daniel Coussirat (1841–1907): Apostle to the French Roman Catholics or Closet Liberal." *Society of Presbyterian History, 1994 Papers,* 75–102.

Strout, Richard. "The Latter Years of the Board of Evangelization of the Presbyterian Church in Canada 1895–1912." Student essay, Bishop's University, 1986.

Vogt-Raguy, Dominique. "Les communautés protestantes francophones au Québec: 1834–1925." PhD diss., Bordeaux University, 1996.

Zuidema, Jason, ed. *French-Speaking Protestants in Canada: Historical Essays.* Leiden: Brill, 2011.

Middle Years

CHAPTER 5

The College and the North
Andrew S. Grant

By William J. Klempa

The Reverend Andrew Shaw Grant (1860–1935), always referred to as "Dr. Grant" though he did not earn an MD and refused a DD. This is the only photo available; with credit to the Presbyterian Church in Canada Archives.

ANDREW SHAW GRANT IS deservedly praised as a notable Canadian. His colourful career and numerous achievements earn him a high position on the honour roll of Presbyterian ministers, and also of outstanding graduates of the Presbyterian College of Montreal. He served as a medical missionary during the Klondike gold rush and came to be known simply as "Grant of the Yukon." He built a log church, St. Andrew's; a log hospital, the Good Samaritan Hospital of Dawson City;[1] and served diligently in his roles as a parish minister, general superintendent of missions of the Presbyterian Church before 1925 and general secretary of the Board of Missions thereafter. All these contributions were marked by his profound moral passion and social activism.

Grant was born on October 10, 1860 in Huntingdon County in rural Quebec, near the American border. A quiet, peaceful village, it belied its name of La Guerre. His father, Thomas Grant, came to Canada from Inverness, Scotland, and his mother was a Canadian of Scottish ancestry. The Grant household was associated with the Calvin Presbyterian Church in that community. Young Andrew Grant took his primary schooling at the Huntingdon Academy. It is likely he worked on a farm or taught school for several years before entering McGill University in 1882 to prepare himself for the Christian ministry. His intention, it would seem, was to become a medical missionary on a foreign mission field. While enrolled in arts, he also took three sessions at the McGill Medical College. Though there is no proof he earned a license to practise medicine, nevertheless he was known as Dr. Grant all his life. In one of these sessions, he studied under the distinguished Canadian surgeon, William Osler, who later received an appointment to Oxford University and was made a baronet for his outstanding contributions to medical science. Grant graduated in arts in 1885. Subsequently, he took his theological studies at the Presbyterian College, Montreal, where he was taught by Principal Donald MacVicar in theological studies, Professor John Campbell in Old Testament, and Professor John Scrimger in New Testament, and received lectures from such notables as Principal Sir William Dawson and Professor J. Clark Murray of the Department of Philosophy at McGill.

During one of the summers while a student at the college, he served on the Western Mission field to which he was recruited by the redoubtable Dr. James Robertson, superintendent of Western Missions and a honorary graduate of the college (1888). Ralph Connor, in his biography of Robertson, relates an incident during Andrew Grant's summer work near Edmonton, Alberta. On one occasion, he had been requested to visit and to pray for

---

1. Dawson City was named for Dr. George Mercer Dawson, the son of McGill's principal Sir William Dawson who was a noted geologist and geographer.

a native woman near death. When he entered the house, he found she was in a state of mortification with a broken and seriously diseased leg. There was no doctor available in the vicinity and it was clearly evident to him that the woman had to lose either her leg or her life. Immediately, he took action by locking the room in which the woman was lying and then, taking his own small medical kit and a bucksaw that he sterilized by placing in boiling water, he administered chloroform. With the assistance of a homesteader, he amputated the diseased portion of the leg, tied the arteries, and stitched down the flap, while the members of the family raged outside the locked door. Later, he had the joy of seeing her stump around on a wooden leg he had provided.[2] This feat was voiced far and wide. Grant came to be known as a courageous and daring person.

He graduated in 1888 with his bachelor of divinity degree and, in the winter of 1889, took post-graduate studies in Edinburgh, Scotland. His specific studies are unknown, but it is highly likely that he attended lectures at New College from such notables as Professors Robert Rainy, Church History; A. B. Davidson, Old Testament; and Marcus Dods, New Testament.

Grant returned to Canada in the summer of 1889. He was licensed to preach the Gospel by the Presbytery of Montreal. A Call was extended to him by the Presbyterian Church of Almonte, Ontario, to be its minister, succeeding the late Dr. John Bennett. He was ordained by the Presbytery of Lanark and Renfrew and inducted into the Almonte charge in August 1890. Interestingly, the town of Almonte was also home to one of the Presbyterian College's most famous graduates, James Naismith, the inventor of the game of basketball. Like him, Andrew Grant was of an athletic build and a devout disciple of "muscular Christianity."

He married Caroline Wetherald of Richmond, Indiana, that same year in the Presbyterian Church in Whitby, Ontario. Two children, Oswald and Jamie, were born to Caroline and Andrew Grant while they were in Almonte. He remained minister of the congregation for the next seven years. In 1897, he was approached by Dr. James Robertson to go as a missionary to the Yukon, where the Klondike gold rush was well underway. Dr. Robertson was convinced that a Presbyterian witness was needed there. The Roman Catholics and the Anglicans had ministered in the Yukon long before the Gold Rush had begun, but there was no Presbyterian presence.

To set the stage for the church's Call to Andrew Grant to go to the Yukon, it is necessary to relate the following events. In the summer of 1896, a Scottish Presbyterian and Nova Scotian, Robert Henderson, found gold

---

2. Connor, *Life of James*, 358–59.

in the Yukon while panning in a creek near the Indian River.[3] In August of that year, three prospectors—the American George Carmack and the Tagish Canadians "Skookum" Jim and Dawson Charlie—stumbled upon a much more valuable deposit of gold nuggets after Henderson told them where to look. Consequently, the Canadian government credited Henderson with the gold find and named the others as co-discoverers. The honour, however, of being the first nonnative Canadian to find evidence of gold in the Yukon in 1834 belongs to Robert Campbell, another Presbyterian of Scottish decent. Presbyterians, it appears, were particularly prone to being afflicted with "gold fever."

When the 1896 discovery was first reported on July 17, 1897, in the Seattle *Post-Intelligencer*, whose headlines shrieked "GOLD! GOLD! GOLD! GOLD!" Presbyterians in particular, but also many non-Presbyterians, perked up their ears. Thousands of prospectors, miners, and other seekers after gold rushed to the Klondike. After the ship the *SS Portland* returned to Seattle carrying gold nuggets valued at over a million dollars (in today's currency, roughly a billion dollars), even more gold seekers stampeded to the Klondike. This included a great number of Seattle policemen, seriously weakening the Seattle police force. The gold seekers travelled by steamship from San Francisco, Seattle, and Vancouver converging on Skagway, Alaska, the closest Pacific port to the Klondike gold fields. Amusing as well as tragic stories abound about the Klondike gold rush. Hundreds, indeed thousands, made their way to Seattle, Washington, only to be told that they had missed their destination by about a thousand miles. A woman arrived in Seattle and asked if she could walk from there to the Klondike.[4] Her purpose is unclear, yet it is unlikely that she was a gold prospector. Many of the tragic stories involve men who died of exhaustion, pneumonia, or violence on the treacherous Chilkoot Path on the way to Lake Bennett in the Yukon.

When Robertson witnessed prospectors and miners leaving from the port of Vancouver to go to the Yukon, he determined that Presbyterian missionaries should be sent there as well. Dr. Robertson was firmly persuaded that the church should be first in the field and not give way to the evil influences of the rum-runner, the gambler, the con artist and the harlot who tended to be first in the new settlements of the West. When he returned to Winnipeg, he conferred with C. W. Gordon (Ralph Connor) who was minister of St. Stephen's Church. They decided to approach Robert Dickey, a second-year student at Manitoba College, to go to the Klondike. Robertson's

---

3. Berton, *Klondike*, 36.
4. National Park Service, "Hard Drive."

mind also fastened on Andrew Grant whose feat on the Edmonton mission field he had remembered.

Dr. Robertson made two visits to the Almonte manse. On his first visit to recruit Grant, Grant hesitated to accept the challenge but did not refuse absolutely. On the second visit, Mrs. Grant said, "Dr. Robertson, I do not know how you dare to come into our home again, trying to break up our family." The superintendent felt a twinge of conscience; he had hesitated to recruit married ministers to go to the Klondike. He replied that he was aware of the sacrifice he was asking for and expressed regret for his daring. Nevertheless, a final decision had to be made. On the morning of the Presbytery meeting, Mrs. Grant said to her husband, "Do not hesitate on our account; go and do your duty." This was the first time they dared to face the question together, and when the Presbytery concurred in Dr. Robertson's Call to him, Grant accepted the challenge.

The Klondike gold rush stirred the interest and captured the imagination of both miners, and the Canadian public. At the end of the nineteenth century, Presbyterians were strongly mission-minded, and thus when the church announced it had plans to send three missionaries to the Klondike, the news was greeted with both enthusiasm and financial support. Not surprisingly, Grant's acceptance of the challenge was an event to be celebrated in a very public way. His designation as a missionary to the Yukon took place at St. James Square Presbyterian Church, Toronto, on December 30, 1897. The church was packed to the doors. The venture appealed to many outside the Presbyterian community. Sir Oliver Mowat, lieutenant governor of Ontario, was in the chair and Principal George M. Grant of Queen's University was the main speaker. The various church offices were well represented: besides the Rev. L. H. Jordan, minister of St. James Square, there were Dr. Cochrane, convener of Home Missions; Dr. Warden, clerk of assembly; and Dr. Robertson, superintendent of Northwest missions.

Sir Oliver's address dealt with the importance of the work in the home field from the viewpoint of patriotism as well as of religion, and with the unique power of the Gospel of Christ to save men from all manner of sin, and to keep them clean, honest and law-abiding in the midst of widespread immorality and worldliness. "It is an honour," he declared, "to the Presbyterian Church to be first in the Klondike field. It would have been an honour to be second or third. But the pioneer, the Church, to first face the hardships, is worthy of all honour." Principal Grant focused on words from the book of Esther and stressed that the missionary-designate Andrew Grant had come to the kingdom "for such a time as this." He praised the Presbytery and the whole church for taking such immediate, decisive action in sending missionaries to the Yukon. He added that the committee had seen the opportunity—an opportunity "which comes to few Churches once, to no Church twice"—and acted. "We will show," he continued, "that they have rightly estimated the Presbyterian Church."

Then the missionary, Andrew Grant, responding to the chairman's invitation, said:

> Missionary work was always attractive to me. It was not my privilege to go to the foreign field. Klondike was the last place I should have chosen . . . When the superintendent faced me with the question "Will you go to the Klondike?" every personal and selfish consideration said "No!" but all that was best in me said "Yes!" But I would not go, were I not overwhelmingly convinced that I am called. I believe all my training and experience have been training me for the work. I know something of life on the frontier. It attracts me because I believe that by God's grace some poor fellow may be saved from going down, and some who are down may be helped back.

Grant travelled by rail to Vancouver and boarded the steamship the *SS Danube* bound for Skagway on January 2, arriving nearly three weeks later on January 22, 1898. Grant was preceded in Skagway by Robert Dickey, an Irishman and graduate of Manitoba College, Winnipeg, who had been ordained in Vancouver and arrived in Alaska on October 9, 1897. The very next day he preached at the first Presbyterian service held in the area at Burkhart Hall.

Grant stayed in Skagway for two days. He arranged for Dickey to go to Dawson City, some six to eight hundred miles distant. In a letter to the *Westminster*, a Presbyterian newspaper, A. S. Grant gave a detailed account of his journey from Skagway to Lake Bennett.

Grant left Skagway with a small party, carrying with them their own provisions. Those who undertook the journey were required by the North-West Mounted Police to carry a year's supply of food with them (1,200 pounds). Otherwise they would be turned back. The supplies had to be carried in relays and the journey repeated over and over again. Grant stated that it was the most arduous trip he had ever undertaken. He spoke of the hardships encountered by those undertaking the journey as almost inconceivable. Progress on the trail was painfully slow and even a minor accident would delay the progress of the entire party. While on the trail, it seems that an accident took place and one of the party blamed Grant for the delay that resulted, uttering a stream of profanity and threatening Grant with a beating. Grant accepted the challenge and a fisticuff fight was about to begin. A companion of Grant said, "Better not fight him, you may have to preach to him tomorrow." Grant replied, "I'll lick him today, and preach to him tomorrow." The bully considered prudence the better part of valour and withdrew.

Next, Grant surmounted the tortuous Chilkoot Pass. The vast majority of the parties turned back before reaching the summit, so terrible were the hardships of the journey. Many were stranded, sickness took a heavy toll and many froze to death. Grant gave medical attention to some fifty patients who had spent hours on the trail, often going considerable distances to see them. In the mornings, he roused himself from his bed in the snow by the consideration, "God did not bring me here to die on the trail."

The Canadian government, faced with the threat of lawlessness and social unrest, had established a police presence on the Yukon Trail. The legendary Sam Steele from Montreal, an officer of the North-West Mounted Police,[5] a distinguished Canadian soldier and police officer (1848–1919), was sent to Lake Bennett in the Yukon, where he established his headquarters.

Grant arrived in Lake Bennett on April 22, 1898. In Bennett he picked a church site and ordered a 24-by-40-foot meeting tent. He started a subscription list headed by a contribution from Major James Walsh, Yukon Commissioner. To this, he added $60 in donations he had collected along the trail.

During his time in Lake Bennett, Grant reported, "We are all here safe and well. This is to me additional proof that I am called upon by God for this work and have assurance that he will prosper us." Grant wrote Dr. Robertson to urge a replacement for Dickey, so he too could come to Lake Bennett. Meanwhile, Commissioner Walsh was pushing both Grant and Dickey to accompany the prospectors to Dawson City when the waterways opened. Dickey arrived in Bennett where he again conferred with Grant. They decided that Dickey would serve in the Bennett area until the ice breakup, and then go to Dawson City. Grant immediately proceeded overland to the north end of Lake Laberge to take an early boat to Dawson City where his medical skills were much needed.

Interestingly, the previous summer, the Home Mission Board of the Presbyterian Church in the USA had sent the Rev. S. Hall Young to the Yukon to "penetrate the Interior to seek out the seekers of gold—for God." Young arrived in Dawson City that year and, supposing that it was in American territory, he established a church and took services. When he became aware that Dawson City belonged to Canada, he turned the work over to

---

5. Major General Sir Samuel Benfield Steele, KCMG CB MVO, distinguished Canadian soldier and police officer (1848–1919) was sent to Lake Bennett in the Yukon, where he established his headquarters.

the Canadian Presbyterian missionaries. In his history of the Klondike gold rush, Pierre Berton gives us the following account:

> Hal Young, one of Alaska's best known Protestant ministers . . . was replaced the following summer by a Canadian, Dr. Andrew S. Grant, a surgeon who had studied under Osler and then taken to the cloth. Young's makeshift church had burned to the ground, and Grant held services in the Pioneers' Hall until the building was submerged in the spring floods. Nothing daunted, the minister gathered up his flock and marched them to St. Paul's Anglican Church, walking in through the doors just as the congregation commenced to sing the second stanza of a grand old hymn: "See the mighty host advancing, Satan leading on."[6]

Grant proceeded to build a log church for the Presbyterians, and, with the assistance of the other churches, established and built the Good Samaritan Hospital, which would also be a log structure. Now historical sites of the National Parks of Canada, they are visited annually by great numbers of tourists to the Yukon. Before the gold rush, Dawson City was a town of about four thousand residents. After the gold rush (particularly when the Wagon Trail and the railroad connection had been built) the population soared to about fifteen thousand.

When the unknown author of the 1935 obituary of Andrew S. Grant visited Dawson City on September 5, 1898, Grant had already been there since early summer. The writer was to recall that Grant, whom he described as "that athletic parson" had helped build his own log church and hospital ("The Good Samaritan"), and also assisted Rector R. J. Bowen with the construction of his Anglican chapel. Grant had already won a name for himself on the trail, and as a student missionary, for his medical and surgical work. By this time, Dawson City being well served by medical professionals, Andrew Grant would relinquish that aspect of the work and concentrate on his ministerial and allied duties. Grant's memorialist provides us with another account of a leg amputation:

> In a rude shelter, heated by a small stove, and with only one man there, in addition to the invalid, he amputated a man's leg in an almost hopelessly gangrenous state, a triumph of medical surgery even under most favorable circumstances. He told the man that under the best conditions he had one chance in a hundred, but there he had not one in a thousand. The man pleaded,

---

6. Berton, *Klondike*, 288. The line appears to be a misreading of the first line in the second verse of "Onward! Christian Soldiers" by Sabine Baring-Gould (1834–1924); the original reads as follows: "At the sign of triumph, Satan's host doth flee."

"For God's sake, take that chance, for I have a wife and children in Chicago." Subsequently the man offered Grant an incredible sum of money for his services. This he refused absolutely, but reported that both his hospital and church would benefit from the man's gratitude and generosity.

After the building of the hospital in Dawson City—a rude building of logs without glass—this heroic and resourceful man, with the assistance of only one nurse (his patients on mattresses of hay) successfully coped with an epidemic of typhoid fever, saving many lives.

Soon after, the hospital was enlarged. Ultimately, it accommodated over two hundred patients. For its support Dr. Grant was himself responsible, except for a per capita grant from the government. In an address, he stated that not one dollar had ever come from the outside for that service, the heavy responsibility resting on him alone.

Letters, Address and Resolution

While Grant was in Dawson City, he wrote to Sam Steele, the superintendent of the North-West Mounted Police, who has been called the "Forrest Gump of Canadian history" for his involvement in so many historical incidents: "The Fenian Raids, the Long March West, the 1870 Riel Uprising, the establishment of the North-West Mounted Police, the construction of the Canadian Pacific Railway, the 1885 Northwest Uprising, the Klondike gold rush, the Second Boer War, the First World War, the Spanish flu epidemic, and the Winnipeg General Strike."[7] The letter, addressed to Colonel Steele, is dated May 26, 1899, and reads:

> Dear Sir,
>
> I cannot tell you how much I appreciate the stand you have taken in establishing law and order in this territory.
> You have maintained the dignity of our British institutions here, among a class of American citizens, many of them not of the highest grade; which will always reflect credit on your Administration and go far to promote the cause of morals and religion here and elsewhere. I highly appreciate your action in stopping those Sabbath Performances; I fully endorse your action in bringing up Newman under the [word unclear] act; and am strongly in favour of the introduction of an ordinance making it criminal to allow children on the stage.

7. Wheeler, "Reviving."

I hope the ordinance will carry,
Yours respectfully,

Andrew S. Grant.[8]

He also wrote a letter to the Canadian Prime Minister, Sir Wilfred Laurier, about the appalling social and moral conditions in the Yukon Territory, asking him to reverse the law temporarily legalizing gambling houses and dance halls. The letter reads as follows:

Dawson, Y.T., 19th March, 1901

To the Hon. Sir Wilfrid Laurier, Premier
of the Dominion of Canada.

My Dear Sir,

I have been in this country since 1897, and have watched closely the trend of events here, and last year when outside, addressing large meetings in centres like Montreal and Toronto I always stood up for the Government in its Yukon Administration on general principles.

Your Government is aware that open gambling and dance-hall business has been carried on in this city from the first, much to the disgrace of both the people and the Government. We were promised more than once by the authorities here, that these things would be put under the ban of the law; and at last the imperative order came from your Minister of the Interior, that on the 16th of March these places would be closed, and much to the delight of the great majority of the people they were closed on Saturday the 16th at 12 mid-night. At noon on Monday the order came to re-open until the first of June, and there was a regular carnival song among the sporting fraternity of this place, and the thing was flouted in the face of the decent people; and citizens of other countries resident here, expressed their surprise and disgust with our Government. It is not with me as much a matter of allowing open gambling and prostitution, with all their con-commitant [sic] evils, for ten weeks more, as it is that the majesty of our British Law should be trampled under foot, and that our Canadian Government should for a moment sanction this evil. It is nothing more or less than a standing disgrace to our country and an insult to the people of Dawson. I never for one moment thought that the message sent by these people would receive any consideration from your Government,

---

8. Grant, "Letter."

or we would certainly have sent another and a very different petition. Pardon my intrusion but this thing must be set right.

Your obedient servant,

Andrew S. Grant
Pastor St Andrews Church.
A citizen of the Empire.

Grant returned to Toronto in 1900 in order to make arrangements to move his family to Dawson City where they lived until 1908. Caroline Grant was born in 1902 and Alan in 1905.

In 1901, work was begun on the construction of a Gothic church building. St. Andrew's Church and manse were impressive structures by any standard, as the following will attest:

> The church and the manse were designed by Skilling, an American architect. The new church had an oak interior, a seating capacity of 600 and a massive pipe organ. The construction cost was $16,250 for both buildings.
>
> St. Andrew's Church was built in the Gothic Revival style characterized by a massive appearance, asymmetry, openings with pointed arches, and the use of a corner tower with buttresses. The Gothic Revival style was associated with morality and goodness in the early 1800's. Skilling designed St. Andrew's Manse in the more modern Second Empire style as defined by its Mansard roof.
>
> Dormer windows in the second floor and the bay window also reflects its Second Empire design. The Classical Revival design can be seen in the columns, pilasters, and trim over the front door, the pediment, the entablature, the cornice, and the stairway.[9]

In early 1908, the Grant family bid farewell to the Yukon in order that Grant might assume the position of general superintendent of missions following in the footsteps of Dr. James Robertson, who had enlisted him for the Yukon ministry. They returned to Toronto where they resided in Rosedale and became associated with the newly established Rosedale Presbyterian Church.

In 1911, he became convener of the Home Mission Committee for the Presbyterian Church in Canada. That same year, Grant was appointed president of the newly formed Moral and Social Reform League whose purpose was to arrange for a large congress of Canadian Presbyterians in order

---

9. Dawson City, "South Dawson."

to educate church members regarding current moral and social problems. Grant organized the congress, which took place in Toronto at Massey Hall beginning on June 13, 1913. It was a mammoth undertaking and speaks volumes of Grant's organizational skills. It was billed as a Pre-Assembly Congress to which ministers, missionaries, their wives and one male representative of every congregation were invited. There were dozens of speakers and it is estimated that about four thousand attended the various sessions. The congress was opened by C. W. Gordon, the novelist and historian, who spoke of the challenge that Canadian Presbyterianism faced at the beginning of the twentieth century. Dr. John G. Shearer (1859–1925) spoke on the theme of "The Redemption of the City." Other speakers addressed the issues of prostitution, gambling, white slavery, and child labour. When W. H. Smith, a self-proclaimed "progressive," spoke of the suppression of the traffic in liquor by the state, A. S. Grant introduced a series of resolutions on the issue, calling for total prohibition, the text of which follows:

> Mr. Chairman,—I regret exceedingly that the Temperance part of our programme was shut out this morning. It will be absolutely impossible for us to hear the three men who were asked to speak to this Congress on this vital question.
>
> I want to tell you as a man who has pioneered this country that God will not save Canada until the Christian men of Canada say regarding the liquor traffic, "Get off the map." I am not saying that He cannot do it, but it is my humble judgment that He will not, because there is in our camp that sin which we have fostered and which to-day is our great national sin. We shall never have a strong nation on the North American continent unless, before this great influx of immigration comes to our shores, we teach men that this traffic is a horrible crime. We have indulged this sin and have allowed it to eat into our very life until it has destroyed the basis of our best success. We have started the work and have counted the cost, but we cannot build successfully until we have cleared away the rubbish. My soul is pained within me because of the young men of Canada who in armies are trudging down to the way of destruction and physical ruin.
>
> I wanted, more than anything else, to get an expression of opinion from the Presbyterian elders in Canada in regard to the liquor business, because we can put it off the map. (Hear, hear.) I am sure of this, that the moment we begin to move there are forces that will move along with us. Do you think you could for one short day separate yourselves from your politics and take your stand upon a great national issue and say that this thing

must go? My liberty does not extend to the destruction of my brother, and I have no right as a citizen to put forth any effort to work the destruction of my brother. I am my brother's keeper. I have put too much time and too much money into this thing to stop now. I want to tell you that I am a man who has been forced to spend his life and money taking care of wreckage caused by this infernal business; I am sick of it. I am looking for vengeance, and I am going to have it. (Applause.) The Presbyterian Church has committed itself already to the theory; but it is not on the job; it has never taken the thing seriously. You are afraid to take your stand because of commercialism and because of vested interests. It is said that it cannot be done. Take it to God and He will cast out the devil.

There is no question at all but that the use of spirituous liquor is a detriment to the physical, social, intellectual, and spiritual life of our people. There is no question at all about that. Science has accepted the fact. What right has an ignorant, brutish man to deal out poison promiscuously to his fellow citizens even if he has the authority of the law? He has no right, and ought not to be given it. This is the resolution I wish to submit:

> "(1) Whereas recent scientific investigation has revealed that alcohol is a poison and injurious to life, even when taken in small quantities; and
>
> "(2) Whereas the liquor traffic has become a great economic burden; and
>
> "(3) Whereas it is the enemy of all social progress, and the cause of much social distress, inefficiency, poverty, insanity, crime and death; and
>
> "(4) Whereas the highest demand of individual and national life demands the suppression of the liquor traffic; and
>
> "(5) Whereas the progress of the kingdom of God is greatly hindered through the traffic in intoxicating liquor;

"Be it therefore resolved:

> "(1) That in the opinion of this Congress, consisting of all the ministers and representative laymen from all the congregations in the Presbyterian Church in Canada, the time has come when legislation should be secured in Canada prohibiting the manufacture, importation and sale of intoxicating liquor for beverage purposes;

"(2) That this resolution be forwarded to the General Assembly for action;

"(3) That it be a suggestion to the Assembly to invite all other religious bodies and temperance organizations to cooperate in a movement having for its object the total suppression of the liquor traffic in Canada."

I want this business prohibited by law, and afterwards it will be a matter of what the penalty shall be—not a fine, but imprisonment. That may seem a drastic measure, but it is the spirit of the resolution, and the time is opportune for it.

I want to know as your representative in leading our country in great missionary enterprises what your position is regarding this business. Are you prepared to take your stand as citizens and members of the great Presbyterian Church in Canada, responsible for your brothers going down to death? I say, cut out this business and you will cut the nerve of the social evil and will make it absolutely impossible for many other evils to exist, and the dens of iniquity will go out of business of their own weight. If you are going to build up the kingdom of God in Canada this thing must be rooted out of our civilization. It is said that we cannot do it, that it has been here and that it will always stay. Let us arise and show the world that it can be done. Put it on the drug shelf with other drugs.

This resolution was carried unanimously by a standing vote amid a wild outburst of applause.

The 1913 Pre-Assembly Congress had reached a fitting climax and conclusion. Grant was firmly persuaded that state prohibition of alcohol was the answer to the ravages created by alcoholism that he had seen in Dawson City. Besides this address, he actively campaigned for the ending of the liquor trade; at his own expense, he had leaflets dropped from an airplane in various Ontario towns and cities, making the argument for prohibition.

Commentary on Grant's Letters, Address and Resolution

Our focus will be on this resolution and the two letters Grant wrote while in Dawson City, the first to Superintendent Steele and the other to Prime Minister Laurier. They constitute the literary remains of A. S. Grant that we know with certainty are from his hand. There are mission reports from 1925–35 in the Acts and Proceedings of the General Assembly of the

Presbyterian Church in Canada that bear Grant's name, but it is difficult if not impossible to determine whether Grant is their sole author.

The resolution and letters reveal a man of strict moral code, almost verging on puritanism, for example, he links dance halls with prostitution. Grant believed that it was the responsibility of governments to enact legislation that would keep people from self-destructiveness, caused by specific social evils. He was strongly influenced by the Social Gospel movement that dominated the end of the nineteenth and the first two decades of the twentieth centuries. He was of the conviction that the kingdom of God would not come in Canada until some of these social evils had been eradicated through parliamentary legislation. Basically, this was his approach to the whole question of the liquor traffic and its suppression. Grant firmly believed that liberty did not include the freedom to destroy one's fellow man, and he took seriously the principle that we are our brothers' keepers, as outlined in his speech above.

At the beginning of the twentieth century, alcoholism posed an enormous problem in most industrial societies. For instance, in Switzerland at this very same time, alcohol constituted one of the main problems among workers, causing severe disruptions in family life. Karl Barth, then pastor of a Reformed congregation in the Swiss village of Safenwil, was the president of the Blue Cross Total Abstinence Society that advocated *Alkoholfrei* hotels. In his July 26, 1914 sermon, Barth lists alcoholism, along with tuberculosis, capitalism, and war, as one of the major social problems that plagued European society.[10] Prohibition of all alcohol seemed to be the solution. It was this law that Andrew Grant believed was needed in Ontario and the whole of Canada. As he said in his pre-assembly resolution: "God will not save Canada until the Christian men of Canada say regarding the liquor traffic: 'Get off the map.'" In his address, he railed against the "great national sin" Canada had fostered—liquor traffic—that he considered to be a horrible crime, and thus a national issue requiring a firm stand.

In critique of Grant's position, it has to be said: first, that science is less clear in its view of the poisonous nature of alcohol for individuals than Grant claimed. Medical science today, for instance, speaks of the beneficial aspects of a glass of red wine daily. Moreover, wine was used and recommended in the Bible, although men like Grant and his teacher Sir William Dawson did not think so. Moreover, there are many biblical warnings about the misuse of alcohol, for example in the book of Proverbs.

Second, while Grant was rightly concerned about alcohol's destructiveness for his fellow man, his resolve to prohibit the trade of alcohol

---

10. Barth, *Predigten*, 388.

constituted an interference with personal liberty. It is clear that the imposition of prohibition in Canada and the United States did not work. Bootlegging and illegal bars, called speakeasies, became common. Consequently, the liquor traffic was never suppressed. Our contemporary approach provides more personal liberty in the matter of alcohol consumption, and accepts the fact that there will be drunkenness. The money raised through taxation of alcohol is often then devoted to the care and cure of alcoholics. Alcoholic drinks are restricted to some extent, of course, through laws that prohibit minors from purchasing them, and are often accompanied by messages encouraging moderation. No perfect solution exists, but the more contemporary approach seems better suited to Western societies with their emphasis on personal liberty.

Also in 1913, the Women's Home Mission Society (WHMS) and the Women's Foreign Mission Society (WFMS) of the Presbyterian Church in Canada were considering an amalgamated Women's Missionary Society that would be one unified society in the Presbyterian Church encompassing both home and overseas missions. The decision was made by the women at a large meeting held at Cooke's Presbyterian Church at the same time as the Pre-Assembly Congress. At the June Assembly in 1913, Andrew Grant made a motion, seconded by Dr. Alfred Gandier, that the two Women's Missionary Societies unify and that the Montreal Women's Missionary Society join the synod. This motion was subsequently carried by the Assembly.

Church Union with the Methodists and the Congregationalists was in the air and it dominated the affairs of the church courts during the next few years. Andrew Grant, unlike his fellow Presbyterian College alumnus, George Pidgeon, a fervent Unionist, took a gradualist approach to Church Union. Grant firmly believed in spiritual unity, but thought that a longer period of time would be required to achieve this in order to avoid a disruption in the Church. The disruption he feared, of course, did occur, despite the fact that about two-thirds of Presbyterians favoured Church Union. Grant left his position as general superintendent of missions in 1915 to oppose the Unionist movement. That year was a difficult one for the Grant family. Their son Oswald was killed in action in France. It was also in 1915 that Andrew Grant was invited by Queen's University to accept an honorary doctorate of divinity. He responded by thanking Queen's but declining the honour, giving as his reason that he was unworthy of it. To soften the abruptness of this refusal, he mentioned that he had already declined a similar offer from his own alma mater, the Presbyterian College of Montreal.

Records are not available to inform us of his activities thereafter, but we do know that in 1919 he travelled to Europe to help with the demobilization of the Canadian Armed Forces. After Church Union, Andrew Grant was invited by the continuing Presbyterian Church in Canada to serve as secretary of the Board of Missions. Along with A. E. Armstrong, Grant's counterpart in the newly formed United Church of Canada, he worked out an arrangement that was subsequently approved by the Commission on Church Union, a task made easier by Grant and Armstrong's mutual respect and the fact that neither had ever visited an overseas field.

Dr. Grant's ten-year tenure of the general secretaryship of the Board of Missions spanned a difficult time. The period after Church Union was one of retrenchment and reconstruction, when mission charges needed ministers who came from the British Isles and the United States, some of dubious quality, to fill the vacancies. Next came the Great Depression, triggered by the 1929 stock market crash, which caused deficits in church budgets and consequently mission cutbacks. The national church was greatly assisted by the WMS, which contributed a fund to defray the deficit. In 1929, Andrew Grant even gave up his annual stipend for the same purpose. One of the last letters that we have from Grant was written in 1935, expressing gratitude to the WMS for the role that they played in making up the deficit:

> I am writing to convey to you and to your Council Executive and to all those who took part in raising this large sum of money, amounting to $25,000, for the work of the Presbyterian Church in Canada through this period of depression, our sincerest thanks.
>
> This in itself is one of the most magnanimous, self-sacrificing things that has come under my observation in the history of our Church. Your Board during this period of depression and with the tremendous volume of work for which you were responsible has made this additional contribution to the general funds of the Church, and as one who made this request of you I wish to convey my sincerest thanks . . .[11]

That very year, Dr. A. S. Grant underwent an operation from which he never recovered. He died on July 22, 1935. Among the many tributes paid to Grant was that of Dr. W. M. Rochester, editor of the *Presbyterian Record*, who wrote: "A most extraordinary man and a most colourful figure passed to his reward quite recently, leaving a great gap in the ranks of the workers in the Presbyterian Church in Canada."

Since no sermon is available to us from the pen of Andrew Grant, this essay has relied on and has quoted extensively from his letters and the lengthy resolution he introduced at the 1913 Pre-Assembly Congress, so that the still voice of this remarkable man, this seeker of gold-seekers, might

---

11. Klempa and Doran, *Certain Women*, 207.

still be heard by us almost a century later. In a real sense, the life and career of Andrew Grant continues to be stirring and an eloquent sermon proclaiming the Master to whom he belonged and who he sought to serve, at great cost to his family and to himself. Like Dr. James Robertson, he believed that there was something more precious than gold, and so he went to the Yukon to communicate the treasures of the Gospel to the gold seekers. The Presbyterian Church in Canada and the Canadian community were greatly enriched by the incomparable work and witness of this extraordinary man. As the college celebrates its 150th anniversary, it honours this renowned graduate, and exclaims with the psalmist: "Bless the LORD, O my soul, and all that is within me, bless his holy name. Bless the LORD, O my soul, and do not forget all of his benefits" (Psalm 103:1–2 NRSV).

Dedication

This essay is dedicated to the memory of Mrs. James (Jane) Grant, Dr. Andrew Grant's daughter-in-law, a long-time member of Rosedale Presbyterian Church, Toronto, whose kindness and generosity during our time in Rosedale (1970–78) to my late wife Lois, our two daughters, Catherine and Mary-Margaret, and our son Michael are gratefully remembered.

I am grateful to my son Michael and to Ms. Kirsten Shute for their valuable assistance with the research and the writing of this essay, and to Bob Anger for his kind help with the Andrew S. Grant collection compiled by Grant's daughter, Caroline Grant, in the Presbyterian Church in Canada Archives, accession number #1973-5003.

The Author

William Klempa is principal emeritus of the Presbyterian College, Montreal and adjunct professor of Christian theology in the McGill Faculty of Religious Studies. He has been recording secretary, and on the Theological Committee, of the World Alliance of Reformed Churches, and a delegate to the World Council of Churches. He served as moderator of the Presbyterian Church in Canada and was a convener and member of the Committee on Church Doctrine of the Presbyterian Church for over thirty years. His most recent book is a collection of essays in Reformed history and theology, entitled *Exploring the Faith*.

Bibliography

Barth, Karl. *Predigten 1914*. Zurich: Theologischer Verlag, 1974.

Berton, Pierre. *Klondike: The Last Great Gold Rush, 1896–1899*. Toronto: McClelland & Stewart, 1972.

Connor, Ralph [C. W. Gordon]. *The Life of James Robertson, D.D.* Toronto: Westminster, 1908.

Dawson City Museum & Historical Society, Parks Canada, Government of Yukon, Department of Tourism and Culture, "South Dawson City Walking Tour," 6. www.tc.gov.yk.ca/publications/South_Dawson_City_wt.pdf.

Grant, Andrew Shaw. "Letter to Colonel Steele, May 26, 1899." Bruce Peel Special Collections Library, University of Alberta (2008.1.2.1.1.50.1). http://coventry.library.ualberta.ca/units/2008/1/2/1/1/50/1.

Klempa, Lois, and Rosemary Doran. *Certain Women Amazed Us: The Women's Missionary Society, Their Story 1864–2002*. Toronto: Women's Missionary Society, 2002.

McNab, John. "A Prospector of Souls." In *They Went Forth*, 123–39. Toronto: McClelland & Stewart, 1933.

Moir, John S. *Enduring Witness*. 3rd ed. Toronto: Committee on History, Presbyterian Church of Canada, 2003.

National Park Service, Washington. "Hard Drive to the Klondike: Promoting Seattle during the Gold Rush." http://www.nps.gov/klse/forteachers/hrs1c.htm.

Wheeler, Lauren. "Reviving the Canadian Hero." 2012. http://activehistory.ca/2012/08/reviving-the-canadian-hero/#more-9019.

CHAPTER 6

The College and Athletics
James Naismith

By David S. Mulder

The Reverend Dr. James Naismith, MD, MPE, DD, (1861–1939). The handwritten caption on the reverse of the photograph reads: "Dr. Jim Naismith, as he appeared when he received his theological degree in late 1880s." This is not quite correct. Dr. Naismith graduated from the Presbyterian College in 1890, but did not pursue a BD. This shows him, robust and resolute, wearing the BA hood from McGill University, the institution from which he graduated in 1887. This is a print of a cabinet card by Summerhayes and Walford, Montreal, courtesy of Springfield College, Babson Library, Archives and Special Collections.

THE COLLEGE AND ATHLETICS

IN THE SPRING OF 1939, Presbyterian College, Montreal, awarded its highest accolade, an honorary doctorate in divinity, to its best-known graduate: the Reverend Dr. James Naismith, BA, MD, MPE of Lawrence, Kansas. Many felt that the college had waited too long. James Naismith died before the year ended. Why had it taken so long to acknowledge not only the man, but the principle he espoused, that Christian ministry is not limited to the pastorate?

To fully understand Naismith's contribution, it is necessary to return to his roots. He was born in Ramsay Township, just west of Ottawa, to first generation Scottish Canadians. His mother, Margaret, was the daughter of Robert and Annie Young, who reached Canada in 1832 and became successful farmers. His father, John Naismith, left Scotland for Upper Canada at the age of nine. He eventually relocated to Ramsay Township to work with his uncle Peter where he met and married Margaret Young.[1]

When James was nine years old, the Naismith family moved nearby to Almonte where his father was a saw hand in a lumber mill. Shortly afterward, the family met with tragedy: grandfather Young died, the mill burned and within three months both parents had died with typhoid fever. This left three orphans, Annie, James and Robert, to the care of their maternal grandmother Young. James was devastated and desperately grieved his mother. These circumstances accelerated his self-identity, industry and spirit of innovation and may explain his poor performance in school and his preference for all athletic activity. With the direction of his uncle Peter, he was required to do his share of chores on the farm and in the woods. An avid outdoorsman, James enjoyed hunting, fishing and trapping. His real passion was playing games with neighbour boys which included tag, "duck on a rock,"[2] tobogganing, swimming, and ice hockey. His construction of a pair of ice skates from two files and a block of wood was early evidence of his innovative skills when faced with family financial constraints.

His love of physical activity, farm work and sports led him to drop out of Almonte High School in 1877 to work as a lumberjack. He immediately emulated his coworkers in terms of rough language and drinking whiskey. On one occasion, a bar patron asked him: "Ye're Margaret Young's son, aren't ye." "Aye," James replied, reaching for his drink. "She'd turn over in her

---

1. See Rain and Carpenter, *James Naismith*, 2.

2. A local game where a large rock (3–4 feet) was chosen. The guard placed his rock on the large rock and others attempted to dislodge his stone ("the duck") by throwing their own stone at the target. If their stone missed, it must be retrieved before being tagged by the guard. Players learned that a lob shot was most successful, perhaps used by Naismith in designing the game of basketball.

grave to see ye." Humiliated and respectful for his mother, James put down his glass and never touched alcohol for the rest of his life.[3]

Heeding the advice of his uncle Peter, who insisted, "James, make your living with your head not your hands,"[4] he returned to high school after an absence of five years and completed high school in two years, including languages French and Latin, to meet the entrance requirements of McGill University. His uncle promised financial support if James would ultimately make a career in the ministry and if he would return to help on the farm each summer. His uncle gave him a wall plaque for his room at McGill: "Do not let anybody work harder than I do."[5] His high school principal also encouraged the ministry and Naismith felt that Christianity would put him in the best position to be a positive role model and to serve his fellow man.

Early at McGill, two fellow students convinced him to participate in other campus activities, such as athletics rather than becoming an academic recluse. This was a real conflict for Naismith, who grew up with the prevailing thinking that organized athletics were a tool of the devil. His time at McGill was characterized by a high level of academic performance along with a leading role in McGill football, rugby, soccer, lacrosse and gymnastic teams. His bachelor's degree in April 1887 was a prerequisite to entering the Presbyterian College of Montreal.

When he graduated from the Presbyterian College of Montreal (April 1890), he was expected to seek a call to a congregation, the necessary step within the Presbyterian Church to secure ordination. Twenty-seven years later, in order to become a chaplain in the US Army during World War I, James was ordained by the American Presbyterian Church, but at this juncture of his life, Naismith felt strongly that he would not take up a pastorate. Instead, at the urging of D. A. Budge from the Montreal YMCA, he enrolled in the YMCA International Training School in Springfield, Massachusetts, (known today as Springfield College), where for a second time, Naismith again met Amos Stagg who had so influenced his decision against ordination.

While pursuing his studies in theology, he maintained a major interest in physical education activities. When the Director of McGill's gym classes was unable to continue, James Naismith took over as director of physical training for McGill in 1891 when the director (Frederick Barjum) died. By this time, he was a rare four-sport varsity athlete, having played varsity

3. Rains and Carpenter, *James Naismith*, 11; Cosentino, *Almonte's*, 20; Naismith, *Best*, 10.
4. Rains and Carpenter, *James Naismith*, 14.
5. Ibid., 17.

football (he never missed a game); varsity lacrosse, varsity rugby and he won the prestigious Wikstead silver medal, and the following year the Wikstead gold medal as varsity gymnastics champion.[6] A pivotal event for Naismith was a visiting lecture by Amos Alonzo Stagg from Yale. He spoke at McGill while playing football at Yale University. His message emphasized the bond between sports and religious faith early in his career.[7] Naismith would later play football for Coach Stagg at Springfield College. Stagg also earned his MPE at Springfield College[8] and became a famous coach in American College Football (1862–1965). He pointed out that it takes many of the same qualities to become a good athlete as it does to become a good Christian including enthusiasm, perseverance, and hard work. This raised the idea that he might provide more service to young men with athletics than by the traditional activities of the ministry.

During Naismith's McGill student days, Budge encouraged a relationship with the Montreal YMCA (one of the earliest YMCAs in North America: 1851). He was attracted by the YMCA core values and the practical role it played in guiding young Christian men in how their lives should be lived. The role of educational opportunities in the form of evening classes was an additional plus. It is of note that a university evolved in 1926 named after the founder of the YMCA: Sir George Williams. This university merged with Loyola to become the present-day Concordia University. The Montreal YMCA was a major influence in Naismith's ultimate career.

Naismith's decision to forsake the ministry and a pastorate for a career in physical education was monumental! However, he was not prepared at this time to take the next step towards ordination: seeking a Call to be a minister of a congregation. Naismith felt strongly that God was calling him to a career in physical education. It was strongly opposed by family (especially his sister) and his faculty. His childhood companion from Almonte, R. Tait McKenzie[9] expressed it best: "It took courage at that time to leave the time-honoured and well-beaten path for unknown and comparatively unexplored regions, but the decision once taken he never faltered and I think never regretted it."[10]

6. From "History of McGill Athletics," http://www.mcgill.ca/channels/news/history-mcgill-athletics-176215.

7. From http://www.mcgill.ca/aoc/james-naismith-3.

8. From the University of Chicago faculty, A Centennial View, 9, http://www.libiuchicago.edu/e/spd/centcat/Fac/Facch06-01.htmail.

9. Tait McKenzie was the son of Reverend William McKenzie, the minister of the Free Presbyterian Church in Ramsay Township Ontario. See the Virtual Museum, http://www.virtualmuseum.ca/important-notices.

10. Rains and Carpenter, *James Naismith*, 27.

Naismith's career goals were strongly influenced by two men he met on his first day at Springfield College. Dr. Luther Gulick, the director of physical education, emphasized the original core values of the YMCA in developing a sound mind, body, and spirit. He also encountered Amos Alonzo Stagg who coached Naismith in football and summarized his role with this quote: "Jim, I played you at center because you can do the meanest things in the most gentlemanly manner."[11] His position at centre prompted Naismith to produce the forerunner of the modern football helmet. Gulick challenged Naismith's innovative skills to develop a game for physical education students that could be played indoors because of the challenge of New England's harsh winters. The game would fill the hiatus between football, baseball and soccer. Naismith began by studying the popular attributes of football, lacrosse, soccer and hockey. He chose a soft soccer ball, and incorporated passing, rather than running with the ball to minimize injury with the target for the goal high above the player's head. The janitor offered two old peach baskets for boxes at both ends of the gym. They were nailed to the railing of the gym gallery that happened to be exactly ten feet in height (identical to today's basket). Naismith wrote out thirteen rules for the new game and posted them on the gym bulletin board prior to the first game played with nine men on each team in December 1891. Many refinements to the game have taken place, such as the open net basket making retrieval of the ball after each score unnecessary and dribbling was added to passing as a means to advance the ball. By 1893, this "new game" became an international phenomenon via the YMCA. Inventing the game of basketball would become Naismith's greatest accomplishment.

In 1895, Naismith was offered a position as director of physical education at the YMCA in Denver. While his YMCA position was full-time, he enrolled in the Gross Medical School at the University of Denver and was granted his doctor of medicine degree in 1898. The demands of his job and his medical studentship were further compounded when his wife's sister died in childbirth and the Naismiths raised this new infant for three years, until the baby's father remarried. This stretched Naismith's motto that each of life's challenges was an opportunity. His success in Denver led to his next academic promotion.

The University of Kansas was recruiting a new physical education instructor and a chapel director. The chancellor of the university, Francis H. Snow, received a most positive letter of support from Amos Alonzo Stagg for James Naismith to fill this position: "I recommend James Naismith, inventor of basketball, Presbyterian, teetotaler, all around athlete,

---

11. Baker and Naismith, *Basketball*, 28.

non-smoker, and owner of a vocabulary without cuss words."[12] This sealed his appointment and life-long career accomplishments, including a losing record as basketball coach. More importantly, he mentored Forrest "Phog" Allen who became the "Father of Basketball Coaching." He influenced Dean Smith (North Carolina) and Adolph Rupp (Kentucky), all of whom have entered the Basketball Hall of Fame as coaches along with Naismith.

Naismith's time in Lawrence, Kansas, at the university was characterized by his role as a teacher and friend of the students. In the classroom, he encouraged a well-conceived argument or debate as a sound teaching device. He personally mentored many student athletes to change behaviour and develop important life skills. He also became known for his popular talks to community organizations and his Sunday sermons in local small town Presbyterian churches. One of his messages to the community was: "Athletics and the playground furnish the laboratory in which the great lessons of fair play and the square deal are being taught to children."[13] His sermons in the local churches became legendary. It was late in his career in Kansas that Naismith sought to be ordained, a requirement to serve in the National Guard (1916). In this capacity, he served as a chaplain and emphasized "social hygiene." He accomplished this goal through education of soldiers and vigorous exercise programs such as basketball and boxing. He also worked with local authorities to ban houses of prostitution. His work occurred at the Texas-Mexico border at the time of a revolution. His work was widely respected and at the outbreak of World War I he was encouraged to join the US Army in 1917. This required American citizenship, which he did not acquire until 1925. He nevertheless served as chaplain for the US Army in Paris 1917–1919. Touching letters to his wife reflect his thought about war and his compassion for individual soldiers.[14] This is likely the incentive for writing a book entitled *The Basis of Clean Living* (1919).[15] He never forgot his Presbyterian roots in rural Ontario and Presbyterian College Montreal. His sermon on "Athletics and Religion" has been chosen to show Naismith's contribution and influence on sports, the college and the church.

Naismith Legacy, the Game of Basketball

There is no question that Naismith's celebrity relates to his discovery of the game of basketball. He is included in all of Canada's Sports Halls of Fame.

12. See Rains and Carpenter, *James Naismith*, 71; and Cosentino, *Almonte's*, 65.
13. Rains and Carpenter, *James Naismith*, 97.
14. Ibid., 122.
15. Naismith and Johnson, "Bulletin."

In the United States, he is recognized at the University of Kansas as a coach, professor emeritus, university's Hall of Fame. The street in front of the basketball arena is named in his honour. At the national level, the Naismith Memorial Basketball Hall of Fame includes many of his students and coaches at the University of Kansas. It is the ultimate tribute to his contributions to the game of basketball at every level. In 2014, the original hand written 13 Rules of Basketball was sold at Sotheby's auction for more than four million dollars. The purchaser donated it to the University of Kansas, where it will be the centrepiece of a new field house at the university.

Athletics and Religion

An Address by James Naismith from Typed Notes[16]

Less than half a century ago, to have mentioned athletics and religion in the same breath, except to express extreme antagonism, would have been anathema. But today we are beginning to look on each of these as an expression of different phases of the same individual, perfectly compatible and mutually necessary for the full development of man.

In the early 1890s a young theological student was publicly censured for playing on a college football team, because it was a Godless game and one that no Christian should encourage. This incident shows the attitude of the clergy towards athletics at that time.

Last week, I attended a boxing tournament where the referee was an active ordained minister; one of the judges was a minister and the other was a graduate of a Y.M.C.A. College. "Verily, athletics and religion have met and kissed each other."

It is interesting to note how this change has come about, and to look forward and anticipate the result of this understanding between those who obey the physical laws of the Creator, and those who obey the spiritual.

This antagonism is older than the Christian Religion. We get our religion from the Hebrews; and they were a people that took little or no interest in sports of any kind.

We get our athletics, mainly, from the Greeks who had some very advanced ideas of various sports. In their case athletics was closely related to their religion, as they were associated with some of their religious ceremonies.

---

16. These notes are kindly provided by the William L. Clements Library, University of Michigan.

These two nations do not seem to have come into direct contact, so that there was no opportunity for our forefathers to see the highest form of athletic activity.

The point of contact between religion and athletics came when the Romans conquered the Hebrews, and this naturally produced an antagonism to everything of a Roman character. Herod tried to introduce the Roman Games, and spent large sums of money to establish the Roman Sports. This was doomed to failure because of its being Roman, in the first place; and because the Roman Sports were such as had no appeal to the Hebrew people.

The circus opposed every tradition of the Jews and the attempt to introduce it ended in contempt for the promoter and caused antagonism to sport. The Roman Sport, as the early Christians knew it, was not likely to heal this breach, especially when it was used as a means of entertaining the Roman Populace by pitting the Christians without weapons against the wild beasts in the Arena. As a consequence of such a Sport it is little wonder that the antagonism was intensified rather than diminished.

In the following centuries there was little to bring them together for the mass of the men had warfare as an occupation, and Jousts and Tournaments as a recreation. While the Soldier was developing his body for warfare, the clergy were developing the spirit by crucifying the flesh and making their lives holy by other forms of bodily suffering.

It is not to be wondered at that our immediate ancestors who had this heritage of hatred for sports should look upon them as the work of the Devil which should be shunned in every way possible.

The life and work of a number of acknowledged athletes began to show that an athlete could be a Christian and that a Christian could be an athlete. The Studd brothers of England, Gale and Cowan of Princeton, Stagg of Yale, Elliot of North-western, Gulick of Oberlin, Black and Bond of Knox, Seerlen and Kallenberg of Iowa, Hagerman from Pomona and a host of others too numerous to mention, paved the way for a closer relationship between Athletics and Religion.

It was not until the middle of the nineteenth century that there was any definitive attempt to heal the breach, and even then Athletics were looked upon as a necessary evil to be tolerated, because we could not abolish them. In 1860 the Y.M.C.A. in San Francisco established a Gymnasium where young men could take part in Gymnastics. This innovation was tolerated, rather then welcomed, but there were some who saw, in athletics, a point of contact between the religious and the athletic. Athletics were introduced into the work of the Young Men's Christian Association, not because of their intrinsic value, but because they gave an opportunity for religious contact.

Jahn introduced the German System to develop men for warriors; and Ling developed the Swedish as educational and medical systems. But it was America that saw the possibilities of athletics, in the formation of character.

In 1890, Dr. Gulick, seeing the value of athletics for individual development, modeled the athletics of the Y.M.C.A. after the Greek System, and arranged an American Pentathlon designed to benefit the participant, and to build up an all around man. A few years later there was organized, in the Y.M.C.A., The Clean Sport League, designed to develop sportsmanship and the spirit of fair play. In this Organization each member pledged himself to play the game according to the rules and to accept the penalty for any of their infringements.

This, so far as I know, was the first deliberate attempt to mould character by the use of Athletics. The athletes of the colleges were not ready to accept this idealism in athletics and the League did not continue long enough to see the results of its efforts. Today, a player would not be condemned if he failed to lie for his team. The principles which these men panned and looked forward to are actually coming to pass.

In 1892, Dr. Wey introduced basketball into the Elmira Reformatory as an aid in developing the right kind of a spirit in the inmates. In 1898, Hull House began to play Basketball; in 1902, The M.E. Church at Northhampton had a basketball team that played twenty-eight games. Basketball is being played in nearly every high school in America. Minnesota has a High School league of 254 teams:

High school basketball leagues	Number of players
South Dakota	181
Wisconsin	390
Kansas	540
Ohio	431
Indiana	600
Illinois	725

These are simply used as an illustration of the number of young men who are taking part in this one form of sport.

Most of those who have been active in High School Athletics, when they enter business have the same instincts of play and are anxious to have an opportunity of taking part in athletics in their leisure time. It has been said that we make a living in our working hours, but we build our character in leisure time. If this is true, then the people who supervise the working hours, and neglect the leisure time, may expect an advance in efficiency and a decline in character.

A few churches have been aware of this for some time. Fifteen years ago, Old Trinity in Brooklyn carried on in connection with their religious work, an elaborate program of organized athletics, but it is only within the last few years that our churches have awakened to the opportunities and possibilities of athletics as a part of their work for mankind; and have opened their doors week days as well as Sundays. Some of them are turning their old buildings into recreation centres, others are building gymnasiums.

The big problem of athletics has been to widen its range so that every man would have a chance to take part in some form of athletic activity. It was planned that Basketball should accommodate a large number of players on the floor at one time. Cage Ball and Pushball were developed with this idea in mind; but the evolution of sport has shown that a great many small teams give opportunities to a greater number of persons, and at the same time they get more of the benefits of competition.

In Kansas City, there are this season three hundred basketball teams playing in organized amateur leagues. Many of these represent Sunday Schools and practice in their own buildings.

Present indications are that the extension of athletics will be through the Churches and organizations of that kind.

Athletics as well as other factors in human life that have no higher ideal than the gratification of selfish desires soon become not only useless but a menace to character. But athletic activity directed by Christian Ideals is bound to have a wholesome effect on all the participants. A player reflects the spirit of the organization that is back of the team. It has been noted that a person playing on two different teams, with different ideals, exhibits the spirit of the team with which he is playing at the time. Therefore, if we keep a young man constantly playing with the right ideals and under the right environment, his actions will soon become a fixed habit and will thus affect his character.

Prohibition is attempting to make a country where we cannot obtain liquor. Sunday School Athletics are attempting to make a nation of young men who have no desire to obtain it. A fraction of the amount of money spent on enforcing the prohibitory law, if used to promote properly directed athletics, would soon build up a generation of young men proud of their athletic ability rather than of their power to absorb nicotine or alcohol.

One preacher of a conservative denomination said, recently from his pulpit "that basketball had brought more young men into the Sunday School and into Church membership than any other one factor."

The leader of one of the large men's classes on being asked how he could reconcile Sunday school teaching with Basketball, said: "Man alive! Athletics is one of the best factors that we have to develop the spirit of the class."

Religion can be of great benefit to the right kind of athletics, and athletics can be a splendid servant of religion. Instead, then, of these two being antagonistic and driving the athletic youth away from religion and making the religious depreciate athletics these two may, and are in many cases, working hand in hand for the common object of developing a better mankind.

Commentary on Naismith's "Athletics and Religion"

During his memorial service at the University of Kansas, Rev. Theo H. Aszman summarized Naismith's philosophy of athletics and religion in this way: "He preferred to do his preaching in active living rather than from the pulpit."[17] I believe this is the message he was trying to impart in his address.

Naismith's background as an accomplished athlete, coach, athletic director, an ordained Presbyterian minister with an MD gave him the podium to expound on this theme. He relates the original conflict to the Greeks' emphasis on athletics and the Hebrew role in religion. He often points to the awareness of the Greeks to the value of athletic competition.

First Corinthians 9:24–27 is the biblical source that supports the value of athletics and exercise.[18] The Apostle Paul is reminding his fellow citizens with a rhetorical question (v. 24) on how to run a race. All Corinthians knew about the Isthmian Games and thus understood this athletic metaphor.[19] Naismith often added the exhortation from Ecclesiastes 9:10: "Whatever your hands find to do, do it with your might." His message is that Christian life requires the same preparation, perseverance, and passion, as an athletic event. With his medical background, he was aware of the physiological role of regular exercise that includes prevention of heart disease, high blood pressure, obesity, back pain, mood elevation and stress control, to name a few. He constantly emphasized the discipline of self-control to diet, sleep, and a rigid training regime for the conditioning that optimal performance demanded.

17. Rains and Carpenter, *James Naismith*, 193.
18. All biblical Scriptures are from the New International Version of the Bible.
19. The Isthmian Games or Isthmia were one of the Pan-Hellenic Games of Ancient Greece, named after the Isthmus of Corinth, where they were held.

Naismith was a firm believer in the application of the character traits of an athlete to daily striving for the prize. Competing in any athletic program requires endurance and focus on the required skills. Naismith always emphasized the social benefits of playing a team sport in terms of loyalty, dependability, fair play, appreciation of diversity, and honesty.

Verse 24 (1 Cor 9:24–27) emphasizes the manner of running the race and the requirements for victory: levels of effort, self-control and dedication. More recently, another famous basketball coach John Wooden at UCLA defines victory or success as: "Success is peace of mind which is a direct result of self-satisfaction in knowing you made the effort to become the best of which you are capable."[20] He also had a firm opinion about Naismith relating athletics to character building. His conclusion was that sports do not build character, they reveal it! The Apostle Paul further observes that the Christian trains with a purpose, not as a fighter shadow boxing. He emphasizes the role of self-control: "I punish my body and enslave it." This athletic imagery was meant to convince the Corinthians of its importance in living the daily Christian life.

Dean Smith was coach of the University of North Carolina basketball team for more than three decades (1961–97). He shared Kansas roots with Naismith. Smith claimed that his parental emphasis on genuine caring for the individual that "all men are created equal" and that the balance between athletics and academics shaped his basic principles of coaching basketball. Smith's principles were simple: "play hard, play together and play smart."[21] While remaining highly competitive, he concentrated on a process for success rather than the outcome. This process was based on his principles and required optimal performance (excellence) by each individual for a team goal. He felt that the leadership skills developed during this basketball-based philosophy were transferable to life needs as a teacher, business leader, lawyer, minister, physician or parent.

While Smith supported his three principles, clearly playing together was his highest priority and the secret of his success as a coach. He emphasized "we" rather than "me," and encouraged playing as a unit to accomplish a team goal. Off the court, he encouraged support of each other as an unselfish family unit. Many of his players commented on the use of the togetherness culture in their future career. Coach Smith was always modest in the face of victory and took responsibility in the case of a loss. He judged each game by how the team performed relative to his principles rather than the outcome.

20. Wooden and Jamison, *Wisdom*, 17.
21. Smith, *Carolina*, 28.

Personally as a surgeon, my athletic background in amateur hockey has resulted in my considering each surgical operation as a team sport. Everyone from the admitting clerk, the patient transporter, to the team in the operating room, is essential to a successful outcome. The teamwork between nurse, anaesthesiologist and surgeon is of greater consequence than any game. An optimal outcome must be recognized and celebrated by all involved.

A biblical reference to athletics is found in 1 Timothy 4:8: "For physical training is of some value, but godliness has value for all things, holding promise for both the present life and the life to come." This message relates to the essential balance between athletics and religion in our daily lives.

James Naismith, John Wooden, and Dean Smith are legends in the game of basketball. Each emphasized the physical and social benefits of athletics at the elite level. Smith examined the post-basketball careers of many of his Carolina players and how they embodied the principles they learned as a college athlete in achieving their career goals. These values included self-discipline, self-control ("run the race to win"), and hard work ("play hard"). He always spoke of timeliness, endurance, and focus, but his mainstay was team work ("play together"). In many aspects, James Naismith had the same philosophy as St. Paul: he supported the effort and determination in running the race, rather than the victory itself. Naismith's career was dominated by this philosophy. He applied it to his every day Christian way of life.

Mike Babcock coached the Canadian men's hockey team to a gold medal in the 2010 Vancouver Olympics. As a motivational tool, he posted "The Credo" on the dressing room wall which emphasizes preparation, commitment, determination, destiny, and team character. It begins and ends with three words: "Leave No Doubt." It summarizes the coach's philosophy for an athlete, but also provides the principles for daily life.[22]

Naismith's speech addresses the negativism of prohibition as a means of controlling alcohol abuse. He proposes instead support of a generation of young people who strive to avoid alcohol related to the demands of high level athletic performance. Roy Williams notes that "Naismith supported his players as people first, as students second, and as athletes third."[23] His deep-seated motive with his students was always to develop both their moral and physical profiles. He used the sport of basketball to attract young men of character and expose them to his way of life which emphasized teamwork, cooperation along with the nurturing of physical skills. Naismith violently opposed segregation and demanded that African Americans have equal

22. See Babcock, *Leave*, 5–6.

23. Rains and Carpenter, *James Naismith*, viii. Roy Allen Williams (born August 1, 1950), an American basketball coach is currently the head coach of the men's basketball team at the University of North Carolina.

opportunity on the basketball court, in the classroom, or in the community. This was also a part of both Wooden's parental creed and Dean Smith's golden rule that all men are created equal. These men were forward thinking for their times. This concept should resonate strongly today. Georgetown coach John Thompson proclaimed that "basketball had done more to bridge the gap between the races than anything else in society."[24]

Naismith placed a great deal of emphasis on the important role the game of basketball had in dispelling the concept of athletics as the devil's work. He points out with pride how popular the game became in churches and how it attracted young adults to the church and religious concepts. This is reflected in Montreal when shortly after Naismith's graduation, Erskine Presbyterian Church, where the first classes for Presbyterian College were held in 1867, planned a new sanctuary on Sherbrooke Street. Built by the well-known local architect Alexander Hutchison, it was later pronounced a heritage site. In 2007, the church was purchased by the Montreal Museum of Fine Arts to become the Claire and Marc Bourgie Pavilion. When the Erskine Church opened in 1894, it boasted not only a large suite of halls for Sunday School, but a full-sized gymnasium.

Another indicator in the college's attitude in sporting endeavours comes from the minutes of the senate of the Presbyterian College at McGill (April 13, 1920). When Dr. James Barclay, minister of St. Paul's Church, Montreal, (1883–1910), died in 1920, he was lauded not only for his services to the college and community, but for "his strong personality, broad culture, gift of utterance, athletic prowess, genuine interest in everything that affects human welfare." Dr. Barclay was an internationally renowned curler and president of the Royal Montreal Golf Club. Dr. Barclay's sermons attracted many young men to the church and afterwards to the manse. Dr. John McCrae, the poet of "Flanders Field" fame attended and possibly young James Naismith, drawn by Barclay's championship of so-called Muscular Christianity. Barclay's message was enhanced by his significant involvement in sports.

Further evidence of the Church's attitude towards sports is found in the *History of the Presbyterian College, Montreal 1865–1986*: "By 1901 the Calendar was listing a Hockey Club and a cooperative athletic association embracing the four affiliated theological colleges. The death of Professor Campbell who had for several years been patron and Honorary President of the Hockey Club led to its dissolution. By 1910, however, the Athletic Association had been revived and included football, basketball as well as hockey."[25]

24. John Robert Thompson, Jr. (born September 2, 1941) is an African-American former basketball coach for the Georgetown University Hoyas. See Rains and Carpenter, *James Naismith*, 182

25. Markell, *History*, 67.

A story from the Rev. James Peter Jones, a graduate and former senator of the college, now retired in Brockville, Ontario, illustrates that old prejudices die hard. A former Mountie, Jones had been a boxer in his day and was urged by his fellow students at Presbyterian College to enter the ring as their representative. He emerged McGill champion and was to enter the Inter-Varsity competition on behalf of the university. However, Jones was made to withdraw by the principal of Presbyterian College, Dr. Robert Lennox, who deemed it unseemly that a theological student be seen as a prize fighter. To make matters worse, the man Jones defeated was declared the winner of the Inter-Varsity competition.[26]

While Naismith's coaching record at the University of Kansas was a losing one, he mentored many coaches in his life principles, including Phog Allen, Adolph Rupp and Dean Smith. All went on to hall-of-fame coaching careers and all fostered Naismith's life lessons in their athletes. This emphasizes Naismith as a teacher and mentor at heart whose honest message to all was "do the best with what you have," and "to be thankful for what you have."[27]

Naismith's ultimate goal in life when he entered the Presbyterian College at McGill was "to find a way to help people." His career took an entirely different turn when reasoning how he could be most effective in this goal he chose a career in physical education over the ministry.

Even those who opposed his decision have since agreed that his career choice was exemplary and allowed him to live out his life's motto: "I want to leave the world a little bit better than I found it." One of Naismith's classmates who became moderator of the general assembly sent a letter to Naismith's sister stating: "You with your athletics have done more for the welfare of humanity than any member of our class."[28]

There is no question that James Naismith is probably the most famous graduate of the Presbyterian College and McGill. His sermon's message in "Athletics and Religion" has been adopted by countless students, fellow coaches and citizens. The message in the address "Athletics and Religion" still rings true as does the impact of his life. Naismith's personal reflections on his life's work are summarized in a poignant letter to his wife prior to his return from France. In his words, what was most meaningful to him was "The knowledge that I have tried to help the people of the world to make it a little better and that I have tried to love my neighbor as myself."[29]

26. Confirmed by a telephone interview October 15, 2014.
27. Rains and Carpenter, *James Naismith*, xv.
28. Ibid., xii.
29. Ibid., 125.

We celebrate James Naismith's contribution of service to the world: the still voice of a Presbyterian College Graduate still heard wherever athletes meet.

The Author

My personal background includes an upbringing in a small Saskatchewan farming community (Eston). Amateur athletics, hockey, baseball and football were always front and centre in this prairie town. My childhood dream was to be the next Gordie Howe or Maurice Richard. A stellar hockey coach convinced me that an academic career would be more satisfying. This led to the College of Medicine at the University of Saskatchewan that was followed by a surgical residency at McGill and the University of Iowa. My entire surgical career has been based at the Montreal General Hospital and McGill University, serving as Surgeon-in-Chief and McGill Chair of Surgery.

Early in my surgical residency, I provided medical care to McGill football and hockey teams. This led to working as team physician with the Montreal Junior Canadiens, the Montreal Voyageurs, the Montreal Canadiens, and the Montreal Alouettes. To have worked with two magnet organizations as McGill University and the Club de Hockey Montreal Canadiens has been the ultimate honour and privilege.

I am a member of the congregation of The Church of St. Andrew and St. Paul in Montreal.

Bibliography

Babcock, Mike, and Rick Larsen. *Leave No Doubt: A Credo for Chasing your Dreams.* Montreal: McGill–Queens University Press, 2012.

Baker, W. J., and James Naismith. *Basketball: Its Origin and Development.* Lincoln: University of Nebraska Press, 1996.

Cosentino, Frank. *Almonte's Brothers of the Wind: R. Tait McKenzie and James Naismith.* Burnstown, Ontario: General Store, 1996.

History of McGill Athletics. http://www.mcgill.ca/channels/news/history-mcgill-athletics-176215.

Markell, H. Keith. *History of the Presbyterian College, Montreal 1865–1986.* Montreal: Presbyterian College, 1987.

Naismith, Ian. "The Best Sportsman That I Ever Knew." NBA.com. http://www.nba.com/history/players/naismith.html.

Naismith, James. Notes for "Athletics and Religion." With carbon copy, undated, box 1: The James Naismith Collection 1893–1962. William L. Clements Library, University of Michigan.

Naismith, James, and G. E. Johnson. "Bulletin of the Section of Hygiene." In *The Basis of Clean Living.* American YMCA Expeditionary Forces, July 1918.

Rains, Rob, and Hellen Carpenter. *James Naismith: The Man Who Invented Basketball.* Philadelphia: Temple University Press, 2009.

Smith, Dean, et al. *The Carolina Way: Leadership Lessons from a Life in Coaching.* New York: Penguin, 2005.

Wooden, John, and Steve Jamison. *The Wisdom of Wooden: My Century On and Off the Court.* New York: McGraw Hill, 2010.

CHAPTER 7

The College and Ecumenism
George Campbell Pidgeon

By Joseph C. McLelland

The Very Reverend George C. Pidgeon, DD, LLD, (1872–1971), first moderator of the United Church of Canada, 1925–26. This 1946 portrait by Kenneth Forbes was commissioned by, and is the property of, Bloor Street United Church, Toronto. Dr. Pidgeon is wearing the DD hood from the Presbyterian College of Montreal, a degree he earned by examination in 1905. The image is used by permission of Bloor Street United Church and was photographed especially for this book by Andrew Liszewski.

GEORGE C. PIDGEON WAS at the centre of a moment of high drama in Canadian church history. It was June 9, 1925, in College Street Church, Toronto. The fateful moment had come, the motion to end the Presbyterian Church in Canada and begin the United Church of Canada. Pidgeon was moderator of the first body and soon became moderator of the second. After the benediction, however, the seventy-nine commissioners loyal to the Presbyterian Church in Canada gathered in a corner to maintain the continuity of their highest church court, adjourning to reconstitute at 11:45 in Knox Church. Their voices had to contend with the organ blaring out, the organist egged on by none other than C. W. Gordon (Ralph Connor). So began an era of division and union, with George Pidgeon a leading player on this ecclesiastical stage.[1] The dramatic shift in his position reflected his role as leading advocate of ecumenism in that era. His career had prepared him well, from academic youth through ministry and leadership positions. This graduate of our college represents a dimension often overlooked in its commitment to the "continuing" Presbyterian establishment. As he led the opening worship service of the new church, surely he experienced the sorrow of leaving behind the church in which he had been raised, educated and ordained.

George Campbell Pidgeon was born on March 2, 1872, the eldest son of Archibald Pidgeon and Mary Campbell of New Richmond, near the Cascapedia River, Quebec. In 1887 he enrolled in Morrin College in Quebec City, an affiliate of McGill University. Two years later he transferred to honours English at McGill, under Professor C. E. Moyse, graduating 1891. After experience in ministry to summer parishes, in 1891 he and fellow student W. D. Reid took joint charge of Victoria Church in Pointe St. Charles, Montreal. Here he met Helen Jones whom he would later marry. He followed the advice of the Presbyterian College professor of practical theology, Dr. James Ross, to write out the morning sermon in full but prepare notes for the evening.

In 1894 he graduated (diploma) from Presbyterian College as gold medallist; on May 29 he was ordained and inducted into the pastorate of Montreal West. He began work on a thesis that earned him the bachelor of divinity in 1895. He then prepared for the doctor of divinity (by examination at that time) at Presbyterian College, choosing the field of the Greek New Testament, and receiving the degree in 1905, the youngest Canadian (aged thirty-two) to have obtained the earned doctorate.

It was a stirring period in Canada's story, with industrialization transforming economic and social life. Urbanization posed a challenge to the

---

1. The year 1925 launched a new denomination, while the "continuing Presbyterians" claimed to be the legitimate heirs to the Presbyterian tradition. Years of quarrel and legal wrangling led to peaceful coexistence.

churches, whose tradition of social reform faced new issues, but also new questions of how to meet them. Two chief concerns dominated the evangelical field: evangelization among French Canadians and prohibition. Two names signify differing strategies: Principal D. H. MacVicar of Presbyterian College and Principal George M. Grant of Queen's. They symbolize the options of the Scottish ideal of a covenanted nation as against seeing the Gospel as the leaven in the secular lump. Pidgeon's biographer notes: "Pidgeon related better to the MacVicar line."[2]

Pidgeon's Montreal ministry included Mount Royal Vale and Kensington. The temperance question was to the fore, not least because of a notorious "Half-way House" illegally open on Sundays. Efforts to close it succeeded only when local support was mobilized, a lesson in social action.

In 1898 he moved to Ontario, serving first in Streetsville, bringing with him his new bride Helen Jones. Now he found time for a thorough preparation of sermons. He spent the mornings from Monday to Wednesday in his study, giving two hours to New Testament Greek and exegesis, then working on the sermons for two more hours. He spent all day Thursday on the sermon and then reworked it for oral delivery.

At that time the Christian Endeavour[3] hold on Christian education was being challenged by the growing Sunday School movement. The International Sunday School Lessons[4] provided standard curriculum, along with joint training for teachers. Pidgeon made this curriculum the theme of his mid-week addresses.

In 1903 a Call came from Victoria Church, Toronto Junction. In contrast to Streetsville, this was a congregation in difficulties. This former boom town suffered from the real-estate crash and the congregation faced bankruptcy. Fortunately for its new minister the economic situation soon improved. More serious was the temperance issue. Hotels open on Sunday and a nearby gambling house galvanized the ministerial association. Two petitions helped their successful campaign.[5]

---

2. "Grant carried more weight in the country as a whole, but in a crisis MacVicar could carry a General Assembly." Grant, *Pidgeon*, 31.

3. The Young Peoples' Society of Christian Endeavour was founded in 1881 by F. C. Clarke of Portland, Maine. This interdenominational and evangelical movement spread widely and proved a rival to the Presbyterian Young Peoples' Society.

4. L. C. Parkhurst, a graduate of the University of Oklahoma and Princeton Theological Seminary, developed this nondenominational curriculum, which continues worldwide popularity.

5. Grant notes that the merchants' reported that local option helped business; the other, signed by the undertaker alone, that removing liquor damaged his business. Grant, *Pidgeon*, 37.

A positive feature of the times was that young people crowded the evening service and the Bible class. In 1906 the *Toronto Globe* asked Pidgeon to make his Sunday School lessons the basis of weekly articles; in 1923 the series was taken over by *Winnipeg Free Press*, continuing the series until 1960.

Meanwhile, the temperance issue concerned all denominations, with a new emphasis on political weight. Pidgeon was a leading figure, helping to persuade Presbyterian and Methodists to establish national boards. In 1911 he was named convener of the Presbyterian Board of Social Service and Evangelism. This period shows that the tradition of social radicalism owes much to evangelicalism.

A major career shift occurred in 1909, when Pidgeon was asked to join the faculty of Westminster Hall, Vancouver. This upstart Presbyterian institution attracted students by offering summer courses, leaving students free to serve parishes in the winter. Principal John B. McKay[6] gathered a stellar cast of teachers, including James Denney, James Moffat, George Adam Smith—famous British names. Pidgeon became registrar and professor of practical theology. George and Helen with their children Alice, Arch and Helen, enjoyed the ambience of West Point Grey. In 1911 he was named president of the Christian Social Council of British Columbia, and in 1913, a member of the executive of the Social Service Council of Vancouver. Moral reform had to deal with prostitution and gambling, but economic injustice spelled the new direction for reformists.

In 1915, Toronto's Bloor Street Presbyterian Church was looking for an associate pastor. This was an attractive congregation, many members relocating as the city moved northwards, making it a downtown church. Its proximity to the university was a bonus for George Pidgeon, given his enjoyment and success with young people and students. His responsibility was alternate morning and all evening services. Finding times changing, foreshadowing the decline of the evening service, he turned his energies more to the morning sermons.

A new challenge came from the YMCA, inviting him to lead Bible studies at Geneva Park on Lake Couchiching, about one hundred miles (162 kilometres) north of Toronto. One result of this was the YMCA secretaries' formation of the Toronto Business Men's Noon-Day Bible Club, meeting in Simpson's Arcadian Court in downtown Toronto. Much of the material from this was published in *The Vicarious Life* (1945) and *The Indwelling Christ* (1948).

---

6. Later, principal of Manitoba College. John W. Grant mistakenly has "John A. Mackay," famed principal of Princeton Seminary (ibid., 41). John B. (1870–1938) had a similar knack of attracting famous theologians to his staff.

THE COLLEGE AND ECUMENISM

Another outcome of WW I was the YMCA decision to send ministers to Canadian troops at the front lines. W. A. Cameron was to look after the first division, George Pidgeon the second, and John McNeill the third.[7] Pidgeon was in France from September 1917 to May 1918 when he was forty-five. Returning to Bloor Street Presbyterian Church, he soon found himself sole minister of a growing congregation. Help came in the form of a secretary, a deaconess, and a director of Christian education. He became convener of the new Presbyterian Board of Home Missions in 1917 and the next year president of the Social Service Council of Canada.

His scholarly interests were well met by the formation of the Canadian Library of Religious Literature, projected at twenty volumes. Pidgeon was named chief editor, arranging for publication by Hodder & Stoughton. The outbreak of war and then funding problems limited the success of this venture. His gifts, however, were clearly homiletical. "There is no harder taskmaster than the ambition to excel in the pulpit, he declared in a 1914 sermon."[8]

His greatest struggle was about to begin. Canadian Presbyterians had long talked of union with other denominations. One pioneer in this view was John Cook, principal and professor of theology at Morrin College in Pidgeon's student days. Principal MacVicar of Presbyterian College agreed. In 1904 Presbyterians, Methodists and Congregationalists began formal discussions and by 1916 voted to unite. George Pidgeon was not a leading figure at this stage, indeed he had doubts about aspects of the proposed Basis of Union, and the way it was being presented to the people. At the 1911 General Assembly he was one of a group arranging a meeting between leaders of both union and anti-union forces; the attempt failed. Like other church executives, he was well aware of the new phenomenon of Western expansion. With so many moving west to small towns unable to support three churches, practical logic took root as a major factor in the union cause. Indeed, on the prairies, especially Alberta, congregations were forming "local union" churches on their own. Church Union seemed to assure a substantial Christian presence in the West. Pidgeon concluded, "The Union movement has gained such headway that nothing can stop it."[9]

Since the topic of church union has been covered exhaustively we will simply highlight his role.[10] Even this is difficult, since he was in the cen-

---

7. All three were prominent Presbyterians.
8. "Fifty Years Trying," quoted in Grant, *Pidgeon*, 59.
9. Quoted in Morrow, *Church Union*, 55. See Pidgeon's own discussion of local union, in *United Church*, 55.
10. E.g., Morrow *Church Union*; Silcox, *Church Union*; Walsh, *Christian Church*.

tre of a stormy issue—hero to one side, villain to the other. It does seem that he hoped that Presbyterianism would be maintained without losing its national character. He maintained a love for his alma mater; in 1917 he was one of the fiftieth anniversary preachers. But the bitter struggle that ensued saw the lines hardening: on one hand, a group of anti-unionists who argued for a form of federalism among the three churches gave way to form the militant Presbyterian Church Association.[11] On the other, by 1921 a wave of local unions in the West anticipated organic union. Like acts in a drama, the movement involved high rhetoric and low flyting, even a truce that did not work and at last a General Assembly union committee that included anti-union members. George Pidgeon was named its convener, as well as chairman of the joint union committee of the three negotiating churches. From being a strong advocate of organic union he became the midwife of its birth.

When the 1916 Presbyterian General Assembly, with the assent of two-thirds of presbyteries (under the Barrier Act) adopted a unionist proposal, endorsed by the 1922 Assembly, he saw organic union as assured and its consummation a moral imperative.[12] From now on he was wholly committed to the cause.

In 1921 he was offered the chair of homiletics at Knox College; he declined in favour of returning to the pastorate. In 1922 he reported, "The old bitterness is gone, and must not be allowed to return."[13] To say the least, this was highly optimistic, for the debate within the Presbyterian Church was worsening. It was complicated by the Anglican Primate, following the 1920 Lambeth guidelines, who sought meetings with the other churches. The timing, if not the substance, proved difficult for the Presbyterian unionists, as did the intervention of D. R. Drummond on behalf of a federalist model.[14] The case was now before the courts, as both sides sought legislative approval, the issue turning on the human and material resources that would enter union. All compromise was past, and with legislation now in play, his hope of a strictly ecclesiastical settlement faded. Both he and his committee wished him to remain impartial, but by the fall of 1922 he felt called to a positive and public advocacy of the unionist cause. While the parties wrangled in and out of court, the "enabling legislation" was finally obtained.

11. Hamilton was a stronghold of the association; in my boyhood I heard their side alone from my minister Dr. C. L. Cowan.

12. He argued from the Presbyterian system of government by courts, as against the "will of the people" through popular votes.

13. Grant, *Pidgeon*, 79.

14. See "Is There Not a Way Out?," April 6, 1923, in Morrow, *Church Union*, 435–44.

In a final speech in Ottawa he succeeded in so alienating his erstwhile friend Ephraim Scott, a staunch anti-unionist that the latter refused to shake his hand.[15] He was also upset by two Presbyterian College friends, Principal Fraser and Professor Thomas Eakins, who had allowed their party to accuse the unionists of heresy. In March 1925 he sought affidavits from students testifying to their theological statements.[16]

The sorry state of the church (that is, of both churches) in 1925 is full of tragic stories of separation and loss, of pastors without churches and vice versa. In the new United Church, George Pidgeon had to play the role of comforter, advisor and conciliator. He tried to preserve his character as a man of integrity and conscience, but his key role in the drive for union marked him as militantly pro-union. No doubt the partisan leadership of his outspoken brother Leslie helped to reinforce this image.[17]

His last act in this drama was to constitute the Presbyterian General Assembly of 1925 and to arrange for the inception of the United Church of Canada, celebrating its first Holy Communion. He introduced a custom now common, distributing individual cups throughout the pews and asking members to hold them so that all could drink together.[18] At the election of moderator, the favourite, Dr. S. D. Chown, Methodist general superintendent, declined to stand and stated that it were better to elect a former Presbyterian, and moved that a ballot be cast for George Pidgeon. The vote was unanimous.

His next act was to press for the acceptance of the United Church of Canada by the World Presbyterian Alliance. This was successful as was that of the nonconcurrent Presbyterian Church as member. More difficult personally was the fate of many, including continuing Presbyterian ministers whose advice to their congregations to vote union was unheeded, leaving them without a church. So many complaints to be heard, so much advice to be given!

---

15. Scott, *Church Union*, sums up the anti-union arguments with passion; he does not mention Pidgeon by name. He is consistently dismissive of the steps taken by "the 'union' committee," especially in what he termed the "first period"—i.e., 1903–1912.

16. Grant, *Pidgeon*, 100.

17. Also a Presbyterian College graduate (dip. '01) and Minister of Erskine and American Church, Montreal; and Augustine Church, Winnipeg. He prepared the unionist argument for presentation to Parliament: "It is difficult to imagine how the bill could have passed without his assistance." Grant, *Pidgeon*, 96. Compare with: "There's no fighting the Pidgeons, Leslie is too clever and George is too good." Quoted in MacLeod, *Stanford*, 37.

18. Prof. David Hay of Knox College called this practice "turning a sacrament into a toast."

Back at Bloor Street Church, only pressure from his former associates kept him from accepting offers from churches in Montreal and Vancouver. He would serve there as minister for thirty-two years until retiring (in 1948) at the age of seventy-six.

During the hard years of the Great Depression, there were also positive causes to challenge him, particularly the peace movement. He was co-chairman with Harry E. Fosdick of the campaign for peace and disarmament, until Hitler's rise which compromised efforts for peacemaking. The United Church had gained the reputation of espousing radical views on the economy, including anti-capitalistic rhetoric. The Fellowship for a Christian Social Order reflected the radical turn for many scholars and churchmen. A report on Evangelism and Social Service to the 1933 Toronto Conference declared that "the principles of Jesus" implied "the end of the Capitalistic System." Fifty-six dissenters signed their protest, the first name being that of George Pidgeon.[19] Not that he was a complete dinosaur, but his evangelicalism muted his sense of economic justice. (The tension remains today, as is evident in the evolution of the twin emphases in one national Presbyterian board.)

The need for evangelization made common cause across denominations. An Inter-Church Committee was formed, with Pidgeon as chairman, arranging mass rallies across the land. Although not very successful in its aims, after World War I the example of Rhineland revivalism[20] and the rise of the Christian group movement offered new scope. Pidgeon was drawn to the Oxford Group that was founded in 1931, though not uncritically, judging its spirituality not wholly biblical.

His work at Bloor Street kept him more than busy; in 1934 when sixty-two, he suffered a physical collapse; the congregation sent him south to recover. He resumed his pattern of thorough sermon preparation, and broadened the scope of Christian education to include social and athletic activities. The sanctuary was redesigned as amphitheatre, with a semicircle of pews facing a central pulpit.

The new "ecumenical movement" became a central concern of his mature years. He was appointed a delegate to the Faith and Order conference at Lausanne in 1927, and despite being unable to attend was appointed a member of its continuation committee. Ten years later he attended the twin conferences of Life and Work (Oxford) and Faith and Order (Edinburgh). The result was membership on the consultation committee preparing to

---

19. See Grant, *Pidgeon*, beginning 121.

20. The native pietism of the Rhine-Palatinate in western Germany burgeoned in the eighteenth century into the "holiness movement" that spread to England (notably the Oxford Group) and North America (Charles Finney was the outstanding representative).

establish a World Council of Churches (1948). At the same time, preparations for a Canadian Council of Churches were in the hands of two agencies he had led, the Inter-Church Committee for the Evangelization of Canadian Life, and the Christian Social Council of Canada. The parallel development of the World Alliance of Reformed Churches garnered his attention. In 1938 he was elected to a term as chairman of its western section, encouraging a series of theological papers which proved material to the 1948 meeting where official standards were adopted.

The years of World War II saw little flagging of vigour, as he threw himself into the debate on school curriculum. He followed the MacVicar line that religion should be an integral part of public education. He became the leading voice for organic union and for the teaching and ethos of the United Church of Canada.[21]

His thirtieth year at Bloor Street was marked by sitting for his portrait painted by Kenneth Forbes, and receiving a cheque from President Sidney Smith of the University of Toronto to fund the George C. Pidgeon postgraduate scholarship at Emmanuel College. In 1947 he was made honorary doctor of laws by the University of Toronto, joining his other honorary doctorates from Victoria University and Yale, and in 1955 another from McGill University. He retired on June 30, 1948, after thirty-two years at Bloor Street, aged seventy-six; he was named minister emeritus.

So this graduate of our college, so important for the ecclesiastical shape of Canada, reflects well on his Presbyterian background and education, a worthy doctor of divinity. Indeed, he saw ecumenism as the biblical and theological future for the church, and all in all, remains a "still voice" still worthy of being heard.

George Campbell Pidgeon died June 15, 1971 at the age of 99.

The Word of the Cross[22]

Preached at Bloor Street Presbyterian Church,
Toronto, sometime before 1925

1 Cor 1:17—2:5[23]

Here is a story from a popular Canadian novel of a generation ago. A congregation of Highlanders in Glengarry sent for a young minister from Montreal to preach at their service preparatory to the Communion. He was

---

21. For example, Pidgeon's four addresses to the Conference of Montreal and Ottawa in 1935 were published as *Communion*.

22. Published in *The Indwelling*.

23. Dr. Pidgeon used the King James Version of the Bible.

stately in appearance and in his style of speech, and he had behind him the rich religious tradition of the Scot. Although young, he was grounded deeply in Christian doctrine and was noted in that region for strong exposition of the attributes of God in their bearing on the lives of men. On this occasion he chose for his text John 3:16, and he drove that message of the divine love home to loveless hearts. There was no escaping the judgment of that text and his application of it to every corner of loveless lives, the coldness of their hearts toward God, their lovelessness in the home, in society, in the church, and toward the world for whom Christ died, and the people's conviction of failure rose with Highland emotion in response to his message. Now, inspiration gives the preacher, like Browning's musician, the gift to frame out of three sounds, not a fourth sound, but a star; over the horizon of that little congregation a divine light arose that day; they were the first to see it, but their surprise turned the eyes of the whole county in its direction. To change the figure, the answer to that people's devotion to the love which the preacher proclaimed and the sacrament symbolized, was like the sacrifice on Elijah's altar on Mt. Carmel, and in answer to their prayer the divine fire descended and spread until it became a conflagration. The famous Glengarry revival arose out of that service, and for generations the religion of that people was governed by it. . . .[24]

I am sorry for the preacher who is master of his moods; it means that there is no give and take between his soul and the author of his message. The Christian preacher is the commissioner of love; he aims at conviction and decision in the loveless. The content of his message is the truth about love and he cannot deliver it with heart unstirred. Besides, the miracle of the new creation cannot be wrought in a hearer without the cooperation of the divine Spirit with the speaker. Often his consciousness of that Spirit whose agent he is grows clear and strong; sometimes there seems to be nothing but gray ashes where once the fire burned. But if his dependence is on God, he will be used by God whether his feelings are aroused or not.

How perfectly Paul expresses this in I Corinthians 2:3-4: "I was with you in weakness, and in fear and in much trembling. And my speech and my message were not in plausible words of wisdom but in demonstration of the spirit and power." His mood kept the man himself in the background but only to give place to the power of God. And this was by far Paul's most effective mission. God used him miraculously while he felt all alone.

Here is a story behind this passage. After a strange series of restraints and constraints Paul had been called into Europe on his second missionary

---

24. The lengthy sermon is shortened to comply with the allotted space. A paragraph of about a page is omitted here.

journey. His ministry was fruitful and a church grew up in every place that he visited. But no sooner did his message catch the imagination of the people than wanton persecution drove him away. He was racked with anxiety about his converts, particularly in Thessalonica; mere babes in Christ they were, lambs of the flock surrounded by wolves and robbers. From Athens he sent his companions to revisit these scattered groups and to confirm them in the faith. While they were away he met the philosophers of Athens on their own ground with a speech remarkable for its skill and comprehensiveness, but he was laughed at when he mentioned the resurrection of the dead. Alone and disheartened he went to Corinth, at that time the Glasgow or Chicago of Greece, and as famous for its wickedness as for its wealth. In the face of the luxury, power and misery of its paganism, he decided to change his methods and confine himself to the story of the Cross. The results astounded him; converts were multiplied; and the most brilliant congregation of the period was built up around him.

Years after he wrote the story of his mood and message on that occasion. During Paul's mission in Ephesus the Judaisers who had caused the trouble in Galatia, came to Corinth and turned a section of the church against Paul. Then Apollos from Alexandria, intellectual and eloquent, took up the work in Corinth, and while sympathetic with Paul, he presented Christianity in a philosophic garb which attracted the Greeks with their love of wisdom. Splits appeared in the little church, some saying "I am of Paul," others "I am of Apollos," and so on. Paul felt constrained to explain the method he had used and the reason for it, and to point out that it was his preaching of the Cross which had brought them to Christ. The result is the chapter before us, the most splendid vindication in literature of Christian evangelism and of its method, the word of the Cross.

I would therefore suggest as the motto of this sermon Moses' words to Israel at the Red Sea: "Stand still and see the salvation of our God."[25] Paul's argument is that these Corinthians' salvation is due solely to God's sovereign grace.

The means which God had used to save them was Paul's message of Christ as crucified, but it was God the Creator who had used that message to create them anew. Ideal Christian preaching is the quiet presentation of God's way of salvation delivered in dependence on the Holy Spirit who can be counted on to use this word as His instrument for claiming His own. When the riots arose in Corinth the Lord said to Paul one night, "Don't be afraid, but speak and do not be silent; for I am with you, and no man shall

---

25. Exod 14:13.

attack you to harm you; for I have many people in this city."[26] That is to say, Christ aimed through Paul's preaching to reach many whom He had already chosen and to bring them into His light and love, and the word of the Cross was splendidly effective in Christ's hands.

This message of salvation through a crucified Messiah was offensive to the natural man, whether Jew or Greek. Note Paul's careful choice of words, "The Jews *asked* a sign; the Greeks *seek* wisdom." The Jews *demanded* signs, *i.e.*, action from God as the only evidence of divinity which could be accepted. The Greeks *sought* wisdom, a discovery and attainment to be reached by intellectual effort. Nothing seemed clearer to the Jewish mind than the argument of Mark 15:32: "Let the Christ, the King of Israel, come down now from the Cross, that we may see and believe." In other words, your helplessness proves you an imposter; your Messiahship would be demonstrated even now by the nails springing out and you descending to the discomfiture of your foes. They did not see what Paul saw and the ages acknowledge, that His divinity was proven by the love that persisted right through the agonies of Calvary in bearing to its doom the sin of man. The Greeks reached after a conception of God which they could prove by their own reasoning, and accept as reasonable, thus demanding that it harmonize with their preconceived ideas. Paul's irony in assuming that the Greek wisdom of his time was really wise was turned, not against the noble seriousness of thinkers like Socrates and his successors, but against the subtlety of the Sophists whose object was not to discover truth but to win a verdict by the cleverness of their speeches. . . .[27] Over against all this Paul set the fact of the Cross. Here is something which God has done, and has done once for all. It is something which He has done for men which they could never do for themselves; their part is to accept it. Because it takes them in the condition in which it finds them and lifts them into union with God.

Paul's horror of sin was always in the back of his mind, particularly when he is thinking about the Cross. He went through the world open-eyed, not dreaming of ideal manhood, but seeing men as they are; and what he saw of the vice and wickedness of his time drove him to such appalling descriptions of human degradation as we find in Romans 1 & 3. And he felt involved in it. Had he not persecuted to the death the saints of God, redeemed by the blood of His Son? We can appreciate this now as we could never have done a generation ago. We have found a capacity for cruelty in human nature that no one thought was there before the war. The tragedy of the ages has befallen our race in our time because man's will to power over

---

26. Acts 18: 9–10.
27. Twelve lines are omitted.

his fellows has driven him to extremes in crime which have surpassed anything recorded in history. The "will to power" in the history of conquerors is all too familiar to us, but never had it more disastrous consequences than in our time. Look at the horrible things which men's lust is driving them to do now in Christian Ontario.[28] This has arisen out of our common life; we are somehow involved in what we abhor. Paul saw sin in these identical forms everywhere he turned. He saw it in its relation to God and in the light of God's holiness before whose unapproachable purity even the seraphim veil their faces. He saw it in relation to God's love. And he saw God meeting it in a head-on collision on Calvary. There human wickedness came to a head in the crucifixion of the Son of God. There the love of God came to head in bearing sin at its worst in order to turn men from it forever. With the sin of man so appalling in its nature and its consequences, the action which would overthrow it must be on a range wider and an intensity deeper than the evil. That is what we find in the Cross. Do you wonder that when Paul thought of Rome with its depths of depravity and its world-conquering might he exclaimed, "I am not ashamed of the Gospel; for it is the power of God unto salvation to everyone who believes."

Gospel preaching then and now is a statement of fact, a tragedy and a transaction which has taken place in the history of our race. As such it requires plain, straight telling, "not with wisdom of words, lest the Cross of Christ be emptied of its power." . . .[29] That was the fault of the Sophists of Paul's day; they wanted admiration for their brilliant style without regard for the truth which their sentences contained. As Cicero said, "Their poor little syllogisms only prick like pins; even if they persuade the mind, they effect no change of heart, and the listeners go away just as they came."

Paul felt the lure of the intellectual and determined not to let it turn him from his purpose, so he decided to present the fact of Christ and His Cross with a directness which no one could misunderstand or evade. The effect was that he reached all classes and conditions of men. It was to man as man that he spoke, and men as men answered. . . .[30]

Not many, but some; there were a few converts in Corinth who had stood high in its religious and social circles, but the masses of his converts were from the poor and the slaves. True religion lifts the submerged to places where their capacities find the inspiration, recognition and opportunity which develop them, but it does not pass by those already privileged. In its early years it penetrated even to the Imperial circle. Russia liquidated her

28. Presumably the Evelyn Dick murder case in Hamilton.
29. Twenty lines omitted.
30. Eleven lines omitted.

middle and upper classes including her intelligentsia, and look at the mess that her leaders are making in world affairs without them.... France made the same mistake in her revolution with equally catastrophic consequences. In every reform and revolution Britain has retained the loyalty and ability of those whose privileges she curtailed, while she gave the common people more and more of their rights. When Kaiser Wilhelm's soaring ambition threatened the liberties of Europe, it was David Lloyd George, a son of the common people and committed to the cause of the common people who put the drive into Britain's campaign and kept it there to the end. Dr. Glover has said, "Hesitation is the badge of the scholarly tribe";[31] it certainly was not the badge of this tribune of the people. When a graver peril threatened his country later, it was Winston Churchill, adventurer, author, authority on the history and the science of war, and proud descendant of Marlborough, who gave utterance to her spirit of defiance and through her defended the liberties of the world. Paul himself belonged to the intelligentsia and bore the proudest titles of his time. In Jesus' day, the carpenter had a standing above the rank and file, and as long as the Magnificat remains the greatest hymn of the Christian Church, we must recognize that in the human parentage of the Son of God there was genius of the first order as well as David's royal blood.[32] But Jesus and Paul both recognized the capacities for God and His service to be found in men as men without regard to race or rank; why, even the nonentities God chose to bring to naught the entities, the people who thought they were everything....

The plain fact is that when Christian truth is embodied in profound arguments it wins no converts; when the Gospel is offered in simple faith, it changes people into the likeness of Christ. No period has had such examples of its effectiveness as our own. In mission halls in the cities, in remote frontier settlements, and in the work of missionaries in other lands, the simple story of the Cross has been the power of God unto salvation.

The effectiveness of this appeal is due to the fact that it presents a person to persons for their personal acceptance and trust. Christianity is primarily not a system of truth to be understood but a person to be relied upon. And a person in two aspects, suffering or having suffered, and active.

Does not the revolutionary character of the Christian revelation overwhelm our imagination? A God who suffers! A Creator, omnipotent and eternal, who will not withdraw the freedom which He gave to His creature, man, even when it is turned against His Son, but will, in love, bear the worst

---

31. Quoted in *Indwelling*, 85.

32. The Magnificat (Luke 1:46–55) is attributed to Mary, thus "genius of the first order" [author].

that free men can do to make provision for their salvation and to move them to accept it! We cannot fathom the depths or scale the heights of a love like this...

In all the churches which we visited in Roman Catholic Quebec, we saw the Stations of the Cross, representations in form or colour of the incidents of the Saviour's way to Calvary. In one chapel the figures were the work of a retired business-man, who had finished his life work in the world, and in his closing years added to it his conceptions of the suffering Servant of the Lord. Patriarchal in appearance, with flowing white beard and sensitive fingers, he saw in the blocks of wood that he could buy those features which he was called to bring out for the inspiration of the people. The images of Christ were carved in wood; he must have entered into the Master's humiliation and pain to carve such perfect expressions of them; and each figure was given a setting peculiarly its own. My thought as I studied them one by one was: This actually happened. The one in whom I live really bore these things for me. The Son of God who went through all this sore abuse and scorn for the redemption of men now lives to make that redemption effective in everyone who will accept Him as Saviour and Lord. Do you wonder that the lives of earth's best have been devoted to reflecting that love into every open heart?

It was not an accident that Christianity is the religion of the Crucified. The Cross is but the culminating expression of a spirit which was characteristic of it throughout. Its peculiar note is Victory through Suffering. An idea like that of Islam, making its way by the sword, was abhorrent to it from the first. Jesus came to be the Messiah of the Jews, but the narratives of the Temptation teach us that, from the very beginning of His career, he stripped off from His conception of Messiahship all that was political, all thought of propagating His claims by force. A new mode of propagating religion was deliberately chosen, and carried through with uncompromising thoroughness. The disciple was not above his Master; and the example which Jesus set in founding His faith by dying for it, was an example which His disciples were called upon to follow into all its logical consequences. Christianity, the true Christianity, carries no arms; it wins its way by lowly service, by patience, by self-sacrifice....

There is a quality which Christ brought into human nature, accepting responsibility for saving men in every way in which they will accept salvation, putting oneself into meeting supreme need without regard to the consequences of oneself, and then finding Christ with him as he walks in Christ's way.

Commentary on "The Word of the Cross"[33]

In the foreword to his collection of fourteen sermons, published in 1948, Pidgeon explains that "in these closing months of my active ministry" he had been trying to "give the essence of the Gospel" that formed his preaching over the years. This essential Gospel is "the living Christ." He lauds St. Paul as "the greatest exponent of Christianity according to Christ." In particular he explores Paul's flights of inspiration, which he calls "Poems of the Christian experience." For Pidgeon, faith means a personal acceptance of "the religion of the Crucified . . . the simple story of the Cross."

Such expository preaching reflects the biblical knowledge of a bygone era. It also springs from a former clerical lifestyle now overcome by demands of ageing congregations, empty pews and techniques of communication far removed from the study with its bookshelves (including Hebrew and Greek Bibles) and no landline. Consider Pidgeon's method of preparation: three or four days of study, working with the Greek New Testament, with a final rehearsal on Saturday. The seminaries of his day, including the Presbyterian College Montreal, centred on a curriculum that gave the original biblical books central place, systematic theology and church history were worthy adjuncts, but the variety of courses in non-theological topics—means and methods—were scorned. The aim was to produce preachers able to produce sermons of exposition and exegesis for a people who knew their Scriptures.

He was an evangelical of the classical model formed in the nineteenth century, not least in Scotland, whose theologians he knew from his visit there, while some were colleagues at Westminster College, Vancouver. Most notable is James Denney, famed as preacher of the atonement focused on the crucified Lord. "This core of the Gospel—'a God who suffered'—is joined with another that makes it personal: That phrase 'in Christ' is found one hundred and sixty-four times in Paul's writings, expressing our solidarity with the Redeemer." So he takes Paul as chief source in his meditations. For this is Paul's "favourite phrase." But it is Paul's "experience and achievement" that makes him the model, his own suffering the key to his grasp of the Gospel. This echoes Calvin's doctrine (the famous turn in *Institutes of the Christian Religion*, book 3) of "union with Christ," the "benefits" of Christ's work are of no use to us unless the Spirit joins us to him.

One more observation in this preamble. He is an inveterate teller of anecdotes and quoter of poets, including Tennyson, Pope, Browning, Spenser, Keats and Shakespeare. In one sermon he quotes from a string of seven poets. He can also refer to our appreciation of bodily strength in Barbara Ann

---

33. Pidgeon, *Indwelling*, 76–90.

Scott. The sermon before us should hold no surprises, its solid evangelical message clear on every page. Let us gloss it a little.

The sermon begins with an anecdote about the Glengarry Revival of 1900. It is familiar through Ralph Connor's *The Man From Glengarry* (1901), which devotes two chapters to it. Now the "guest preacher" who inspired the revival was presumably the Rev. James Ross of Perth, professor of homiletics, pastoral theology, sacred rhetoric and church government at Presbyterian College, whom Pidgeon names as influential on his preaching style. Revival is much on the preacher's mind but of an individual kind, the "person to person" mode of communicating the Gospel, as in Paul's "ideal Christian preaching."[34]

Pidgeon does not value philosophers highly, but excepts Socrates and Cicero, blaming "the subtlety of the Sophists" who spurned Paul in Athens.[35] His love of poetry reflects his homiletical sense of communicating the Gospel through homely speech, understandable by everyone in the pews. His sermons were thirty minutes long, the result of an intense preparation that seems unimaginable today. He spent three mornings and one full day in writing the sermon, assisted by his Greek New Testament and obviously compendia of poetry. Gone are those days when the Hebrew and Greek Bible were used by the parish minister as weekly tools of preparation.

Why preach? "The preacher's practical object" is the conversion of souls. Thus it is the most personal of human speech, and the preacher must identify with his message: "I am sorry for the preacher who is master of his moods" for then he lacks connection between "his soul and the author of his message." He preaches love and cannot be himself loveless. The preacher is "the commissioner of love." (Is he aware of the irony in that very Presbyterian noun?) Pidgeon is relentlessly evangelical in addressing his hearers as sinners in need of the forgiving love of the Crucified. His purpose is to lead them to "the experience of Christ as Saviour and obedience to Him as Lord." And since Gospel is *fact*, "it requires plain, straight telling." Like Paul, Pidgeon feels but rejects "the lure of the intellectual," with its "profound arguments."

His confidence in the saving power of the Gospel does not yield an easy optimism. He sees the roots of evil in man's "will to power." He does not expand on this famous phrase of Nietzsche, concentrating rather on its fruits, "extremes in crime."[36] He refers to the World War I still of fresh memory, and to events in "Christian Ontario." The Ontario incident is probably the infamous "Torso" murder trial of the scandal involving Evelyn

---

34. Ibid., 80.
35. Ibid., 79.
36. Ibid., 82.

Dick in Hamilton, 1946. She and her father were imprisoned on charges relating to murder.

George Pidgeon is included in this anniversary volume as an example of a Presbyterian College graduate worthy of our college's theological tradition. The fact that he chose a path removing him from our ecclesiastical family should not blind us to the fact that he does indeed continue that tradition, and in such a way that he embellishes its scholarly character. In both his undergraduate and the doctorate of divinity studies, his is an outstanding record. Indeed, the sermon is replete with Presbyterian doctrine: organic union did not entail his rejection of his familial and academic heritage. The "sovereignty of God," God the "omnipotent and eternal," Providence, the divine attributes, are on display in an appropriate homiletical modality. If he reflects an older orthodoxy no longer much alive among us these days, this in itself witnesses to his loyalty to his roots. It is indicative of the open-mindedness of this staunch Presbyterian as he remained in doctrine and polity that he is able to draw devotional value from the Stations of the Cross that he observed in Quebec.

The Author

The Rev. Dr. Joseph McLelland was born in Scotland, and came to Canada in 1927 with his family. At McMaster University he earned a BA in English literature, followed by a BD from Knox College, Toronto, and an MA in philosophy from the University of Toronto. Dr. McLelland served as the minister of St. Paul's Presbyterian Church in Val D'Or, Quebec and then went to the University of Edinburgh where he received a PhD in historical theology. Upon returning to Canada, he became the minister to congregations at Bolton and Nashville in Ontario. In 1957 he joined the faculty of the Presbyterian College, Montreal, as the Robert Professor of History and Philosophy of Religion. In 1959, he became an associate professor of philosophy and religion at McGill University, Montreal. He is now the McConnell Professor Emeritus. He was also dean of the Faculty of Religious Studies at McGill University from 1975 to 1985. Dr. McLelland is a prolific author, editor and reviewer. In 1985 he was elected moderator of 111th General Assembly of the Presbyterian Church in Canada. Dr. McLelland is the recipient of an honorary DD from Knox College, Toronto, and Diocesan College, Montreal. In October 2007, the Presbyterian College renamed the college library in honour of Dr. McLelland in recognition of his fifty-year association with the college.

Bibliography

Grant, John Webster. *George Pidgeon*. Toronto: Ryerson, 1962.

MacLeod, A. Donald. *W. Stanford Reid*. Montreal: McGill-Queen's University Press, 2003.

Morrow, E. Lloyd. *Church Union in Canada: Its History, Motives, Doctrine and Government*. Toronto: Allen, 1923.

Pidgeon, George Campbell. *The Communion of Saints*. Toronto: United Church, 1935.

———. *The Indwelling Christ*. Toronto: Clarke, Irwin, 1948.

———. *The United Church of Canada*. Toronto: Ryerson, 1950.

Scott, Ephraim. *"Church Union" and the Presbyterian Church in Canada*. Montreal: Lovell, 1928.

Silcox, Claris Edwin. *Church Union in Canada*. New York: Institute of Social and Religious Research, 1933.

Walsh, H. H. *The Christian Church in Canada*. Toronto: Ryerson, 1950.

CHAPTER 8

The College and Politics
W.G. Brown

By Dan Shute

The Reverend Walter George Brown, MP, (1875–1940), pictured on his wedding day 1904, wearing the white tie customary for ministers at that time. This photo is used by permission of its owner, Mr. Andrew Billingsley, grandnephew of W. G. Brown.

DURING HIS SIXTY-FOUR YEARS, Walter George Brown waged constant war against what he deemed to be forces destructive to God's purposes in the world: war itself, market capitalism, theological modernism, church union, communism/fascism, and millenarian fever, to name but a few. As odd and confusing as his convictions may appear to us today, W.G. Brown was, in fact, very much a product of family, church, college, and age.[1]

Walter Brown's grandfather, James, immigrated to Canada from Scotland to carve out a farm south of Montreal in the Chateauguay River Valley. James' son, Charles, who took over the farm, married Christine White, and they had three daughters and one son who came into the world September 6, 6, 1875. Young Walter was in the unenviable position of being the only son of a farmer whose success depended on rugged work, Walter's included. The Browns almost lost their son to rheumatic fever, and Walter lived out his life with a rheumatic heart condition. Damaged heart or not, Walter developed a powerful physique and a legendary stamina. In his adult life, "many a time in his sermons and addresses, he would refer proudly to his humble home and to his father whom he often referred to as 'a great horseman.'"[2] The Browns were active in the leadership of the local Presbyterian Church. By an uncanny coincidence, the year of Walter's birth, the man who would become the great champion of the continuing Presbyterian Church in Canada, also saw the birth of that church, an amalgam of Church of Scotland, Free Church, and Secession Church traditions.

Walter's parents provided him with a fine education. In view of their modest means, this would have represented no little sacrifice on their part; such a commitment gives evidence of the high priority placed by Scots Presbyterians on education. Walter first attended Huntingdon Academy, where he won a four-year scholarship to McGill University. There is every reason to believe that Walter went to McGill for the express purpose of preparing to enter the Presbyterian College, Montreal, which he did in 1888.[3]

Martha Ann Rowat, daughter of the Brown's family pastor, the Rev. Andrew Rowat, graduated from Huntingdon Academy at the same time as Walter. Unfamiliar as we are today with delayed gratification, their wait

---

1. A more technical version of this biographical essay will be found in *The Dictionary of Canadian Biography* XVI.

2. Baptismal register (still extant 2014) for Athelstan Presbyterian Church records, 1 April 1940, in *Quebec, Vital and Church Records*; Andrew Billingsley, grand-nephew of Brown, personal communication, May 2014; Donald Grace, grandson of Brown, personal communication; Ephraim Scott, "Rev. W. G. Brown, B.D.," 129, an anonymous tribute, May 1940, the Presbyterian Church in Canada Archive, Rev. W. G. Brown collection accession #1973-5017 Folder 8 (hereafter PCA, Brown collection).

3. Billingsley; Reid, "Reporter's Folio," 62; Woodside, "College Note Book," 294.

until 1904 to wed may seem excessive. As we will see, Brown's life was not, until then, sufficiently stable to contemplate marriage responsibly. As near as we can tell from the records of their life together, Martha was indeed "a Martha" (Luke 10:38–42). Throughout his ministry, Brown was often away from home to look after scattered Presbyterians in the hinterlands of Alberta and Saskatchewan. It was left to Martha to look after the house, their four children, and, no doubt, pastoral emergencies that arose during the pastor's frequent absences.[4]

In order to understand Brown's career, a number of things must be kept in mind. The Presbyterian Church in Canada was, at the time, the largest and wealthiest Protestant denomination in Canada. World War I had not yet shattered the confidence in human moral progress. Great Britain was the richest and most powerful country in the world, and optimism was in the air that those of British extraction breathed. Canada was still considered by its citizens as a Christian nation. Clergy were respected professionals, the equals of medical doctors, and were expected to play large roles in the civic as well as religious sphere. There was a general feeling among Christian clergy that nascent secularism was a mere flash in the pan. Nor had Protestant theological liberalism made great inroads as yet, and the major tenants of the historic Christian faith were still believed to be intellectually superior to the alternatives. Still less was the rise of Holiness and Pentecostal churches dreamt of. In short, Presbyterian clergy had every right to presume upon a brilliant future both for themselves, their church, and their nation. Such was the boundless enthusiasm reflected in the ambience of Presbyterian College where the young Brown went to study.

At Presbyterian College, Principal MacVicar was the sole voice of Westminster Confessional Calvinism. The rest of the teaching staff were moderately conservative and engaged in exploring and incorporating ideas current in the intellectual climate of the era into traditional Christian doctrine. Brown found this sort of moderate conservatism serviceable enough to continue in it throughout his ministerial career. The academic standards that the college expected of its students were high. Most entering the college had at least some university training, and about half held a university degree. In relation to the classics, whether English or Latin or Greek, the average student of the time was well read with strong written English.

Students formed the Philosophical and Literary Society, which published a substantial periodical, the *Presbyterian College Journal*, from 1881 to 1908. College faculty provided many of the articles, though students

---

4. Photos of W. G. Brown's Huntingdon Academy graduating class and his wedding photo from Billingsley's collection; Mingie, "Graduates' Column," 128.

and visiting worthies also contributed. It is from this *Journal* that we get a picture of the young earnest theologian. In February 1899 Brown was elected reporting editor of the *Journal*, and as such, he was for the space of a year responsible for "Reporter's Folio." Brown proved to be a clear writer, as demonstrated in his first effort that November, where he showed a bias for missions, camaraderie, and muscular Christianity. The young Brown touted sports as excellent spiritual training. He also showed an early interest in politics and entertained the then current question as to whether or not ministers of the Gospel should participate in politics.

Presbyterian College was one of four Protestant colleges in the city, the others being Methodist, Anglican, and Congregationalist. These colleges engaged in fiercely contested athletic events. In 1899 Brown placed second in the shot-put. A year later he was first (tossing a sixteen-pound shot thirty feet ten inches). The December *Journal* mentioned that Brown was chosen by the Philosophical and Literary Society "to represent the College in the Intercollegiate Debate" ("intercollegiate" presumably meaning the theological colleges). We now begin to get a picture of Brown as he was to be throughout his ministry: fierce debater, powerful physique, vivid engagement in missions, and sincere desire to work with fellow Protestants, all the while upholding the Presbyterian side. The April 1900 *Journal* announced that its new editor-in-chief was none other than Mr. W. G. Brown, BA.[5]

In his editorials, Brown gave a clear picture of what he thought important, not only in the life of theology, but also in the wider church. Against dumbing down or shortening the college's curriculum, he championed "a thorough knowledge of the Hebrew and Greek languages." Brown vigorously supported foreign missions. He firmly defended the skills developed in debating societies, he being a master of the art. He believed that pastors should keep up with their reading. Brown was very much a creature of his time and spoke of Queen, Empire, and the Boer War with admiration. He was also a "College man," and showed nothing of the conservative Calvinist reacting against contemporary theological investigations. He spoke in glowing terms of Professor Campbell's reviews of books and Professor Scrimger's musing on ethical issues in the *Journal*. Both Campbell and Scrimger were intellectually adventuresome by the standards of the time, Campbell having had the distinction of a heresy trial (1893) and Scrimger becoming progressively more liberal in his views as time went on.[6]

---

5. Brown, "College Note-Book," (18 Apr 1899) 472; (Nov 1899) 39–43; (Dec 1899) 131; (Jan 1900) 207; (Nov 1900) 49.

6. See Brown, *PCJ*: "Training," 340–42; "Watchman," 151–52; "Triumphs," 256–59; "Debating Societies," 253–56; Editorial, 259; "Portable Library," 428–29; "Our Late Queen," 339–40; Markell, *History*, 23, 29.

Brown was always near the top of his class. He also showed promise as a public speaker. For instance, in the 1901 convocation when he took first prize in elocution. As further evidence of his skill as a public speaker, he was elected "President of the Dining Hall." The college dining hall and the chapel, the major foci of college life, were places of recitation, singing, and oratory. For his many achievements and his general likeability, Brown was unanimously elected valedictorian of his class. He also received the silver medal, the second highest academic prize and was among only three of the ten graduates who received the BD in addition to the diploma in theology on the night he graduated.

Valedictorian Brown's graduation photograph still hangs in Presbyterian College's gallery of graduating classes–his visage is in the centre of his classmates. He was a clean-shaven, earnest, square-jawed young man, with a hank of hair evidently not easily tamed. Perhaps Brown's professors believed that he was destined for an academic career, but that was not to be. Brown's personality was better suited for the public sphere rather than the private study. His ministerial career was driven by anxiety for the lost and underprivileged, and, although he kept up in his reading, his waking hours were largely taken up with pastoral visitation and endless rounds of committee meetings.[7]

Presbyterian College was able to give scope to Brown's natural talents in the areas of athletics, debate, journalism, and oratory. It should come as no surprise that he was courted by many prominent pulpits. He would turn a deaf ear to calls to prestigious congregations, choosing to spend his days on the Canadian frontier. In September 1902, he received a year's appointment as an ordained missionary to several northern Ontario lumber camps, where his fluent French and rugged physique came in handy. At his own request, Brown was appointed the following year to mining camps in New Denver, Sandon, and Silverton, British Columbia. In a dispatch to the *Presbyterian College Journal*, he remarked that "the average hard-fisted workingman ... will go to church where he receives an honest welcome, where the service is simple, the sermon good, and the minister a manly man." Brown was able to build up this pastoral charge sufficiently that he could finally wed Martha Rowat.

In 1906, his presbytery (Kootenay) elected him moderator, and that same year he completed his thesis ("Socialism in British Columbia"), which earned him an MA in the Political Science Department of McGill

---

7. Brown, "Reporter's Folio," 488; Reid, "Reporter's Folio," 62; Presbyterian College, "Order of Convocation, 1901," 430.

University.⁸ The following year, the Kootenay Presbytery accepted his resignation, allowing him to do a semester of of post-graduate studies in Scotland. In 1908 the Browns were back in Canada, in his old home in Athelstan, where Martha gave birth to their first child. Within a year, Brown accepted a Call to the frontier church of Red Deer, Alberta. Here he settled down to build up his own congregation and, as missions convener of presbytery to plant or to nurture a sizable number of missions in central Alberta. It was while he was in Red Deer that Brown became one of the most prominent leaders in the movement against the soon-to-be-formed United Church. Brown was proud of his Scottish heritage, it is true, but more problematic in his eyes were the high-handed tactics of church unionists and their easy compromises with the humanistic philosophies of the age. Brown promoted an American alternative to organic church union, namely planned cooperation among the Protestant denominations.⁹

The Presbyterian churches in the Canadian West were more likely to go into Union than those in the rest of the country. Presbyterianism in Saskatchewan was particularly hard hit. Only one Presbyterian congregation in Saskatoon stayed in the continuing Presbyterian Church. The remnants of diehard Presbyterians from the three congregations that went into Union formed a building-less church and raised enough money for a decent stipend to allow them to issue a Call. This was a Call that only a fool would answer, or perhaps, someone with sufficient confidence to start a church from scratch. So the continuing Presbyterians threw the gauntlet down at the feet of none other than the Rev. W. G. Brown, easily the most famous continuing Presbyterian pastor in Canada. Brown, in spite of increasingly severe arthritis, could not resist the challenge; he and his family moved from Alberta to Saskatoon to build a congregation and pick up the shards of Saskatchewan Presbyterianism. Brown quickly got his congregation on a firm footing. Its building was affectionately known as "St. Andrews in the basement" or "the Root Cellar" since it was but one story and partially below ground level. Its

---

8. See the following from *PCJ*: Duguid, "College Note Book, " 45; "Graduates' Column," (Nov 1903) 48, (Dec 1903) 123; Brown, "Among the Mountains," 300–302; Mingie, "Graduates' Column," (Nov 1904) 63, (Dec 1904) 128; Foote, "Graduates' Column," 314. *Acts* (1902) app., 432–33; (1904) app. 470–71; (1905) app. 454–55, (1906) app. 554–55. Raynald Lepage, Curator of Rare Books, McGill University, personal communication, December, 2014.

9. MacDonald, "College Note Book," (Apr 1906) 314, (Nov 1907) 47. Scott, "Rev. W. G. Brown," 129. *Acts* (1905) app. 448–49, (1911) app. 462, (1915) app. 556, (1925) 88–90. *Acts* (1925) (continuing PCC edition) app. 90, 118. "Memorial Tributes to the Rev. W. G. Brown, 1940," PCA, Brown collection; Moir, *Enduring Witness*, 218. Clifford, *Resistance*, 27, 50, 61, 68, 85, 93, 131–32, 152–53.

stalwarts were initially successful as well in gathering non-unionist remnants into organized, if marginal, congregations.[10]

Unfortunately, history was not on Brown's side. Five years into his ministry the stock market crashed and drought hit the Prairies. Widespread poverty and bands of itinerant unemployed were the immediate result. Brown did what he could to alleviate the suffering around him. But he also did some hard thinking. Never impressed with free-market capitalism, he was also wary of the panaceas of socialism and communism. We saw Brown in his Alberta ministry avoiding the extremes of sectarian Presbyterianism on the one hand, and Church Union on the other. So in his Saskatchewan ministry, he preached against the extremes of capitalism and socialism/communism. All the same, it was radical politics, and, even in those days, radical politics rarely went hand-in-hand with Christian convictions. In his words, "I classify myself as an orthodox-radical. By that I mean that I am orthodox in religion, that is, I accept and believe the great fundamental doctrines of our Christian faith as ordinarily understood. In social, economic and political reform, I am a radical." As we might say today, it worked for him! "I get most of my philosophy of life from my own experience or reflecting on my observations of the experience of other people."[11]

Brown's high profile in the continuing Presbyterian Church in Canada led to his being nominated as moderator of General Assembly. This position Brown accepted in 1931, and being moderator had its perks. Offers of a DD (Doctor of Divinity *honoris causa*) could be expected; his alma mater, Presbyterian College, offered him one, but he graciously turned it down. Another of the perks was (and is) a junket to an overseas mission of the Church. Brown characteristically chose to go to the most far-flung mission: Japan, Korea, Manchuria, and Taiwan (then Formosa). In Formosa, Brown ran into theological modernism invading even the mission field and he was scandalized. On his return, he protested to the General Assembly's mission board. Brown was politely heard, and his complaint prudently dismissed. In his disposition to the mission board, Brown proudly claimed that he was "100% an evangelical." He did not mean that he necessarily accepted all Scripture as historically accurate, but that he believed that "the one outstanding reason for and justification of Foreign Missions is the uniqueness of the way of salvation for sinners through Jesus Christ." As with denominational affiliation, and as with politics, Brown was groping for a middle way

---

10. Brown, "Why I remained with the Presbyterian Church in Canada and did not leave it to enter the United Church of Canada in 1925," in *Sermons*; *Acts* (1924) app. 444–45, (1929) app. 23–24. Burt, "Church focus of Brown's life," PCA, Brown collection; Billingsley.

11. Brown, "Competition and Co-Operation"; "War and Peace," in *Sermons*.

and saw hope in the emerging dogmatism of Karl Barth. As well, Brown heartily approved of the influence of W. W. Bryden at Knox College. Bryden came increasingly under the influence of Barth and was the major figure in the renewal of Reformed theology in the Presbyterian Church in Canada.[12]

With his decreasing mobility as the result of arthritis, Brown would turn to radio (CFQC Saskatoon) to get his sermons to go where he could no longer go. He also had published fifteen of his sermons as pamphlets, which he had stitched together in book form with the cover title *Sermons in Answer to Questions*. This slim volume is W. G. Brown's literary legacy, about which you may read more in the commentary that follows the excerpt from the pamphlet sermon reprinted below.[13]

Lest we be tempted to make an idol of our remarkable Mr. Brown, we must admit that he made at the least one very public mistake, one that hastened his death. Brown was exceedingly well known and well liked in Saskatoon, and his reformist politics much appreciated. He and his friends created the United Reformed Party, an ad hoc coalition of labour and agricultural movements. Brown was its only candidate. In December 1939, Brown crushingly defeated his opponents, but the strain of the campaign and the move to Ottawa broke his health. The horrific war he had predicted had broken out four months earlier. The frail Brown sat in the House but one day. The ruthless Mackenzie King prorogued Parliament under the pretense of needing a firm mandate to pursue the war. Though too ill to travel back, Brown again won his seat with an even larger majority, but he was not to savour his victory. On April 1, 1940, Brown's damaged heart stopped beating before he could resume his seat. And a mercy it was, since Brown would have had both to witness the war and the death of his only son in that war, and to chafe under King's authoritarian rule. Yet we cannot imagine that Brown went to his reward with many regrets. Few Presbyterian pastors in his generation had been able to use their talents so fully, and to make such an impact both locally and nationally. As his obituary notice in the General Assembly minutes put it: "As he was perhaps the best known minister in our whole church, we do not need to mention his outstanding qualities, suffice to say he quit himself like a man, was a good soldier of Jesus Christ,

---

12. Martha Brown gave a detailed report of their visit to the Far East in *Glad Tidings* 8:7–8 (July–Aug 1932) 245–52; W. J. Pellow, "Miscellaneous memories of W. G. Brown," PCA, Brown collection; Brown, "War and Peace"; *Presbyterian Record*, 65:5 (May 1940); *Acts* (1940) app., 313; "Statement of Rev. W. G. Brown about the serious situation in the Presbyterian Mission in North Formosa to the General Assembly's Committee on this question," PCA, Brown collection; Vissers, *Bryden*, 101–2.

13. Thanks to Billingsley for the identity of the radio station. The volume was bound in Saskatoon by Fred B. Williams and was deposited in Presbyterian College Library in 1938.

was eloquent and mighty in the scriptures, was of help to the Timothys and Tituses, and cared for the poor and needy."[14]

What Is the Alternative to the Present Social Order?[15]

Text: John 11:44. Loose him and let him go.

Custom of long standing has led most ministers to choose a text. There is no doubt much to be said for the custom so long as we do not make ourselves slaves to this or to any other custom. I have not chosen this text to make it the basis of an exposition of the miracle recorded here even if I were capable of doing that, which I am not, nor indeed is any man qualified to give an exposition of a miracle. Sir Andrew Fraser, a great British statesman, for over thirty years governor of Bengal, made this statement at a missionary conference many years ago in Calgary at which I was present: "The power of prayer is limitless because the power of God is infinite." If I might adapt it I would say that the possibility of miracles is as great as the infinitude of God. I once heard Sir William Dawson say: "The strange thing was not that Jesus performed miracles, the strange thing would have been, if Jesus, being the Son of God, had not performed miracles." Great scientists like Jeans and Eddington, who place the spiritual before all other realities, realize that a miracle is not a violation of law but the introduction of a higher law that brings about a result that otherwise would not have happened. Lazarus is a good type of a man bound in the grave clothes of sin. To all such men the words of Jesus are as life from the dead: "Loose him and let him go." But Lazarus to me is also a type of human society bound in the grave clothes that we have made for ourselves. It is impossible for human society to live while it is bound in the grave clothes with which it is now bound hand and foot.

There have been great epochs in the progress of the understanding of the mind of Christ. The Protestant Reformation of the sixteenth century, when the truth that "the just shall live by faith" and that every believer has the right of direct access to God through Jesus Christ, the only Mediator,

---

14. Torehy Anderson, "Saskatoon Parson Headache to Grits," from Edmonton's Ottawa Bureau, copyright 1940, the Soutam Co.; "W. G. Brown Minister served one day in Commons," PCA, Brown collection; *Acts* (1940) 313; Johnson, *Public Archives of Canada*, s.v. "Brown, Walter George."

15. The following sermon has been condensed to fit the requirements of this volume. The original was preached at the regular Sunday morning service at St. Andrew's Presbyterian, Saskatoon and can be found in its entirety as no. 13 in *Sermons in Answers to Questions*.

shook Europe to its foundations.¹⁶ Another epoch was the first recognition of the right of all people to have the Bible in their own mother tongue; that [epoch] reached a climax in the establishing of the British and Foreign Bible Society. Yet again, the abolition of slavery and the recognition of the claim of Foreign Missions. Every one of these and more were inspired by the spirit of Jesus Christ manifesting its power in the lives of some of His disciples. In nearly every case their most bitter opponents were people who were nominally among the people who called themselves Christians. As the Pilgrim Fathers were setting out for the land of Liberty, John Robinson, one of their loyal band preached to them and in the course of his sermon he said: "Fresh light shall yet break out from God's word."¹⁷ The reason that every one of these epochs went straight forward was because of an aroused Christian conscience that was ready to bear the cross for the truth that had taken possession of it. It is my firm conviction that we are today standing on the threshold of another great epoch in the understanding of the Word of God in the New Testament. That new epoch will be marked in history as a new appreciation of the application of the Principles of our Christian faith to every circumstance of our social order. Let no one say that the Sermon on the Mount won't work. . . .

Jesus says that part of His mission was to set at liberty them that were bound, bound not only by the fetters of sin, but His example in cleansing the temple and on other occasions makes it quite clear that He includes sinful conditions as well as sin.¹⁸ For that work He said that the Spirit of the Lord was upon Him.¹⁹ If any man have not the Spirit of Christ he is none of His.²⁰ Let us study this question from three points of view. . . .

(1) The Fruit of the Present Social Order.

. . . Years ago I was a missionary among the shantymen of Northern Ontario.²¹ I saw the lumber kings of that day sweeping the country of its finest timber, becoming millionaires in the process and leaving not a twig behind.

---

16. "The just shall live by faith": the KJV's translation of Rom 1:17, a verse often quoted by Martin Luther. "Only mediator": 1 Tim 2:5.

17. For a short biography of Robinson, see *Cyclopedia*.

18. "Set at liberty": Luke 4:18. "Cleansing": Matthew 21:12–13 and parallels. "Other occasions": e.g., Matthew 21:1–4.

19. Luke 4:18.

20. "None of his": Rom 8:9 KJV.

21. In 1902 Brown was ordained as a missionary to Northern Ontario lumber camps, where his fluent French came in handy.

Most of the shantymen and river drivers that I knew in those days I venture to say are now living on an old age pension supported by the tax payers of the country.... Part of the fruit of our present social order is caused by too much ecclesiastical domination—not confined to one church, remember—in the administration of the public affairs of our country.... Two weeks ago a friend asked me to go and see a moving picture entitled, "Forward America."... The burden of the picture was to show how the chain store was pushing the independent business man off the street; the purpose was to rally support for the local man. Most people would sympathize with the purpose of the picture. As to the effectiveness of it, I would say that you might as well put on a picture to protest against the gang plow pushing the walking plow off the farms in Saskatchewan. This is part of the fruit of our present social order.

... The idea that progress is inherent and inevitable is probably the biggest lie that the devil is promoting today. The world war and the world hunger show this up in its true colour. Progress does not come from beneath but from above. "In all thy ways acknowledge Him. He shall direct thy paths" (Prov 3:6). We seem to forget that the religion of Jesus Christ is not a spiritual life insurance policy to get us into heaven, but it is a call to join a company of spiritual adventurers for the Kingdom of Heaven's sake. Timid people and legal people are prone to ask, "Is there a precedent?" Rugged men rather ask "Is it true? Is it right?" ...

In the last six or seven years in this Province we have spent over $100,000,000 on relief and what have we to show for it? In face of that, we had more people on relief last fall than one year ago. In Canada we have spent over $1,000,000,000 for relief and, if I am not mistaken, [we have] still more people on relief. Am I blaming the government either provincial or federal? There is no use trying to unload our sins onto the government. ... Last week I had a most interesting privilege of worshipping with two hundred men in the Prince Albert Penitentiary. While no one can turn away from personal responsibility the question that kept hitting me in the face was: How much is our present social order responsible for this fruit? ... What baffles me is the way that we are affected by eating this fruit. Last year certain men set off on a trek to Ottawa. The first result was a riot in Regina. The next move was a commission to sit on the riot. The sum total of the whole thing, so far as getting to the cause of the situation was concerned, was, in my most humble opinion, a great big zero; but it cost the people of this country more than $51,000 to write that cipher into the history of this province.[22] ... Always remember that it is your privilege to disagree with

---

22. Brown referred to the 1935 On-to-Ottawa Trek by protesters of the appalling

every word I speak. My concern is, with the help of God and hard work, to speak what I believe to be true and do what I believe to be right. What I say is this. If the people of this country don't face these facts seriously there is going to be a stampede to Communism.... The people who will lead that stampede for the most part will not be the people who are compelled by civic and church authorities to meet on the market square to discuss their problems, but they will come from the men and women who are now among the undergraduates of our universities. A lot of people would like to have their religion on the top of the Mount of Transfiguration [in] singing psalms and saying prayers. Now the Mount of Transfiguration is a necessity for all of us; but let us watch how Jesus looked at the question. When Peter wanted to stay up there Jesus said, "But there is a boy down there in the valley who is bound by an evil spirit, let us go down and loose him and let him go."[23] Religion without the mountain top will be anaemic, Religion without the valley will have no virility. Let us turn to the next picture. [5]

(2) *What are the Roots of the Present Social Order?*

... My sense of wonder at the greatness of Jesus grows every day. The Scribes and Pharisees of His day tied the people hand and foot with petty rules. As Jesus and His disciples went through the corn or wheat fields they rubbed out the kernels of wheat, but the Scribes and Pharisees said, "Aha, a Sabbath breaker, eh!" Jesus said, "The Sabbath was made for man, not man for the Sabbath."[24] [This is] a principle that will never pass away, no matter what organization under the guise of charity and for the sake of gain tries to make the Sabbath a day of amusement, a holiday but not a holy day. Principles are eternal. Rules become antiquated. Let me take an illustration that will make some of you very angry. Loyalty to Jesus Christ as Saviour and Lord: I believe [this] to be the outstanding principle of Christian discipleship and of membership in the Christian Church. I don't know any other essential principle. Some people tie that up with many rules. For example, certain people say that cigarette smoking should debar a person from church membership. That's a real condition and I would never think of making

---

conditions of government-sponsored work camps in British Columbia. Howard, "On to Ottawa Trek."

23. Matt 17:1–18 and parallels in Mark and Luke. None of the Gospels imply that Peter wanted to stay on the mountain, and Mark specifically says that he was terrified. Nor does Jesus claim foreknowledge of the ill child that awaited them. Brown is using homiletic license here to be able to use his original catchphrase, viz., "loose him and let him go."

24. Mark 2:23–27.

light of the sincere convictions of any person; . . . The millionaire tobacco manufacturers are the only people that I know who are the beneficiaries of this habit that will leave its mark on the next generation. . . . In spite of that, I wouldn't dream of saying to a man, "You can't join the Presbyterian Church if you smoke cigarettes." Are you loyal to Jesus Christ as Saviour and Lord? That's the root question. . . . Jesus never spoke to the Jews as Jews nor the Gentiles as Gentiles; but to man as man. Herein lies the note of Catholicity (which, as you know, properly means Universality) of the appeal of Jesus. He goes to the roots of things. . . . Capitalism has been a magnificent success when you think of the way it has speeded up production and, in that way, has made a real contribution to the progress of human society; but it has been a magnificent failure when you think of the way it has refused to distribute the proceeds. . . . If it were not fear of a rising up of the people all types of business would be merged much more rapidly than is being done. Much of it, in my opinion, is already done though not openly proclaimed. If labour people want to organize, these same people vigorously protest by highly organized propaganda that many people will believe. The real roots show up in a situation like this. Suppose the government sets out on a program of public works to relieve the present distress. The manufacturer of steel and cement at one raise their price because of the increased demand, their dividends increase, and the tax payer carries the entire burden of the public works program. Unless private business is stimulated by this government enterprise, the last state is worse than the first.[25] . . . Under the present system we are bound to have recurring booms and depressions. . . . Each boom will steadily develop more monopoly and every depression will grow steadily wider and more severe. . .

(3) Better Fruits from Better Roots of a Better Social Order.

. . . The greatest attempt to find an alternative in our day is in Russia. . . . If I had been brought up under the regime of the Czar and had been led to believe that the perversion of religion that there and then existed was the only kind of religion that there was, I have not the least doubt that I would have been anti-clerical and anti-religious too. What exasperates me is to find people who know what the real essence of religion is or ought to be [and who have] thrown overboard the true with the false. . . . If communism is not the answer, . . . I am quite sure that Fascism or Nazism is not the answer

---

25. This is an allusion to the demonized man who was exorcised but then demonized more severely (Matt 12:43–45), which meant that the root cause of the man being demonized was not dealt with.

because both of these, as I understand them, are capitalism organized on a basis of tyranny and fear.... It amazes me to hear men denounce Hitler for his Aryan superiority snobbery and, in the same breath, turn round and exalt their British superiority snobbery and wonder why people don't swallow it. In Christ Jesus there is neither Jew nor Greek: racial distinctions are gone; there is neither bond nor free: social distinctions are gone; there is neither male nor female: sex distinctions are gone; all are one in Him. I am not satisfied that socialism is the alternative. Public ownership, which has no necessary connection with socialism, will become, I believe, increasingly necessary and operative. Jesus was a revolutionist of the first order, but He was not a revolutionist who believed in force. He took what was good out of the old, for He came not to destroy but to fulfill. He knew that spiritual regeneration was the beginning of religion, but He also knew that it was *only* the beginning. He ate and drank with publicans and sinners because He saw unlimited possibilities in them.... The ideal must be [to put] good men in charge of a good system, and you can lift the world to new heights of power, service, and happiness....

The new and better social order must be based on the principle that we will help ourselves when we help other people. That is thoroughly sound and fully Christian.... What we must set ourselves to do is to think our way through to a system where we can do our own financing and develop a system that will have all the merits of capitalism in its productive capacity and will be free from its demerits in the matter of distribution.... That new economic system ... is Co-operation, whose principles are thoroughly sound from an economic point of view and fully Christian. The more fully this system that recognizes these two truths is carried out, the more it will be in accord with the ideals of the system. The last of the benefits of this system are probably the financial benefits, though these are almost overwhelming as they cover not only the necessities of life and all the ordinary merchandising but also life insurance and all types of protection.... About 1900 a French Canadian, Adolph Desjardins, introduced this type of self-help into the Province of Quebec. The capital to begin with was $26.40. The Credit union idea has spread and today their assets in Quebec amount to over $16,000,000. They have spread all over [8] Nova Scotia and are a phenomenal success.... Since 1929 more than 5,000 regular banks in the U.S.A. have closed their doors; but in that time not one of the 3,000 credit unions has closed its doors.... It isn't a question for them now of running to the government and the big financial interests for help, it is a question of these people helping themselves.... Do we want to help ourselves by helping other people or do we want to continue to be bound hand and foot as we are today? For my part I want to be free and I want to help other people to be free. . . . A few years ago I crossed the St. John River in the City of St, John, N.B. At noon time the current was running toward the sea and the waterfall of several feet was tumbling oceanward. At 5 o'clock I crossed the river again and by this time the current was running up the river and the waterfall was up stream. What had happened? The moon by some mysterious power had lifted up the ocean and it was rushing up the narrow banks of the Bay of Fundy and up the St. John River. I thought at the time, that's the best illustration of the power of God to convert a man's life and of Benjamin Kidd's thesis that a great idea will transform a nation in one generation.[26] . . . The trouble is not in God but in ourselves that we are underlings. We can do IF we will. By the Grace of God shall we not say, "We can do it *and we will.*" Amen.

Commentary on "What Is the Alternative to the Present Social Order?"

Brown's sermon printed above was, strictly speaking, no sermon at all, but rather a diatribe against free market capitalism, to which was appended a sketchy defence of the still nascent co-operative movement. No biblical text could be found to support his arguments (capitalism, needless to say, was not invented in biblical times), and Brown's socioeconomic vision is based on Christian wisdom. Therefore to find a text, *any* text, for his sermon, Brown resorted to a symbolic interpretation of a Scripture passage and to a plea for continuing revelation based on Scripture. As for symbolic interpretation, Brown saw Lazarus coming out of the tomb and swaddled with grave clothes (John 11:44) as "type" of contemporary society, bound with the deadening wraps of capitalism. As for continuing revelation, Brown appealed to the Pilgrim Father John Robinson's notion of "Fresh light shall yet break out from God's Word." Brown optimistically predicted "that a new epoch will be marked in history as a new appreciation of the application of the Principles of our Christian Faith to every circumstance of our social order." Beyond these two homiletic moves, Brown did not go but straightway plunged into his damning analysis of the "Present Social Order."

In all the suffering and chaos of Depression-era Saskatchewan, Brown had not stopped thinking. He was appalled at the lack of response to the Depression from the governments in power, and he was in equal measure upset at appeals to laissez-faire capitalism. In his fifteen years of Saskatoon

---

26. Benjamin Kidd (1858–1916) was a self-taught sociologist, who, though not religious, had positive things to say about Christianity's teaching of altruism as a positive contribution to western civilization. See *Social Evolution.*

ministry, Brown advocated the *via media* of cooperation. Rather than the state taking over agriculture and industry, the co-operative movement envisaged capital being raised by workers themselves and the workers having a share in management. Brown, ever the Renaissance man, was an amateur economist. He set co-operation against the other grand economic systems current in his day: capitalism, fascism, communism; and he recommended co-operative credit unions. Thus Brown was involved in that part of the agrarian-labour movement that was then coalescing into the CCF (Co-operative Commonwealth Federation).[27]

Our best way forward is to try to understand Brown's focus on the co-operative movement in the light of what he called his "philosophy of life," which was quite comprehensively represented in *Sermons in Answer to Questions*. For Brown, the pulpit was a proper forum for more than purely spiritual concerns, though he preached such sermons. Of the fifteen sermons, seven were directly related to the social questions of the day. And even in those sermons not directly on the social crisis, Brown usually managed to include some social commentary.

We may wonder at Brown's audacity that he supposed himself to be qualified to speak with authority on so many questions. Brown was not an academic, but by the standards of the time, he was an intellectual in the sense of well educated. Brown respected theological scholarship, and this would have been one of the reasons he refused an honorary doctor of divinity offered him by Presbyterian College. He continued to read as time permitted, and shared with his congregation his thoughts on the great issues of the day. For example, he mentioned that he had just finished reading William P. Paterson's *The Rule of Faith*. Paterson was no strict Calvinist, nor even particularly conservative theologically, but Brown was able to distil what he considered good for his hearers. Nor did Brown neglect the biblical languages that he had championed as a theological student. Brown was not an original thinker, but he was a shrewd one. He read widely and worked tirelessly for the good of his church and his community. He showed a familiarity with science and faith issues. His critique of the Darwinism of his day, while not profound, did display an acquaintance, if only second hand, with the then current intellectual discussions. Brown made no attempt to interpret the first eleven chapters of Genesis in a strictly historical manner but steered a middle course between a six-day creation (he did not mention it) and a philosophical acceptance of blind chance as the motor in the development of life. Thus Brown took an interest in the science that pointed beyond

---

27. No. 13, "What Is the Alternative to the Present Social Order?," in Brown, *Sermons*.

purely mechanistic causation to a spiritual basis for reality. Sir James Jeans was hardly a traditional Christian in his philosophical explorations but did write a series of works popularizing advances in science, particularly in the area of speculative physics. Brown mentioned Jeans as an ally of those protesting against pure materialism: "Great scientists like Jeans and Eddington, who place the spiritual before all other realities, realize that a miracle is not a violation of law but the introduction of a higher law that brings about a result that otherwise would not have happened."[28]

In Brown's day, of course, the universe was thought to be orderly and placid, unlike today's violent and unpredictable one. All of these things show Brown to be open to intellectual currents in the modern world and less likely to hold more stubbornly to traditional economic solutions.

Brown the intellectual was also Brown the idealist. At the close of what was essentially a polemic against capitalism, Brown made what he called "a prophecy." In this prophecy he predicted "within twenty years" a golden era of personal religion and national and international cooperation. It is uncertain how to take Brown here. He rightly foresaw the horrors of World War II, and he perhaps believed that humanity would learn its lesson and found a new world on better principles. In any event, the Cold War ensued.[29]

Brown championed causes that would be quaint in the beginning of the twenty-first century. He also retained something of the Calvinist and the Puritan in making a distinction between the ceremonial law and the moral law of the Old Testament. On that basis, he strongly urged Sabbath-keeping and tithing as part of the healthy Christian life. He believed, as did many in his day, that beverage alcohol was a positive evil. Brown had a visceral dislike of Roman Catholicism (in his day, the pre-Vatican II variety, of course). Like many of his compatriots he, innocently or not, equated civic freedoms and freedom of religion with Protestantism.[30]

Brown had no use for war. At the same time he was not a pacifist in the strict sense of the word. Even in 1937, he shuddered at the coming world war: "Fifty years from now, when the people read the files of our daily press they will agree that the chief mark of the people who lived in the year 1937 was stupidity.... We are rushing into the devils' inferno that will turn this world into a human slaughterhouse."

As with his doctrinal position, Brown sought, in the question of participation in war, a middle position. He wished to warn against "Jingoists

---

28. No. 12, "The Church and the Kingdom of God"; No. 4, "Evolution"; No. 13, "What Is the Alternative to the Present Social Order?," in *Sermons*.

29. No. 10, "Co-operation and Competition," in *Sermons*.

30. No.14, "Christian Stewardship," No. 3, "Why I Am a Protestant," in *Sermons*.

who want war for its own sake" and "Pacifists who will not fight under any circumstances." Brown wanted his flock to be "militant people who believe in and demand peace and are ready to put themselves into a fight to secure the conditions upon which peace is possible." By this fight, Brown meant that the Christian churches, hierarchy and ordinary members, should work militantly for disarmament, international cooperation and mutual understanding.[31]

Thus we see that the co-operative movement was a natural fit for W. G. Brown. We cannot end our study without reference to Brown's physical condition. Surely part of Brown's asperity was a product of his deteriorating health during his Saskatchewan ministry. W. J. Pellow recalled: "His arthritis in the knees was obvious to all and his familiar walking stick was his indispensable companion. His determination in carrying on when other men would have given up must have gone a long way in commending the Christian faith to people. I have seen him climbing those steps to the pulpit in St Andrew's in the Basement to speak and preach and his face was grey with pain."[32]

Not even Brown could maintain his grueling pace of pastoral duties and visits to outlying missions without damage to his health. Then, too, his rheumatic heart condition grew worse with the passage of time. His vitriolic rhetoric was in part a reflection of the constant pain with which he lived. Brown, however, being Brown, was not so much concerned with personal pain as with the social pain around him as the Great Depression continued one gray year after another. He was haunted by the mobile armies of the unemployed, and scandalized at the inaction of government leaders and the captains of industry. His *cri de coeur* should not surprise us, but make us pause to ask ourselves why we are silent as rich nations pull away from areas in the world that are so poor that they cannot be rightly called developing, but are more properly understood as a permanent underclass. Brown's small literary deposit is a witness against us.

The Author

Dan Shute is a minister of the Presbyterian Church in Canada. He is married to Elaine Richardson and they have two children. He served as an ordained missionary in New Brunswick 1975–1977 and was appointed librarian of Presbyterian College in 1980, a position he continues to hold. He has a doctorate from McGill in historical theology, and his focus in academic

---

31. No. 7, "The Bible on Its Own Terms," No. 8, "War and Peace," in *Sermons*.
32. Pellow, "Miscellaneous memories," PCA, Brown collection.

research has been on the Italian Reformer, Peter Martyr Vermigli. He has taught Presbyterian polity, Bible content, and Hebrew at Presbyterian College and at Faculté de Théologie Évangélique. He has published short biographies of the following ministers of the Presbyterian Church in Canada: Daniel Coussirat, Robert Campbell, and W. G. Brown. He is at present interim moderator of two congregations of the Presbytery of Montreal, and, time permitting, continues his research into the Psalms.

Bibliography

Brown, Martha. "The Diamond Jubilee of Our Formosa Mission." In *Glad Tidings* 8:7–8 (July–Aug 1932) 245–52.

Brown, W. G. "Among the Mountains and Miners." In *Presbyterian College Journal* 23:5 (Mar 1904) 300–302.

———. Collection. Presbyterian Church in Canada Archives.

———. "College Note-Book: Reporter's Folio." In *Presbyterian College Journal* 18:6 (Apr 1899) 472; 19:1 (Nov 1899) 39–43; 19:2 (Dec 1899) 131; 19:3 (Jan 1900) 207; 20:1 (Nov 1900) 49.

———. "Debating Societies." In *Presbyterian College Journal* 20:3 (Jan 1901) 253–56.

———. Editorial. *Presbyterian College Journal* 20:3 (Jan 1901) 259.

———. "Our Late Queen." In *Presbyterian College Journal* 20:4 (Feb 1901) 339–40.

———. "A Portable Library." In *Presbyterian College Journal* 20:5 (Mar 1901) 428–29; 20:4 (Feb 1901) 339–40.

———. *Sermons in Answer to Questions*. Saskatoon: [the author], 1937.

———. "The Training We Need." In *Presbyterian College Journal* 20:4 (Feb 1901) 340–42.

———. "The Triumphs of the Gospel." In *Presbyterian College Journal* 20:3 (Jan 1901) 256–59.

———. "Valedictory Address." In *Presbyterian College Journal* 21:5 (Mar 1901) 432–38.

———. "Watchman, What of the Night?" In *Presbyterian College Journal* 20:2 (Dec 1900) 151–52.

Clifford, N. Keith. *The Resistance to Church Union in Canada, 1904–1939*. Vancouver: University of British Columbia Press, 1985.

Duguid, Colin. "College Note Book, Our Graduates." In *Presbyterian College Journal* 22:1 (Nov 1902) 45.

———. "Graduates' Column." In *Presbyterian College Journal* 23:1 (Nov 1903) 48.

Howard, Victor. "On to Ottawa Trek." In *Canadian Encyclopedia*, edited by James H. Marsh, 3:1566. 2nd ed. Edmonton: Hurtig, 1988.

Johnson, J. K. "Brown, Walter George." In *Public Archives of Canada: The Canadian Directory of Parliament, 1867–1967*. Ottawa: Queen's Printer, 1968.

Kidd, Benjamin. *Social Evolution*. New York: Macmillan, 1894. http://www.ask.com/wiki/Benjamin_Kidd?o=2801&qsrc=999&ad=doubleDown&an=apn&ap=ask.com.

MacDonald, A. B. "College Note Book, Our Graduates." In *Presbyterian College Journal* 25:5 (Apr 1906) 314; 27:1 (Nov 1907) 47.

Markell, H. Keith. *History of the Presbyterian College, Montreal 1865–1986*. Montreal: Presbyterian College, 1987.

McClintock, John, and James Strong, eds. *Cyclopedia of Biblical, Theological, and Ecclesiastical Literature*. New York: Harper, 1867–1887.

Mingie, George W. "Graduates' Column." In *Presbyterian College Journal* 24:1 (Nov 1904) 63; 24:2 (Dec 1904) 128.

Moir, John S. *Enduring Witness: A History of the Presbyterian Church in Canada*. 3rd ed. Toronto: Committee on Church History, Presbyterian Church in Canada, 2004.

Presbyterian Church in Canada. *Acts and Proceedings of the General Assembly* (1902) app. 432–33; (1904) app. 470–71; (1905) app. 448–49, 454–55; (1906) app. 554–55; (1911) app. 462; (1915) app. 556; (1924) app. 444–45; (1925) 88–90; (1925 continuing Presbyterian Church in Canada edition) app. 90, 118; (1929) app. 23–24.

Presbyterian College, Montreal. "Order of Convocation, Wednesday April 3rd, 1901." In *Presbyterian College Journal* 21:5 (Mar 1901) 430.

Quebec, Vital and Church Records Drouin Collection, 1621–1967. http://search.ancestry.ca/search/db.aspx?dbid=1091&geo_a=t&geo_s=us&geo_t=ca&o_iid=41015&o_lid=41015&o_sch=Web+Property.

Reid, Allen S. "Reporter's Folio." In *Presbyterian College Journal* 19:6 (Apr 1900) 488; 20:6 (Apr 1901) 460; 21:1 (Nov 1901) 62.

Vissers, John. *The Neo-Orthodox Theology of W. W. Bryden*. Eugene, OR: Pickwick, 2006.

Later Years

CHAPTER 9

The College and the Nation
Cairine R. Mackay Wilson

By Andrew J. R. Johnston

Senator Cairine Reay Wilson, née Mackay, (1885–1962). From her Fonds, circa 1930, oil on canvas by G. Horne Russell, Library and Archives Canada, accession number 1997-212-1, MIKAN number 2837777, reproduction copy number C-018713.

CAIRINE R. WILSON WAS never a student at Presbyterian College Montreal, nor did she ever serve on its senate. However, her family had been instrumental in the founding of the college. She was raised just blocks from the college. She remembered the college in her will. In the context of this book, Cairine Wilson may be considered as an outstanding example of a life shaped by God through the Presbyterian Church in Canada, to which the Presbyterian College has contributed so fully since 1865.

To the seventh of their eventually eight children, born February 4, 1885, Robert and Jane Mackay gave the name Cairine, Gaelic for Catherine.[1] Two dimensions of this child's family life—dimensions which were to prove formative for the perspectives and priorities she would develop—were Christian faith and national politics.

The Presbyterian Church was very much part of Cairine Wilson's heritage. Her great uncle Joseph Mackay had arrived in Montreal in 1832 when he was only twenty-one and built up a very successful wholesale dry goods business. He was respected both for his ability and integrity in business, and also for his strong Christian faith. Joseph was committed to a particular congregation, the St. Gabriel Street Presbyterian Church in which he was elected an elder, and also to the witness of the wider church. He was instrumental in the establishment of the Presbyterian College, Montreal in 1865, contributing generously to the construction of the College and endowing a chair of systematic theology, and thereafter serving on its board of management. He personally underwrote the calling and settling of up to a dozen ministers from Scotland to serve the growing Presbyterian population in Canada. Upon retirement from his business activities, he extended support to Canadian Presbyterian missionaries, entertaining them in his home and visiting them on his travels. His Christian endeavours were shared by his bachelor brother Edward and nephew Hugh, all of whom were generous benefactors of the college.

Cairine's father, Robert followed his uncle in the family business, and also into Christian faith, and she grew up in a home infused with the disciplines and theology of the Presbyterian Church. She was baptized at Crescent Street Presbyterian Church and attended worship there regularly with her family. As a teenager, she committed the answers of the *Westminster Shorter Catechism* to memory. And, with the centrality of the Scriptures in both public worship and personal devotions, Cairine often heard the reminders from both Old and New Testaments that those who have been blessed are called to become a blessing unto others, and those to whom much is given, much will be expected.

1. Great debt is acknowledged to Valerie Knowles for *First Person*.

Another significant dimension of Cairine's family life was political activity as an appropriate realm for Christian service. The Canadian Presbyterian tradition traces its roots back to the activities of Jean Calvin in Geneva and John Knox in Scotland, both of whom were actively involved in the political and social dimensions of their day. Wilson's father, Robert Mackay, was a central figure in the Liberal Party of Canada. In acknowledgement of his significant contributions to the Liberal Party, he was appointed a senator in 1901, the last named by Queen Victoria. Prominent guests and discussions concerning the nation filled the family home. As a young woman, standing in for her oft-infirm mother, Cairine accompanied her father to meetings and gatherings in Ottawa, sometimes staying with family friends Sir Wilfred and Lady Laurier and accompanying them on occasion to Rideau Hall.

These twin cornerstones of her family—faith and politics—provided a sure foundation for Cairine Wilson. What is exceptional is the life she built upon this foundation.

Cairine Mackay was introduced to a most eligible Ottawa bachelor named Norman Wilson by Lady Laurier at a Rideau Hall ball. Norman was both a Presbyterian and a member of the Liberal Party. Twenty-nine years of age, he was the Member of Parliament for Russell County, Ontario. Four years later, in February 23, 1909, they were married by the minister of Crescent Street Presbyterian Church. From a life of privilege in the centre of Montreal, she was transported to the small town of Rockland, Ontario, where Norman managed the W. C. Edwards and company lumber mill that dominated the community. Most of her time was focused upon their family, giving birth to the first four of their eight children: Olive (1910), Janet (1910), Cairine (1913), and Ralph (1915). She participated in the life of the Presbyterian congregation, organizing knitting to support Canadian troops fighting overseas, and was known for acts of kindness to ill and retired employees. With the death of her mother in 1911, Cairine Wilson had increasing responsibility for her father and his sizeable household in Montreal. When her father died in 1916, she and her siblings each inherited a significant sum, and two years later, Norman and Cairine (now in her mid-thirties) moved to Ottawa.

Norman and Cairine became members of St. Andrew's Presbyterian Church in the centre of the capital, and the Wilson family continued to grow with the addition of four more children: Anna (1918), Angus (1920), Robert (1922) and lastly, Norma (1925). Cairine Wilson also became directly involved in the Liberal Party. In June 1921 she was appointed joint president of the Eastern Ontario Liberal Association with twenty-two constituencies, just in time to provide organizational support for the federal election of December 1921. This was the first election in which Canadian women were granted the right to vote, and the election that brought the Liberals to national victory under the leadership of William Lyon Mackenzie King. The new prime minister had been a friend of the Wilsons since the year he shared a desk with Norman in the House of Commons, and had been a member of St. Andrew's since 1901.

This joint presidency of the Eastern Ontario Liberal Association brought Wilson into a position previously occupied only by men. She set an example and proved a hard worker, using her extensive social and honed organizational skills to create opportunities for other women and indeed youth to grow in political awareness and activity. She chaired the committee that established the Ottawa Women's Liberal Club in 1922, and served as its president for three years. Furthermore, she chaired the committee that brought together a large gathering in Ottawa in 1928 that led eventually to the establishment of the National Federation of Liberal Women of Canada, serving as its honorary president, then as acting president and finally president from 1934–1947. In 1928 she led a committee created to form a "League of Youth" that resulted in the establishment of the Twentieth Century Liberal Association of Canada in 1930.

On October 18, 1929, Viscount Sankey, Lord Chancellor of the British Privy Council, ruled that "yes, women are persons . . . and eligible to be summoned and may become Members of the Senate of Canada." He stated further that "the exclusion of women from all public offices is a relic of days more barbarous than ours. And to those who would ask why the word 'persons' [in the British North America Act] should include females, the obvious answer is, why should it not?"[2] This landmark decision was the culmination of many petitions and much activity, beginning in 1917 with the refusal to make Magistrate Emily Murphy of Alberta a senator, to the 1927 petition and subsequent appeal of the "Famous Five" Canadian women whose monument is now found on Parliament Hill. Four months after this decision, Prime Minister Mackenzie King appointed Cairine Wilson as Canada's first woman senator, a first also for the British Empire.

The appointment of Cairine Wilson was something of a shock to many. Some felt the honour belonged by right to a woman like Emily Murphy who had fought long and hard for women's rights in the nation. Regional considerations elicited criticism of the appointment of an Ottawa resident. Many felt that a mother of eight children (with seven still at home) had prior and higher responsibilities to her family. The appointment was something of a shock to the Wilsons themselves, with Norman initially declining on

---

2. Munroe, *Person's Case*.

their behalf. It was Cairine who convinced him that the appointment was an appropriate one. Even the notice in the April 1930 issue of the national monthly, the *Presbyterian Record*, is succinct to the point of telling.

> It is pardonable that our Church should feel gratification that the first lady to take her seat in the Red Chamber at Ottawa as a senator for the Dominion of Canada is a Presbyterian. She was formerly a member of Crescent St. Church Montreal, with which church her father, also a senator, was long identified. She is now a devoted member of St. Andrew's Church, Ottawa. As a member of the senate she is known as the Honourable Cairine Mackay Wilson. Naturally at the opening of Parliament she was the centre of attention being the first lady appointed to that body. It was expected by all who knew her that she would occupy well her high position, an expectation confirmed by her first address which was delivered in both French and English. With the introduction of Mrs. Wilson to the Senate there is now a balance between the two chambers, there being a lady member in each.[3]

This understated paragraph was found tucked away between announcements of a church being built in the West and a letter from a missionary overseas. Was the exclusively male leadership of the denomination itself somewhat ambivalent about this development in the governance of the nation? It is also interesting to note that the *Presbyterian Record* published no article by Cairine Wilson, consummate publicist though she was, until 1956; and that article ("Helping Our Sisters in Distress") dealt not with national politics but an initiative of the Presbyterian Church in Canada—a new home for unwed mothers named Armagh—that Senator Wilson had steered into being.

It is clear that Cairine Wilson received the honour of being Canada's first woman senator due to partisan and social connections. She was not involved in the struggle that granted women the right to vote in 1921 or in the petitions and appeals that opened the door for women to serve in the senate in 1929. What becomes equally clear, however, is that Wilson had the strength of character to accept the opportunity it presented. When unveiling a portrait of Wilson in the Senate Reading Room in October of 2013 (a portrait that is believed to have been commissioned on the occasion of her appointment in 1930), the Honourable Noel A. Kinsella, speaker of the senate noted: "From our modern vantage point, the remarkable courage and aplomb of Ms. Wilson in accepting this appointment might be overlooked. On her first day in the Senate, she would have taken her seat in the Senate

---

3. *Presbyterian Record*, April 1930, 114.

Chamber, the lone woman among 95 male colleagues."⁴ Wilson not only accepted but also shaped the position on her own terms as an individual of principle and faith.

An even cursory review of her first years as senator reveals that Wilson focused intentionally on concerns of women and children. This was not a matter of constraint, a woman restricted to women's issues, but of encouragement and advocacy. She responded to an incredible number of invitations, addressing associations from women teachers to Canadian Clubs of cities across Canada, repeatedly articulating the progress that women had made in society as a whole, and the opportunity women now had to shape the coming generation by being active in community and political affairs.

For the most part, women and their children continued to be entirely dependent on men, and it being the Great Depression, this made them particularly vulnerable. In the senate, Cairine spoke to issues that she felt affected women most, including preventative medical care and health insurance, women's working conditions and education. A couple of examples provide a sense of her priorities. In 1938 Wilson spoke in the senate in support of widening the grounds for divorce beyond adultery, a position that attracted much public notice. The bill was passed by the Senate, but defeated in the House of Commons. In 1943 there was much debate about the establishment of universal family allowances. Against vocal personalities such as Charlotte Whitton, the colourful and Conservative mayor of Ottawa, who considered family allowances an inappropriate intervention, and Prime Minister Mackenzie King, her fellow St. Andrew's member and party leader who opposed them on financial grounds, Wilson spoke passionately in support of universal family allowances as a means of social equity and justice.

It was not that Cairine Wilson was a great orator in the senate or beyond. Her speeches are remembered for their sincerity, clarity and underlying compassion. Indeed it was well beyond Senator Wilson's speeches that her greatest service was offered. She was a diligent and perceptive member of thirteen very different senate committees over the years, where much of the work of the senate was actually accomplished.⁵ Within months of being appointed, she became the first woman chair of a Senate Standing Committee (Public Buildings and Grounds). Beyond the senate, she served on the boards of organizations like the Victorian Order of Nurses, the Ottawa branches of the YWCA and the Canadian Save the Children Fund (which she helped launch), the Bronson Home for Elderly Women, and the Mackay Institution for Protestant Deaf Mutes in Montreal (named after her great-

4. Kinsella, *Speaking Notes*.
5. Parliament of Canada, *PARLINFO*.

uncle Joseph, a benefactor of both land and finances). Besides all this, she maintained a commitment to the care of others in a very personal way. On Sundays after public worship at her church, she made visits to Saint Vincent's Hospital, a long-term care facility.

Cairine Wilson began her career as Canada's first woman senator with one focus in mind: the challenges and possibilities of the nation's women and children. Stemming from this, her compassion and commitment led her into ever-expanding circles of concern and activity. One of the earliest was the League of Nations, inaugurated January 10, 1920. From the slaughter of "the war to end all wars," its mission was to maintain world peace. To prevent further wars, the signatory nations committed to collective security and disarmament and the settling of disputes through negotiation and arbitration. In a resolution she presented to the senate on November 16, 1932, one can hear how her aims for the nation led her into the international realm: "Resolved: that in the opinion of the Senate there should be no curtailment or interruption in the continuity of the work of the League of Nations dealing with social and humanitarian questions and particularly with that section which relates to the opium traffic, the traffic in women and children, and child welfare."[6] Despite opposition, and despite its rejection by the United States, the resolution carried and Canada maintained its support for the social and humanitarian work of the League.

Wilson believed that an organization like the League would not only help shape a better world for women, but also that women had a particular contribution to play in this development. Reflecting upon Wilson's work as she followed her into the Red Chamber decades later, Senator Sharon Carstairs, in her book *Dancing Backwards*, notes: "Wilson believed that women needed to take up the cause of world peace, because war grew from men's greed and ambition and only women could change history's direction. Wilson used her position in the Senate to openly campaign for world peace."[7]

In 1933 Wilson accepted an invitation to sit on the national council and executive of the League of Nations Society of Canada. Despite the failure of an international disarmament conference, the withdrawal of Germany from the organization, and then the withdrawal of Japan, she continued to speak and act in support of the League of Nations. She was elected chair of the national executive of the Society in 1936, and the following year was made its first woman president, serving in that position until 1942. Even with so many other claims upon her time and energy, this cause lay so close

---

6. Canada. The Senate, *Debates*, November 16, 1932, is quoted in Knowles, *First Person*, 176.

7. Dempsey, "Remembering."

to her heart that, when fundraising fell short, she personally maintained its continued operation.

Notwithstanding her commitment to collective security, Wilson was no pacifist. When the leaders of Britain, France and Italy agreed on September 30, 1938, to allow Hitler to occupy the German-speaking part of Czechoslovakia in an attempt to avoid war, Prime Minister Mackenzie King and most Canadians rejoiced in Neville Chamberlain's promise of "peace in our time." Courageously and (so it proved) correctly, Cairine Wilson spoke out four days later denouncing the so-called Munich Agreement. She knew that such a public statement would anger many, including her prime minister, and could put her very position as senator in doubt, but she was convinced that appeasement would only encourage further aggression, and would result in only greater suffering for both soldier and civilian, including the women and children.

The clarity and courage with which Cairine Wilson held to her humanitarian principles is perhaps even more impressive than the fact that history vindicated her perspective. Cairine remained a senator. With the German invasion of Poland on September 1, 1939, and the declaration of war by Britain and France two days later, the League of Nations ceased to be relevant, and Cairine turned her attention increasingly to a new organization that had been created by the League of Nations Society of Canada on October 15, 1938: the Canadian National Committee on Refugees and Victims of Political Persecution. Her work with this committee is acknowledged by many as her greatest contribution to her nation. And, one could add, her most distinctive witness as a Christian and Presbyterian.

Wilson's work for and with refugees is the focus of the speech and commentary that follow this biography. It was not a concern that many Canadians shared. Because of the extensive unemployment of the Great Depression, the doors of immigration to Canada had been almost completely closed. There were increasing numbers of refugees in Europe, but they were considered a European issue and a responsibility of the European powers. Protectionism and isolationism predominated in popular thinking and in government policy. But her involvement in the League of Nations Society provided Cairine Wilson with a broader perspective, and her compassion for the vulnerable brought her to the side of the refugees. Her work in launching a financial appeal to assist eighty thousand Czech refugees through the winter of 1938 soon developed into a commitment to offer refugees shelter in Canada.

The Canadian government actively resisted such a development. In 1938, Canada's director of the Immigration Branch, F. C. Blair, articulated the thinking of many when he stated: "Ever since the war, efforts have been made by groups and individuals to get refugees into Canada, but we have fought all along to protect ourselves against the admission of such stateless persons without passports for the reasons that coming out of the maelstrom of war, some of them are liable to go on the rocks and when they become public charges, we have to keep them for the balance of their lives."[8]

In December 1938 a delegation led by Senator Wilson met with Prime Minister Mackenzie King, appealing for Canada to accept refugees on humanitarian grounds, with no success. The private diaries of Mackenzie King reveal his personal prejudices: "We must seek to keep this part of the continent free from unrest and from too great an intermixture of foreign strains of blood."[9]

With a view to remove such bureaucratic barriers and to change government policy, Wilson poured her energies into the establishment of the Canadian National Committee on Refugees and Victims of Political Persecution. She co-chaired a national conference on refugees on December 6, 1938, that was sponsored by this new group. The CNCR would become Canada's most active and influential refugee advocacy organization, with local chapters across the nation, and an office in Toronto. Cairine Wilson gave of herself fully, serving as its chair for the length of its history from 1938–1948, speaking publicly whenever possible, and fundraising, at times providing the funds herself in order that the work might continue.

With Canada's declaration of war on Germany on September 10, 1939, Wilson and the CNCR changed tact. Instead of seeking a revision of general government policy that would allow for the immigration of refugees, they would now seek the means whereby individuals and groups might sponsor particular refugees for admission. In support of such a direction, she would mention a particular example, such as that of Thomas Bata, whom the CNCR had worked hard to be accepted into Canada as a refugee after fleeing Czechoslovakia, and who established a shoe manufacturing plant in the Belleville area that employed seven hundred by the autumn of 1940. Despite many other examples she shared in speeches and broadcasts, there was little engagement by the public or the government.

An added dimension of challenge was presented by the fact that most of the refugees were Jewish. The policies of the Nazi regime made Jews stateless refugees in their own country, first in Germany itself by the Nuremberg Laws, then in the annexed territories of Austria, Sudetenland and Czechoslovakia. Those who had the opportunity to flee did so, often with nothing. The Canadian public learned more and more about the brutal persecution

---

8. Canadian Council for Refugees, "Brief History."
9. Canadian Broadcasting Corporation, "Hate at the Top."

of the Jews in Europe, and about the growing numbers seeking refuge, but public response was limited.

Anti-Semitism was most strident in Quebec, but latent through most of Canada and certainly its government. After Kristallnacht (November 9–10, 1938), Frederick Blair, Canada's top immigration bureaucrat, stated that "pressure on the part of the Jewish people to get into Canada has never been greater than it is now and I am glad to be able to add, after thirty-five years experience here, that it was never so well controlled."[10] No better illustration can be given than the rejection of the *St. Louis* on which over nine hundred Jewish German refugees set sail from Hamburg on May 13, 1939. They held valid Cuban visas but by the time they arrived, the Cuban government had revoked their visas and refused them entry. So did the government of the United States and, despite pleas from the CNCR as the ship approached these shores, so did the government of Canada. It is believed that after their return to Europe, approximately one quarter of the ship's passengers died in concentration camps. The next month, with the fall of France imminent and faced with a massive migration of children, the CNCR placed newspaper ads from coast to coast pleading for the admission of at least these most vulnerable ones: "This week the lives of hundreds of thousands of children are in our hands. Next week the deaths of thousands may be on our heads."[11] But most of these children were Jewish and the government balked.

For ten years, Cairine Wilson and the CNCR advocated for the reception of these stateless ones, including and especially Jewish refugees. In the context of the prevailing anti-Semitism, her persistence was not only demanding but radical. The senator was not shy in involving cabinet ministers and communicated directly with bureaucrats on behalf of countless individual refugees. In the autumn of 1943 the CNCR organized a nation-wide petition demanding the government grant entry to more victims of Nazi persecution. The opening and closing sentences alone convey the passion and strength of the senator as she pleaded for signatures of support in a speech entitled "The People of Canada's Conscience": "365 days a year, year in and year out for the last decade, we have been reading stories of Nazi bestiality, stories of mass murder of men, women and children, stories of imprisonment and torture and starvation of millions of innocent people. . . . Reason, and even self-interest, the dictates of our own hearts and the teachings of our Christian religion demand that we Canadians signify in

---

10. Ibid.
11. Keshen, *Saints, Sinners and Soldiers*, 194.

no uncertain terms our determination to accept refugees and modify the restriction of our immigration law."[12]

While acknowledging the energy and devotion of the CNCR as a whole and of Cairine Wilson in particular, the cause attracted few supporters and failed to convince the government to adopt a more humane policy. Only one hundred Jewish orphans were finally granted admission into Canada, and because of the stringent regulations imposed, only two of them were actually received. In the 1933–1945 period of Nazi rule in Germany, Canada admitted fewer than five thousand Jewish refugees, "one of the worst records of any democracies."[13] It was this persistent explicit advocacy for Jewish refugees that marks Wilson's most distinctive Christian witness, fearlessly speaking out for justice and compassion even if most of her fellow Christians and Canadians would not accompany her. The *Ottawa Journal* claimed that Wilson was "the mother of lost causes." Regardless of political considerations and prospects of success, Cairine Wilson clearly wished to align herself with God's causes.

From a deep reservoir of compassion for the most vulnerable, and an incredible dedication of energy and influence in their service, Cairine Wilson continued to extend her commitments. In 1940 Canada had accepted seven thousand individuals of German and Italian descent, many of whom had fled to Britain for safely from the Nazis but ended up being lumped together with individuals feared to be sympathetic to the fascist cause. They were held in Canadian prison camps under terrible conditions. In January 1941 the Central Committee for Interned Refugees was formed, bringing together representatives of the CNCR and the United Jewish Refugee and War Relief Agencies. Cairine agreed to serve as its chair. Until the Canadian government relented and reclassified civilian interns as refugees, Cairine dedicated precious time to visit the camps and write letters to government officials, pleading for their humane treatment and seeking sponsors for their possible release.

When a mass rally was called in Toronto on January 10, 1946, to protest the planned deportation of Japanese Canadians to Japan, Cairine Wilson was one of the main speakers. Again, when the senate reactivated its Standing Committee on Immigration and Labour in 1946, Wilson was a leading member and eventually its chairperson, the second time she was named to chair a senate standing committee. An initial report by the committee under Wilson moved the government to open up immigration, both

---

12. Cairine Reay Wilson Collection, *H-2301*, 176.
13. Canadian Council for Refugees, "Brief History."

in numbers and categories accepted, with explicit mention of European displaced persons.

By late 1948, the Canadian National Committee for Refugees came to an end. Its reputation and influence had grown, but as a volunteer organization dependent upon freewill contributions, its finances had remained precarious and ultimately unsustainable. Cairine Wilson could look back not so much as a success but as a witness made and seeds sown. Between 1946 and 1962, Canada admitted nearly a quarter of a million refugees.

Cairine Wilson continued to work in the senate in support of progressive social legislation and to serve the nation in a variety of areas. She was asked by Prime Minister Louis St. Laurent to share her expertise in refugee matters as a Canadian delegate to the fourth General Assembly of the United Nations in the autumn of 1949, the first woman in Canada to be so appointed.

While Wilson did not receive much success in her humanitarian advocacy initiatives, she was not without acknowledgement. She received honorary degrees from Acadia (1941), Queen's (the first woman so honoured, 1943) and Gallaudet (1960), and was acknowledged within her lifetime by Trafalgar School for Girls in Montreal as its most distinguished graduate. When in 1950 the American Mothers Committee of New York sought to acknowledge women who promoted world peace, the National Council of Women named Cairine Wilson as the Canadian representative. In the same year, she was appointed Chevalier de la Légion d'honneur by the government of France for her services to France (and French refugees) during the war. During the illness of the senate's speaker in 1955, she was asked to assume his chair—an honour repeated several times thereafter.

After the death of her ever-supportive Norman on July 14, 1956, and following some years of declining health, Cairine Wilson died on March 3, 1962. She was a life-long member of the Presbyterian Church in Canada, committed in worship with and support of congregations in each of the communities in which she lived: Crescent Street Church in Montreal, the Rockland Church, St. Andrew's in Ottawa, and the Greenock Church of St. Andrew's-by-the-Sea, New Brunswick. While Wilson did not receive much support for initiatives close to her heart from the Presbyterian community in Canada, she accepted its failings without giving up on God's use of it, or her. She left bequests to both the Presbyterian Church in Canada and the Presbyterian College Montreal, in addition to several other organizations with which she had been involved.

There are many facets to the life of Cairine Wilson: a daughter of privilege; a wife and mother of eight; a woman who encouraged other women to become active in shaping their nation through politics; a serving senator for thirty-two years; an advocate for global peace through collective security; and a relentless champion of refugees and vulnerable minorities. But, through every facet and phase of her life, there ran strong Christian faith. Raised up by God through the Presbyterian Church in Canada, she honoured the church most fully by reminding the church of a key dimension of its calling, the summons to work beyond the church and to welcome God's realm of peace and justice for all humanity.

In November 1954, Cairine Wilson addressed the venerable Women's Missionary Society of St. Andrew's Church Ottawa. On small typewritten pages, she left the following notes:

> Three types of Christian
>
> 1st Christian who stands aside to let somebody else assume responsibility.
>
> 2nd Christian who is willing to undertake the work if it does not place too great demands upon her time and money...
>
> 3rd type Christian, who really works ... Militant Christians, seek out places where they may serve, may give freely of themselves, their resources and their time....[14]

Cairine Wilson was definitely a "3rd-type Christian," and that of the first order!

A Talk Recorded at Canadian Broadcasting Corporation, Toronto, April 29, 1943

"Canada's Population Problem"[15]

We have been listening to the story of Canada's development and have learned something of the debt we owe to those who came to our country seeking refuge from oppression and poverty in their native lands. These pioneers showed courage in undertaking hazardous journeys by sea and land and in forsaking friends and familiar surroundings to win freedom to exercise their religion and their political opinions for themselves and their children.

Today, we are living through a more critical time than at any previous period in the world's history, and we have the opportunity to show individual and national greatness or alternatively the weakness of Pontius

---

14. Cairine Reay Wilson Collection, *H-2301*, 159.
15. Cairine Reay Wilson Fonds, *H-2301*, 982–84.

Pilate, who by the futile washing of hands, sought to absolve himself from responsibility.

Our imagination refuses to grasp the full extent of the horror although we read and hear daily of brutalities far more calculated and wide spread than the persecutions of Nero or excesses of Ivan the Terrible.

In the past, great refugee movements have often been the beginning of new developments in the countries to which they came. When the Spanish Jews were driven to Holland in 1492, they laid many of the foundations for the Dutch colonial empire; when the French Huguenots were forced to leave France after the revocation of the Edict of Nantes, they brought with them to England and to many of England's American colonies, many of the fine arts of France in which they were highly trained and efficient. The Flemings went to England in the 18th century and through them the woollen industry was established in which Great Britain has ever since maintained her lead. When the Pilgrim Fathers were forced by religious persecutions to seek a new life in the wilds of America, and landed on Plymouth Rock in 1620, they left their mark on the political and culture development of the entire continent. When the United Empire Loyalists found themselves deprived of their rights at the close of the War of the American Revolution, they were welcomed to Canada and laid new foundations for the whole Dominion. What has happened before may happen again; those whom Europe is rejecting will help to build a new and more prosperous Canada, and to make more solid the broad basis of the justice and freedom of the British Commonwealth of Nations.

Recently, an appeal was made in Great Britain by the Archbishops of Canterbury, York and Wales, the Moderator of the Free Church Council and by Cardinal Minsley from which I quote a few lines:

"That the sufferings of these millions of Jews and their condemnation, failing immediate rescue, to a cruel and certain death, constitute an appeal to humanity which it is impossible to resist. They believe that it is the duty of civilised nations, whether neutral or allied, to exert themselves to the utmost possible extent to provide a sanctuary for these victims."

Our own and our country's honour are at stake for he who watches murder without making any kind of attempt to save the victims cannot avoid sharing to some degree the guilt involved.

Canada has a very sparse population, in fact, only one country in the world has a lower ratio of inhabitants to the square mile than our Dominion, and practically all who have studied the problem agree that every province would benefit by an increased population. We boast much of our natural resources, but these are of little avail without the human hands and brains by which they may be developed.

At this time, we have the chance not only to secure most desirable new citizens but the privilege of saving many of those who stood as our first defence against the onslaught of Nazism and Fascism from a horrible fate. In the Atlantic Charter we proclaimed lofty sentiments and endorse Roosevelt's principals [sic] of the four freedoms but these cannot be reserved for ourselves alone. We live on this happy Continent relatively safe from the horrors of war but surely we have a duty to those less fortunate, for did not the Master, whom we profess to serve, say, "For unto whomsoever much is given, of him shall be much required."[16]

Commentary on "Canada's Population Problem"

The year is 1943. The words sound measured and rational. It would be easy to underestimate their strong and even radical character. It is quite a remarkable speech. The nation's first woman senator proceeds not in compliance as a token presence but by personal conviction. An individual of considerable wealth and connection chooses to stand publicly with the struggling and the stranger. In the depths of war with all resources mobilized for combat, here is a plea for the care of refugees. In a culture permeated with anti-Semitism, clear support for the Jewish people is articulated. A Christian, who knew first-hand the pastoral and familial dimensions of a nation at war, calls the church to be true to the larger frameworks and responsibilities of its witness.

The cries of the refugee resonated deep within Cairine Wilson. She had been raised in a home known as Kildonan Hall, a large house at the corner of Montreal's Sherbrooke and Redpath Streets. Kildonan had been built by her great uncle, Joseph Mackay. At the time of his death in 1881, Joseph was one of the nation's financial elite but at the age of twenty-one he had immigrated to Canada in 1832 out of economic necessity. The Mackays had been crofters along the "Strath of Kildonan" in the Scottish Highlands, and among the fifteen thousand tenant farmers ruthlessly cleared from the land by the Duchess of Sutherland in order that she might more profitably raise sheep. Joseph, then a small boy, never forgot the day his father, an elder of the kirk, became a refugee. The wholesale dry goods business that Joseph owned on rue St. Paul and later McGill Street prospered. When he died, he left his estate to his sister's three sons, with Robert taking over the business and house, where he and his wife Jane welcomed their seventh child to whom they gave the highland name of Cairine. Growing up in Kildonan Hall, Montreal, she must have learned from her earliest years the sense of

---

16. Luke 12:48 KJV.

injustice and loss that a refugee would suffer before being welcomed to a new and free land.

Of equally profound influence in the life of Cairine Wilson was her Christian faith. She was raised in the Presbyterian Church in Canada, with worship centred upon the reading and preaching of the Word of God. Over her many years of participating in public worship and private devotions, she would have heard not only of the experience of God's people with oppression and in exile but also God's repeated call for God's people to care for the stranger and the refugee. With the arrival of the first refugees from Czechoslovakia in 1938, both family history and scriptural exhortation evoked a deep personal conviction and response in Cairine.

Refugees were not a concern of the Canadian people. They had suffered greatly through the Great Depression and anxiety arising from unemployment and eviction lingered long in the common psyche. Out of fear that newcomers would deprive Canadians of work, the nation resisted immigration of any sort, including and now especially, penniless refugees who spoke different tongues and worshipped different gods. In her broadcast Senator Wilson addresses this fear directly and clearly. She appeals to history and even self-interest. She shows how refugees have grown economies and wealth in other eras of history when welcomed by other lands. She counters emotions of scarcity by conjuring up images of abundance in the vastness of Canada and its resources.

Wilson is speaking in the midst of a long and demanding war. In the previous year, at Dieppe alone, 3,623 soldiers, mostly Canadian, were slaughtered in less than ten hours. The energies of Canadians were focused upon prayers for Canadian troops, the production of armaments, and "victory gardens." Rather discordantly, Senator Wilson is advocating that precious resources be diverted to the care of refugees. Emotions of anger and hatred against the "enemy" ran strong across the nation, but she urges Canadians to retain a sense of their humanity in the care of humanity. She suggests that the integrity of victory is at stake. Canada has arrived at a time of testing.

The United States joined the allied cause in December 1941, and, if still far distant, victory was now at least a possibility. Just a month before this broadcast, in March 1943, the government of Canada had released the framework for a post-war welfare society. In the senate, Wilson had pleaded with her co-legislators that such a framework would recognize the needs of women, and include initiatives such as family allowances; universal health care insurance; and the allocation of resources to address issues ranging from mental illness and venereal diseases to infant mortality. Now Cairine

Wilson addresses the nation and pleads that Canada needs to be dedicated to caring for others as well as its own.

Wilson names anti-Semitism, and she denounces it. In the months just before the outbreak of war, she had spoken to the Ladies Aid of Knox Church Ottawa (March 3, 1939), and using the narratives of the Christian Scripture had criticized Canada's restrictive immigration policies: "Over 1900 years ago two Jews and their Jewish baby fled to a neighbouring country because the king of the country they belonged to was killing all Jewish babies. Egypt had no passport system: Egypt did not say that no refugee Jews could be admitted unless they were kept by private charity and unless they did no work, paid or unpaid. If that had been Egypt's policy—and perhaps Egypt had some unemployed too—there might never have been a Christian religion."[17]

Now she warns that as Pontius Pilate was complicit in the death of a Jew named Jesus, Canadians will be complicit in the death of Jewish men, women and children if they wash their hands of them. She asks that Canadians consider Jews as fellow human beings in need. A refusal to stand up for them, to assist and embrace them in their hour of need, she describes as participating in "murder" and sharing in the guilt.

Her words are direct and strong. What makes this broadcast so impressive is that Wilson has been making this same plea since 1938, and has encountered apathy at best and stubborn resistance at worst (and more often) at every level of Canadian society. For five years Wilson had been pleading for Canada to take seriously the suffering of the European refugees, and especially the Jewish refugees, and in this broadcast, she passionately and prophetically perseveres. Indeed, just a few months after this address, Wilson, and the Canadian National Committee for Refugees that she chaired, would launch a nation-wide petition urging the government of Canada to accept more refugees, and particularly the victims of Nazi persecution.

Wilson concludes her broadcast with words from the New Testament. They are not words of blessing, perhaps because Wilson felt Canadians were already greatly blessed, but words of accountability. She shares them as a sincere Christian: "I feel that there is no more stabilizing influence in my life, nothing that gives it a deeper and sweeter significance than religion. I'm afraid my faith is very simple but it is sure. It has always been a part of me."[18]

She shares a passage from the Christian Scriptures with her fellow Canadians, revealing her own motivations and inviting a professedly Christian

---

17. Cairine Reay Wilson Collection, *H-2301, 672*.
18. Knowles, *First Person*, 164.

nation to join her in honouring the way of Jesus Christ. Cairine Wilson was called not to success but to faithfulness, and faithful she was.

On Holocaust Remembrance Day 2014, a tribute to Cairine Wilson by Valerie Knowles was printed in the *Ottawa Citizen*. In a subsequent letter to the editor, Harvey Goldberg writes:

> Before and during the Second World War, Wilson was one of the very few Canadians who spoke out for the Jews of Europe. Wilson helped found the Canadian National Committee on Refugees in 1938, one of the few non-Jewish organisations that worked for refuge and rescue. The Committee, under Wilson's leadership, worked tirelessly on refugee issues throughout the war, with very limited success. Canada had the worst record of all the Allies in accepting Jewish refugees. After the war, until her death in 1962, Wilson continued to advocate for immigration reform and the resettlement of refugees. In the 1930s, genteel anti-Semitism among the Canadian establishment was considered by most as the norm. Wilson, however, fought against the tide and her class to speak for those who had no voice. We could use more senators like her.[19]

The Author

The Reverend Andrew Johnston is a minister currently serving the congregation of St. Andrew's Church, Kingston, Ontario, after ministries with Briarwood Church, Beaconsfield, Quebec and St. Andrew's Church, Ottawa, Ontario. He has studied at the universities of Toronto, Edinburgh and McGill. The Presbyterian College, Montreal awarded him an MDiv in 1986 and a DD in 2007. His father, the Reverend John A. Johnston, PhD, DD was also a graduate of Presbyterian College (1954) and for many years was editor of *Presbyterian History*. Andrew's mother, Dr. Heather Johnston, was president of the Canadian Council of Churches in 1979.

Bibliography

Blais, Flora M. "Cairine Reay Mackay Wilson: Canada's First Woman Senator." In *Called to Witness: Profiles of Canadian Presbyterians*, edited by W. Standford Reid, 1:162–75. Toronto: Presbyterian Publications, 1975.

Cairine Reay Wilson Collection. *H-2301*. Library and Archives Canada.

19. Goldberg, *Ottawa Citizen*.

Canadian Broadcasting Corporation. "Hate at the Top." In *Canada: A People's History*. http://www.cbc.ca/history/EPISCONTENTSE1EP13CH4PA2LE.html.

Canadian Council for Refugees. "Brief History of Canada's Response to Refugees." 2009. http://ccrweb.ca/en/brief-history-canadas-responses-refugees.

Dempsey, Karen. "Remembering Our First Woman Senator." In *National Council of Women of Canada Newsletter* 9, no. 1, Spring 2010.

Goldberg, Harvey. Letter to the editor. *Ottawa Citizen*, March 30, 2014.

Keshen, Jeff. *Saints, Sinner, and Soldiers: Canada's Second World War*. Vancouver: University of British Columbia Press, 2004.

Kinsella, Noel A. Speaking notes on the occasion of the unveiling of a portrait of Senator Cairine Wilson, October 16, 2013. http://sen.parl.gc.ca/nkinsella/PDF/Speeches/wilsonportraitunveiling-e.pdf.

Knowles, Valerie. *First Person: A Biography of Cairine Wilson, Canada's First Woman Senator*. Toronto: Dundurn, 1998.

Langmuir, Kay. "Queen's Chronicles Honorary Degree Recipients." In *Queen's Gazette*, April 24, 2006. http://www.queensu.ca/registrar/currentstudents/convocation/hondegrees/Queens_Honorary_Degree_History.pdf.

Munroe, Susan. *The Person's Case: A Milestone in the History of Canadian Women*. http://canadaonline.about.com/cs/women/a/personscase.htm.

PARLINFO of the Parliament of Canada. Wilson, the Hon. Cairine Reay. http://www.parl.gc.ca/parlinfo/Files/Parliamentarian.aspx?Item=176923a1-4b32-4b92-8bee-1d447764ec79&Language=E&Section=ALL.

The Presbyterian Record 55, no. 4. Toronto, April 1930.

CHAPTER 10

The College and Chaplaincy
John Weir Foote

By Thomas J. (Tom) Hamilton

Lieutenant Colonel The Reverend John W. Foote, VC, CD, DD, (1904–1988). The portrait was most likely taken in conjunction with the awarding of Foote's VC. The photo shows the crown on the shoulder of his uniform signifying his rank of major. His military ribbons include: Victoria Cross, 1939–45 Star, Canadian Volunteer Service Medal (including the Dieppe Bar, a clasp worn to indicate participation in the Dieppe Raid), Defence Medal, War Medal 1939–45, and the Order of St. Lazarus. In September 1945, Foote was posted to CFB Borden as senior Protestant chaplain and promoted to major, a rank he held until 1948 when he was released to pursue a career in provincial politics. Photo credit Canadian Department of National Defence.

THE COLLEGE AND CHAPLAINCY

FEW WORDS WERE SPOKEN as the Canadian soldiers sat in their landing crafts. From New Haven on England's south coast, they had confidently climbed the gangway to their infantry landing ship, Glengyle. Their morale was high, thanks to years of training in Canada and England and the conviction that Europe desperately needed to be liberated from Hitler's Nazi regime.[1] But now, hours later, as they approached the French coast, their thoughts were more subdued. Their eager excitement was tempered with a growing and gnawing apprehension: "What would the first taste of battle be like?" As if he could read their thoughts, the one military member who carried no gun, opened a small Bible and interjected these words into the thoughts of the comrades who surrounded him: "Finally, my brethren, be strong in the Lord, and in the power of his might . . . Put on the whole armour of God, that ye may be able to stand."[2] The padre[3] continued to read the remaining seven verses of Ephesians, Chapter 6 and then closed his New Testament.[4]

The padre was a long way from home. He was a long way from the carefree days at Presbyterian College, in Montreal. But the past eleven years with its seminary training and pastoral experience had helped prepare him for this moment. It was 4:45 a.m., August 19, 1942, and the assault on Dieppe, France, was about to begin. That day, few of the nearly five-thousand-strong Canadian attack force would be able to stand physically against the enemy's onslaught of bullets and shrapnel. Whereas for Honorary Captain John Weir Foote, "being able to stand" involved faithfully living out his calling as a military chaplain, and fulfilling his duty as an agent of morale despite the worst of circumstances. Foote consistently pursued this calling throughout his life as he repeatedly sought to raise the morale of those around him in the midst of death and life.

Throughout history, numerous victorious military leaders described "morale" as one of the key factors that separates victory from defeat."[5]

---

1. Brown, *Semper Paratus*, 192–93.

2. *Hamilton Spectator*, "Those Who Gave"; "Promised to Go Back"; "To Honour Dead."

3. The word "chaplain" in its Latin form first appeared to identify clerics who carried religious relics into battle, but the word "padre" was first coined by British units in India and quickly spread throughout the British Army. In contrast to "parson," "padre" was reserved for military chaplains who had earned the respect of soldiers. See Bergen, Introduction, 6; and Crerar, *Padres in No Man's Land*, 12, 91.

4. Eph 6:10–11 KJV.

5. For a comprehensive analysis of morale as it relates to the military and to chaplains, see Hamilton, "Soldiers', Sailors' and Airmen's Greatest Ally: Morale Defined" ch. 1 in "Padres under Fire," 17.

Morale also proved to be a key element in combatting "battle exhaustion."[6] Other descriptions of morale included such phrases as "esprit de corps, strength of soul, and more recently spiritual resiliency."[7] Over the centuries, military chaplains played vital roles in sustaining and raising the morale of the soldiers in wartime. This practice continued in the Second World War as military chaplains ministered to Canadian military personnel. In *Instructions for the Canadian Chaplain Service*—required reading for all military chaplains in the Second World War—Brigadier G. A. Wells, principal chaplain (Protestant), and Brigadier C. L. Nelligan, principal chaplain (Roman Catholic), wrote that the chaplain's role was to "seek the spiritual and moral welfare of the men . . . by maintaining a high morale among them." In fact, Wells and Nelligan noted further that: "The personal work of the Chaplain among officers and men may be of the greatest possible value . . . to the unit to which he is posted: (a) by creating and fostering a strong esprit de corps, and (b) by maintaining a high morale among the men."[8]

Describing the potential value of a chaplain's role in raising morale is one thing; however, providing examples of their effectiveness is another. In his work as a padre, Foote served as an example of a chaplain who personified and who raised the morale of others. Whether in death or life, Foote consistently endeavoured in his "personal work as a chaplain" to "foster a strong esprit de corps," and to "maintain a high morale among the men."[9] Foote's method of accomplishing this was twofold: first, his actions were motivated by consistent and deeply held religious convictions, and second, his actions were primarily directed in a practical way to meeting the needs of those he felt "called to serve."[10] Foote's ability to sustain and raise the morale of the soldiers he served was particularly evident during the raid at Dieppe and his subsequent captivity as a German prisoner of war (POW).

As an historical figure, John Weir Foote, VC—"Jack" to his friends[11]—remains enigmatic, elusive, and overlooked. Inside the Canadian Chaplain School at Canadian Forces Base Borden is a prominent portrait of Foote with

---

6. This was the term used in the Second World War. Mental fatigue in the First World War was called "Shell Shock," and in recent decades referred to as "Post-Traumatic Stress Disorder" (PTSD), and "Operational Stress Injury." See Hamilton, "Padres under Fire," 276; and Copp, *Battle Exhaustion*, 132.

7. Pargament. "Building Spiritual Fitness in the Army," 58–64. Cacioppo, "Social Resilience," 43–51.

8. Hamilton, "Padres under Fire," 33.

9. Ibid.

10. "Called to Serve," this current motto of the present-day Canadian Armed Forces, Chaplain Branch, finds it origins in the ministry and service of individuals like Foote.

11. Atkinson, "Military Honours," *Guide*, 1.

the citation for his Victoria Cross. Missing, though, are details describing his ministry and life. This is indicative of Foote's renown: a one-time heroic action under fire that was honoured with the Commonwealth's highest military medal, the Victoria Cross. But some prominent military historians have overlooked his prestigious recognition and ignored him in their historical writings on the Dieppe Raid. In their recent ground-breaking texts on the battle, David O'Keefe, and Tim Cook failed to mention Foote, although they recognize Lt. Col. Merritt, Canada's other VC recipient at Dieppe.[12] There is a definite need for a comprehensive biography of Foote because the VC did not define him. It was only a small part of a unique and quite remarkable life: graduate of the Presbyterian College, noteworthy Presbyterian minister, public servant, twice-elected member of the Ontario provincial legislature, patron of the arts, humanitarian, musician, and one of sixteen Canadians awarded the Victoria Cross during the Second World War.[13]

Part of the issue relates directly to a lack of historical sources and Foote himself. Foote intentionally left no biography, no memoirs. Trying to find sermons or personal papers proved unrewarding. Much of this was Foote's own choice. For instance, Foote was reluctant to speak about his achievements at Dieppe, and while proud of serving "his boys," the VC left him uncomfortable because he felt that so many others had sacrificed more than he had. When he was awarded the VC in 1946 he felt embarrassed and was reluctant to speak about it. For instance, in February 1946, when Foote was asked to speak at St. Giles Presbyterian Church in Ottawa, even though it was in front of a congregation—the type of audience Foote had addressed for years—he shuffled on his feet, repeatedly mopped his brow and admitted that he was not "very glib" in summing up the things he had done in war. He was, however, pleased to comment on his mission as a POW. In that meeting it fell to others to describe the heroism of the padre.[14] For the rest of his life,

---

12. In his official history of the Canadian Army during the Second World War, Stacey includes a brief summary of Foote's actions in his chapter on the Dieppe Raid. O'Keefe and Cook, however, fail to even refer to Foote, even though they describe Merritt, the other VC at Dieppe. Stacey, *Six Years of War*, 377; O'Keefe, *One Day in August*, 271–72, 356–57, 374; Cook, *Necessary War*, 269.

13. Despite his service and work in the Presbyterian Church, the Canadian military, and the Ontario government, there are no primary or secondary sources relating to Foote in denominational, government or local archives. Notwithstanding the excellent assistance of the archivist and deputy archivist at the Presbyterian Church in Canada Archives, there were only a few general references to Foote in the "General Assembly's Acts and Proceedings," and in the *Presbyterian Record*. Inquiries at the library and archives of Presbyterian College Montreal revealed nothing. There were also no records at the Cobourg Archives, while the Port Hope Archives (PHA) holds a few local newspaper articles. Foote's personal papers remain elusive.

14. Cragg, "Chaplain Who Won VC," *Globe*.

he was not interviewed by historians, and was even reluctant to speak with journalists. This reluctance may have been from genuine humility or Foote's own means of dealing with a terrifying event that may have forced him to take actions that contradicted his own ethical and moral understanding of a chaplain's proper actions in battle.[15]

On the eve of the Second World War, an eclectic group of citizens gathered at the Union Cemetery in Port Hope, Ontario.[16] With the Port Hope Citizens' Band leading the procession, Orangemen, Odd Fellows, and private citizens had marched from the Independent Order of Odd Fellows headquarters on Walton Street to the cemetery. They assembled for the sixty-first annual Decoration Day service to decorate the graves of deceased members with small silk flags and flowers. Leading the service was Rev. John W. Foote. His theme of "from death unto life" permeated the service. In his opening remarks he complimented members of the lodges not only for their "graciousness in remembering the *deceased* brethren, but for their consideration to the *living*."[17] In the local paper, Foote's theme continued in his sermon, and was summarized:

> In speaking of our attitude towards death, Mr. Foote urged his hearers to build up during days of health and happiness, a philosophy which would enable them to meet bereavement with peace of mind and spirit. Taking his text from St. John's Gospel, Chapter 14 verse 19, he showed that belief in Christ was a guarantee of immortality, "Because I live ye shall live also."
>
> He pointed out that Christ seldom spoke of death, rather, he spoke of "being with the Father," that he, speaking of his own death said to his followeres [sic] "if ye loved me ye would rejoice because I go to the Father."
>
> The churches and the lodges stress both the importance of this implicit belief in God and the quality of life that is pleasing to God. For people who believe and who live out their beliefs there is no death. "He that believeth in me hath already passed from death to life," he quoted, urging his audience to live as members of a church and a lodge holding such comforting and inspiring faith.[18]

15. See Appendix A for a brief biography of Foote's life.

16. Not to be confused with the similarly named cemetery in Cobourg where Foote and his wife Edith (née Sheridan) would be buried in 1988.

17. Italics are mine.

18. *Port Hope Weekly Guide*, "Large Crowd."

Foote's sermon reflected the orthodox biblical Christology of his Reformed theology as a Presbyterian.[19] It was also what one might expect in the sermon presented at this type of memorial service. But it also identified Foote's own personal understanding of faith and his conviction that his faith should genuinely benefit the lives of others. Foote believed that Christ was the soul's "guarantee of immortality" and that Christian faith would therefore enable all "to meet bereavement with peace of mind and spirit." Armed with this spiritual conviction, Foote had a philosophical basis that propelled him to raise the morale of soldiers in their own experiences "from death to life."

Shortly after the Canadian Parliament approved the declaration of war against Germany on September 8, 1939, Foote applied to the Committee on Chaplaincy Service of the Presbyterian Church in Canada.[20] Like all Canadian clergy who became padres during the Second World War,[21] Foote needed the recommendation of his denomination's chaplaincy committee who then forwarded his name to Brigadier George Anderson Wells, principal chaplain (P) for approval as a military chaplain in the Canadian Chaplain Service (Protestant).[22] On November 8, 1939, the Presbyterian Committee on Chaplaincy Service forwarded twelve names including Foote to Wells.[23] Denominational endorsement did not ensure a commission as a chaplain. Foote's was one of only five names that Wells approved.[24] On December

19. Moir, *Enduring Witness*, 235-36. Wright, "Canadian Protestant," 152-54.

20. The committee responsible for chaplaincy in the Presbyterian Church in Canada initially referred to itself as the "Special Committee re: Chaplain Service" and the "Chaplaincy Service Committee." By May 14, 1940, the minutes call the committee the "Committee on Chaplaincy Service." This is the same name that appears in the denomination's "Acts and Proceedings" throughout the war. Chaplaincy Service Committee Minutes (CSCM), Board of Administration, the Presbyterian Church in Canada Archives.

21. To avoid the controversies and difficulties in the First World War when there was only one Chaplain Corps (see Crerar, *Padres*, 36-62), in the Second World War, Canadian military chaplains were divided into two distinct and separate chaplain branches—the Canadian Chaplain Service (Protestant) and the Canadian Chaplain Service (Roman Catholic). Hamilton, "Padres under Fire," 38-79.

22. The four largest Protestant denominations in Canada—the Church of England in Canada (Anglicans), the United Church in Canada, The Presbyterian Church in Canada, and Canadian Baptists—established chaplaincy committees to receive and vet applications before submitting names to Wells in Ottawa. All Roman Catholic "secular" clergy in diocesan ministry and those in religious orders were required to receive the official sanction of their ecclesiastical authority before their names were sent to Brigadier C. L. Nelligan, Principal Chaplain (RC) for his approval as military chaplains.

23. "8 November 1939," Minutes: CSCM, PCA.

24. The recommendation of a denominational chaplaincy committee did not ensure approval in the CCS. Mostly, Wells tried to ensure that chaplains fairly represented

20, 1939, Foote was attested and commissioned as an honorary captain in the Canadian Army. In January 1940, Foote was attached to the chaplains' pool at military district number 2. He received basic training at CFB Borden and worked at the Exhibition Grounds in Toronto. In the spring of 1940, Foote was posted to the Royal Hamilton Light Infantry (RHLI). Before the RHLI left Hamilton, Foote displayed his commitment to the morale of the soldiers and officers. He visited hundreds of homes, ensuring that the padre had visited "the kin" of every family in the regiment.[25] He believed in the importance of such visiting should he have to write letters of condolence to families back home in Canada.

The RHLI travelled overseas with the 2nd Canadian Infantry Division in the summer of 1940,[26] and Foote trained with the regiment as their padre.[27] In England, Foote came to a greater understanding of the soldiers and their needs. In addition to accompanying them in their training, he was tasked with a unique position and suffered an unexpected and difficult crisis. Shortly after he arrived in England, Foote served as director of education for the 2nd Canadian Infantry Division. He was responsible for arranging educational courses for soldiers to help them plan for their careers in a post-war world.[28] Furthermore, in June 1941 he suffered a "serious illness," so serious that the Committee on Chaplaincy agreed to write to Mrs. Foote "conveying the sympathy of the committee and expressing hope for his early recovery." While his illness remains unknown, it must have been serious because it was very unusual for the committee to convey such a sentiment.[29]

Throughout RHLI training in England Foote employed various means to sustain the morale of the soldiers he served. In addition to providing church parades and expected religious ministrations, he tried to implement a practical devotional for the "spiritual welfare of the men."[30] Foote also tried to raise morale by intentionally living and training alongside the soldiers of the RHLI, even though it was not required as an officer and military chaplain. Such actions, however, won the admiration of the soldiers he served. Not surprisingly, when the attack on Dieppe was imminent Foote

---

the denominational numbers present in the army, but there were certainly instances when personal bias appears to have influenced his decisions. Hamilton, "Padres Under Fire," 121–25.

25. Baldwin, "Stayed Behind," *Globe*.
26. "8 January 1940; 12 December 1940," Minutes: CSCM, PCA.
27. Brown, *Semper Paratus*, 224.
28. Anon., "Story," 3.
29. "2 June 1941," Minutes: CSCM, PCA.
30. "12 December 1940," Minutes: CSCM, PCA. "Chaplaincy Service," *Presbyterian Record*, 15.

confronted Lt. Col. Robert Labatt, Commanding Officer of the RHLI and declared, "I know what's in the wind, Bob, I want to go." His commanding officer had no intention of allowing the padre to accompany the soldiers to Dieppe—especially when he would be in the first wave of attack—but surprisingly he relented and permitted his padre to go. It may have been another indication of the close relationship between the soldiers and their padre, and subsequently of Foote's ability to raise morale. After all, the padre respectfully referred to them as "his boys."[31]

In the early morning darkness of August 19, 1942, hundreds of soldiers of the RHLI boarded assault landing crafts and began the eight-mile run to the French coast. The plan, *Operation Jubilee*, called for the Essex Scottish Regiment and the RHLI to make a frontal assault on Dieppe. To the east at Puys, the Royal Regiment of Canada and the Black Watch attacked, while west of Dieppe, the South Saskatchewan Regiment landed at Pourville.[32]

At 4:45 a.m. the RHLI assault crafts were only a few hundred feet from the beach. Some thought it was strange that they could clearly see the outlines of buildings in the early morning twilight when they had been told that the buildings would be indistinguishable because of Allied bombing. They soon learned why. Suddenly the air was filled with enemy machine gun, shell, and shrapnel fire. "C," "B," and "D" companies led the initial assault. "D" company was immediately cut down and unable to advance. The other two companies were also hit hard, but some managed to scramble across the shingle beach to the sea wall and the casino. "A" company and battalion headquarters landed next.[33] Foote and Captain D. W. Clare, the medical officer (MO) were hit by enemy fire in one of the landing craft carrying the battalion headquarters. For the next eight hours they worked together to try to save the lives of their comrades.

Finding themselves on the beach in the midst of a hailstorm of enemy fire, Foote and Clare made a quick reconnaissance of the situation. Tank Landing Craft 5 had taken a direct hit, leaving her with a gaping hole amidship. Exploding ammunition ricocheted from within, while black smoke drifted from her blown engine, yet she was almost straddling the beach and provided some protection from enemy fire and so was quickly turned into a makeshift Regimental Aid Post (RAP). For hours the padre crisscrossed the beach carrying and dragging wounded soldiers to the MO at the RAP.[34] In

---

31. Whitaker and Whitaker, *Dieppe*, 232.
32. Brown et el., *Semper Paratus*, 190.
33. Ibid., 196–202.
34. Ibid., 207–9.

this act of complete unselfishness, Foote's commitment to save the lives of "his boys" must be considered the ultimate act in raising morale.

Foote's actions at Dieppe have been described somewhat placidly as "collecting the wounded . . . as he walked about."[35] But Foote was in the midst of an inferno of death and destruction. To act as an agent of morale under such circumstances required the utmost resolve: physical, mental, emotional, and spiritual. Foote's resolve was evident in six dangerous and herculean factors. First, he was subject to constant small arms, machine gun, mortar and shell fire as he repeatedly crisscrossed the beach, yet he survived. From the relative safety of Tank Landing Craft 5, even the MO suffered wounds to his head,[36] but Foote avoided becoming a casualty. Standing six feet tall and weighing more than two hundred pounds, his stature presented an unmistakable target on the shores of Dieppe. It was miraculous that he came physically unscathed through the inferno of battle. In fact, it was something that stayed with him for the rest of his life. Decades later, Foote remarked that he was still shocked that he survived Dieppe.[37] Second, the human carnage around Foote was unspeakable. Major Richard McLaren, the RHLI's intelligence officer, described the broken humanity that the padre was trying to carry to the MO at the makeshift RAP: "Padre Captain John Foote had moved calmly throughout the entire terrible morning searching out the wounded . . . the injuries were appalling: men had limbs torn off, muscles spilling out of their thighs, guts being stuffed back into stomachs, ears ripped off, eyes blinded."[38] Third, Foote dragged wounded to the makeshift RAP, and also helped with bandaging the wounded and administering morphine injections to the sick and dying. Prior to Dieppe, Foote had never administered a needle and decades after the raid, MO Clare expressed his ongoing amazement that Foote was able so calmly and effectively to learn that medical procedure and not shirk from helping the wounded despite the severity of their casualties. Fourth, Foote's actions were not accomplished in the midst of a controlled attack lasting a few minutes; his ordeal of fire lasted almost eight hours.[39] It is also estimated that Foote's actions directly saved the lives of thirty soldiers.[40] Fifth, when General Roberts gave the order to retreat, and assault craft moved in, Foote was on the forefront, loading the wounded for evacuation to England. While he

35. Ibid., 208.
36. Ibid., 207.
37. Brayley, "Modest Chaplain," *Hamilton Spectator*, 1.
38. Whitaker, *Dieppe*, 264.
39. Bishop, *Victoria Cross*, 179.
40. Ibid.

moved the wounded from the makeshift RAP, he noticed a new group of casualties. As soldiers sprinted from the sea wall across the stony beach to the water's edge, the enemy attacked the retreating Canadians. Foote dashed throughout the beach grabbing, carrying and dragging wounded soldiers to the waiting landing craft. Well aware that their window for retreat was limited, he called out "every man, take a man." Sixth, there remains significant historical evidence that Foote was required to deal quickly with a serious dilemma that forced him to take actions that contradicted his own ethical and moral understanding of a chaplain's proper actions in battle. Private W. F. Konkle claimed that he was the last wounded soldier to speak to Foote and Clare, before safely embarking from Dieppe. From his hospital bed in England, Konkle stated: "Captain Clare and Captain Foote had established a Red Cross base. Clare was fixing up the boys who had got it principally from machine gun fire, although there were mortars breaking around . . . Foote was with him and they continued to administer to the wounded. The Germans opened up on their base with machine gun fire. They stood it so long and the last I saw of them as I went down to the water was Captain Foote shooting a tommy gun at the Germans to hold them off."[41]

Konkle's claim that Foote fired a weapon was substantiated by others.[42] If Foote actually fired a gun at Dieppe it would have occurred after hours of demanding and exhausting work with Clare. Foote's quick response further underscores his resolve to protect the MO and the soldiers he was determined to serve. It may also help explain his ongoing reluctance after the war to discuss his actions at Dieppe. Finally, when Foote had the opportunity to be evacuated with the wounded he voluntarily chose to remain behind. In the later stages of the withdrawal, two soldiers grabbed him aboard one of the assault vehicles, but he slid into the water and went ashore. According to Foote years later: "It seemed to me the men on the beach would need me far more in captivity than those going home."[43] Others reported at the time that Foote had said, "The men in the prisoner of war camp will need me more than the men returning to England."[44] It would seem irrefutable that Padre Foote stubbornly refused to be evacuated from Dieppe, so that he could stay with "his boys" even in captivity as prisoners of war. One hundred and ninety-seven RHLI died on the beach at Dieppe, and one hundred seventy-

41. Wemp, "Gallant Doctor," *Telegram*, 1.

42. Major Bell, RHLI, claimed in an interview with the *Hamilton Spectator* that "I was told by a reinforcement officer overseas that Captain Foote was last seen on the beach with a tommy gun in his hands covering a medical officer who was tending some wounded." *Hamilton Spectator*, "Padre's Gallant Deed," 1.

43. Dunkin, "The God," *Fellowship Link*, 15.

44. Fletcher, "War Hero," 1.

five more were marched into captivity as POWs.[45] Besides the actions of Foote, the tragic raid at Dieppe had numerous examples of loyalty, bravery, sacrifice, and courage under fire. One of those was Corporal Al Comfort, a medic with "D" company. Despite shrapnel wounds in both legs, shoulder, and chest, he bandaged the wounded on the beach until all of his dressings were used. Only then, were his wounds attended to and he helped evacuate the wounded. In fact, it might be argued that Corporal Al Comfort was more deserving of recognition than Foote. Despite numerous wounds, he did work similar to Foote's, and also became a POW. In the years that followed, Foote noted the exceptional bravery of others, especially those who made the ultimate sacrifice and was extremely reticent to accept praise for what he had accomplished. But Foote's selfless actions on August 19, 1942, were recognized as exceptional because of who he was and what he had accomplished. All military personnel receive training in how to defend themselves. All Canadians who attacked Dieppe carried weapons except the padre. If he picked up a gun to provide covering fire for Clare and the wounded, it was only after dodging enemy fire for hours on the beach and being unable to defend himself. Furthermore, his resolve to raise the morale of his soldiers resulted in the lives of thirty soldiers being saved. For courage and bravery under fire, Foote was awarded the VC.[46] In the decades since Dieppe, the question has been asked: how was Foote able to maintain his own sanity—his own morale—let alone the morale of others in the midst of such an inferno of death? The answer for Foote directly related to his Christian faith.

When Foote was taken into captivity, the soldiers who were evacuated back to England spoke of their padre, "the Padre who chose to stay behind."[47] With the identity of those who became POWs intentionally kept confidential, the media referred to him as Padre X.[48] A telegram was sent to Foote's wife listing him as missing in action. She was also asked to keep his identity hidden from the media. Someone who knew Padre X was Col. J. Logan-Vencta, Foote's senior chaplain who searched the landing crafts and who despaired when Foote was not found, fearing he had been killed.[49]

In captivity Foote tried to raise the morale of his fellow prisoners of war. As he had demonstrated in England, and at Dieppe, Foote's efforts were intended to be practical, spiritual, and meaningful. Foote was first

---

45. Whitaker and Whitaker, *Dieppe*, 232, 265.
46. Appendix B provides the citation for the VC for Padre Foote.
47. Baldwin, "Stayed Behind," *Globe*, 1.
48. Anon., "Story," 3.
49. Cragg, "Chaplain Who Won VC," *Globe*, 1.

incarcerated in Oflag 7B at Eichstadt, Bavaria. In January 1943, Foote "refused the easier option of staying in the officers' prisoner of war camp and volunteered to be transferred to the notorious Stalag 383 prison with the enlisted men, where for fourteen months Canadian soldiers were manacled, against the rules of war."[50] In captivity Foote believed he should be with those he could help the most. He wanted the POWs of other ranks to know that he was the padre first, and an officer second.

Foote was reluctant to discuss his heroism at Dieppe, but quite willing to discuss his mission in Nazi prison camps. In one address, "The Dieppe Raid and Thirty-Four Months in a Prison Camp," he said very little about his own role. In fact, in describing five POW camps he constantly referred to others and only mentioned himself briefly. He described services in fields and barns and had high praise for the Canadian Engineers who constructed a church out of Red Cross boxes. It was noticed that Foote used the personal pronoun "I" only once in his entire address.[51]

Foote tried to provide religious ministrations that were practical and meaningful. During one of their Christmases in captivity, Foote gathered soldiers together in a small room for worship. Despite the presence of armed guards they recited the twenty-third Psalm together. When they repeated verse 5, "thou preparest a table before me in the presence of mine enemies," there was a gasp of astonishment at the sudden understanding of those words.[52] Foote was inspired by the role of faith to raise the morale of the POWs. Some Sundays his congregation could be a thousand men or more,[53] and he led Protestant services and Mass.[54] Despite the cruelty of chains and manacles, Canadian prisoners came to worship services. Foote was amazed "to see line after line standing to sing or to read with the chains dangling from their wrists made one feel certain that religious convictions held as much vitality as in the days of the early church."[55]

Foote's mission was directly connected to raising the morale of others. Foote told a neighbour that he voluntarily became a POW "because he believed it could be of the most help upholding the morale in the German POW camps."[56] Furthermore, Victor Sparrow, president of the Toronto and

50. Montagnes, *Port Hope*, 187.
51. Cragg, "Chaplain Who Won VC," *Globe*, 1.
52. Dunkin, "The God," *Fellowship Link*, 15.
53. Steven, *In This Sign*, 72.
54. Greenfield, *Forgotten*, 149.
55. Steven, *In This Sign*, 72.
56. Dr. Don Mikel, as quoted in Atkinson, "Victoria Cross Recipient," *Guide*, 1. PHA.

Western chapter of the Dieppe Veterans and POW Association, described Foote with the words, "I loved the man, he was some kind of guy." Even though it was decades after the fact, Sparrow noted that "members of the association revere as well the chaplain's courage in the prison camps."[57] Foote's comrades appreciated his efforts to raise the morale of other POWS. In serving the needs of POWS he was described as "a tower of strength for all."[58]

In captivity, Foote also continued to envision ways of helping veterans in the post-war world. Building on his work as director of education in England, Foote worked as a teacher and chaplain. He also contemplated new means of helping veterans. It was as a POW that he first considered politics as a way of helping veterans once the war was over.[59]

Foote's final days in captivity might be considered the most difficult. Along with hundreds of other Canadian and British prisoners, Foote endured the deprivation of a thirty-seven-day forced march from their prison camp west because their Nazi captors were trying to evade the advancing Russians. During this journey, Red Cross food parcels were virtually nonexistent so Canadians had to scrounge for their own food. Foote praised Sapper Maurice Gauthier who "practically kept us from starving" because of the way he somehow managed to scavenge a pocketful of grain, a few eggs, or a chicken. Foote described how during the last seven days of their journey, fifty of them were forced to stand crowded into a single box car. Their captors gave them only one loaf of bread and they were refused water even though Canadian soldiers were dying of dysentery.[60] Foote was finally liberated by British soldiers near Bremen, Germany.[61]

At the end of the Second World War, Rev. Dr. F. Scott MacKenzie, the principal of Presbyterian College, remarked that more than one-third of the graduates from Presbyterian College had served in the armed forces and most were military chaplains. He noted further that they "have served with devotion and ability and some have won outstanding distinction."[62] Although Foote continually shied away from ever acknowledging it about himself, his distinction was more outstanding than all the others. The eight hours he dodged enemy fire to drag wounded Canadians to a makeshift regimental aid post, and the thirty-four months he spent in captivity as a prisoner of war surpassed the service of his colleagues and forever changed

57. Atkinson, "Military Honours," *Guide*, 1. PHA.
58. Fletcher, "War Hero," 1.
59. Anon., "Story," 3.
60. Brayley, "Modest Chaplain," 1.
61. *Hamilton Spectator*, "Propose Major Foote," 1.
62. MacKenzie, "Presbyterian College," *Presbyterian Record*, 235.

his life. In the decades that followed, what mattered to Foote was the experience not the recognition. Three days following his funeral, noted political cartoonist B. King paid his own tribute to Foote. Under the title "Lt.-Col. John Weir Foote, 1904–1988" was an upturned soldier's helmet. Inside was a book bearing the inscription "Holy Bible" and resting on the side of the helmet was a Victoria Cross.[63] In response, longtime friend Edith McConnell commended the simplicity of the drawing and remarked in a letter to the editor of her local paper, "The helmet, the Bible, and the medal was the story of a great man's life."[64] On the fourth anniversary of the Dieppe Raid, Foote addressed RHLI veterans and members at a cenotaph memorial service: "I think that everything we face today is a religious problem and I feel that we will make a great country with the men and women we have today if we have faith.... All men need faith so that they can fill their obligations to their fellow man."[65] Those simple and straightforward words, reflected in B. King's memorial cartoon, appropriately defined Foote—the practical humanitarian and the devout Presbyterian minister—and underscored his own understanding of morale. And it was the conviction to live out that understanding of morale that propelled him into a landing craft and caused him, moments before battle, to try to inspire the soldiers around him with the words, "Finally, my brethren, be strong in the Lord, and in the power of his might.... Put on the whole armour of God that ye may be able to stand." Those words and the selfless actions which followed were but another example of the way in which Foote's life personified morale from death to life.

Appendix A

Biography of John Weir Foote

John Weir Foote was born on May 5, 1904, to Gordon and Margaret Foote in Madoc, Ontario. His parents had three daughters, Mary, Barbara and Alice, and two sons, Donald and John. Foote's father was a successful merchant.[66] Foote was a lifelong Presbyterian. His earliest spiritual formation occurred at home and at St. Peter's Presbyterian Church in Madoc, Ontario with his family during the weekly services. Foote acquired a love of music inspired

---

63. King, "Lt.-Col. John," political cartoon, *Independent*, 4.
64. McConnell, "A Fitting Tribute," *Independent*, 12.
65. *Hamilton Spectator*, "Honour Memory," 1.
66. Anon. "Story," 3.

from his father who was the local bandmaster in Madoc.[67] In his teens Foote served as the church organist.

Foote's first job was in a brickyard. He then worked on farms in Ontario and Western Canada; in a smelter in Delora, Ontario; and taught public school in Kenora, Ontario. He also worked his way to England on a cattle boat. He returned to Canada and earned a bachelor of arts degree from the University of Western Ontario.

Foote attended Presbyterian College from 1931 to 1934. Upon graduation with his bachelor of divinity degree, he was ordained in 1934 at Bristol, Quebec, and was sent to Fort Coulogne, Quebec, as a mission appointment. In 1936 he accepted the call to St. Paul's Presbyterian Church in Port Hope, Ontario. Foote enlisted in the Canadian Chaplain Service in the fall of 1939. He returned from overseas service in 1945 and returned to England in 1946 to receive the Victoria Cross.

After the war, Foote and his wife Edith[68] lived on Lakeshore Road in Port Hope[69] where he kept a small farm.[70] He was appointed senior chaplain, Camp Borden, then staff chaplain, Headquarters in Ottawa, and finally command chaplain (Protestant), Central Command. He resigned these positions on April 30, 1948. His name was moved to the reserve officers list because he was named chairman of the Liquor Control Board of Ontario,[71] and eventually was asked to accept the Progressive Conservative nomination for Durham County.[72]

On January 22, 1947, Foote was nominated by the Presbytery of Ottawa to be considered for the post of principal of Presbyterian College.[73]

Beginning in 1948, Foote served two terms as MPP for Durham County. As an elected official he was Minister of Reform Institutions. In 1957 he suffered two heart attacks forcing him to resign his seat.[74] Between 1960 and 1969 he worked as sheriff of Northumberland County.

In the mid-1970s he wrote a popular column for the *Cobourg Star* and the *Port Hope Guide*. He and his wife spent their summers in Conception

67. Ibid.
68. Ibid.
69. Mann, "Legion Named," *Port Hope*, 1.
70. Anon., "Story," 3.
71. Foley, "Lt.-Col. Foote," *Independent*, 2.
72. Anon., "Story of Major," 3.
73. *Hamilton Spectator*, "Propose Major Foote," 1.
74. Sweanor, *Military Contributions*, 103.

Bay, Newfoundland, where Foote built a cottage. He also built a trout pond, cleared heavy overgrowth, and enjoyed operating a small motorboat.[75]

On July 3, 1982, Royal Canadian Legion Branch No. 580 was renamed Lt.-Col. John Weir Foote in an elaborate ceremony with representatives of the Korean Veterans Association, OPP, RCMP, and regional and district directors of Veterans Affairs. In addition to local and provincial politicians, veteran George Hees attended. This unique event had three VC recipients present: Foote, Lt. Col. David Currie, and Captain Charles Rutherford.[76]

Foote served as honorary lieutenant colonel to the RHLI from December 1964 to December 1973. The former James Street Armoury in Hamilton was renamed "The Lieutenant-Colonel John Weir Foote, VC, Armoury" on September 8, 1990. At the unveiling Major General Stewart, Commander, Land Forces Central Area, in his remarks stated, "I know you will recognize this Armoury for what it represents."[77] Foote's legacy as an effective agent of morale lives on.

In his retirement, John and Edith Foote attended St. Andrew's Presbyterian Church in Cobourg, Ontario. After she passed away, Foote frequently joined Dr. Fred Robertson for lunch after church. They worked closely as trustees of St. Andrew's. Dr. Robertson described Foote as "one of the most outstanding men I ever met." Another neighbour, Dr. Don Mikel, described Foote as someone whom "everyone loved . . . he never put on airs, and had a good sense of humour."[78]

An accomplished musician, Foote was patron of the Northumberland Symphony Orchestra. He was also an honorary life member of the Royal Canadian Military Institute, and an honorary member of the Rotary Club of Cobourg. He loved the outdoors and always had a bouquet of flowers in his home.[79]

Foote died at home on May 2, 1988, apparently succumbing to ongoing heart-related issues exacerbated by a sudden onset of the flu. The obituary noted his siblings as Donald Foote, Mary Martin, Alice Snelling, and Barbara Armstrong. Legion comrades held a memorial service at MacCoubrey Funeral Home, in Cobourg, Ontario, on May 5.[80] At 2:30 p.m. on Friday, May 6, the Rev. Stephen Hayes led Foote's funeral service at St.

---

75. *Cobourg Star*, "Padre X," 6.
76. Mann, "Legion Named," *Port Hope*, 1.
77. Fletcher, "War Hero," 1.
78. Atkinson, "Victoria Cross Recipient," *Guide*, 1. PHA.
79. Ibid.
80. Port Hope Archives, 3 May 1988.

Andrew's Presbyterian Church, in Cobourg, Ontario. Foote's interment in Union Cemetery immediately followed.[81]

Foote's funeral was attended by four generals, including the chaplain general. At the funeral Rev. Stephen Hayes noted: "I think John Weir Foote was a great man whose life reflected something of the greatness of God. There was in his life a certain generosity that pointed to what the Gospel is all about." Hayes also commented that Foote never stopped learning. Four years earlier he had taken Spanish classes at Trent University and just two weeks earlier he had taken cello lessons. He was buried with full military honours including a sixty-man escort from the Royal Canadian Horse Artillery, Royal Canadian Dragoons. Eight warrant officers served as pall bearers and Foote's casket was taken to the cemetery by gun carriage. At Cobourg Union Cemetery he was given three twelve-gun salutes and the playing of the Last Post.[82]

Appendix B

Citation for the Victoria Cross

His VC award was gazetted after the Second World War on February 14, 1946, the citation read:[83]

DEPARTMENT OF NATIONAL DEFENCE, OTTAWA.

14th February, 1946.

THE CANADIAN ARMY.

The KING has been graciously pleased to approve the award of the VICTORIA CROSS to:—

Honorary Captain John Weir FOOTE, Canadian Chaplain Services.

At Dieppe, on 19th August, 1942, Honorary Captain Foote, Canadian Chaplain Services, was Regimental Chaplain with the Royal Hamilton Light Infantry.
 Upon landing on the beach under heavy fire he attached himself to the Regimental Aid Post which had been set up in a slight depression on the beach, but which was only sufficient to give cover to men lying down. During the subsequent period of

81. Foley, "Lt.-Col. Foote," *Independent*, 2.
82. Atkinson, "Military Honours," *Guide*, 1. PHA.
83. *London Gazette*, 941.

approximately eight hours, while the action continued, this officer not only assisted the Regimental Medical Officer in ministering to the wounded in the Regimental Aid Post, but time and again left this shelter to inject morphine, give first-aid and carry wounded personnel from the open beach to the Regimental Aid Post. On these occasions, with utter disregard for his personal safety, Honorary Captain Foote exposed himself to an inferno of fire and saved many lives by his gallant efforts.

During the action, as the tide went out, the Regimental Aid Post was moved to the shelter of a stranded landing craft. Honorary Captain Foote continued tirelessly and courageously to carry wounded men from the exposed beach to the cover of the landing craft. He also removed wounded from inside the landing craft when ammunition had been set on fire by enemy shells. When landing craft appeared he carried wounded from the Regimental Aid Post to the landing craft through heavy fire. On several occasions this officer had the opportunity to embark but returned to the beach as his chief concern was the care and evacuation of the wounded. He refused a final opportunity to leave the shore, choosing to suffer the fate of the men he had ministered to for over three years.

Honorary Captain Foote personally saved many lives by his efforts and his example inspired all around him. Those who observed him state that the calmness of this heroic officer as he walked about, collecting the wounded on the fire-swept beach will never be forgotten.[84]

The Author

Capt. Rev. Tom Hamilton, BA, MDiv, MA, PhD, has been researching, writing and teaching about Canadian religious and military history for more than twenty-five years. His doctoral dissertation from the University of Toronto, "Padres Under Fire: A Study of the Canadian Chaplain Services (Protestant and Roman Catholic) during the Second World War" examined the role of Canada's military chaplains between 1939 and 1945. For thirteen years he taught as a sessional lecturer in the history department at the University of Prince Edward Island and has worked as a historical consultant to Veterans Affairs Canada. He also served as convenor of the Committee on History of the Presbyterian Church in Canada. Dr. Hamilton is the military chaplain to the Prince Edward Island Regiment, and since 1998 he

---

84. Perrett, *For Valour*, 271–72.

has served in team ministry with his wife, Rev. Paula Hamilton, at St. Mark's Presbyterian Church, Charlottetown, PEI and St. Columba Presbyterian Church, Marshfield, PEI. Tom and Paula have two daughters, Rachel and Susanna.

Bibliography

Anonymous. "Story of Major John W. Foote." Short essay. Bowmanville: The James, 1948.

Atkinson, Suzanne. "Military Honours for Foote." *Port Hope Evening Guide*, May 9, 1988. In "John Foote," Port Hope Archives.

———. "Victoria Cross Recipient 'Loved by All.'" *Port Hope Evening Guide*, May 3, 1988. In [Foote, John VC (07-03)] Port Hope Archives.

Baldwin, Warren. "Stayed Behind to Aid Injured after Dieppe." In *Globe and Mail*, February 12, 1946.

Bergen, Doris L. Introduction to *The Sword of the Lord: Military Chaplains from the First to the Twenty-First Century*. Notre Dame, IN: University of Notre Dame Press, 2004.

Bishop, Arthur. *Victoria Cross Heroes*. Toronto: Kay Porter, 2008.

Brayley, Jack. "Modest Chaplain Thinks Heroism Ordinary Work." *Hamilton Spectator*, February 12, 1946.

Brown, Kingsley, Sr., et al. *Semper Paratus: The History of the Royal Hamilton Light Infantry (Wentworth Regiment), 1862–1977*. Hamilton, Ontario: RHLI Regimental Association, 1977.

Cacioppo, John, et al. "Social Resilience: The Value of Social Fitness with an Application to the Military." *American Psychologist* 66 (2011) 43–51.

"Chaplaincy Service." *Presbyterian Record*, January 1941.

Chaplaincy Service Committee Minutes, Board of Administration, the Presbyterian Church in Canada Archives.

Cook, Tim. *The Necessary War: Canadians Fighting the Second World War, 1939–1945*. Toronto: Penguin, 2014.

Copp, Terry, and Bill McAndrew. *Battle Exhaustion: Soldiers and Psychiatrists in the Canadian Army, 1939–1945*. Montreal: McGill-Queen's University Press, 1990.

Cragg, Ken. "Chaplain Who Won VC Describes His Mission To Nazi Prison Camps." *Globe and Mail*, February 12, 1946.

Crerar, Duff. *Padres in No Man's Land: Canadian Chaplains and the Great War*. Montreal: McGill-Queen's University Press, 1995.

Dunkin, Gil. "The God of Al Comfort." In *The Fellowship Link* (Quarterly Publication: Seniors' Committee Fellowship of Evangelical Baptist Churches Central Region, Fall 2009), 14–16.

Fletcher, Capt. Tim. "War Hero Honoured in Hamilton Armoury Re-dedication" InfO [Information Officer], HMD [Hamilton Military District], HQ [Headquarters], [no date]. In [Foote, John VC (07-03)] Port Hope Archives.

Foley, Linda. "Lt.-Col. Foote Buried Here." *Independent* (Brighton, ON), May 11, 1988.

Greenfield, Nathan. *The Forgotten: Canadian POWs, Escapers, and Evaders in Europe, 1939–1945*. Toronto: HarperCollins, 2013.

Hamilton Spectator . "Honour Memory of Men Who Died in Dieppe Raid." August 19, 1946.

———. "Padre's Gallant Deed Was Typical of Him, So Friend Declares." September 12, 1942.

———. "Promised to Go Back after Grim Encounter on Beaches Two Years Ago—Keep Word." August 1, 1944.

———. "Propose Major Foote As Head of College." January 22, 1947.

———. "Those Who Gave Their Lives on Flaming Beaches Recalled." August 19, 1943.

———. "To Honour Dead of Dieppe Here and at Battle Scene." August 18, 1945.

———. "Wives and Mothers of Dieppe Officers at Gathering Here." April 2, 1943.

Hamilton, Thomas J. "Padres under Fire: A Study of the Canadian Chaplain Services (Protestant and Roman Catholic) during the Second World War." PhD diss., School of Graduate Studies, University of Toronto: 2003.

"Large Crowd Attended Decoration Day Services At Union Cemetery." *Port Hope Weekly Guide*, August 11, 1939.

King, B. "Lt.-Col John Weir Foote." Political cartoon. *Independent* (Brighton, ON), May 9, 1988.

MacKenzie, Rev. Dr. F. Scott. "Presbyterian College, Montreal." *Presbyterian Record*, September 1945, 235.

Mann, Kay. "Legion Named for VC Winner Foote." *Port Hope Evening Guide*, July 5, 1982.

McConnell, Edith. "A Fitting Tribute for Foote." *Independent* (Brighton, ON), June 14, 1988.

Moir, John S. *Enduring Witness: A History of the Presbyterian Church in Canada*. Toronto: Eagle, 1987.

Montagnes, Ian. *Port Hope: A History*. Port Hope, ON: Ganaraska, 2007.

O'Keefe, David. *One Day in August: The Untold Story behind Canada's Tragedy at Dieppe*. Toronto: Knopf, 2013.

"Padre X." *Cobourg Star*, November 5, 1976. In [Foote, John VC (07-03)] Port Hope Archives.

Pargament, Kenneth, and Patrick Sweeney. "Building Spiritual Fitness in the Army: An Innovative Approach to a Vital Aspect of Human Development." *American Psychologist* 66 (2011) 58–64.

Perett, Bryan. *For Valour: Victoria Cross and Medal of Honor Battles*. London: Weidenfeld & Nicolson, 2003.

Stacey, Colonel C. P. *Six Years of War: The Army in Canada, Britain, and the Pacific*. Official history of the Canadian Army in the Second World War. Vol. 1. Ottawa: Queen's Printer, 1955.

Steven, Walter. *In This Sign*. Toronto: Ryerson, 1948.

Sweanor, George, and Peter Bolton. *The Military Contributions of a Small Town*. Port Hope, ON: Sweanor/Bolton, [no date]. In [Foote, John VC (07-03)] Port Hope Archives.

Wemp, Major Bert. "Gallant Doctor and Padre Wouldn't Leave Wounded Stayed to Face Hun Fire." *Toronto Telegram*, September 4, 1942.

Whitaker, Brigadier General Denis, and Shelagh Whitaker. *Dieppe: Tragedy to Triumph*. Toronto: McGraw-Hill Ryerson, 1992.

Wright, Robert. "The Canadian Protestant Tradition, 1914–1945." In *The Canadian Protestant Experience, 1760–1990*. Burlington, ON: Welch, 1990.

CHAPTER 11

The College and the Pastor
Clifford Ritchie Bell

By Malcolm Campbell

The Very Reverend Professor C. Ritchie Bell, DD, DCL, (1905–1982), moderator in 1948 of the 74th General Assembly of the Presbyterian Church in Canada. With credit to the Presbyterian Church in Canada Archives.

"I BELIEVE IN PREACHING with all my heart, soul, mind and strength. I believe it to be the greatest of all the vocations, greater than industry, commerce, politics, literature, art and education; It is the only one that deals solely in spiritual values and ends. I so believe, because its theme is God—his righteousness, love, grace in Jesus, eternal care and immortal hope."[1]

Professor C. Ritchie Bell addressed these passionate words to graduating students and colleagues in the Presbyterian College Student Society publication entitled *Thought*, Centennial edition (1867–1967), in which the inside cover included the following words of dedication: *"To THE REVEREND DOCTOR C. RITCHIE BELL, whose high standards in the pulpit and the pastorate have been an inspiration to a whole generation of students."*

Clifford Ritchie Bell graduated bachelor of divinity from Presbyterian College in 1929. Twenty years later, he was inducted into the Lord Strathcona Chair of Pastoral Theology (1951–1966), and subsequently served as the college's acting principal from 1969–1973. During that time, Dr. Bell played a pivotal role in the life of the college and the church, and is remembered with great fondness by those who knew him. Following Dr. Bell's death, editor James Ross Dickey wrote in the December 1982 *Presbyterian Record*:

> In the middle years of this century there could be, I suppose, several claimants to the imaginary title of "Mr Presbyterian." Dr. C. Ritchie Bell would certainly have had to be among them. Successive years of graduates from the Presbyterian College will have their own memories of the man, who at age forty-two, was the youngest ever to be elected moderator of the General Assembly. He himself would put little store in that or any other distinction, beyond that of being considered a good minister and servant of the church he cared about so passionately. If anyone ever lived "abundantly," it was Ritchie Bell. He had largesse of spirit, a delight in people that was contagious. There are literally thousands who have been touched by his generosity, helped by his wise counsel, moved by the good he saw in them when they saw little, the hope he found in situations that seemed to everyone else to be hopeless.[2]

Professor Joseph McLelland, moderator of the 111th General Assembly, said at rededication of the C. Ritchie Bell Memorial Chapel at the college on November 17, 1985:

> C. Ritchie Bell shared in the first three places for worship (in this college) indeed as Strathcona Professor of Pastoral Theology.

1. Bell, "Preaching," 16.
2. Dickey, untitled, 10.

His has been the single most decisive influence in forming the spirituality of our college community and in encouraging a certain style of pastor and preacher among our graduates. As one privileged to be his colleague for a quarter century, I well know his sense of wholeness, of the central place which the chapel should hold in our life together. His love for the Church and for the college is proverbial, as is his emphasis on the pastoral dimension of ministry, an office in which regular visitation of the People, is as significant as responsible teaching.

The Reverend Dr. John Simms, a former student of Dr. Bell, and co-chair of the fundraising committee for the new Presbyterian College erected on University Street, spoke at Ritchie's memorial service in 1982: "I think the tribute that the world paid to Sir Christopher Wren at his death, is appropriate here: 'If you seek his monument,—look about you.' Sir Christopher was the remarkable seventeenth-century architect who rebuilt St Paul's Cathedral and fifty other London churches after the Great Fire of 1666. Dr. Bell similarly rebuilt our college, our congregations, and churches in Montreal, in the synod and across the land, and helped staff them with ministers inspired by his own vision, faith and academic competence."

Those who knew Dr. Bell recount his zeal for life; his unwavering love of the congregations he served and his strong personal faith. All emphasize his devotion to Presbyterian College, his talent for fundraising; his insistence on academic excellence from his students; and the powerful way he presented the Gospel in a non-judgmental and courteous manner. This is his legacy and why he remains a significant voice from the past.

Early Life and Education

Clifford Ritchie Bell was born in Sherbrooke, Quebec on August 11, 1905, to proud parents William Bell and Jean Copeland. He graduated from Sherbrooke High School in the spring of 1924, and was accepted into the Arts and Divinity program at Bishop's University, Lennoxville. At an early age, there was evidence young Ritchie knew what he wanted to do with the rest of his life. In 1924, Bishop's *The Mitre* included the following comments on freshman C. Ritchie Bell (age 19): "Hobbies: writing, studying, movies, preaching sermons. Aspirations: Doctor of Divinity and an Author."

Ritchie Bell graduated bachelor of arts from Bishop's University in 1928. Simultaneously, he studied for a bachelor of divinity from the Presbyterian College that he completed in 1929. Later, his services to the church and community were recognized by the conferring of two honorary degrees: doctor of divinity (Presbyterian College, 1949) and doctor of canon law (Bishop's University, 1969).

Marriage and Children

Ritchie Bell met his wife, Margaret Farnie Clark, the daughter of Captain George Watson Clark and Jennie McLeod of the village of Melbourne, Quebec, while he was a student minister and she was a deaconess and organist. They were married on August 23, 1930, at St. Andrew's Church, Asbestos, Quebec. Their two children, Janet and David, were born in Truro, Nova Scotia. Today, Janet and Ian Campbell live in Huntingdon, Quebec, while David and Doreen Bell reside in Fonthill, Ontario. Margaret and Ritchie were blessed with six grandchildren, Linda, Barbara, Richard, Brian, Ronald, and Lesley, seven great-grand children, Meghan, Christopher, Krysten, Shannon, Kristine, Kim, and Ryan, and one great-great grandson, Bradley.

Both of Dr. Bell's children have fond memories of their father. Janet recalls her father as being a lot of fun to be around. While he clearly loved his work, he always made time for his family, including at his suggestion, impromptu Saturday afternoon movies with the grandchildren. Janet recalls that her father was extremely accepting of people, never judging them.

Son, David, recalls his father being very friendly, honest, and taking people at their word. He was a man who thoroughly enjoyed meeting people and listening to other points of view. Though quite ready to engage in debate, he was always respectful of others. David Bell recalls with amusement an instance when he once skipped Sunday school, choosing instead to be with friends outside passing the ball. When Dr. Bell learned of this, he was not shy in giving his son feedback. That was the last time David recalls he missed Sunday school!

A Life of Service to God

The Bell's first home was in Truro, Nova Scotia. Ritchie accepted a Call, to the new St. James Presbyterian Church, shortly after graduation. It was brand new, a beautiful church, dedicated in 1930, the former Presbyterian congregations of Truro having entered Church Union in 1925.[3]

At the age of twenty-five, Ritchie Bell had his hands full: new minister, new church, in a new part of the world for him, and of course, newly married. However, Presbyterian College prepared him well and records show

---

3. St. James Kirk, *Celebrating*, 10.

that St. James grew substantially during his six-year ministry. From the start, preaching and worship were important. Church services were advertised in Saturday's paper, followed by a summary of the sermon and other highlights of the service in the Monday edition of the paper. According to daughter Janet, her father loved to sing. A photograph of the choir taken in 1930 shows fifteen ladies, ten men and the minister. Mrs Bell was also mentioned as a soloist.[4]

In July 1936, came a Call to MacVicar Presbyterian Church, Outremont, Quebec, named for the first and longest serving principal of Presbyterian College. As described in the history of the congregation: "Along with the tang of the sea, Mr. Bell brought with him the vigour of youth, and an inexhaustible capacity for work and an abiding joy in the ministry of service."[5]

Though remembered primarily as a preacher and pastor, Bell of MacVicar found time for the wider community. During World War II, he served as a chaplain in the Royal Canadian Navy. Active in the Bible Society, he served as its national vice-president and president of the Montreal District. Despite his busy life, he found time to become president of the Canadian Christian Endeavour Union, an interdenominational organization dedicated to youth. An active mason, he became district chaplain of Royal Arthur Masonic lodge, A.F. & A.M., Montreal in 1939 and worshipful master in 1949.[6] He was also much in demand as a speaker.

Dr. Bell lived through a challenging and formative period of history, faithfully preaching God's word for over fifty years to those in need of divine truth in searching for answers to the problems they faced. His first calling to Truro was born out of a strong desire to preserve Presbyterian heritage and church traditions, following the disruptive events of Church Union in 1925. It was also a time when society was still recovering from the tragic memories of World War I. The year of his ordination was 1929, the beginning of the Great Depression that swept across the land causing business closures, high unemployment and personal misery. As at Truro, Bell remained a communicator of God's Word. World War II began while he was preaching at MacVicar Memorial and humankind was once again challenged by a lengthy period of human loss and suffering. One can only imagine the impact that the times had on CRB (as his friends and colleagues called him) and how it influenced his faith and preaching.

---

4. Ibid., 26.
5. Sixtieth Anniversary, *Sixty Years*, 16.
6. Johnston, "C. Ritchie Bell," 3.

And communicating was exactly what he loved to do: his weekly Sunday morning radio broadcasts entitled *Make Life Worthwhile*, distributed later as handouts; his typed morning and evening sermons made available to those who were absent; and the numerous poems and prayers he composed and shared with his parishioners, a practice he continued with his students.

All his life, "Mr. Presbyterian" never neglected the courts of the church. In 1944, he was elected moderator of the Montreal Presbytery, a position he held for two terms, later becoming its hardworking and all-knowing clerk. On September 30, 1947, he was named moderator of the Synod of Montreal and Ottawa and the following year, moderator of the General Assembly. To be moderator in 1948 was an exciting time. That summer, The Right Reverend C. Ritchie Bell was a delegate to both the Pan Presbyterian Alliance held in Geneva, Switzerland and the very first meeting of the World Council of Churches in Amsterdam, Holland.

And, what an outstanding ministry it proved to be! John Simms, in his tribute at Richie Bell's memorial service, reminded his audience of all that had been accomplished at MacVicar during his friend's twelve years there. On the eve of the congregation's fiftieth anniversary, CRB encouraged MacVicar to pay off its mortgage and then inspired them to undertake a complete renovation of the church building, a monumental task. It was completed by January 1968 to much rejoicing. Disaster struck. On March 6, 1968, the entire building was destroyed by fire. But Ritchie Bell, in the words of Dr. Simms, was "a man of indomitable courage," and under his leadership, the decision was made to rebuild as soon as possible. Within the year, the cornerstone of the new MacVicar Memorial was laid. Eight months later, on November 23, 1969, the modern sanctuary with impressive facilities for Sunday school and youth work was opened. It still stands and today is the home of the Montreal Chinese Presbyterian Church.

MacVicar could not have been prouder of their minister. "In June of 1950, the Reverend C Ritchie Bell was appointed by the General Assembly to the chair of Pastoral Theology, and it is with great regret that this congregation received the news, even as they rejoiced with him in this new appointment. Thus was brought to an end a ministry whose influence in the life of the congregation and in the lives of its members is quite beyond calculating."[7]

---

7. Sixtieth Anniversary, *Sixty Years*, 23.

His Contributions to the College

Ritchie Bell was no stranger to his alma mater. In 1946, he had been a sessional lecturer in pastoral theology and had formed his own ideas regarding the training of ministers. One of his earliest innovations was the introduction of supervised fieldwork that began the year of his induction. His colleagues at Presbyterian College, Joseph C. McLelland, professor emeritus, and William J. Klempa, principal emeritus, recall Ritchie's passion and focus on the importance of pastoral ministry. Dr. McLelland remembers a favourite phrase used by Dr. Bell to his students: "A home-going minister makes for a church-going people." Dr. Klempa also recalls how strongly CRB believed in the importance of "going out and visiting your people in their homes, knowing them and loving them." A former student, Dr. Harry Kuntz, recalls his teacher as someone who emphasized the importance of preparing well-structured sermons, yet being ever mindful of their length. A recurring theme in many of his lectures was the importance of a minister "being a gentleman." This need of "courteousness" was repeated in a memorial address by his close friend Dr. R. Stuart Johnson, district secretary of the Bible Society.[8] Harry Kuntz also remembers Dr. Bell's skill at "putting out fires," inevitable during the course of college life. Eager to play a leadership role (so important for his students), Ritchie knew much about "conflict management resolution" as it is called today. A strong leader must be a good mediator, teacher, mentor, colleague, and also a fundraiser, a skill at which CRB clearly excelled.

As colleague and friend, Professor Keith Markell recorded in his history of Presbyterian College that the college was faced with a substantial financial shortfall during the construction of its new building on University Street. Together with Alex Duff of Montreal West, they launched a campaign to raise over a quarter of a million dollars to help build the college. "Thanks to their dynamic leadership, and the generous response of the church at large, this objective was reached and surpassed."[9]

Of one thing, everyone is agreed. Ritchie Bell loved his college and his students. His daughter Janet recalls how much he looked forward to his annual recruiting trips to the Maritimes, where he would speak to aspiring students, and encourage them to attend the college. And this love was reciprocated, as evidenced by his students who insisted that Presbyterian College set up a scholarship fund in his name to mark the fiftieth anniversary of his ordination in 1979. Rather touchingly, "Alumni have arranged

---

8. Johnston, "Obituary," 3.
9. Markell, *History*, 103.

for a 'Speaking Clock' to be sent to Dr. Ritchie Bell and the cost ($85) was advanced by the college."[10]

In 1985, following his death and in recognition of his lasting contribution to The Presbyterian College, family and friends raised funds to refurbish the college chapel, which was rededicated as the C. Ritchie Bell Memorial Chapel. Sadly, like the old MacVicar Memorial, a fire destroyed the new chapel on November 3, 1990. In the spirit of the one for whom it was named, it was rebuilt soon afterwards and remains in active use.

His Last Ministry

In 1968, while teaching at Presbyterian College, CRB began preaching at the Margaret Rodger Memorial in Lachute, north of Montreal. Upon retirement from the college, he became their full-time minister until 1979, after which he served as minister emeritus until his death in 1982. Clerk of session, Mrs. Edna Forrester-Young remembers her former minister as someone who was "caring, listened well, and always had time for you." She, too, recalls Dr. Bell's exceptional leadership at fundraising. Whether it was to provide for a new church roof or to purchase the beautiful stained-glass windows that adorn the church, Dr. Bell was never hesitant in asking others to give to worthy causes; but he was equally insistent that they be thanked for what they did.

Ritchie Bell's love for people of all ages was never more evident than while he was minister at Lachute, Quebec. Despite his age and failing health, he made countless visits to the elderly and shut-ins. His fondness for youth never left him. Edna remembers how before each Sunday morning service, Dr. Bell would hold an hour-long Bible Study for teenagers. Unlikely perhaps to attend regular services, they were only too happy to sit and talk with their minister as he expounded the Scriptures to them in a very personal way.

C. Ritchie Bell died October 9, 1982. His dear wife and unpaid assistant, Margaret—in every way, the true biblical "helpmate"—died seven years later on February 15, 1989. Let John Simms, CRB's friend and colleague have the last word: "We shall remember him as a man of great joy. I have seen him bring joy through his exuberance in the Lord Jesus Christ to students in class, to worshippers in Church, to weary businessmen, and to seamen. He could have written these words of Paul, 'Farewell; I wish you all the joy in the Lord. I will say it again: all joy be yours.'"[11]

---

10. *Presbyterian College Senate Minutes 1982*, 122. From a meeting held April 29, 1982.

11. Simms, "Memorial." Copy was provided by Janet Campbell.

The Limitations of Love

A Sermon Preached in MacVicar Memorial Presbyterian Church

Outremont, July 18, 1943

> *For we know in part, and we prophesy in part. But when that which is perfect is come, then that which is in part shall be done away.*
>
> —1 Cor 13:9–10 KJV[12]

In this chapter Paul has demonstrated the necessity of love in every sphere and emergency of life. Other measures and gifts fall short sometimes. They are none of them equal to the strain of the wear and tear of life. But love never faileth. It can cure any malady which society suffers. It can bring peace to any home and any heart. It is the one thing always needful.

Now Paul takes another turn in his argument. In my study this last week I came upon an expositor who insists that the passage beginning "we know in part" has nothing at all to do with love, and rather apologized for Paul because he introduced it here. But to my mind the limitations of our knowledge have very much to do with our lack of love. Paul was too keen a dialectician to introduce into his argument anything that did not have a direct bearing upon the subject in mind. He is merely moving out here in his discussion from the narrow sphere of individual relationships to those which encompass society.

The limitation of our knowledge is everywhere apparent. We all recognize it in our relation to the material world in which we live. Knowledge, which seemed a few years ago to be the last word in human wisdom, is no longer so. A century ago the stage coach was the most up-to-date method of travelling. Then came the steam train, and then the electric car and the gasoline propelled motor, and now it is the aeroplane. As we look back over the past and see how far we have come since the days of our great grandfathers, we understand how small was the mechanical knowledge of men in those days. And we also realize how limited probably is the knowledge which we now have compared with what the future may reveal.

Men have always known in part, and the part they have known has had in it great truth, but always beyond it there were vast stretches of truth which they did not know. Shortly before his death, Newton, the greatest

---

12. KJV used throughout.

scientist of his time, said: "I do not know what I may appear to the world; but to myself I seem to have been only like a boy playing on the seashore, and diverting myself in now and then finding a smoother pebble or a prettier shell than ordinary, while the great ocean of truth lay all undiscovered before me."

To what does this lead us? Is it not to this? Since we only know in part ought we not to be extremely careful not to condemn others who profess to see some other side of truth which has not yet been revealed to us? They burned the Maid of Orleans at the stake because she professed to see visions which were hidden from the eyes of her generation. We love her now for what she saw. Let us love these men who, in our own day, in workshop and laboratory, with microscope and test tube, are thinking the thoughts of God after Him, and are opening to us the wonders of His love.

We pass in our application of these words "we know in part" from our knowledge of the material world to our reactions with our fellow men and women. Why is not that love of which Jesus and John said so much, and about which Paul wrote here so feelingly, why does it not dominate human society? Paul has already given some of the lesser reasons. There are envy and pride and selfishness and the spirit of revenge. All these he has mentioned as foes of love. But there is a greater enemy. It is lack of knowledge. We do not love people because we know them only in part. Someone has well said that to love people all we need is to know them. Those who seem to us from the distance to be unlovely and unloveable, if we could live among them, and could know their hearts and their heartaches, we would love them. It is not something in them that makes us shun them. It is something in us, a lack of knowledge.

How often we have passed critical and harsh judgment on others and then later have learned of extenuating circumstances that have made us sorry and ashamed. It is said that a professor in one of the Scotch universities was one day before a new class discussing a subject on which there should have been agreement among the students. He asked all who assented to hold up their right hands. Every hand went up but one. Turning to that one student he sharply said, "Stand up, sir, and tell us why your hand was not raised." The student rose slowly to his feet and then was seen for the first time the empty sleeve hanging down his right side. Hurrying down from his desk the professor put his arm about the boy and said, "I am sorry, sir, I did not know." When we do not love it is usually because we do not know.

Most, if not all, of our national prejudices are due to ignorance. During World War I we thought and said many things on both sides which we would not have said had we known more of what we were speaking. I have heard of a large metropolitan church where Luther's great hymn, "A Mighty

Fortress Is our God," was banned. Sometime after the war closed a young soldier who had been wounded in battle and had been a prisoner behind the German lines was talking to the minister of that Church. He did not say much—few of them ever did. But his heart was heavy and resentful against all war. He spoke of how hard it was to mow down with machine guns the boys who were coming up to the attack singing as they came that hymn of Luther's "*Ein Feste Burg ist unser Gott.*" "Every one of them, like each of us, when we knew him, was a living, loving human soul. Every one of them also came from a home where there was a mother or a wife or a sweetheart who was praying for his safe return. All of them too detested a war which was not of their making." Men can hate when they know only in part and are looking through the lenses of prejudice and ignorance. But when they come close together, and know each other, love comes to take the place of hate.

I thank God that in this war there is so much less hate. In the letters which I receive from the men and women from this church on active service there is no hate. They do not want this awful business. They see an evil and realize that it must be wiped out. They want to get the business over with and get home here again, but there is no hate in their hearts. They realize that there are mothers in Germany who are just as concerned over their boys as you dear people to whom I speak this morning are concerned over your boys. Thank God we have at least made that much progress that we no longer believe that God is a tribal deity but that he belongs to us all.

Why are there conflicts and misunderstandings between labour and capital, between employer and employee? Is their secret not found in the words Paul used here, "We know in part"? The labourer is sometimes bitter and resentful toward the wealthy owner of the shop where he works. He sees his fine home and the apparent luxury in which he lives, and envy fills his heart. But he only knows in part. If he could know more, if he could see the weary days and sleepless nights which that employer gives to the business; if he could only know the hosts of appeals for help that come to him, and the great sums he every year gives away, if he could know the grinding care and worry which are breaking him down in middle life, his envy would change to sympathy, and perhaps to love.

In the same way the employer despises the employee. He wonders at the squalor and shiftlessness, and the sodden indifference to better things, the readiness among the poor to listen to the voices of unrest and discontent. Is it not also because he only knows in part? He does not know the meaning of poverty and of lives for whom the future holds no hope, when existence is little more than keeping at bay the wolf that is always at the door. If he knew more, if like the prophet Ezekiel, he could go and sit where they sit, he too would be moved to a sympathetic love.

When in the Old Testament story Balak called for Baalam to curse Israel he was careful to put him at a point where he could see only part of the people. Men who see only a part, as someone has well said, are very liberal with their maledictions. Much of the intolerance and prejudice and hate, the absence of love, in society and churches and nations, are due to a lack of understanding. They know only in part.

It is when we come to think of God and His plans and purposes that we are overwhelmed with the limitations of our knowledge. But is it strange that our knowledge of God is so limited? An event which occurs today as Bushnell puts it, "is the last link in a train of causes reaching downward from a past eternity, and is to be connected also with every event on a future eternity." How can a mortal placed between these two eternities without knowing either, understand what is transpiring in the divine mind?

More than this we have only just begun to be. If life is eternal, then we are in our infancy. We have no more right to expect to know everything concerning the providential government of the universe than has a baby to comprehend the minds of his parents. A little child does not know the plans and the purposes of his father. He would not understand if the father tried to tell him. He knows only in part. He is willing to take the rest in trust, for he knows instinctively that the love of the father which cares so tenderly for him embraces those purposes also.

Realizing that we can here know only in part, ought we not therefore to love and trust and wait for the divine purpose to unfold itself? We are like a man who is looking off over a city he is visiting. He sees in the distance a fragment of a tower which seems to have no place in the landscape. From where he stands it appears badly proportioned and ugly, and utterly out of relation to anything around it. But a day or so later he is in another part of the city and sees there the great cathedral of which that tower is a part. As it rises before him with its symmetry of nave and transept and arch and window he understands the beauty and perfection of it all, and realizes that that tower, which he did not understand, and could not place before, is the crowning glory of it all.

When Joseph was sold into Egypt by the envy of his brethren, when he was falsely accused and cast into prison, it would not have been strange if he had doubted the God whom he had been taught to worship. It seems as if Jehovah had forgotten him, or did not care. But a few years later he realized that it was all a part of God's wise and loving purpose for him and his race. He could see only in part. We can never see more than a little at a time of the divine plan for us. But we too may rest in confidence that all things are working together for good to them who love God.

Of death, that mystery which lies before us all, we know only in part. We know the fear of dissolution, the sorrow of those left behind, and the returning through corruption of the body to its kindred dust. But that which we see is only a part, a very small part. The Bible declares that the real death we do not see at all. Death in reality is a day of victory. It is a day of graduation when you and I will begin to live as we have never lived before! "For I reckon that the sufferings of this present time are not worthy to be compared with the glory which shall be revealed in us." "For eye hath not seen, nor ear heard, neither have entered into the heart of man, the things which God hath prepared for them who love Him."

Let us not then quarrel with our limitations of knowledge. They are a part of the youth of our existence. There will come a time when all limitations will be removed. "For now we see through a glass, darkly; but then face to face; now I know in part; but then shall I know even as also I am known." "He that loveth not knoweth not God; for God is love."

Commentary on "The Limitations of Love"

Before reviewing a sermon of Dr. Bell, it is helpful to read a few of his words:

> I believe that the origin and end of this college is to produce able preachers of the Word, for all other forms of public religious expression, particularly liturgical and sacramental religion, are dependent upon preaching for their interpretation, freshness and support.
>
> To really preach in days like these, the preacher must announce a message that is based upon the sovereign reality of the living God. It will do no good to start with the shifting human situation, which is always in flux. It is not enough to start with the crisis of democracy, in human personality, in international affairs, in the Church. We shall get nowhere with such a diagnosis of the predicament of man. Besides, we are all quite aware of the dangerous situation which we inhabit, and many of us are overwhelmed with a feeling of guilt for what we humans have done. We know the violence of our age quite well. We must use proper standard in our diagnosis, and we must go beyond mere analysis. The word of God is healing judgment. It throws the brilliant light of divine truth upon our pseudo-civilization and our false, man-made standards. It will offer no healing to those who are unwilling to be told the truth about their "sickness unto death." The resurrection comes after the Crucifixion.

In a sermon, congregations have a right to receive the Word of God as He has Himself given it in his own mighty and redeeming acts.[13]

These were the inspiring words of Reverend Dr. C Ritchie Bell in 1967 to graduating students in The Presbyterian College's centennial year. A proud professor, wishing new graduates all the best, these passages provided his students a few final thoughts on what makes a good sermon. These words also demonstrate the utmost importance Dr. Bell placed on the role of preaching in our church and society, and the critical role that the college has had in producing able preachers of the Word.

In his 1943 sermon entitled "The Limitations of Love,"[14] Dr. Bell addressed a congregation and society in the midst of a terrible worldwide conflict. Countless families and communities were impacted in some respect in the city, the nation and the entire world, as the century's second major World War persisted into its fourth year. One can't imagine a more relevant and timely sermon theme than the subject of love, and the passages referred to in Paul's letters to the Corinthians.

With surety, Dr. Bell takes as his text 1 Corinthians 13:9–10: "For we know *in part*, and we prophesy *in part*. But when that which is perfect is come, then that which is *in part* shall be done away."

As context for his text, Dr. Bell begins by saying: "In this chapter Paul has demonstrated the necessity of love in every sphere and emergency of life. Other measures and gifts fall short sometimes. They are none of them equal to the strain of the wear and tear of life. But love never faileth. It can cure any malady which society suffers. It can bring peace to any home and any heart. It is the one thing always needful." What comforting words spoken to a society ravaged by war, and yet reaping the benefits of economic prosperity, a cruel irony.

In the second paragraph, Dr. Bell moves quickly to focus his analysis on verses 9–10, and his interpretation of what Paul meant by these two verses. Here, he disagrees with the opinion of an unnamed expert concerning "we know *in part*." He suggested that this passage had nothing to do with love, and that Paul was wrong in introducing the passage in this context. On the contrary, Dr. Bell concludes Paul was far too particular to have made such an error, and this passage speaks directly to the limitations of our knowledge, which in turn has everything to do with our lack of love.

In the development of his sermon, Dr. Bell introduces the theme: "limitations of knowledge" to explain that man has always "known *in part*."

13. Bell, "Preaching," 17.
14. Bell, "Limitations."

The preacher provides many illustrations to support this argument, showing the rapidity of man's evolving scientific knowledge. He then chooses a quote from one of the day's great scientists to indicate that man has only scratched the surface. There is so much more to learn. He then applies this principle of partial knowledge to our interaction with our fellow men and women. Dr. Bell's *first conclusion and call to action* is: "Shouldn't we be extremely careful not to condemn others who profess to see some other side of truth which has not yet been revealed to us?"

After posing the question "Why is not that love of which Jesus and John said so much and about which Paul wrote here so feelingly, why does it not dominate human society?" Dr. Bell mentions several of Paul's lesser reasons: envy, pride, selfishness and spirit of revenge, all of which are described as the foes of love. Dr. Bell concludes however, "The greater enemy is lack of knowledge." "We do not love people because we know them only *in part*." What a profound and provocative statement, yet so important and relevant, especially at a time of war.

Dr. Bell goes on "Someone has well said that to love people all we need is to know them. Those who seem to us from the distance to be unlovely and unloveable, if we could live among them, and could know their hearts and their heartaches, we would love them. It is not something in them that makes us shun them. It is something in us, a lack of knowledge."

Having reached the middle of his sermon, the preacher goes on to say how ignorance can result in unexpected outcomes. Much of the intolerance and prejudice and hate (the absence of love) in society and churches and nations are due to a lack of understanding. He concludes, with Paul: "They know only *in part*."

One is impressed by the number of illustrations used to reinforce God's message that we "*know in part.*" I counted twelve.

The second conclusion and call to action is achieved by posing a rhetorical question: "Should we be surprised by this limitation of knowledge?" To which he responds: "Absolutely not!" So how does God want us to live our lives? Answer: "Realizing that we can here know only *in part*, ought we not therefore to love and trust and wait for the divine purpose to unfold itself?"

In Dr. Bell's call to action, he provides two illustrations of individuals working and living with knowledge "in part." The story of Joseph being sold into slavery I found particularly powerful. But the second illustration—the visitor to a city who can't truly understand the true beauty of a city—is also telling. Both men could see only *in part*.

The preacher concludes this section of his sermon by speaking of death as Life's greatest mystery. Even here we should not be afraid because our knowledge is incomplete.

"Of death, that mystery which lies before us all, we know only *in part*. We know the fear of dissolution, the sorrow of those left behind, and the returning through corruption of the body to its kindred dust. But that which we see is only a part, a very small part. The Bible declares that the real death we do not see at all. Death in reality is a day of victory. It is a day of graduation when you and I will begin to live as we have never lived before! "For I reckon that the sufferings of this present time are not worthy to be compared with the glory which shall be revealed in us." "For eye hath not seen, nor ear heard, neither have entered into the heart of man, the things which God hath prepared for them who love Him."

Dr. Bell's *third conclusion and call to action* is that there will come a time when all limitations will be removed. "Let us not then quarrel with our limitations of knowledge. They are a part of the youth of our existence. There will come a time when all limitations will be removed. "For now we see through a glass, darkly; but then face to face; now I know in part; but then shall I know even as also I am known." "He that loveth not knoweth not God; for God is love."

I believe Dr. Bell's message is as relevant today as it was seventy-two years ago—just as it was to the Corinthians nearly two centuries ago—a direct word from God. In every age, despite much advancement in human sciences and knowledge, humankind continues to seek answers to many questions, and yet really knows only *in part*. Our understanding must always be incomplete, just as, at Corinth, the young church set up by Paul fell into disunity, immorality and confusion in regard to church discipline and worship, so the church of today is faced by the same seemingly intractable problems. Yet, once again, to use Richie Bell's won words concerning a good sermon: "To be relevant, the Word of God must 'strike home,' it must profoundly move, it must radically challenge, it must probe deeply, it must beckon lovingly."[15]

I believe this sermon receives high marks on all fronts. All who have read or listened to this beautiful sermon will surely take something from it. Whether it serves to spark further interest in other important writings of Paul; or as a lesson to give us pause before passing judgment on others, it reminds us to give thanks for what we know and what we then shall know in the fullness of God's eternity. Meantime, let us not quarrel with our limitations for as Dr. Bell so aptly put it: "We can never see more than a little at a time of the divine plan for us. But we too may rest in confidence that all things are working together for good to them who love God." This still voice is heard again from one of Presbyterian College's greatest pastors.

15. Bell, "Preaching," 18.

The Author

Malcolm Campbell, retired railway executive and past convenor of the board at Briarwood Presbyterian Church, Beaconsfield, Quebec, grew up in Montreal. As a youth, he attended the First Presbyterian Church of Montreal. His wife, Heather Campbell, serves as elder at Briarwood. They have three children: Colin, Eric and Alison. Malcolm's grandfather was the Very Reverend Dr. Malcolm A. Campbell, past moderator of the General Assembly, lecturer at Presbyterian College, and minister of First Church (1911–1963). His Aunt Janet is Dr. Bell's daughter.

Bibliography

Bell, C. Ritchie. "The Limitations of Love: A Sermon." Delivered at MacVicar Memorial Presbyterian Church, Outremont, July 18, 1943.

———. "Preaching and the Contemporary Scene." In *Presbyterian College Thought: 1867-1967 Centennial Edition*, 16–18. The Students Society of the Presbyterian College, 1967.

Dickey, James Ross. Untitled piece. Presbyterian Record vol. CVI, No.11 ISS 0032-7573 (1982), 10.

Johnston, R. Stuart. "The Very Rev. C. Ritchie Bell." In *Presbyterian College Newsletter, A Publication of Presbyterian College*, 3. Montreal, 1985.

Markell, H. Keith. *History of the Presbyterian College, Montreal 1865-1986*. Montreal: Presbyterian College, 1987.

Presbyterian College Senate Minutes 1982, 122. From a meeting held April 29, 1982.

Simms, John. "Memorial to the Very Rev. Dr. C. Ritchie Bell." Copy provided by Janet Campbell.

Sixtieth Anniversary Committee. *Sixty Years: MacVicar Memorial Presbyterian Church Outremont 1898-1958*. Montreal: MacVicar Church, 1958.

St. James Kirk Session Worship Committee. *Celebrating Our Heritage: A History of St James Presbyterian Church, Truro N.S.* 2001.

CHAPTER 12

The College and Women in Ministry
Alison Stewart-Patterson

By David Stewart-Patterson

The Reverend Lady Alison Stewart-Patterson, LRAM, BTh, STM, DMin, (1931–1992). Photograph provided by her family.

LADY ALISON BRUCE WAS a child of hierarchy and a rebel. She was the youngest daughter of a Scottish noble family with a long history of defiance. Her ancestor, King Robert the Bruce, cemented Scottish independence in 1314 with his underdog victory at the battle of Bannockburn. Her great-grandfather, the 8th Earl of Elgin, was the governor general of Canada who first upheld the principle of responsible government in 1849 by signing into law the Rebellion Losses Act, passed by the legislature but against the wishes of most English-speaking Lower Canadians because it offered payment to francophones for property losses during the rebellion of 1837. A riot led to the burning of Parliament House and Lord Elgin was chased out of town by a stone-throwing mob and expelled from the St. Andrew's Society of Montreal. In 1956, equipped with nothing more than a licence from the Royal Academy of Music, Alison spurned the structure of British society and followed the footsteps of her great-grandfather to Montreal. For years, she remained a typical woman of her time. She married, bore three children (David, Iain and Christian) and raised them while her husband, Cleveland Stewart-Patterson, climbed the corporate ranks at Bell Telephone. But her need to love, to nurture, to minister, could not be confined to family.

The call to make a difference beyond the home first found expression in the mid-1960s. After a two-year assignment in New York, the family settled into a century-old farmhouse in Senneville, Quebec, where she began cultivating an extensive garden. At the same time, they joined St. Giles Presbyterian Church in nearby Baie d'Urfé, where Alison quickly put her musical talents to work.

In the years that followed, she inspired a growing flock of young people to sing. She created a junior choir and filled the church with new voices and new songs. She led them into competitions, took them to music camps, and had them featured on television. She arranged a recording of their performance of *Joseph and His Amazing Technicolor Dreamcoat*.

But a deeper song was building in her heart: a call to serve that went beyond children, beyond choirs, beyond St. Giles. And with her own children grown to high-school age, she listened to God's voice within and took the plunge.

In the early 1970s, women in ministry were rare creatures. The Presbyterian Church in Canada had begun accepting women as ministers and elders only a few years earlier. Alison entered McGill University in 1973, and was one of only twenty-seven women who graduated from Presbyterian College and went into the ministry in the twelve years from 1976 to 1988. The College was still feeling its way as the cradle of a new ministry combining men and women as equals, and Alison was one of its early experiments.

Those days were not without struggles. Having been educated by tutors, Alison came to the college without even a formal high-school diploma. At home, her husband and children had to get used to the idea that she too had become a full-time student and that they would have to share the load of looking after the home. At the college, she was warmly welcomed, if still as "one of the boys." On graduation, her colleagues dubbed her "Rev Al," a moniker her children had emblazoned on a vanity licence plate that now rests over her grave in rural Scotland.

The sermon that follows is important because it speaks so eloquently to the tension that inevitably accompanies human progress. The church, like Canadian society at that time, was struggling to reconcile its deeply seated patriarchal conventions with the changing realities of an increasingly connected world. The 1960s and 1970s were an era when the mantra of youth was to question authority, to challenge boundaries, to upset the established order. It was the raucous assault of rock and roll on ears attuned to gentle jazz. It was students preaching free love and an end to war even as they occupied and trashed the computer centre at Sir George Williams University (later Concordia). Men had landed on the moon, but most were a long way from seeing women as CEOs, as members of their clubs or as ministers in their churches.

The central tension for the church was to sustain its core mission—to bring people into a meaningful relationship with God—while adapting to a new generation and an evolving society. A message seen as irrelevant can have no impact. To continue to thrive, the church had to find ways to speak in new ways to new ears, with new voices and new words.

This was what led the Presbyterian Church in Canada in 1966 to open itself to a fundamental change in gender roles, and Presbyterian College to become the launching pad for its first generation of women ministers. In 1991, barely a year before her untimely death at age sixty, Alison celebrated the first twenty-five years of women in ministry with the following sermon to the congregation of The Church of St. Andrew and St. Paul in Montreal, where she first served as Assistant Minister after her ordination in 1977.

It is an important sermon on two counts. First, most of Alison's sermons have survived only in memory, not in writing. She rarely wrote out what she wanted to say. Indeed, most Sundays she spoke without any notes. She chose words in the moment, letting God flow freely through her, and sharing that fully with those around her in that particular time and place. Second, this sermon captures the three elements of her style and approach to preaching. It begins with a polite but blunt challenge. It proceeds through gentle, persuasive reasoning. And it concludes with joyful, passionate inspiration.

Not Counting the Women

Matthew 14:13–21 and Luke 23–24

Then the disciples took up twelve baskets full of what was left over. The number of men who ate was five thousand, not counting the women and children.

—Matt 14:20–21 Today's English Version

The story, as it has been told to us, is about the miraculous feeding of the five thousand. But what about the women and children? How many people were really fed? Did the women and children eat? How many of them might there have been?

If present congregations are any clue, what we really have is a story about the feeding of fifteen thousand—men, women and children—with only five loaves and two fish. That is an even greater miracle.

It is that greater miracle which we are celebrating here today—the miracle of what happens when the women are counted. Get one thing straight: the women were there. They just were not counted. The women were eating, listening, responding to Jesus; but the Gospel writers did not consider their presence and their response vital to the story.

Not being counted has been the experience of women for centuries in Hebrew, Greek, Roman, European and North American societies. It is still the experience of millions of women in Africa, the Middle East, and India. All major faiths have treated women in this way and, until 1966, The Presbyterian Church in Canada was one of the offenders.

Not being counted robs each of a feeling of completeness, for it implies that one is not good enough or important enough to count. Let us ask by whom are the women not counted? They are not counted by those who have the power to do so: by the author of the Gospel and those who told him the story; by those with the vote, or the money, or who think they have the ear of God.

It is not so with God. If God counts each hair on our head and every sparrow, surely God counts women. It is not so with Jesus. Jesus spent some of his most intimate, deeply theological and spiritual times with women. It is not so with the writer of the Gospel of Luke. Through many, tiny, tantalizing portraits of the women who were closest to Jesus, Luke paints a clear picture of a group of women whom we know by name. Alongside the male disciples, through three years of wandering, they followed Jesus all the way from Galilee to Jerusalem.

The word in Luke's text which is translated as "follow" is the same word that Jesus used when he said: "Follow me." It is the same one which is used to describe Levi's response to Jesus' call (Luke 5:27–28). This word has deep theological significance because it describes the relationship between Jesus and those who followed him and remained with him to the very end. It is a relationship of master/teacher and disciple/learner. Here, the word is used to describe a group of women, uncounted and mostly unnamed.

Feminist historians tell us that in order to recapture women's history in the Bible, we must learn to read between the lines. There it is possible to garner, from all the corners of the Gospel stories, a list of twelve or more women: Mary Magdalene, Mary and Martha; Mary, the mother of the sons of Zebedee; Joanna, the wife of Chuza, Herod's steward; Susanna; the mother of John Mark; four unmarried women whose healing stories are told in the Gospels; the woman of Samaria at the well. These women may not have been "counted" by the Gospel writers, but what they did was counted; it was told over and over again. Their encounters with Jesus were considered necessary for the teaching of the Gospel.

It is important to realize that women have always been ministering, working as disciples and being counted by Christ as valuable in bringing about the Kingdom of God. It is the Church, ruled by men, which has denied women the right to be counted, to be named, to be treated as equally valuable and respected. Early in the life of the Christian church, the men established these rules, and the women reluctantly accepted their ruling.

The women described by Luke ministered to Jesus, serving him all the way from Galilee to Jerusalem as they "provided for him out of their resources" (Luke 8:3). What were these resources? Did they use their housekeeping money? Were they rich? Did they wash clothes, go bargain-hunting, glean from the hedgerows? Did they bandage sore feet and provide resting places at night for the one who had nowhere to lay his head? We can only guess at how this little group of women and men managed to live as they went day by day from town to town.

These women stayed with him from Galilee to Jerusalem. They were there at the end: watching, praying, keeping an eye on what happened to the body. They prepared his body for burial. Just as they had ministered to Jesus while he was alive, so they continued their ministries after his death. As they hurried in the very early morning to do these last ministries, they suddenly found themselves caught up in a new ministry—they found themselves thrust into the role of evangelist, telling the story of a resurrected Lord. They were the first to see, to understand, to tell.

I imagine the women, troubled but excited, hot with running and almost incoherent, as they tried to tell the others what they had experienced.

And once again, they were *not counted* by the men. "An idle tale," they said, meaning: these women speak nonsense.

In 1966, The Presbyterian Church in Canada started to count the women. Now in 1991, we celebrate twenty-five years of ministry by women who have been ordained as pastors and elders. We know their names. They have been counted. Does being counted change everything? Should it? Jesus' model is one of service—washing feet, healing relationships, feeding the spirit, challenging to serve.

The women who followed Jesus give us some examples of the strengths women bring into the family of faith: service and evangelism, speaking about what we have seen and believe; caring for the living and the dead; perseverance, audacity and courage; the ability to be behind the scenes; and the ability to be out front. This balance is crucial.

As a community where faith must be nurtured, we can no longer afford leaders who can only be on top or out front. We need leaders who can be both out front and behind the scenes. Building a community of the faithful who will lead society into the kingdom of peace demands the strong gifts of nurturing, teaching, feeding, caring, healing, reconciling, bringing together, binding up, making whole. For generations all of this has been part of the ministering life of uncounted women.

Now that the women are counted, can we begin to influence, change, reshape the structures and systems of a patriarchal church and society which have brought so much pain and violence? If, in spite of hindrances caused by structures, titles and hierarchies, we could get to the place where Jesus Christ really is king and head of the church, then all of us, Jew or Gentile, free or slave, male or female, clergy or lay, session or people, might learn to minister to and with one another as Christ ministers to us.

We will not need to climb the ladder of hierarchical success, for their will be no ladder. We will not need to trample on others in order to reach the top, for there is no top. What the women demonstrated then, and what women in ministry say now, is that everyone counts; each person is valued and no one is valued more than another.

Christ calls to us—men, women, and children—saying, "Follow me." In Christ's name, our ministry is to help each one to be counted, valued, needed and loved. It is a ministry of speaking about what we have seen and experienced. It is a ministry of reconciling what is broken in our world. It is the ministry of all of us, for we are all counted. It is a ministry for which we are still being trained.

Friends, I have seen the difference which being counted makes. I have seen communities where all are becoming one.

I have seen. I run to tell you . . . !

Commentary on "Not Counting the Women"

Challenge, reasoning, inspiration: in her sermon, Alison tackles the issue of women in ministry as would a mother. She first challenges her listeners as she would a growing child—to notice what is wrong and to understand why it is wrong. Imagine, she says, feeding five thousand men with just two fish and five loaves of bread—a miracle indeed. But think about fifteen thousand men, women and children being fed by that same paltry handful of sustenance. Does counting the women not create a greater miracle—not just once in that long-ago time, but all around us, every day, now?

She is unsparing in her description of the treatment of women by all major faiths through centuries, and in many societies around the world even today. She explicitly names her own church as an offender until all too recently. And she goes so far as to equate not counting women as robbery, a theft of their feeling of completeness, implying that one is not good enough or not important enough to count.

She then goes directly from the issue of why not being counted matters to the painful question of who does the counting. Women are not counted, she says, "by those who have the power to do so." Within the early Christian church—as in other major faiths and in so many societies across time—men made the rules, and women had to make the best of it. She recognizes this behaviour as all too human, but deeply flawed: "If God counts each hair on our head and every sparrow, surely God counts women."

This particular passage in her sermon emerges from her own anguish. More than once during her career in ministry, she was wounded deeply by men who felt their power and prestige threatened by her ease in inspiring faith in others. Before her congregations, she maintained a brave face, but in private, she agonized over the very questions she mentions in this sermon: "Why is this happening? Have I misunderstood what God wants from me? Am I just not good enough?"

This nagging self-doubt drove her to try harder, to tackle tougher challenges. From the privileged Anglophone enclave of The Church of St. Andrew and St. Paul (where years later she would deliver this sermon), she returned to McGill, beginning her engagement with women's and minorities' studies, and earning an STM in 1980. She then was called to become le Pasteur à l'Église St. Luc, where she ministered for seven years to a highly diverse community in her initially shaky second language. (She recalled that in her early days, when she spoke with parishioners after services, most of their comments gently addressed her grammar rather than her messages.) She went on to become responsible for all French work for the Presbyterian Church in Canada within Quebec.

Feeling "dis-counted" as a woman also pulled her deeper into theological exploration of how she and other women could help to transform the practice of ministry. In the academic world, she went on to complete her doctorate in ministry at the Fuller Theological Seminary in Pasadena. In ministry, she followed Cleve on a posting overseas, serving at the First Church of Otago in Dunedin, New Zealand, before returning to Montreal in 1989 to minister to Maisonneuve St. Cuthbert's Presbyterian Church, a congregation badly hurt by the English exodus from Quebec and seeking help to rebuild their confidence and their mission. On her death, she established the Alison Stewart-Patterson Endowment Fund at Presbyterian College to provide financial aid to women students and, when possible, to fund lectures at the college by prominent academics on the subject of her doctoral thesis, the mutuality of men and women in ministry.

While the focus of her sermon is on the "pain and violence" wrought by the structures and systems of both patriarchal church and society, she knew all too well that attitudes embedded for centuries would not change easily. Nor were such attitudes limited to men.

During one of her visits home to see family in Scotland, she was invited to preach at the ancient abbey church in Culross, where she and Cleve were married in 1957. After the service, the local newspaper asked parishioners what they thought, and quoted one outraged elderly lady who declared in a rich brogue: "I'll no have a woman in the pulpit! I closed my ears and didna hear a word she said!" Culture—in an institution or in a society—changes slowly and often with great reluctance.

Much had changed in Canadian society between the day Alison was first counted as a student at Presbyterian College in the 1970s and the day she gave that sermon in 1991. But it was slow and uneven progress. Her doctoral thesis mentions that when Supreme Court Justice Bertha Wilson gave a speech in 1990, she made headlines by declaring publicly that male perspectives had led to unsound legal principles and that "some aspects of the criminal law in particular cry out for change since they are based on presuppositions about the nature of women and women's sexuality that in this day and age are little short of ludicrous."[1]

Much more has changed in the decades since. Women have made great progress in many walks of life. They now constitute the majority of young people entering major professions such as law and medicine. Women can be seen as premiers of provincial governments and chief executives of major corporations. In our schools, there is growing worry that now it is boys who are underperforming, in part because brawn counts for less and

---

1. Stewart-Patterson, *Mutuality*, 106.

less in our knowledge-based economy, and in part because the traits Alison talks about as the strengths women bring to ministry also contribute to their growing success in a knowledge-based economy.

Yet around the world, the same patriarchal dismissal of the value of women remains all too common. Canadians went to war in Afghanistan after the Taliban took power and, among other hateful measures, banned women from any meaningful education. Globalization has made great progress in lifting billions out of poverty, both enabling and encouraging changing attitudes toward the value of women. But in too many communities and too many cultures, those who controlled the writing and early editing of the New Testament would still feel at home.

Even within our own society, the contribution of women remains limited by our relentless focus on competition and hierarchy. As Alison describes in her sermon, we don't know much about the women who followed Jesus from Galilee to Jerusalem along with his male disciples. We don't know if they were rich or poor (although probably the latter). All we know is that they "provided for him out of their resources," that they simply gave all they had. They served in the best way they knew how to support a cause in which they believed.

In this way, Alison's sermon of 1991 continues to challenge us today: "As a community where faith must be nurtured, we can no longer afford leaders who can only be on top or out front." At the same time, she holds out a still elusive vision of a better future for men and women alike: "We will not need to climb the ladder of hierarchical success, for there will be no ladder. We will not need to trample on others in order to reach the top, for there is no top."

This is a critical line in the sermon, because it is a distillation of her doctoral thesis, "The Mutuality of Women and Men in Ministry," accepted in 1991. Her thesis starts from a definition of mutual ministry as "a working relationship of two or more ministers, male or female, ordained or lay, who do not have official or implied authority over each other, but who respect each other as mature partners, recognizing each other's gifts and talents and feeling responsible for each other's growth and development in the Lord."[2]

This definition includes two aspects of the issue of "not counting" women. One is about gender. The other is a matter of hierarchy. Alison's vision of an inclusive ministry requires both an acceptance of the equality of women and men, and a willingness to abandon hierarchy within the church. "We need a radical breakthrough so that, once again, there is no longer a division between the ordained and the unordained. We need a leadership

---

2. Ibid., i.

which teaches and models this equality so that the laity may feel permitted and then empowered to take up ministry and claim it as theirs."[3] Alison practiced what she preached, launching within the Presbytery of Montreal a program to train hospital visitors from the laity.

She suggests that in the modern world, a willingness to move in this direction is not just a matter of building a better church. It is a matter of survival. "On the one hand, the church's most precious resource is its lay people. It is they who are needed, out there in the valueless desert. On the other hand, if the church remains primarily an institution, comparatively rigid in structure, unbending in worship, fixed in its patterns of ministry, it will never begin to speak to today's world. In fact if it remains tightly rigid, it will not bend; it will only break."[4]

In Alison's eyes, "building a community of the faithful" demands the same gifts and passions required to raise a healthy, loving family. What mother has not nurtured her infants, taught her toddlers, fed hungry mouths, cared for fevers and healed cuts and scrapes, reconciled squabbling siblings, brought together distant relatives at Christmas, bound up and made whole the fractures of family life?

As she pointed out, women have been exercising these gifts to strengthen the community of the church for generations, whether or not their efforts and their impact were fully recognized. What she argues, though, is that embracing these strengths and giving them full room to blossom has the potential to "lead society into the kingdom of peace" so much faster than living in a world where the ministry of women goes uncounted.

A very consistent leadership style emerges from Alison's thesis questionnaire and interviews with the other women trained at Presbyterian College during her era. It is described with a variety of words: caring, teaching, collegial, egalitarian, facilitators, enablers, cooperation, consensus and empowerment ("power with" not "power over"). Alison sums it up as leading from among, a female tendency to be very cautious about either claiming or exercising authority, telling a story rather than preaching from the pulpit, a style that "helps them to create a climate where there does not need to be authority."[5]

She describes this approach as staying true to Jesus' model as portrayed in Matthew, where Jesus refuses to divulge his authority (Matt 21:27), and contrasts it with the kind of authority considered normal in a patriarchal church: "Father knows best: obey." Alison concludes: "Authority is among

3. Ibid., 33.
4. Ibid., 55.
5. Ibid., 125–29.

us, rather like the Kingdom. Authority is when we are together. It is the visible and invisible God within each of us and all of us. It is only in giving up our human authority that we will become last instead of first."[6]

In her interviews with fellow women in ministry within the Presbyterian Church, Alison heard both positive and negative experiences. Some described how power had been redirected. "Leadership moved from one family to a whole new team. The new leaders learnt to stand up and be counted," said one respondent. "We learnt to risk something new, even if it was not exactly as anticipated," said another. "I felt for the first time I was a full person, speaking and working in my own language: that of a woman," said a third.[7]

At the same time, Alison's research revealed a continued clinging to hierarchy and patriarchy that still frustrated change, even if more subtly expressed. "The discrimination has now gone underground. Because it is concealed, it can be very damaging. It can and has denied women placements. We get labelled with unflattering adjectives. In our small denomination that is all it takes."[8]

The first lesson for the training of professional leaders within the church, she said, "must be to realize that God's people are not sheep, or children. They are adults and want to be treated as adults, taught as adults and allowed to minister as adults, full partners and servants."[9]

Her message was not that the church would be led better by women. "We also need to recognize the God-given goodness of each sex, that both are created with God-within."[10]

In her sermon, she called for balance, for leaders capable of both being out front and behind the scenes. It was not about gender so much as about the value of all individuals: "Everyone counts, each person is valued and no one is valued more than another."

In her own ministry, in English and in French, across cultures in both Canada and New Zealand, she felt she had made a difference. "In each, based on the same theology of God immanent and within, of inclusiveness and the ministry of all, and of shared authority and leadership, I have taught. Together we have learnt and in each place a new community of being Christian grew."[11]

6. Ibid., 130.
7. Ibid., 131.
8. Ibid., 134.
9. Ibid., 211.
10. Ibid., 212.
11. Ibid., 211.

She acknowledged that some might see her vision of a post-hierarchical church as Utopian, but her advice was down to earth, noting that "it is too easy to sit in our corner and complain. The way may not be open, but we need to keep telling our story, keep up the dialogue, keep pushing." She concluded: "There is nothing romantic or heavenly about teaching and serving. They are two of the most practical ways we can act. This is what is needed—the whole people of God beginning to work for the fulfilment of God's plan, that all shall be one. Nothing more and nothing less."[12]

More than two decades after that sermon, the training for "the ministry of all of us" still appears to be a work in progress. But in training Alison Stewart-Patterson and her pioneering sisters in ministry, Presbyterian College laid the foundation for a fundamental change within the church that has amplified the eternal voice still heard, of optimism and excitement with which her sermon concludes: "I have seen. I run to tell you . . . !"

The Author

David Stewart-Patterson, Alison's eldest son, grew up watching her journey to ministry. David has been a journalist with the *Globe and Mail* and *CTV*, executive vice president of the Canadian Council of Chief Executives and is currently vice president, corporate and public affairs, with the Conference Board of Canada, the country's largest independent think tank. David also is a passionate volunteer, currently serving as vice chair of Futurpreneur Canada, which in 2013–14 provided loans and mentoring that enabled eight hundred young Canadians to launch new businesses, and as a member of the board of trustees of Youth Business International, the UK-based global network of organizations supporting young entrepreneurs. In 2006, the sermon discussed here inspired his own words about his mother and her impact:

12. Ibid., 211–12.

Not counting the women

When the Lord spoke upon the Mount
How many were fed
On a handful of fish and a few loaves of bread?
5,000, you said,
Not counting the women.

When the Lord spoke through your mouth
How many were fed
By the warmth in your heart and the words in your head?
Thousands again, the cards and letters said
And all by one woman.

Where was the Lord when you sat on the beach?
How many were fed
By Trinity salmon in the firelight so red?
Two joyful people and thousands of cells in your gut as they bred
Counting out the days of a woman.

When you talked at the end about my beginning
How many were fed
By the tape of your joy, of your sorrows and dread?
Just me in the darkness with a voice from the dead
Of a soul who saved thousands, but lost count of the woman.

How do you speak as you rest by the sea?
How many are fed
Across heather and waves by Rev Al in your bed?
A whole generation around the world spread
Now counting the women.

David Stewart-Patterson
Mothers' Day, 2006
© 2006–All rights reserved. Used with permission of the poet.

Bibliography

Stewart-Patterson, Alison. *The Mutuality of Women and Men in Ministry*. DMin diss., Fuller Theological Seminary, Pasadena, CA, 1991.
Wilson, Bertha (Judge of the Supreme Court of Canada). Speech at Osgoode Hall, Toronto, March 1990.

CHAPTER 13

The College and Missional Leadership

R. Sheldon MacKenzie

By Richard R. Topping

The Reverend Professor R. Sheldon MacKenzie, PhD, DD, (1930–2012), lecturing to students at Memorial University of Newfoundland. Photograph provided by his family.

SHELDON MACKENZIE WAS A missional leader in his time. He was a great preacher who loved the task of research and sermon preparation in the service of faith and the mission of the church. He was a much loved teacher in biblical studies, a prolific writer for the upbuilding of the church in faith, although he could be a disturber of the status quo for the same end. He was a graduate of Presbyterian College and a voice to be still heard.

Roy Sheldon MacKenzie was born July 26, 1930 in New Glasgow, Nova Scotia, the son of Harold Sheldon (1901–1988) and Gladys MacKenzie (1901–1980). Sheldon was the eldest of five children: Shirley (1932), Clifford (1934), George (1938) and Marian (1940). Sheldon married Jenipher (Jay) Butcher July 25, 1962, and they had two children Mark (1964) and Clare (1966). Sheldon was raised on the family farm in Union Centre, Nova Scotia. At fifteen years of age he left school to work at a saw mill. He moved to New Glasgow at seventeen, where he lived in a rooming house and worked at a hardware store. At the age of twenty-one he returned to secondary school to get his high school diploma. This was not a matter of night classes but of taking day-time classes in the regular session of a high school!

Sheldon did his undergraduate studies at Acadia University in Wolfville, Nova Scotia (1952–1955). In 1955, he began his divinity studies at Presbyterian College, Montreal. At graduation 1958, Sheldon, one of six graduates, received the Calvin Gold Medal, given to the student of superlative academic accomplishment; the Forsyth Graduate Award; the Dora Forsyth Award; the MacVicar Prize in Homiletics; and the Ray T. Nettleship Prize. His Presbyterian College field placement took him to Malone, New York, where he was student assistant to the Rev. Ronald Rowat. He also served as student assistant to the Rev. Bill Isaac at Maisonneuve Presbyterian Church, Montreal.

When Sheldon attended theological college the practice was to appoint graduates to their first pastoral charge, more a matter of the destinating powers of the church than one's own free will. After graduation, to his surprise, the Board of Home Missions appointed Sheldon as an ordained missionary to the pastoral charge of Eckville, Benalto, and Hespero in the Presbytery of Red Deer, Alberta. He had expected that his appointment would be to North Sydney, Nova Scotia, or Newfoundland, where he had been returning each summer to start a congregation. However, according to the mission superintendent of the Synod of the Maritimes, there had been some "horse trading" surrounding student placements and, wrote Sheldon, "this horse was going West."[1]

---

1. MacKenzie, *Eckville*, 2.

Sheldon's examination for licensure and ordination took place on May 8, 1958. Examination of candidates for ordination was in the afternoon before the evening Presbytery meeting at First Church in New Glasgow. Sheldon was questioned about predestination, a doctrine taken up in chapter 10 of the *Westminster Confession of Faith*. "It is a doctrine I could not believe then, and have not changed my mind about since,"[2] he wrote in 1997. The examining committee, both ministers and elders, were agitated by his noncompliance on this point of doctrine. One elder in particular felt that given the length of time the ministers were reasoning with this young upstart, some aspect of his theology was obviously deficient. The Rev. Herbie Buntain, the chair of the committee and cousin of Sheldon's father, resolved the impasse by asserting that since he was a graduate of Presbyterian College, he must be orthodox enough.[3]

After one year in Eckville, where he proved a popular appointment, Sheldon left for St. Andrew's University, Scotland, for doctoral studies in New Testament (1959–1962), spending the spring semester of 1962 at the New Testament Institute in Münster, Germany. During his studies at St. Andrew's, Sheldon also served as chaplain at various Canadian Air Force bases in France, Italy and Germany. At the end of his studies, Sheldon travelled to South Africa, where he married his beloved "Jay," whom he had met while a student in Scotland. Together Sheldon and Jay, whom Sheldon reported was "the best thing that ever happened to me,"[4] returned to Montreal for a one-year stated supply appointment at First Presbyterian Church, Montreal. Dr. Ritchie Bell, who was interim moderator and professor at Presbyterian College, invited Sheldon to this position. Sheldon referred to this period as the turbulent sixties and noted that historians and sociologists say that this decade, more than any other in Canadian history, "was a watershed in our beliefs and behaviour patterns."[5] On Tuesday, October 29, 1963, Sheldon was inducted as minister of the First Presbyterian Church. Both Mark and Clare were born in Montreal. The former principal of Presbyterian College, Dr. F. S. MacKenzie, baptized Mark and Dr. Richie Bell, professor of pastoral theology, baptized Clare. "We have always been grateful to these two giants in the church for their willingness to baptize the two people most precious to us."[6]

Sheldon's connections to Presbyterian College and the Faculty of Divinity at McGill during his years of ministry in Montreal (1962–1969)

2. Ibid., 3.
3. Ibid., 4.
4. MacKenzie, *Montreal*, 6.
5. Ibid., preface.
6. Ibid., 98.

were multiple. Beginning in 1964, he taught three evening courses in the Faculty of Divinity at McGill. At the invitation of Father Mark Beaufoy, warden of Diocesan College, he twice gave a series of evening lectures to "a mixed group of accountants, lawyers, school teachers and a few theological students"[7] on the Epistle to the Romans. While in Montreal, amongst the many extra-congregational commitments Sheldon assumed was service on the senate of Presbyterian College (1965–1970). His involvement with students through the national church included appointment to the General Assembly's committee on Reception of Ministers from other denominations.

During his tenure in Montreal, two students from the Presbyterian College were selected to work under Sheldon's tutelage at First Presbyterian. Dr. Richie Bell and Dr. Neil Smith from the college supervised the appointment of students. In April 1964, Sheldon was asked to supervise his first assistant, James Ross Dickey, who had had some trouble finding a suitable venue in which to serve as a student assistant, a college requirement. His registration at the college was in jeopardy. Dr. Smith, knowing that Jim's career was at stake and believing in his potential, asked Sheldon as a favour to receive Mr. Dickey as his student assistant. Sheldon acceded to this request. This was the beginning of a friendship that continued for the rest of Sheldon's life, with the two corresponding from across the country. Sheldon noted with some satisfaction that Jim Dickey's record as a fine congregational minister and his outstanding work as editor of the *Presbyterian Record* justify Dr. Smith's promise. Sheldon wrote with some delight "that he [Jim] has been awarded an honorary doctorate from the [Presbyterian] college from which he was almost kicked out, provides us with no small pleasure and satisfaction."[8] Bob Cruickshank, the other student assistant from Presbyterian College, was placed with Sheldon at First Presbyterian. Sheldon admired Bob's ability as a preacher and pastor and was delighted that he was asked to preach at Bob's ordination in Dundas, Ontario and to give a series of lectures on the Reformed tradition at Banff, when Bob was serving in Western Canada.

Under a heavy load at First Presbyterian and facing some challenges to his health, including exhaustion, Sheldon left First Church in 1969 for the Kirk (St. Andrew's) in St. John's, Newfoundland. In 1971, he was asked to conduct two courses at Memorial University, and after multiple invitations, he resigned his position to become full-time professor at the university in the Religious Studies Department.[9] During these years in St. John's, Shel-

---

7. Ibid., 99.
8. Ibid., 58–59.
9. It took three invitations to lunch at the Starboard Quarter from Ray Lahey

don was also adjunct professor at Queen's Theological Seminary (Anglican). Sheldon maintained an impressive schedule of events alongside his academic responsibilities. He was a regular Sunday preacher in congregations of various denominations, taught Sunday school with Jay for four years and an adult Bible class at the Kirk, and was the theme speaker at the 1979 Presbyterian Church Pre-Assembly Congress at the University of Guelph, Ontario. The presentations made at the Congress were subsequently published as *The Power and Glory: Studies in Discipleship*.[10] Sheldon published *The Passion according to St. John*,[11] a collection of meditations originally presented at a three-hour Good Friday Service at St. Stephen's Episcopal Church in Philadelphia in 1978.[12] In 1988, Sheldon was presented with the President's Award for Distinguished Teaching at Memorial University (the first award recipient), where he attracted multiple students loyal to their teacher. Sheldon retired from Memorial University in 1994 after twenty-two years of full-time teaching. He continued to lecture at St. Francis Xavier University, Antigonish and supply pulpits in Pictou County and Halifax from his new residence in New Glasgow. He was a regular contributor to the religion column in the *New Glasgow Evening News*. On the occasion of the 150th anniversary of the founding of the West River Seminary at West River (now Durham), the Synod of the Atlantic Provinces engaged Sheldon to write a history of the Seminary. In 1998, *Gathered by the River: The Story of the West River Seminary and Theological Hall, 1848–1958* was published. In 1999 this book was awarded first prize by the Committee on History of the Presbyterian Church in Canada. In 2001 Sheldon and Jay moved to Chilliwack, where Sheldon compiled five books of sermons for publication: a volume for each of the Gospels, except for Matthew; a collection of sermons on Acts; and one on the Old Testament.

---

and Morley Hodder before Sheldon accepted the proposal to teach at Memorial. At the third lunch, Prof. Hodder said, "Now, Sheldon, this is the last time we will be asking you about coming to Memorial. After this there are no more free lunches." MacKenzie, *St. John's*, 21.

10. MacKenzie, *The Power*. There were 128 young people in attendance and 715 delegates to the Assembly. Ibid., 4.

11. MacKenzie, *The Passion*. The meditations in this book, as well as the multiple volumes of sermons on the Gospels, are all set out for oral delivery as is the sermon included in this chapter.

12. Sheldon visited First Presbyterian, Philadelphia to lecture in Adult Education in 1966 and St. Stephen's Episcopal Church, Philadelphia for a conference on religion and healing in the late 1970s. He was subsequently invited back to deliver his meditations on the Passion from John's Gospel. Sheldon participated in Holy Week services here three times: 1978, 1980 and 1983. The healing services held at St. Stephen's on Thursday of Holy Week made a particularly powerful impression on Sheldon. They were a source of spiritual renewal for him. See MacKenzie, *St. Stephen's*, 5.

Sheldon's importance to the Presbyterian Church in Canada and to Presbyterian College continues to endure in the enormous influence he had on many friends, students, and former parishioners throughout the Presbyterian Church in Canada and beyond. Reading the endorsements of Sheldon's numerous books of sermons indicates that he had a wide reading public and a wide influence in the Presbyterian Church in Canada. "His sermons are not prose, but rather verse. . . . The sermons trigger the senses and the imagination. . . . As we listen to him we are drawn back to the Spirit. . . . The reader will find faith confirmed, discipleship challenged and experience enriched."[13] His edifying preaching spoke to and instructed others.

Many alumni of Presbyterian College and others will have known Sheldon through his phone correspondence with them. Sheldon was well connected across the country whether he lived on the east or west coast. His range of friendships and his encouraging counsel have been experienced by quite a number of clergy and former students. He could listen and empathize and offer kind advice. I know that he invited sermons from clergy colleagues to be emailed to him. He read these sermons with great interest providing positive feedback and insight.[14] These days in theological education we talk about holy friendships and the importance of mentorship in the first years of ministry. Greg Jones of the Duke Institute for Leadership and Faith writes: "Holy friendships are crucial to sustaining leaders personally, offering perspective and support in a role that is otherwise often isolated and isolating. Indeed, such friendships need to be cultivated intentionally, because close associations within an organization, even between people who consider themselves friends, may be constrained in various ways that those with people more tangential to the organization are not."[15]

We know that agents of change in congregations, for that is what a leader is, need wide circles of friends for support. Sheldon was a practitioner of this fine practice. He cared a great deal for intelligent leadership and diligent scholarship and offered his deep support and prayers for those who worked hard at the task of ministry. He expected that clergy would be prepared for worship services and that thought and care would be given to leadership, the celebration of the sacraments and preaching. He was less enthusiastic about half-hearted efforts or sermons that were pitched at the level of children's stories or pilfered from the Internet. Sheldon was a Bible

13. From reviewers' comments on MacKenzie's previous books of sermons, *Master's Scriptures*, 1–3.

14. I know that Sheldon received sermons from many preachers including the late Ian Victor and me. Sometimes he would pass Ian's sermons to me and mine to Ian.

15. Greg Jones, "Discovering Hope." Sheldon may not have approved of this Internet reference for serious scholarship.

scholar of great ability, and he engaged in scholarship for the sake of the church. He was not in theological education as a refugee from the church or the world. He cared about a thinking faith that was critically reflective and engaged with the neighbourhood, the country, and the world.[16] He rewrote sermons, even to the hour of delivery, when a matter of pressing importance took place and believers needed to make scriptural and gospel sense of world events.[17] The words of the Reformed scholar and theological educator, Michael Jinkins, president of Louisville Presbyterian Theological Seminary, offer a fair summary of Sheldon's hope for the Church and Christian faith: "There have been few moments in Christianity's history when more was at stake than at this moment. There have been few moments in Christianity's history when we have needed a thinking faith, a theologically reflective faith, a generous and critical, imaginative and deeply engaged faith more than we do today."[18]

Presbyterian College, in its hundred and fifty years of service to the church, has produced many fine preachers. Sheldon was chosen, not only to bring the book into the twenty-first century, but because he was, in his own time and place, a missional church leader. I do not think he put it that way. Current literature tells us that missional leaders are leaders who anticipate that God is active in the world. Missional theology[19] says that it is not that the church has a mission; it is that God's mission has a church. To think missionally is to anticipate that wherever you might go to minister, to be a witness to the Gospel, you can anticipate that God is already active in that

16. His son Mark noted at Sheldon's funeral: "My Dad had appreciation for people of all faith backgrounds . . . The only people for whom he had no patience were those whose own rigidity of faith did not allow them to respect and honour the faith traditions of other prayerful and compassionate people . . . And he always defended the need to apply intellectual criticism to matters of faith." MacKenzie, "Funeral Eulogy," 3.

17. For example, Mark MacKenzie remembers his father setting aside a prepared sermon and staying up late on Saturday night to come up with a scriptural configuration of the Jones town massacre including the danger of false prophecy and the source of hope and solace. See ibid., 3.

18. Jinkins, *Church*, 92.

19. Three important books on Missional Theology are: Bosch, *Transforming Mission*; Guder, *Continuing Conversion*; and a more recent book, Hastings, *Missional God*. An understanding of *missional* begins with recovering a missionary understanding of God. By his very nature God is a "sent one" who takes the initiative to redeem his creation. This doctrine, known as *missio Dei*—the sending of God—is causing many to redefine their understanding of the church. Because we are the "sent" people of God, the church is the instrument of God's mission in the world. As things stand, many people see it the other way around. They believe mission is an instrument of the church; a means by which the church is grown. Although we frequently say "the church has a mission," according to missional theology a more correct statement would be "the mission has a church." See Alan Hirsch, "Defining Missional."

place. Christians do not make God present but discern where God is already present and active in the world and go with the grain of the universe. Missional thinkers encourage Christians to get out of the church building and into the world that God so loves: to love the world God loves. Sheldon's account of ministry in the inner city of Montreal at First Church in particular is a wonderful embodiment of missional theology. He interacted with street people, hand-delivered food baskets, engaged in some rather courageous encounters with drug dealers and pimps, spent time in court, it seems, because he expected that God cared for these odd but beloved folks.[20]

At Sheldon's funeral service his son told the following story, which again exemplifies openness to the world and the expectation that there is "wideness to God's mercy":

> My Dad saw all strangers as friends who hadn't had the good fortune of being introduced to him yet, and for this reason they were to be regarded with a certain degree of sympathy. . . . One time in the early seventies we were on vacation in Nova Scotia and we pulled up our big Plymouth 300 into a garage station for gas. As my father was finishing up obtaining the life story of the man filling our car with gas, a biker gang swarmed into the gas pump area with a rumble that shook the car. This was before the days of accountants driving Harleys, biker gangs were real and menacing and they were feared. My father, looking very much the minister on holiday that he was, paid up and got back into the car unscathed. We were in the process of pulling back onto the highway when Clare looked at me in the backseat and said with relief, "Those guys were Phantom Riders." I nodded grimly. Dad looked at us in the rear view mirror: "Phantom who?" "Phantom Riders," I replied. "They're the biker gang from Newfoundland." "*Newfoundland*!" said my father. He stomped on the brakes, threw the door open and ran towards the gas station office waving as he went, "Hey guys! How are you doing? I'm from Newfoundland too!" We waited for the injurious sounds of boots on polyester but it never came. When we opened our eyes, my dad was surrounded by laughing bikers, back slaps, lots of bear hugs. They called him skipper, a term of endearment and

---

20. He was once visited by a group of drug dealers for meddling with their sales outside the church. "Either mind your own _____ business, or you will get hurt. Bad." Sheldon replied, "You fellows have been seeing too many cops and robbers movies. And I cannot tell you that I won't report you every time I see you with the kids." Around Easter of 1963, three bullets came through an upper window in his office. *Montreal*, 17–18.

respect in Newfoundland, and he rapidly found out about their unreasonable probation terms and their sick mothers.[21]

Sheldon was chaplain to the Newfoundland Constabulary, or "Force Padre" as it reads on the plaque they gave to him when he left St. John's in 1994. He held that position for about three years and he enjoyed it very much. He visited the "Constab" headquarters regularly, talking to the men and women there. He was also called to accompany the police when they were delivering bad news to families, and he took part in official functions. He really enjoyed meeting the members of the force and felt that helping them with problems—both personal and Constab-related—was very worthwhile. Some of the officers and their wives are still in touch with Jay.

Homileticians, professors of preaching, emphasize preaching as an irreducibly verbal event. Hearers of sermons experience sermons as spoken. The place and time of sermons, and their live delivery matter. Preaching has a liturgical and theological context. They unfold in the midst of the gathered people of God, the baptized. Preaching in the Reformed tradition is preceded by a prayer for illumination in which the Holy Spirit is invoked so that the words spoken as human testimony to the Word, Jesus Christ, will be heard as the very Word of God. Preaching takes place in the hope that the risen Christ will annex human testimony—both that of Scripture and the preacher—to speak to his people. Preaching is a fragile but exciting enterprise because the one who proclaims the Word has no power to render his or her words effective apart from the presence of the risen Christ to the words spoken about him. Charles Campbell comments: "Preachers accept a strange kind of powerlessness, which finally relies on God to make effective not only individual sermons, but the very practice of preaching itself. Like the Word made flesh, the preacher's words must be 'redeemed by God' to be effective."[22] If *Still Voices* are *Still Heard* through the testimony of preachers to the Word made flesh, it will be because Jesus Christ is still present to words that witness to him. Sheldon was one in a long line of preachers whose fallibility and weakness depended on the work of God to make it live. Effective preaching and preachers still wait on the answer to the prayer, "Come, Holy Spirit."

---

21. MacKenzie, "Funeral Eulogy," 7.
22. Campbell, *Preaching Jesus*, 214.

Can These Bones Live?[23]

Ezekiel 37:1–14; Romans 8:6–11; John 11:1–4, 17, 34–44

Have you ever had a vision?
>Do you know anyone who has ever had a vision?
>>If you do, did he or she tell you about it?

What about dreams?
All of us have and have had dreams
>About someone or something.

Have you ever had a dream so realistic about someone or
>something that when you woke up you were glad
>>it had only been a dream?

Our ancestors used to think dreams were pretty important.
In Scotland and Ireland there were older people
who believed that some kinds of dreams always came true.
>When our ancestors came to live in Canada

they often dreamt of things happening at home,
long before they got letters to tell them it had been so.
Our spiritual ancestors, the Jews, took dreams seriously.
They believed that God would speak to them through their dreams.
Or their visions.
Joseph had a dream.
In it he was told that he should marry the mother of Jesus.
Because she was pregnant by the Holy Spirit.
The elderly mother of John the Baptist had a dream.
Or a nightmare.
At her age she must have been terrified.
She found out she was going to have a baby.
An important baby.
These women lived 2,000 years ago.
Dreams had been important long before them.
Their ancestors depended on dreams and visions

---

23. I inquired of Jay MacKenzie about the occasion and time of this sermon. She was unable to locate the exact date and place of its delivery. She did note that "many of the sermons were used more than once, in different churches, usually with some rewriting." She continued, "I remember that the sermon entitled *A Man Came Running*, from the Mark book, was used too often in the opinion of our children—who said that the man had run faster the first time—and that he was getting a bit tired." Personal correspondence, April 30, 2014. The sermon is used with permission of Fairway Publishing and Jay MacKenzie.

for conversations with God.
Not everyone believed the dreams of other people.
    It depended on who was dreaming what.
If the visions pleased their listeners,
    they were likely to be taken seriously.
If the visions displeased their listeners,
    they were likely to be ignored.
        Or treated with contempt.
Always the person who had the vision
    believed that it had come to him or her from God.
Sometimes a vision was given in a time of crisis,
    political, religious, or personal.
In which case it came as a warning against some action.
Or as a sign of hope in a hopeless situation.
Once upon a time,
    there was a preacher who was deeply involved
        in the political life of his nation.
His fellow citizens had been badly beaten by their neighbours.
Their spirits were broken.
Too broken to be interested in much of anything,
    certainly not in their religion.
        Nor in their national life.
The preacher tried everything to get their attention.
Nothing made any difference.
    They wanted only to survive.
        Both today and tomorrow alike
            seemed hopeless to them.
One night, as he slept, he had a vision.
In his vision he seemed to be having a conversation with God.
He could see himself standing alone in a battlefield.
The battlefield was an old one.
    It was deserted and quiet.
The only sounds were those of leaves moving in the wind
    and the rattle of windblown bones.
All around him,
    for as far as he could see,
        were the bones of men who had one day marched off to war.
The battle had been lost.
    The campaign had been a disaster.
        The losers were left lying where they had fallen.
            The dead had been dead a long time.

He soaked up the atmosphere of the ancient battleground.
    A voice within him asked a ridiculous question:
        "Can these bones live?"
        "Can these bones live?"
What a question!
The only appropriate reply was the one that came to mind:
    "Only God knows the answer to a question like that."
Again a voice within him said:
    "Let's give it a try.
    Speak, why don't you?
    Command the bones to assemble themselves in proper order."
In the dream that is what happened, isn't it?
In the words of the old Southern spiritual:
        "The toe bone connected to the foot bone;
        the foot bone connected to the ankle bone;
        the ankle bone connected to the leg bone . . .
        Now hear the Word of the Lord."
On and on it went.
    "Speak," said the voice within him.
    "Command that the bones be given bodies.
    That the bodies be given uniforms.
    Then let us see what will happen."
In his dream or vision he obeyed the voice within him.
    He gave the orders and got the surprise of his life.
The bodies remained where they were.
    Yet the battlefield had been transformed.
        Something quite fantastic had happened.
            The dry bones had become bodies.
An observer from the outside,
    not knowing what had taken place,
        might have supposed he saw an army taking a rest break.
As yet no one or anything moved.
There was no life.
    Only what appeared to be life.
What a vision!
    It was quite incredible.
        At any moment he would wake up.
            When he did the vision would disappear.
As it was he slept on.
    As he slept he heard a voice speak to him once again:
        "Let us finish what we have begun."

So far we have been dealing with things we can see and hear.
Now we must ask for something we cannot see or touch.
We must ask for "spirit," for "life."
Even in a vision
this must have seemed a request right out-of-sight!
"Can these bones live?"
The preacher was about to find out.
He called on God to put "life" into the forms on the ground.
He called on God, the source of life, as he was told to do,
to breathe "spirit" into the lifeless bodies.
At once the silent army of the dead
became a noisy regiment of lively men.
By this time the vision had begun to fade.
He was about to wake up.
Just before the vision, the dream, left him,
he saw a mighty army, ready to move off
at the orders of its commander.
Then he woke up, a preacher forever changed.
He was now a person transformed.
The vision became the inspiration
for the rest of his ministry amongst his people.
"My ministry, "he said, "is in a nation like that battlefield.
It is in a place of dead souls.
In it there are people who are unconcerned and unresponsive.
It doesn't matter that I speak to them about faith.
Or hope. Or patriotism.
All I get in response to my preaching
is the steady dull glare of their indifferent spirits.
There is a ghastly stillness all around me.
It is the stillness of those who will not hear.
When I speak, no one even pretends
that I am speaking of things real to them.
When I am silent,
no one asks me to begin speaking again.
These are dry bones indeed!"
The message of the vision took real life seriously.
It recognized that the preacher
was living in a valley of dry bones.
In that situation he must continue preaching

just as he had been doing.
To preach, believing that the dry bones had great potential.
It was an amazing vision.
It had to do with the future of the People of God.
It had to do with their nation and their religious life.
Against all odds,
> Ezekiel came out of the vision convinced
>> that the future was brighter than anything
>>> they had known.

What appeared to be death
> held within it the potential for life!

What he saw in his vision,
> and passed on to his people, the People of God,
>> gave them hope for the future.

The nation was afterward renewed!
In terms of time the scene has changed.
> The situation is much the same.

The battlefield of dry bones is much like the Christian church.
Those who are still in the Church
> sense that within it there is motion without meaning.

They hear familiar words that have somehow lost their power.
They listen to a routine profession of faith
> and fail to see it follow through in terms of performance.

In what appears to be a religious wasteland
> the modern Christian disciple cries out:
>> "Can these bones live?"

Is there hope that the People of God will look up and live?
Will these respectable graveyards
> for God ever give up their dead?

The answer from people,
> both inside and outside the Church, is No!

It is too late, they say, for artificial respiration.
In this Year of Our Lord very few still believe
> that a resurrection is possible.

They are wrong!
The vision of the battlefield coming to life
> belongs as much to us as it did to Ezekiel.

Within the Church of Christ
> the potential for transforming our society
>> is as real now as it was 2,000 years ago.

Within the People of God
>   there is still that power which will free us from ourselves
>   >   and leave us open to God.
The impossible is still the order of the day with God.
So we wait for the spiritual renewal of ourselves.
Because that is where it has to begin.
It has to begin with the household of faith.
With each one of us in it.
We know it will happen.
We feel it is about to happen.
The resurrection to life is just moments away.
We don't know when it will happen
>   but the signs of it are unmistakable.
Have you seen them?
Perhaps you are one of them and didn't know it.
If you have made even the slightest progress
>   in your spiritual growth you are a sign of resurrection.
If, because you are a disciple of Christ,
>   you are sometimes able to love the unloveable,
>   >   occasionally to forgive the unforgiveable,
>   >   >   you are a sign of resurrection in the world.
If, because you are a disciple of Christ,
>   the way you behave with other people
>   >   will match the things you believe about God,
>   >   >   the transformation has already begun with you.
If, because you are already loved by God, and you are,
>   you have made even the slightest effort to love yourself,
>   >   you will soon be able to love other people as well.
The dry bones have already begun to move.
At any moment the Spirit of God may break in
>   and transform both us and our present situation.
In the meantime, and for however long it takes,
>   we will go on, guided by the Spirit of God,
>   >   proclaiming and living as the People of God.
One day, believe me,
>   the dry bones everywhere around us will be transformed by
>   >   God into a success beyond our wildest dreams!
>   >   >   "Can these bones live?"
>   >   >   >   You bet! Just wait and see.
>   >   >   >   >   Amen.

Commentary on "Can These Bones Live?"

This sermon, given more than once by Sheldon, is striking in its immediacy to the current life and times of the Presbyterian Church in Canada. The point of the sermon is to encourage and to instill hope in God's people for a promised future of flourishing under God by the grace of God. The sermon is an appeal to the imagination to envision what is not yet but might be, will be, by the power of the Spirit of God who raises the dead. Just like Israel, out of the land, depleted, undone, and in exile, the church is diminished, in numbers ("those still in the church"), power, meaning, and transformative influence on individuals and society. It is a sermon about resurrection and whether it is possible for God's people in this time (of the disestablishment of the church, increasing secularity, perhaps the Quiet Revolution) to be renewed and to be agents of renewal in the world. "Within the Church of Christ the potential for transforming our society is as real now as it was 2,000 years ago. Within the people of God there is still the power which will free us from ourselves and leave us open to God." The sermon is instructive and inspirational for the current life and times of the Presbyterian Church in that it places hope squarely on God.

In preparation for this chapter on Roy Sheldon MacKenzie (July 1930–December 2012), I spoke to a number of people about his preaching. The question they most often asked me was whether or not I had heard him preach. I have not. I have read five volumes of his sermons. Both his family and his students told me, however: "You had to hear him preach."[24] This remark was accompanied by a sense of Sheldon as a pulpit presence, a living voice; someone who performed his sermons in the very best sense. Good preachers lose themselves to what it is they are preaching about. Sheldon wrote about the "freedom," "the thrill"[25] and the "rewarding"[26] work of

---

24. The Rev. Dr. James Ross Dickey, for example, one of the two student assistants that Sheldon had at First Church from Presbyterian College, has made this observation a number of times in telephone conversations. Sheldon's son Mark MacKenzie offered these words at Sheldon's funeral. "My Dad was a great preacher. He could really preach. When he was on a roll he would look at the back of the church, look out over everybody's heads and then, when everyone was waiting for the wrap-up . . . he would take a sip of water. Total cliff hanger." MacKenzie, "Funeral Eulogy," 3.

25. MacKenzie, *St. John's*, 4. Sheldon's excitement about preaching can also be picked up in the prefaces to his multiple books of sermons. For example, in *The Master's Scriptures*, 11–12, he recounts the collegial discussion of sermons with Rod Berlis of The Church of St. Andrew and St. Paul, Montreal, and Norman Slaughter, of Erskine American United Church, Montreal. They would correspond during the week about their sermons on the way to Sunday, rejoicing together when they were "ready to preach." There is a palpable sense of excitement and delight here.

26. MacKenzie, *Montreal*, 87–89. Sheldon also notes on these pages the sage advice

preaching. Of course there is personality, giftedness, scholarship, and the humanity of the preacher. Sheldon would have been the first to admit his own fallibility as a preacher. Preaching is a human enterprise, something people of flesh and blood are trained and shaped to perform with more or less skill and interest. However, the best of preaching gains its strength from the subject matter of preaching. The animation of a preacher for the delivery of a sermon is fueled by the material upon which the sermon is based. I think that is what Sheldon's students allude to when they say, "You had to hear him preach." He got caught up in the Gospel he preached. Sermon study and delivery were full of promise and the expectation that in the midst of human speech about God, with all its fallibility and weakness, God speaks. Sheldon's son, Mark, found a bookmark in his father's Bible when preparing for Sheldon's funeral service. On the bookmark was a prayer in Sheldon's own hand: "Lord Jesus, Son of God, Fill me with your life."[27]

It is not easy to reconstruct the original occasion of this sermon. It was used more than once and so in different times and places. The world it assumes—that the ancestors of the listeners of the sermon come from Scotland and Ireland—has changed. It does assume the diminished influence of the church in public life and Sheldon's days in Montreal were in the midst of the Quiet Revolution, which secularized public institutions across the province of Quebec. There is a tantalizing reference to "patriotism" in this sermon, which indicates that patriotism, alongside hope and faith, is a subject for preaching. I know that Sheldon was very active in Expo 67 for a number of years, on the board of directors for the Christian Pavilion and the Finance Committee, when Canadian patriotism would have been at high tide.[28] He was also in Montreal in June 1968 when, during Trudeau's election campaign in Montreal at the Saint-Jean-Baptiste Day Parade, rioting Quebec separatists threw rocks and bottles at the grandstand where Trudeau was sitting. Trudeau rejected the pleas of his aides that he take cover, and stayed in his seat, facing the rioters, without any sign of intimidation. This image of Trudeau showing courage made a great impression on the country. So much so that Trudeau handily won the election the next day. One can only wonder whether this cluster of happenings in 1960s Montreal was there in the background for the sermon from Ezekiel.[29]

---

of his preaching instructor at Presbyterian College. Dr. Richie Bell told his Homiletics 101 class that when they grew complacent about the task of preaching, it would be best to resign from the congregation and sell insurance or drive a city bus!

27. MacKenzie, "Funeral Eulogy," 4.

28. MacKenzie, *Montreal*, 100–101.

29. Whether or not this sermon is located in the specifics of the cultural common life of 1960s Montreal or not, we can assume that secularity is part of the backdrop for

It is interesting to note that there are no imperatives in the sermon. In the whole of this solicitous invitation to hope, the listener is not directly asked to do anything. This is not preaching as moralizing discourse and a summons to straighten-up and fly right. While it speaks of human potential, it does so in an almost ironic way: "what appeared to be death held within it potential for life!" Dry bones and potential for life! Sheldon moves almost immediately to "the impossible is still the order of the day with God" and "we wait for the spiritual renewal of ourselves." The sermon is realistic about the condition of God's people (dry bones) and at the same time hopeful for God's people and society (new life) because there is theological realism about what God can do (resurrection).

The conclusion of the sermon stirs the listener to wake up to signs of resurrection already at work in the world and in us: God is already active as a real agent of social and personal transformation. Progress is made in spiritual growth, sometimes we love and forgive; sometimes our conduct matches our creed. The listener is encouraged to read in faith the signs of transformation already underway. The beginning of the holiness of the people of God is a first-fruit of resurrection breaking out among us. Sheldon helps us ascribe our own moral and spiritual transformations to the resurrecting Spirit of God. It has begun. It is not finished; but it is begun. To put the matter theologically, sanctification is underway. God is alive and active as an agent of renewal in the lives of God's people here and now. Glorification has yet to make the work of transformation complete. We go on proclaiming and hoping and living guided by God's Spirit in anticipation of what God has yet to bring. The expectation for the more that is yet to come from God does not eviscerate action, but fires it up. The waiting for God is active and engaging, but God brings God's full renewal to our lives and the world. We act but it is not all up to us. There is a very astute treatment of advent ethics here that oscillates between human and divine action. I wonder if the signs of promise might have included some examples of social transformation. Where is the Spirit working transformation in human society in the here and now? The civil rights movement? Personal and ecclesial transformations are envisioned but where in the world was and is the Spirit at work through the church as an agent of resurrection in the commonweal? How is Christ presently the transformer of culture? I think some examples

---

this piece of proclamation. Charles Taylor makes the case that the whole of the North Atlantic World now lives in a secular age. By this he means that: (1) public spaces have been sanitized against references to God and ultimate reality; (2) religious belief and practice are diminished, people are turning away from God and no longer going to church as they did; and (3) belief in God is challenged, "it is one option among others and frequently not the easiest to embrace." See Taylor, *Secular*, 4–5.

of this would have spoken to the question of public transformation also begun (inaugurated) but not complete (consummated) in Christ.

In addition to its powerful central point, this sermon is instructive in its format, use of Scripture, and its sense of context. First, consider the format of this sermon. The sermon has been reproduced as it was laid out in manuscript form. This is a sermon written for oral delivery, as were all of Sheldon's sermons. It is indented to indicate how a sentence ought to be delivered, in phrases that linger and line out, not in complex sentences with subordinate clauses. The sentences are short. The language is lively and never is a five-dollar word used where a fifty-cent word will do. Repetition is used to emphasize the ridiculous question: "can these bones live?" "can these bones live?" A familiar spiritual is included to intone rhythm and provoke memory and draw the listener in "dem bones, dem bones." At the start, questions are posed that encourage a conversation between preacher and listener. It is an interrogative sermon. Sheldon, the scholar, wears his learning lightly, although to the scholar the substructure of the sermon is deeply informed by exegetical work. He manages to describe exilic Israel without the jot and tittle of historical reconstructions. The sermon is written for the ear and not the eye. It is set out more like poetry than prose on the page. The form of the sermon follows the form of the passage from Ezekiel, which is given in a visionary and poetic genre. He does not preach the conceptual distillate of a three-point sermon after boiling off the narrative in good reductive modernist fashion. Instead the sequential order and frame of the sermon is set by the narrative that is the visionary account of Ezekiel.

The biblical passages that were read the Sundays this sermon was preached are still grouped together in the revised common lectionary (fifth Sunday of Lent year A). Sheldon worked primarily with the Ezekiel text from which the sermon title is taken. Allusions to other texts are designed to situate the episode from Ezekiel 37 within the overarching narrative of Scripture and its treatment of visions and dreams. Old and New Testament are read together in a loose unity around Christ, as Sheldon noted in preachers he admired—Dr. Allan Duncan and Norman Slaughter—in the preface to the book in which this sermon was published.[30] The sermon assumes that Scripture is relevant to the life of God's people and that the Bible can be read as a single book. Sheldon uses the phrase "people of God" to talk about Church and Israel, almost as the two forms of the one people of God. The listener is located in this narrative: like the people of Israel, our spiritual ancestors, and like our blood relatives from Scotland and Ireland, we have dreams. I don't think current preachers can assume the same blood relatives

---

30. MacKenzie, *Master's Scriptures*, 10, 12.

in most Presbyterian congregations these days. However, the strategy of assuming that Scripture gathers us to the story it tells is theologically sound. It assumes the work of the Holy Spirit who gathers, up builds and commissions the Church by means of scriptural testimony to Christ. It is a classic Christian reading strategy to identify the Genesis to Revelation story of the Bible as the context within which we live.[31] Sheldon does not so historically locate the passage from Ezekiel in a reconstructed historical context that he undoes the canonical location of Ezekiel as a part of the Old Testament within Holy Scripture. The relevance of the passage to the expectant Christian listener is assumed. This is our story. This material is about us, for us. We inhabit this story of Ezekiel and the valley of the dry bones.

The sermon is more ambitious than most. It is not engaged in moralism or offered in the imperative mood. It assumes we will act but does not command us. One searches in vain for "we must" and "you should." It is not an apologetic sermon that aims primarily to demonstrate that faith is reasonable or useful to the current social order.[32] Instead, the sermon is a grand exercise in scriptural re-description of the life of God's people. Instead of beginning with a sense of the context of the listener and the church in the language of sociology, or psychology, or secularity, or Quebec politics, or the brute historical facts, the preacher describes the situation of the listener in the terms that the text from Ezekiel and the Gospel of John suggest. We are Israel! That is who we are. We need God's resurrection power. That is what is necessary. The context of dried-up Israel and dead Lazarus is our context: we are exiles, powerless, diminished, dead, and no longer influential. Sheldon lays the story of dry bones and resurrection to life over the gathered people of God. He narrates where we are in the world. He does not explain as much as he describes. He trusts the text to more truly name both our trouble and our hope than he trusts himself or statistical prospects for possibility. The sermon recontextualizes those who listen, so that they will know where they are and therefore what to look for and expect in a world where God gives life to dry bones. Sheldon does not place the text in our context but rather allows the texts of Ezekiel and John to become our context in a way that reorients us to its diagnosis and remedies, its prospects

---

31. See, e.g., Frei, *Eclipse*; Levering, *Participatory Exegesis*; and Williams, "Historical Criticism," 217–28.

32. Willimon notes that much contemporary preaching succumbs to the apologetic temptation. By this he means that preaching becomes a demonstration of either the rationality of faith according to the current conventions of what counts as rationale or the usefulness of faith to me or my culture's aspirations. "In these [apologetic] sermons, the faith is argued, not on the basis that 'Jesus is Lord,' but rather that the values of the preponderant social order—history, human rationality, social utility—are Lord." *Conversations*, 179.

and possibilities. I think this feature of the sermon is its most daring and most delightful. A person would have to believe in a God who transforms life to talk like this.

"One day, believe me,
    the dry bones everywhere around us will be transformed by
        God into a success beyond our wildest dreams!
           "Can these bones live?"
              You bet! Just wait and see.
                Amen."

The Author

The Rev. Dr. Richard Topping, principal of the Vancouver School of Theology, holds the St. Andrew's Hall Chair in Studies in the Reformed Tradition. He was minister of The Church of St. Andrew and St. Paul, Montreal, 2000–2009. During these same years he taught at Presbyterian College, as lecturer in Pastoral Theology and the Reformed tradition. He also served on the Board of Presbyterian College, 2004–2009. He is the author of *Revelation, Scripture and Church*, a treatise on theological interpretation of the Bible, and co-author of multiple denominational resources including the *Catechism for Today*, and *Together in Ministry*. He is co-editor of *Calvin@500*, a series of essays celebrating the five-hundredth anniversary of Calvin's birth in 2009. Sheldon MacKenzie was an encouragement to Richard from both the east and west coasts. They often corresponded by phone, Richard arguing the merits of Karl Barth over Sheldon's favourite, Rudolf Bultmann. "Barth was good on Romans," said Sheldon.

Bibliography

Bosch, David. *Transforming Mission: Paradigm Shifts in Theology of Mission.* 26th printing. New York: Orbis, 2010.

Campbell, Charles. *Preaching Jesus: New Directions in Homiletics in Hans Frei's Postliberal Hermeneutics.* Grand Rapids: Eerdmans, 1997.

Frei, Hans. *The Eclipse of Biblical Narrative: A Study in Eighteenth and Nineteenth Century Hermeneutics.* New Haven: Yale University Press, 1973.

Guder, Darrell. *The Continuing Conversion of the Church.* Grand Rapids: Eerdmans, 2000.

Hastings, Ross. *Missional God, Missional Church: Hope for Re-evangelizing the West.* Downers Grove: InterVarsity, 2012.

Hirsch, Alan. "Defining Missional." *Leadership Journal,* (Fall 2008). http://www.christianitytoday.com/le/2008/fall/17.20.html.

Jinkins, Michael. *The Church Transforming: What's Next for the Reformed Project.* Louisville: Westminster John Knox, 2012.

Jones, Greg. "Discovering Hope through Holy Friendships." *Faith & Leadership,* June 18, 2012, http://www.faithandleadership.com/content/l-gregory-jonesdiscovering-hope-through-holy-friendships.

Levering, Matthew. *Participatory Exegesis: A Theology of Biblical Interpretation.* Notre Dame: University of Notre Dame Press, 2008.

MacKenzie, Mark. "Funeral Eulogy for Sheldon MacKenzie." Chilliwack United Church: January 3, 2013.

MacKenzie, R. Sheldon. "Eckville 1958–1959." Unpublished manuscript, 1997.

———. *Gathered by the River: The Story of the West River Seminary and Theological Hall 1848–1858.* Winnipeg: Hignell, 1998.

———. *The Isolated Jesus.* Lima, OH. CSS Publishing, 1994.

———. "Montreal 1962–1969." Unpublished manuscript, undated.

———. *The Master Missionaries: Sermons from Acts.* Lima, OH: Fairway, 2009.

———. *The Master Preacher: Sermons from John.* Lima, OH: Fairway, 2006.

———. *The Master Storyteller: Sermons from Luke.* Lima, OH: Fairway, 2001.

———. *The Master Teacher: Sermons from Mark.* Lima, OH: Fairway, 2007.

———. *The Master's Scriptures: Sermons from the Old Testament.* Lima, OH: Fairway, 2011.

———. *The Passion according to St. John: Meditations on Chapters 18 and 19 of John's Gospel.* Winfield, BC: Wood Lake, 1987.

———. *The Power and the Glory: Studies in Discipleship.* 2nd ed. Winnipeg: Hignell, undated.

———. "St. John's 1969–1972." Unpublished manuscript, undated.

———. "St. Stephen's Church, Philadelphia." Unpublished manuscript, undated.

———. *The Words He Spoke.* Lima, OH: CSS Publishing, 1990.

Taylor, Charles. *A Secular Age.* Cambridge: Harvard University Press, 2007.

Williams, Rowan. "Historical Criticism and Sacred Text." In *Reading Texts, Seeking Wisdom: Scripture and Theology,* edited by David F. Ford and Graham Stanton, 217–28. London: SCM, 2006.

Willimon, William. *Conversations with Barth on Preaching.* Nashville: Abingdon, 2006.

Our Graduates

THE FOLLOWING LISTS OF known graduates indicate only the degrees earned at Presbyterian College: Bachelor of Divinity (BD) or its successor degree Master of Divinity (MDiv) and Doctor of Divinity (DD) whether by examination or *honoris causa*. The date given is the date of graduation (diploma or certificate); the awarding of a degree often came at a later date, though that is not recorded here. Earlier, there were a number of "courtesy" BDs (*ad eundem gradum*). These are listed separately as are the DDs. Permission was given in 2010 to bestow an MTS (Master of Theological Studies) but up to this date none has been granted.

The first graduate of the College in 1869 was Colin Campbell Stewart, MA. As he was the first, let him serve as the representative of all those who follow. Born at Musquodoboit, Nova Scotia, in 1841, Mr. Stewart took literary courses in Dalhousie College, Halifax, and McGill College, obtaining the degree of BA from the latter institution with the Gold Medal in Natural Science in 1867. Colin earned his MA from McGill University in 1870, following his graduation in Theology in 1869. In September 1870, he was ordained by the Presbytery of Owen Sound as minister of Division Street Church in that city, where he died four years later in August 1874. Founder of the Neil Stewart Prize for Hebrew in McGill and author of A Scriptural Form of Church Government, during his student days, Colin Campbell Stewart served as the first Librarian of Presbyterian College, Montreal.

ABBOTT, Chen Chen – MDiv	1997
ABRAM, Louis T.	1900
AFOUAKWAH, Sampson – MDiv	2014
AICKEN, Janice Elizabeth	1982
AIDE, Lisa Marie – MDiv	2007
AIKENS, Eldridge P. – BD	1946
AKITT, W.	1902
ALLAN, George Rose – BD	1914
ALLAN, John – BD	1878
ALLAN, John F. – BD	1960
ALLARD, Joseph	1881

ALLARD, Kermit Cameron	1939
ALLEN-MACARTNEY, Denise P. – MDiv	2009
ALLUM, Helen Ruth	1994
AMARON, Calvin Elijah	1879
ANDERSON, F.J.	1901
ANDERSON, John Alexander	1880
ANDERSON, John Duncan	1896
ANDERSON, John MacDonald – BD	1962
ANDERSON, Robert K. – BD	1964
*ANDREWS, J.C. Elder	1944
ANGEL, S.D.	1890
ARCHER, Russell Clifton	1933
ARMSTRONG, Jean Stewart	1979
ARNOTT, H.	1903
ASHE, W.E.	1899
ATHANASIADIS, Harris – MDiv	1989
*ATHANASIADIS, Nicolas (Nick) – MDiv	1990
AUSTEN, Frederick H.	1967
AVISON, Henry Reade Charles	1925
BAILLIE, John King	1880
BAIN, Carol – MDiv	1998
BALL, William John – MDiv	1991
BALLANTYNE, Robert Leith Tweadle	1894
BALMER, Derek	1973
BALSDON, Heather Lynne	1997
BANNERMAN, Gordon L.	1953
BANNERMAN, John R.	1981
BARBER, William M.	1966
BARKER, George Harvie – BD	1967
BARR, Alan Ferguson	1995
BARRON, Thomas John	1886
BAY, Kee W. – BD	1963
BAYNE, George Dunlop	1881
BAYNE, George T.	1881
BEAN, Everett H. – BD	1946
BEATON, J. MacLean	1909
BEATON, Laughlin	1898
BEATTIE. Walter T.	1910
BEAUCHAMP, Pierre E.	1895
BEGGS, Eric A. – BD	1969
BELL, Clifford Ritchie – BD	1929

BELL, John Wesley	1952
*BENNETT, Thomas	1870
BERDAN, Linda	1981
BETTRIDGE, Nancy A.	2002
*BIGELOW, Jesse Edmiston – BD	1940
BINGHAM, George Edward	1940
BISSET, Robert	1955
BLAKELEY, Malcolm	1880
BLAXLAND, Daphne Ann – MDiv	1991
BLOUIN, A.P.	1908
BODKIN, John A. – BD	1969
BOLINGBROKE, Harold – BD	1912
BONETTO, Richard Allen Ward	2009
BOONSTRA, Anthony (Tony)	1978
BOUCHARD, L.R.	1892
BOUCHARD, Theodore A.	1880
BOUCHER, Joseph E.	1913
BOUDREAU, Moses Frank	1877
BOUGHTON, George W.	1928
BOURGOIN, Jules	1889
BOURGOIN, S.H.	1905
BRANDT, E.H.	1896
BREMNER, W.B. – BD	1897
BRETZLAFF, Katherine – MDiv	2012
BRIARD, Everett J.	1954
BRIGHT, Alfred	1906
BROUILLETTE, Charles	1875
BROUILLETTE, Téléphore	1874
BROWN, A.V. – BD	1902
BROWN, Douglas George	1988
BROWN, James A.	1931
BROWN, Samuel Gorley	1911
BROWN, Samuel Mitchell	1940
BROWN, Walter George – BD	1902
BROWNLEE, Thomas Cornelius – MDiv	1982
BRUNEAU, Ismael P.	1882
BRUNEAU, Timothy David – MDiv	2004
BRUNTON, J.N.	1899
BRUSH, John C.	1957
BRYDEN, Jean Elizabeth – MDiv	1988
BUELL, Mark – MDiv	1993

BUNTAIN, Herbert MacLeod	1940
BURGESS, John	1921
BURGESS, Katherine Anne – MDiv	2009
BURKE, Michael Wayne	1988
BYRON, Moses B.	1899
CAMERON, Andrew – MDiv	2011
CAMERON, A.G.	1901
CAMERON, Daniel George	1883
CAMERON, George	1916
*CAMERON, James – BD	1874
CAMERON, John R. – BD	1956
*CAMPBELL, D.G. – BD	1946
CAMPBELL, David	1889
CAMPBELL, Donald Alexander	1938
CAMPELL, Donald L. – BD	1961
CAMPELL, Duncan John	1915
CAMPBELL, J.D.	1901
CAMPBELL, Malcolm Arthur	1909
CARNEGY, Charles	1936
CARRIÈRE, Samuel Anselme	1882
CARSON, Donald Garth	1978
CARTER, Robert P. – BD	1951
CARRUTHERS, Edward – MDiv	2010
CASSELMAN, Archie Boyd	1939
CATHCART, Joseph	1934
CAUBOUE, Anthony	1881
CAVENEY, Michael Frank	1984
CAYER, Paul Napoleom	1889
CHAMAS, Feras	2014
CHAN, John	1975
*CHANNON, Owen – BD	1947
CHARLES, G.	1891
CHARLES, J.E.	1894
CHATREAU, Delbert R. – BD	1969
CHAZEAUD, Camille A.	1921
CHENARD, Cynthia Jean – MDiv	1991
CHILDS, Bradley Roy	2010
CHO, Ki Sunn – BD	1955
CHOI, Sung-Chui – MDiv	1992
CHOLTUS, Guy Frédéric	1978
CHUDLEY, Reid Easton – MDiv	2004

CLARK, David Austen Robert – MDiv 2009
CLARK, Wylie C. – BD 1894
CLARKE, Christopher – MDiv 2014
CLARKE, James White 1923
CLARKE, Susan Victoria 2006
CLAY, William Leslie 1890
CLEAVER, Richard Charles 2004
CLELAND, J.A. 1897
*CLIFF, H. Welsford – BD 1909
CLOW, W.L. 1946
COBURN, D.N. – BD 1898
COCHRANE, John James 1874
COOK, W.A. 1890
COOPER, James W. – MDiv 1994
COPPIETERS, Joël Albert – MDiv 2012
CORBETT, Edward Annand 1912
CORDNER, Joseph – BD 1909
CORRY, Doreen Linda 1976
COTÉ, Joseph Emery 1889
COUSENS, Henry – BD 1924
COUSENS, John R. – BD 1958
COUSINEAU, Benoit Gilbert – MDiv 2005
COWAN, G.K. 1946
COWPER, Lawrence J. 1972
CRAIG, D.J. 1905
CRAIG, David T. – BD 1966
CRAIG, Douglas William – MDiv 1986
CRANSTON, W.T. 1909
CRAWFORD, Harry A. – BD 1963
CROMBIE, W.T.B. – BD 1899
CROZIER, H.G. 1899
CRUCHET, Alfred B. 1878
CRUCHON, C.F. 1902
CRUICKSHANK, Robert W. 1970
CUNNINGHAM, Robert F. 1967
CURDY, E. 1898
CURRIE, Alexander 1886
CURRIE. Dugald 1884
CURRIE, Maxwell Carleton 1952
DALZELL, Gardiner C. – BD 1954
DAVID, Romeo E. 1909

DAVIDSON, John R.H.	1970
*DAVIDSON, John W. – BD	1969
DAVIDSON, M.B.	1906
DAVIDSON, Ronald A. – BD	1967
*DAVIS, Harry Glen – BD	1963
de BRUIJN, Bertus – MDiv	1983
DeGIER VANDERSPEK, Joyce	2012
DETLOR, W. Lyall	1934
De VRIES, Roland – MDiv	2001
DELANEY, William L. – BD	1957
DELPORT, Dewald – MDiv	2006
DENNY, John O'Neill – BD	1943
DEWAR, David Angus	1980
DEWAR, D.L. – BD	1889
DEWAR, Edgar F.	1972
*DEY, W.J.	1875
DEZHBOD, Shahrzad	2014
DICKEY, James R. – BD	1967
DI GANGI, Mariano – BD	1949
DI GENOVA, Valentino.	1898
DOBIE, George Edgar – BD	1945
DOBSON, John R.	1891
DOEHRING, Carrie	1978
DOIG, Howard Andrew	1936
DONAHUE, Lee Stephen	1984
*DONOVAN, Deanna Lynne – MDiv	1989
DORAN, Gerald E. – BD	1954
DORAN, Maureen Rosemary	1986
DOUGLAS, Frederick Dixon	1934
DOUGLAS, James Ferguson – MDiv	1997
DOUGLAS, Robert James	1899
DOUGLAS, William A. – BD	1962
DRENNAN, Jacob M. – BD	1959
DRYSDALE, Andrew Wishart – BD	1911
DSERONIAN, H.	1897
DUCKETT, James – MDiv	2010
DUCKWORTH, Nelson Jack	2005
DUCLOS, John E.	1887
DUFFY, William F. – BD	1968
DUGUID, Barbara Ellen – MDiv	2009
DUGUID, C.	1903

*DUNCAN, Allan M. –BD	1957
DUNCAN, Gordon Ross	1911
DUNCAN, Graeme E. – BD	1962
DUNCAN, J.S. – BD	1910
DUNCAN, William Scott	1938
EADIE, Robert	1894
EARLS, Robert Keith	1931
EDMISTON, James J. – BD	1950
EENKHOORN, Johan Adriaan	1979
ELDER, David L.	1957
ELMHURST, J.R.	1898
EMERY, Scott Gilman – MDiv	1988
ERVINE, William Joseph Clydesdale	1980
*EWING, Christine Dorothy Wallace–MDiv	1986
EWING, Robert – MDiv	1987
FAIR, John Craig – MDiv	1995
FALCONER, Charles A.	1963
*FANTECHI, Giancarlo – MDiv	2007
FARADAY, Gordon	1944
FARRIS, Allan Peter – MDiv	2007
FAUROT, Jean Hiatt	1940
FAUSER, Gloria Geraldine	1986
FAWCETT, Melvin Grant	1979
FERGUSON, Hugh	1900
*FERGUSON, Roderick Alexander	1976
FERRIER, James Drader – MDiv	1985
FERRIER, Timothy Francis Stuart	2007
FILES, James W.	1961
*FILYK, Steven Arthur – MDiv	2006
FISCHER, Ronald D. – MDiv	2007
FINDLAY, James Slater – MDiv	1987
FINLAYSON, John A.	1974
FLECK, John	1935
FLETCHER, Gilbert Hyndman	1916
*FLETCHER, Jonathan McCullough – BD	1939
FOOTE, Charles Henry	1936
FOOTE, Ernest Gordon Blair	1936
FOOTE, James	1907
FOOTE, John Weir – BD	1934
FORBES, J.J.	1886
FORD, Victor M. – BD	1962

FORTIER, D. John P.	1960
FOSTER, Linda Jill – MDiv	2007
FOURNEY, Lloyd W. – BD	1969
FOWLER, Frederick Gordon – BD	1918
FRASER, Alexander Donald	1894
*FRASER, Daniel James	1893
*FRASER, Ian D. – MDiv	1982
FRASER, John A. – MDiv	1976
*FRASER, John Keir Geddie – BD	1891
FRASER, Marc William – MDiv	2009
FRASER, Murray Young	1938
FRASER, R. Douglas	1873
FREEMAN, James Morton	1938
FRESQUE, Gordon	1981
FRESQUE, Hubert	1916
FREW, Robert	1891
FRIOUD, Jacqueline – MDiv	1990
FRY, Douglas O.	1958
FULFORD, George Lloyd	1934
GALLOU, Goulven	1913
GAMBLE, Robert	1884
GARDNER, David	1919
GAVINO, Victor C. – MDiv	2009
GEDDES, W.H.	1883
GEMMELL, Thomas – BD	1963
GILLIES, Donald John	1934
GILLIES, Malcolm	1929
GILLIS, Raymond L.	1965
GILMOUR, F.W.	1897
*GILMOUR, George	1896
GIROULX, L.R.	1894
GLEN, Raymond E. – BD	1965
GOOD, Robert	1932
GORDON, John Simpson	1896
GORDON, J. Thom	1913
GOURLAY, J.J.L.	1895
GRACE, Byron Malcolm	1994
GRACE, Howard G.	1951
*GRAHAM, Angus A. – BD	1897
GRAHAM, D.J. – BD	1897
*GRAHAM, Elizabeth Angela – MDiv	1995

*GRAHAM, J.H.	1886
GRAHAM, John Joseph	1919
GRAHAM, Kelly Robert – MDiv	2003
GRAHAM, Murray M. – BD	1963
GRAHAM, Robert James	1984
GRANT, Andrew S. – BD	1888
GRANT, J.P.	1884
GRANT(MacDonald) Mary Anne – MDiv	2004
GRAY, L. Dale – MDiv	1998
GREENE, Jonathan	1957
GRIEG, J.G.	1902
GRIER. James	1920
*GROSJEAN, Georges F. – BD	1921
GROULX, A.B.	1887
GUERGIS, Karam	1920
GUTHRIE, Donald	1894
*HALL, Robert – BD	1924
HAMILTON, R.	1877
HANNA, R.M. – BD	1908
HANKINSON, Lawrence D.	1947
HAHN, Joseph – BD	1967
HARDWICK, John	1915
HARDY, Charles Allan – BD	1903
HARGRAVE, I.L.	1888
HART, Edward C. – BD	1957
HASTINGS, C.J.	1890
HATTIE, D.E.	1913
HAUGHTON, C.	1899
HAYWARD, David Richard	1988
HEATH, David Sidney – MDiv	1978
HENDERSON, Albert – BD	1961
HENDERSON, Amanda	2012
HENDERSON, Michael W.A. – MDiv	2002
HENDERSON, R.	1888
HENRY, Douglas Norman	1980
HENRY, J.K.	1881
HERMAN, John	1976
HERMAN, Shirley Jean	1979
*HERRIDGE, W.T.	1883
HEUSTIN, William Harold	1940
HIBBERT, Terence Paul	1978

HIGGINS, J.H.	1888
HILDEBRANDT, Henry Lawrence	1980
HILL, Robert (Bob)	1965
HINCKE, Karen (Provost)	1982
HO, Jonah (Chung Lok) – MDiv	1997
HOBMAN, J.G.	1900
HODGES, D.H.	1886
HOLLINGWORTH, W.D. Grant	1928
HONG, Wally (Won-Hong) – MDiv	1987
*HOOGSTEEN, Mark T. – MDiv	1997
HOPKINS, John Fletcher	1987
HOPKINS HENDERSON, Mabel Velma	1979
HOSKIN, R.H.	1871
HOSTETTER, B. David	1954
HOUSE, Kenneth William	1933
HOUSTON, Adam	1964
HOUTBY, Ruth – MDiv	1998
HOWARD, Geoffrey Peter – MDiv	1984
HOWAT, Alexander Guthrie	1911
HOWSON, James Donald Lochhead	1940
HUBERTS, Henry William	2003
HUGHES, Leo E.	1963
HUGHES, R.	1876
HUGHES, William James	1951
*HUNTER, W.A. – BD	1910
HUTCHINSON, Andrew Thomas G.	1988
HUTCHISON, D. – BD	1895
HUTCHISON, Francis	1928
*HUTCHISON, James W. – BD	1962
HUTTON, Thomas Stanley	1936
HWANG, Chia Sheng – BD	1964
HWANG, Timothy Elisha – MDiv	1997
HYDE, Richard	1882
INGLIS, Robert L.	1966
INGRAM, Terence David	1977
INTERNOSCIA, A.	1879
IARRERA, Alice Eda – MDiv	1983
IRELAND, George Drillio	1897
ISAAC, William J.O.	1947
ITESCU, Henry Hanan – MDiv	1996
JACK, Hugh	1929

JACK, Milton – BD	1905
JEANS, Charles J. St. Clair	1948
JACKSON, Peter	1920
JACKSON-BISSONNETTE, Coralie – MDiv	1987
JAMIESON, D.M.	1890
JAMIESON, J.S.	1908
JAMIESON, S.D.	1898
JAMIESON, W.J.	1890
JAOUNI, Gabriel Jawad	2002
JEANS, C.J. St. Clair	1948
JENVEY, Stephen Frederick – MDiv	2007
JOHNSON, D.C.	1873
JOHNSON, Ian Kenneth	1981
JOHNSON, Lois Cooke	1983
JOHNSON, Robert W.	1965
JOHNSON, William G. – MDiv	1981
JOHNSTON, Andrew J.R. – MDiv	1986
JOHNSTON, Grant	1982
JOHNSTON, John A. – BD	1954
*JOHNSTON, Robert	1889
JOHNSTON, William Grant	1982
JOLIAT, Henri	1905
JONES, Charles Sinclair	1916
JONES, James David – MDiv	1990
JONES, James Peter –BD	1960
JORDAN, Katherine Elaine – MDiv	1990
JUNG, Yeon-Ho – MDiv	2004
KAHUMBU, Charles Mutamba	2004
KALEM, H.T.	1890
KAM, Hye-Sook – MDiv	2001
KANDALAFT, Huda	2004
KANDALAFT, Samer	2008
KATCHIKIAN, Samuel – MDiv	2011
KAY, Andrew – BD	1916
*KEITH, Henry J. – BD	1904
*KEITH, Neil D. –BD	1898
KEIZER, (William) Stirling – MDiv	1987
KELLOCK, John M. – BD	1894
KEMP, Bruce	1981
KENDALL, Ralph – BD	1958
KENNEDY, Cecil Howard – BD	1933

KENNEDY, Duncan Scott – MDiv	1982
KENNEDY, Thomas Elmer	1918
KERR, David McMaster	1936
KERR, Samuel Howard – BD	1964
KERR, Samuel McMaster	1936
KIM, Caleb (Han Gyun) – MDiv	2007
KIM, Duk S. – BD	1961
KIM, Kwang-Oh – MDiv	1996
KIM, Philip (Hyeung-eun)	2010
KIPFER, Peggy	2008
KITT. W.A.	1902
KLEINSTEUBER, Wayne	2001
KNOTT, James – MDiv	2006
KNOWLES, W.E.	1899
KNOX, William Ernest	1955
KRAGLUND, Erik Wayne – MDiv	2013
KRUNYS, Derek George – MDiv	2005
KUNTZ, Harry – BD	1960
KUNZELMAN, Richard C.	1980
KURDYLA, Thomas	1982
KWONG, Johmann Kwok Fai – MDiv	1988
LAKER, Campbell Cameron – MDiv	1995
LAM-BASHA, Gwendolin (Siu-lai) – MDiv	2007
LAMOND, Harrison Livingston	1940
LAMONT, Thomas	1939
LANGLOIS, Gloria – MDiv	1992
LANGTON, J.F.	1888
LAPOINTE, Cleophas	1902
LARIVIÈRE, Henri Alfred	1916
LARKIN, Frederick Howe	1888
LAVERIE, J.H.	1902
LeBEL, Pierre	1910
LEE, A.	1884
LEE, H.S.	1902
LEE, Joshua Sung-Dae – MDiv	2010
LEES, Adam	1988
LEFÈBVRE, T.Z.	1885
LEFNESKI, David Charles	1991
LEFORT (SMITH), Anna – MDiv	2000
LEITCH, Hugh D.	1897
LEITCH, Malcolm L.	1885

LEITH, Magnus J.	1898
*LEMOINE, William Lorne. – BD	1950
LINDSAY, John	1896
LISCOMBE, Kevin – MDiv	1998
LISTER, John Donald	1952
LIVINGSTONE, Duncan	1924
LOCHEAD, A.W. – BD	1904
LODS, A.J.	1889
LOISELLE, H.O.	1887
*LOWERY, Basil – BD	1961
LUNDY, S.	1901
LUTTRELL, H.P.S.	1906
MA, JinPing – MDiv	2012
MacALISTER, J.M.	1872
MacCALLUM, Angus	1896
MacCUAIG, William Wilberforce	1897
MacCUSKER, Samuel F.	1890
MacDONALD, Alexander – BD	1962
MacDONALD, Alexander S. – BD	1955
MacDONALD, Andrew – MDiv	2011
MacDONALD, Charles A.	1956
MacDONALD, Darryl Claude – MDiv	1988
MACDONALD, Duncan Ross	1958
MacDONALD, Edwin Grant	1939
MacDONALD, Glenn Sidney	1977
MacDONALD, John Wilkes	1930
MacDONALD, Kevin – MDiv	2001
MACDONALD, Lloyd G.	1974
MacDONALD, Malcolm Norman	1926
MacDONALD, Peter – MDiv	2010
MACDOUGALL, John	1889
MacDOUGALL, John	1960
MacEACHERN, Norman A.	1910
MacFARLANE, A.H.	1880
MacFARLANE, J.A.	1888
MacGERRIGLE, J.A.	1897
MacGREGOR, A.	1892
MacGREGOR, A.	1897
*MacGREGOR, George – BD	1900
MacGREGOR, Hugh	1873
MacILRAITH, J.S.	1889

MacINTOSH, H. – BD	1897
MacINTYRE, J.	1873
*MacIVER, James Colin	1970
MacKAY, D.	1884
MacKAY, Donald W. – BD	1968
MACKAY, G.	1876
MacKAY, Hector	1900
MacKAY, John D.	1947
MacKAY, J.G.	1923
MACKAY, Murdo – MDiv	1993
MacKELVIE, George	1888
*MacKENZIE, A.D. – BD	1906
MacKENZIE, Angus W.R.	1929
MacKENZIE, E.A. – BD	1894
MacKENZIE, Francis Scott – BD	1916
MacKENZIE, J.	1876
*MacKENZIE, J.A. – BD	1912
MacKENZIE, J. Dugald	1905
MacKENZIE, Murdock	1889
MACKENZIE, Ralph E. – BD	1959
*MacKENZIE, R. Sheldon – BD	1958
*MacKENZIE, W.A.	1884
MacKERACHER, William M.	1897
MacKIBBIN, W.M.	1875
MacKILLOP, C.	1878
MacKINNON, Archibald Donald	1927
MacKINNON, Wallace	1941
MacKINNON, Lydia	2011
*MACKINTOSH, William – BD	1911
MacKNIGHT, R.	1885
MacLAREN, A.S.	1899
MacLAREN, Narcisse	1895
MacLEAN, Alison Osborne	1939
*MacLEAN, Angus Hector – BD	1923
MacLEAN, Charles	1880
MacLEAN, Charles Howe	1938
MacLEAN, C. Ian	1981
MacLEAN, Donald	1886
MacLEAN, G.C.	1901
MacLEAN, J.A.	1889
MacLEAN, John L.L. – BD	1959

MacLEAN, Kenneth	1916
MacLEAN, Randolph Douglas – BD	1941
*MacLEAN, Robert A.B. – BD	1959
MacLEAN, Robert Underwood	1937
MacLEAN, Samuel	1899
MacLEAN, William	1929
MacLELLAN, Archibald Donald	1936
MacLELLAN, D.D.	1872
*MacLELLAN, D.H.	1873
MacLENNAN, F.A.	1877
MacLELLAN, James D.	1932
*MacLELLAN, Kenneth – BD	1893
MacLELLAN, Malcolm	1888
MacLENNAN, William C. – BD	1969
MacLELLAN, William Lloyd – BD	1934
*MacLEOD, A.B. – BD	1903
MacLEOD, Brian Darryl – MDiv	2012
MacLEOD, Donald	1915
MacLEOD, Donald Edward	1975
MacLEOD, D.M.	1900
MacLEOD, F.	1873
MacLEOD, Gordon Clair	1972
MacLEOD, John – BD	1951
*MacLEOD, J.B. – BD	1902
MacLEOD, John Kenneth	1971
MacLEOD, John Rae	1878
MacLEOD, J.W.	1892
MacLEOD, M.J.	1889
MacLEOD, Norman A. – BD	1894
MacLEOD, Norman V.	1903
MacLEOD, Roderick	1939
MacMILLAN, Donald	1937
*MacMILLAN, Donald Neil – BD	1933
MacMILLAN, John Eldred	1948
MacMILLAN, William C. – BD	1909
MacMILLAN, Robert G.	1947
MacNAUGHTON, Lee M.	1953
*MacNEIL, John Cornelius – BD	1936
MacNEILL, Henry F.	1964
MACODRUM, Donald	1935
MacODRUM, Herbert A.	1947

MACODRUM, Murdoch Maxwell	1935
MACODRUM, William Boyd	1928
MacPHAIL, Kelly Carlyle	2003
MacQUARRIE, Kenneth Wayne – MDiv	2008
MacQUEEN, John Murdock – BD	1940
MacRAE, Murdock J.	1967
MacRURY, Hector – BD	1962
MacVICAR, Archibald	1895
MacVICAR, Donald – BD	1892
MacVICAR, J.H.	1889
MacWILLIAM, William Alexander	1916
MacWILLIAMS, Andrew C.	1888
MacWILLIAMS, Wendy – MDiv	2011
MacWILLIE, Gordon J. – BD	1957
*MAHAFFY, A. – BD	1895
MAHOOD, Denis H. – BD	1962
MARK, William J.	1933
MARKELL, Harold Keith	1941
MARSHALL. J.H.	1946
MARTIN, Alexander Denham	1912
*MARTIN, John Campbell	1888
MASON, Bonita (Bonnie) – MDiv	1998
MATHESON, Gael Irene	1983
MATHESON, Gordon J.	1964
MATHESON, J.	1878
MATHESON, James E.	1971
MATHESON, Peter	1903
MATHEWSON, Cornelius Kelley	1920
MATTINSON, Beth Marion	2005
MAWHINNEY, David Lawrence. – BD	1966
MAY, W.H.	1904
MAYNARD, J.	1894
McANDLESS, (William) Scott – MDiv	1992
McAVOY, James	1924
McBRIDE, John S. – BD	1944
McBRIDE, William Crozier	1947
McCALLUM, Robert	1912
McCARROLL, C.	1947
McCOLL, John	1911
McCONNELL, Wm. Fishbourne	1915
McCORD, Robert	1913

McCRAE, David Lamont	1879
McCUAIG, D.A.	1912
McCUAIG, Malcolm – BD	1961
McCULLOUGH, R.	1892
McCURLIE, John Meikelquham	1918
McDONALD, James G.	1944
McDONALD, Kenneth H.	1967
McDONALD, Ranald Somerled Walker	1987
*McGOUGAN, Edward – BD	1907
McGOWAN, James Archibald	1939
McGREGOR, Roy R. – BD	1963
McGURRIN, John	1979
McILROY, James	1908
McINNES, John Lewis – BD	1915
McINNES, John P.	1895
McINTYRE, Kerry James	1980
McKAGUE, Peter D. – BD	1962
McKEE, Irvine Ross	1945
*McKENZIE, Andrew Hugh – BD	1945
McKINNON, Warren K. – BD	1963
McLAGAN, Elizabeth (Betty)	1985
McLAREN, J.	1886
*McLAREN, J.F.	1880
McLENNAN, Mark Rodney	1978
McNABB, M.D.	1946
McNABB, Robert	1883
McNAUGHT, Thomas – BD	1917
McPHADDON, John Martin Hugh – MDiv	1990
McPHEE, A. Floyd M. – BD	1963
McPHEE, N.	1873
McPHERSON, Charles Edward – MDiv	1987
McRAE, Roderick Alexander	1922
McRAE, Donald	1875
McVEY, Robert Wilson	1913
McVITTIE, Thomas Johnstone	1915
MENANCON, J.E.	1898
MÉNARD, Moise	1893
MÉNARD, Wayne Lewis	1992
MENZIES, Scott	1981
MERILLEES, William	1912
MEWS, Donald C. – MDiv	2014

MEYER, Trudie – MDiv 1999
MILLAR, D.D. – BD 1899
MILLER, Frederick A. – BD 1956
MILLER, Jared – MDiv 2010
MILLS, Alexander – BD 1937
MILLS, Paul 1961
*MINGIE, George W. – BD 1905
MISSROON, James Benjamin – MDiv 1982
MITCHELL, Charles Lorne – BD 1936
MITCHELL, George S. – BD 1905
MITCHELL, John – BD 1881
MITCHELL, Thomas A. 1899
MOASE, Waldon B. 1972
MONTGOMERY, I. Adams 1909
MOORE, Donald S. – BD 1964
MORIN, Joseph L. 1885
MORISON, John Archibald 1891
MORISON, Wm. Ralph 1913
MORISON, W.T. 1895
*MORLEY, Frank Selkirk – BD 1935
MORRIS, J.J. Harrold – BD 1956
MORRISON, Alexander – BD 1961
MORRISON, Alexander J. 1953
MORRISON, Allister Evan 1941
MORRISON, Donald R. 1923
MORRISON, J.A. 1882
MORRISON, J.D. 1904
MORRISON, John P. – BD 1966
MORROW, J.D. 1904
MORTON, A.C. 1877
MORTON, James E. 1956
MOSLEY, Sybil – MDiv 2009
MOSS, William T.D. 1893
MOUSSEAU, G.C. 1882
MOWATT, Edward E. 1905
MOWATT, J.A. 1904
MUIR, Peter D. 1895
MUIR, Thomas. 1875
MULLINS, William 1870
MUNRO, Duncan 1935
MUNRO, Gustavus 1873

*MUNRO, J.R. – BD	1895
MURRAY, George	1931
MURRAY, H.T.	1897
MURRAY, Prescott	1930
MURRAY, Victoria Carolyn – MDiv	1995
MURRAY, Wallace J.	1965
NAIRN, James	1898
NAISMITH, James	1890
NELSON, Edwin G.	1967
NELSON, Todd Edward – MDiv	2014
NELSON, T.A.	1880
NICHOLS (Symington) Jo-Anne E. – MDiv	1990
NICHOLSON, Donald	1911
NICHOLSON, John C.	1908
NIMMO, Alexander	1929
NOCBAN, Jules – MDiv	1999
NUGENT, William Oliver	1937
OGILVIE, A.	1886
OLIVER, D.	1899
ORMISTON, Albert	1905
PAGE (van Gelder) Patricia Lynne	1984
PALMER, Florence Clarissa	1979
PAQUETTE, Linda – MDiv	1998
PARADIS, Misael R.	1875
PARK, Linda – MDiv	2001
PARKS, Winston Allan Montgomery – BD	1964
PARTRIDGE, Glendon Forrest	1938
PASMORE, Linda Elaine – MDiv	2004
PATTEMORE, Devon Lesley – MDiv	2003
PATERSON, N. Douglas – MDiv	2012
PATTERSON, James	1981
*PATTERSON, John Hall – BD	1934
PATTERSON, Thomas A.	1905
PATTERSON, William	1895
PAUL, Larry R. – BD	1963
PAULEY, Frederick	1959
PECK, Georges	1914
PELLETIER, E.D.	1879
PENFOLD, Telford E.	1974
PENMAN, John Westland	1879
PETTIGREW, Cedric C. – BD	1969

PETERS, David Ernest	2007
PHILPS, George M.	1966
PIDGEON, E. Leslie	1901
*PIDGEON, George C. – BD	1895
PLATFORD, Joye – MDiv	1999
POFF, John Garth – BD	1964
*POPE, Alexander McKean – BD	1920
PROCTOR, Samuel John – BD	1913
QUINN, Charles Wesley	1945
RAMSAROOP, Neil	1958
RAMSAY, Alison James	1972
RANES, James W. – BD	1954
*RATTRAY, Alexander Aitken – BD	1940
REES, Brian A.	1977
REEVES, Archibald C.	1894
REICHELT, Harvey J.	1974
REID, Andrew D.	1899
REID, Allan Stewart – BD	1904
REID, D.M.	1912
REID, James	1881
REID, J.T.	1900
REID. William Dunn – BD	1893
RENAULT, Leslie – BD	1956
REY, Jean S.	1899
RHODES, Joseph Bernard – BD	1942
*RITCHIE, Gordon – MDiv	1993
ROBERTS, Earle F.	1955
ROBERTS, Gwendolyn May	2004
ROBERTS, W.D.	1886
ROBERTSON, David C.	1970
ROBERTSON, J. Bruce	1960
ROBERTSON, James	1882
*ROBERTSON, John Campbell	1899
ROBERTSON, Norval	1946
ROBINSON, Linda Elaine	1990
ROBINSON, Robert Ritchie – MDiv	1989
ROCHEDIEU, Charles A.E.	1920
ROCHESTER, William M.	1890
RODNEY, Harry Scott – BD	1941
RONDEAU, A.G.	1900
*RONDEAU, Samuel	1887

RONDEAU, S.P.	1892
ROSS, A.R. – BD	1906
ROSS, P.R.	1880
ROSS, Walter	1906
ROTHNEY, W.O.	1901
ROWAT, Charles Andrew Ronald	1934
RUNDLE, Michael Charles Austen – MDiv	2009
RUSSEL, Andrew – BD	1893
RUSSELL, Walter	1889
RUSSELL, William Dawson.	1878
SADLER, T.A.	1896
St. AUBIN, Stanilas	1893
St. GERMAIN, Pacifique E.	1892
SAKASOV, Paul	2003
SAMPSON, Michael Glen – MDiv	2012
SAMPSON, Percy McKechnie	1925
SARCEN. Gerald E. Jr.	1970
SASS. Frederick W. – BD	1953
SAULTERS, Thomas	1986
*SAVAGE (MacDonald), Marilyn S. – MDiv	2002
SAVILLE, Gordon Charles	1979
SCALES. Austin Alexander – MDiv	1997
SCOTT, Andrew C. – MDiv	1993
SCOTT, D.J.	1898
SCOTT, Herbert Crawford	1939
SCOTT, Matthew Henry.	1879
SCOTT, Robert De Witt – BD	1920
SCRIMGER, J. Tudor	1899
SELF, Stanley – BD	1959
SEYLAZ, E.F.	1884
SHARKEY, Norman F.	1931
SHARKEY, Sidney James – BD	1936
SHARPE, Brian Bower – MDiv	1988
*SHAVER, Charles M. – BD	1956
SHAW, E.J.	1898
SHEARER, William	1880
SHEARER, W.K.	1885
SHEPHARD, Donald Malcolm	1994
SHERBINO, David Earl	1976
SHERBINO, Joel Aaron – MDiv	2003
SHORTEN, Barbara Jean – MDiv	1987

SIKKEMA, Henry John	2003
SIM, Robert Bruce – MDiv	1991
SIMMS, John Alwyn. – BD	1947
SIMONDS, Robert W. – BD	1959
SIMPSON, Hugh Lindsay	1937
SIMPSON, John Harry – MDiv	1989
SINCENNES, J.B.	1895
SINCLAIR, A.J.K.	1912
SINCLAIR, Henry	1871
SMITH, Carol Anne	1994
SMITH, David McLean – MDiv	1991
SMITH, E.F.M.	1896
SMITH, Earl Fenton	1947
SMITH, Gilbert A.	1881
SMITH, G.H.	1889
SMITH, John Angus	1940
SMITH, Leslie G.	1969
SMITH, R. Douglas	1909
SMITH, Sheina Balloch	1977
SMITH, Wayne Glenwood	1991
SMITH, Wilson Wylie	1910
SMYTH, William C.	1970
SNOOK, Wendy Lorraine – MDiv	1986
*STATHAM, Todd Regan – MDiv	2003
STEWART, C.C.	1869
STEWART, David Angus – MDiv	1996
STEWART, Donald	1902
STEWART, J.B.	1882
STEWART, John Clark	1896
STEWART, R.G.	1908
STEWART, Robert	1885
STEWART, Rupert G. – BD	1908
STEWART-PATTERSON, Alison	1977
STRANGE, Robert	1916
STUART, J.A.	1900
SULLIVAN, Howard Thomas – MDiv	1992
SURMAN, Stephen Thomas	1984
SUTHERLAND, Alexander David – MDiv	2006
SUTHERLAND, Andrew Donald	1926
SUTHERLAND, Angus	1921
*SUTHERLAND, Hugh Campbell – BD	1892

SUTHERLAND, William Smith	1938
SWAN, William	1919
SYME, Robert Alexander	1977
SYME, Ruth M.	1978
TANGUAY, G.B.	1897
TANNAHILL, George – BD	1960
TANNER, W.P.	1900
TAYLOR, Gordon R.	1936
TAYLOR, James	1895
TAYLOR, John Blaine – MDiv	1986
TAYLOR, Samuel John	1879
TAYLOR, William Scott – BD	1918
THOM, George W.	1901
THOMAS, William	1935
THOMPSON, Andrew – MDiv	2010
THOMPSON, N.E. Ted	1973
THOMPSON, Sarah Marie – MDiv	2011
THOMSON, G.J.A. – BD	1887
THOMSON, Wm. Kelman	1911
TOOMBS, Albert Earl	1936
TORRANCE, E.F.	1874
TOUCHETTE, W.F.	1904
TOWNSEND, J.A.	1881
TOWNSEND, Wm. McNeill	1896
TOWNSLEY, Charles	1958
*TOZER, Vernon Wesley – BD	1964
TREANOR, George Garfield	1914
TREBITSCH, I.T.	1902
TUCKER, W.L.	1906
TULLY, A.F.	1875
TURNBULL, Jill Marie – MDiv	2014
*TURNER, H.H. – BD	1901
TURNER, W.D.	1900
ULLEY, James Albert	1922
URQUHART, John J. – BD	1963
VAIS, George – BD	1961
van BRUCHEM, Arty Lee	1979
van BRUCHEM, Gerrit Arnoldus	1979
VAN DEN BERG, Arie (Jon) – MDiv	2012
VANDERKAMP, Luke	2008
van HARTINGSVELDT, Job – MDiv	1998

VESSOT, Charles H.	1891
VOO, Patrick Ben-Fu	2002
VAUDRY, John Pierce	1977
*VICTOR, (Donald) Ian	1979
VIDAL, Marc-Henri	1995
WADDELL, N. – BD	1887
WALKER, G.F.	1878
WALKER, Peter A.	1897
WALLACE, J.M. – BD	1898
WALLACE, W.E.	1888
WANG, Daniel (Zhi Kun) – MDiv	2011
WARDEN, David Scott – MDiv	1997
WATSON, Bradley John	2003
WATSON, M.	1886
WATSON, Thomas Johnstone – BD	1933
WATT, Robert	1874
WEATHERDON, Brian Ross – MDiv	1982
WEAVER, Stephen James – MDiv	1992
WEIR, George	1897
WELCH, Larry Allen	1977
WELLWOOD, J.M.	1873
WHEELER, J.A.	1900
WHILLANS, George	1885
WHILLANS, Robert	1872
WHITE, Edwin Jenkins	1934
WHITEWAY, John – BD	1960
WHYTE, Charles W.	1890
WILD, Kenneth Charles – MDiv	1989
WILLIAMS, Eugene B. – BD	1957
WILLIAMS, Glynis Ruth – MDiv	1988
WILLIAMS, Gordon E. – BD	1968
WILLIAMS, J.	1947
WILLIAMS, James Henry	1941
WILLIAMS, John W.	1950
WILLIAMSON, Alfred W. – BD	1959
*WILSON, Donald J. – BD	1953
WILSON, Douglas A.	1951
WILSON, Robert Hadley – MDiv	2009
WILSON, Robert James	1916
*WOLLAND, E.J. – BD	1915
WONG, Morgan T.S. – MDiv	1990

*WOOD, Louis A. – BD	1908
WOODBERRY, Frederick Milton – BD	1953
WOODSIDE, G.A.	1896
WOODSIDE, J.H..	1904
WOODSIDE, John W.	1907
WORTH, F.J.	1900
WRIGHT, Dennis Dean – MDiv	2006
WRIGHT, Ernest Arthur	1928
WRIGHT-MACKENZIE, Barbara A.	1995
*WÜBBENHORST, Karla – MDiv	1998
WYBER, James R. – BD	1964
WYNN, Bonnie – MDiv	1999
*YATES, Lawrence Edward – BD	1945
YEE, Mary Anne	1979
YOUNG, Alison Mary	1984
YOUNG, Arthur Clifford	1938
YOUNG, David Allan	1979
YOUNG, H. – BD	1898
YOUNG, S.B.A.	1898
YOUNGER-LEWIS, C.	1931
YULE, George	1901

*Calvin Gold Medalist – Presbyterian College's Highest Honour

Ad Eundem Gradum

BERRY, James Garrow – BD	1938
CAMPBELL, J.L. – BD	1900
CURRIE, John W. – BD	1910
DRUMM, Thomas Porter – BD	1935
DRYSDALE, Robert J. – BD	1909
FOOTE, W.R. – BD	1907
HILL, A.M. – BD	1901
LANG, David – BD	1906
MacIVOR, J.G. – BD	1901
MacLEOD, P.A. – BD	1900
MacMILLAN, Robert – BD	1907
McNAIR, John – BD	1903
SHARO, Samuel F. – BD	1911
SMITH, W.H. – BD	1901
SQUIRES, Charles William – BD	1923
STAVERT, R.H. – BD	1914
STEPHENS, J.G. – BD	1909
SWIFT, P.H. – BD	1889
WEDDERBURN, John Forbes – BD	1927
WEIR, S. – BD	1893

Doctors of Divinity

*ACKERMAN, The Rev. G., BD MD PhD, Buffalo, New York	1888
AIKENS, The Rev. E. Powell, BA BD MTh, Town of Mount Royal, Quebec	1970
ALLAN, The Rev. John F., UEL BA BD, Victoria, British Columbia	1988
ANDERSON, The Rev. J. D., BA, Beauharnois, Quebec	1932
ARMOUR, The Rev. J.S.S., BA BD STM, Montreal, Quebec	1985
BAIRD, The Rev. Frank, MA, Pictou, Nova Scotia	1927
BALLANTYNE, The Rev. R.L., MA, Riverview and Howick, Quebec	1926
BARCLAY, The Rev. W., MA BD, Hamilton, Ontario	1941
BEAN, The Rev. Everett H., BA BTh BD, Glace Bay, Nova Scotia	1972
*BEATTIE, The Rev. Professor F. R., MA BD PhD, Brantford, Ontario	1887
BEAUBIEN, The Rev. Irenée, SJ, Montreal Ecumenical Centre, Quebec	1970
BELL, The Very Rev. C. Ritchie, BA BD, Montreal, Quebec	1949
BELL, The Rev. Linda J., BA MDiv DMin, Elmira, Ontario	2012
*BELL, The Rev. Victor Clarence, MA, Strathfield, New South Wales, Australia	1936
BERLIS, The Rev. R. J., BA BD, Montreal, Quebec	1952
*BERRY, The Rev. James Garrow, MA BD, Martintown, Ontario	1938
BIGELOW, The Rev. Jesse E., BA BD STM, Edmonton, Alberta	1971
BLACK, The Rev. James S., Halifax, Nova Scotia	1896
BLACKBURN, The Rev. Malcolm Stewart, New Westminster	1959
BLAIR, The Rev. D. B., Barney's River, Nova Scotia	1890
BRANDT, The Rev. Principal E. H., BA, Montreal, Quebec	1915
BRIARD, The Rev. Everett J., BA, DMin, Toronto, Ontario	2000
BRYDEN, The Rev. Professor Walter Williamson, MA, Toronto, Ontario	1928
BUSCARLET, The Rev. Amarlic F., BD, Quebec	1911
CALDWELL, Miss Georgine, BA BSc MA ED, Sydney, Nova Scotia	1991
CAMERON, The Rev. Archibald Gardner, BA, Deseronto, Ontario	1934
CAMERON, The Rev. Daniel George, Swift Current, Saskatchewan	1930
CAMERON, The Rev. John Robert, BA BD, Charlottetown	1981
CAMPBELL, The Rev. D. Glenn, BA BD MTh, London, Ontario	1968
CAMPBELL, The Rev. Donald A., BA, Charlottetown, Prince Edward island	1966
CAMPBELL, The Rev. Malcolm A., Montreal, Quebec	1926
CAMP, The Rev. Professor Emidio, ThM DrTheol, Zurich, Switzerland	2009
CARNEGY, The Rev. Charles, Hamilton, Ontario	1958
CARTER, The Rev. Robert P., BA BD MRE, Agincourt, Ontario	1975
CHESTNUTT. The Rev. W.K., The Presbyterian Church in Ireland	1950
CHINIQUY, The Rev. Charles, Montreal, Quebec	1893
CLARK, The Rev. W. B., Quebec City, Quebec	1889
CLAY, The Rev. W. Leslie, BA, Victoria, British Columbia	1913
CONGRAM, The Rev. Charles N., BRE BA MDiv, Tecumseh, Ontario	2007

CORBETT, The Rev. Principal Donald J.M., BA LLB BD PhD, Toronto	1990
COUSENS, The Rev. Henry, BA BD, Brockville, Ontario	1950
CRABTREE, Mrs. Eleanor Knott, BHSc MA, Meaford, Ontario	2004
CRAISE, The Rev. Alexander, New Carlisle, Quebec	1936
CRIDGE, The Right Rev. Edward, Victoria, British Columbia	1895
CROMBIE, The Rev. John, MA, Smith's Falls, Ontario	1895
CRUICKSHANK, The Rev. Robert W., BA BD, Medicine Hat, Alberta	2003
CURRIE, The Rev. Dugald, BA BD, Perth. Ontario	1913
DALZELL, The Rev. Gardiner Carlyle, BA BD STM, Chatham, Ontario	1984
DAVIDSON, The Rev. Macfarlane Bell, MA, Galt, Ontario	1934
DAVIDSON, The Rev. Professor Richard, PhD, Toronto, Ontario	1914
DAVIS, The Rev. H. Glen, BA BD MTh, Agincourt, Ontario	2001
De SILVA, Mr. Danford (Dan), BA MA, Montreal, Quebec	2001
De Visme, The Rev. Principal Jean, Montmorency, Quebec	1918
DEWEY, The Rev. F. M., MA, Montreal, Quebec	1909
DICKEY, The Rev. James Ross, BA BD, Hamilton, Ontario	1998
*DICKIE, The Rev. Henry, MA, Woodstock, Ontario	1907
DICKIE, The Rev. R. W., BA, Montreal, Quebec	1914
DICKSON, The Rev. Principal Irene J., BA BEd AMM BD MTh, Toronto	1989
DOBIE, The Rev. George E., BA BD MTh, Ottawa, Ontario	1977
DOBSON, The Rev. John Robert, BA BD, Montreal, Quebec	1921
DOIG, The Rev. Howard A., Toronto, Ontario	1965
DONALD, The Rev. George Henry, MA, Montreal, Quebec	1927
DOUGLAS, The Rev. George Lee, BA STM MLS, Toronto, Ontario	1967
DOUGLAS, The Rev. R. J., BA, New Westminster, British Columbia	1926
DRYSDALE, Rev. Robert John, MA PhD, Montreal, Quebec	1935
DUNCAN, The Rev. Allan M., BA BD, Brockville, Ontario	1990
DUNCAN, The Rev. George, MA BD, Montreal, Quebec	1919
DUNCAN, The Rev. Graeme E., BComm BD, Brampton, Ontario	1997
FALCONER, The Rev. A., MA, Pictou, Nova Scotia	1899
FARADAY, The Rev. A. Gordon, CD, BA MA, Penticton, British Columbia	1977
FARRIS, The Rev. Professor Allan L., MA BD MTh, Toronto, Ontario	1973
FEILDING, The Rev. Professor Charles R., BA STD, Trinity College, Toronto	1967
FINDLAY, The Rev. Allan, Barrie, Ontario	1900
FLYNNE, The Rev. John, Sydney, Australia	1940
FOLSTER, The Rev. Stewart, Theol Ed Cert, Saskatoon, Saskatchewan	2015
FOOTE, The Rev. John Weir, VC BA BD LLD, Port Hope, Ontario	1949
FOOTE, The Rev. E. G. B., OBE BA, Chaplain of the Fleet, Ottawa, Ontario	1951
FOURNEY, The Rev. Lloyd W., BA BD, Edmonton, Alberta	1999
FRASER, The Rev. Thurlow, BA MA BD, Portage la Prairie, Manitoba	1911
FROST, Dean Stanley B., BD DPhil, Faculty of Divinity, McGill University	1967

GANDIER, The Rev. Principal Alfred, MA BD, Toronto, Ontario	1908
GILLIES, The Rev. W., Kingston, Jamaica	1898
GILMOUR, The Rev. Frederick William, BA, London, Ontario	1935
GLEN, The Rev. Principal J. Stanley, MA, PhD ThD, Toronto, Ontario	1955
GOOD, The Rev. Robert, Erskine Church, Ottawa, Ontario	1950
GRAHAM, The Rev. Professor Angus A., MA BD, Moose Jaw, Saskatchewan	1921
HALL, The Rev. Professor Douglas J., B.A. MDiv STM ThD DD, Montreal	1995
HARDWICK, Rev. John, Morrisburg, Ontario	1958
*HARVEY-JELLIE, The Rev. Professor W., MA DLitt, Montreal, Quebec	1929
HAY, The Rev. Principal James Charles, MA BD PhD, Toronto, Ontario	1980
HERRIDGE, The Rev. William T., MA BD, Ottawa, Ontario	1899
HIBBERT, The Rev. Terence, BA BTh MMin DMin, Coquitlam	2009
HILDEBRANDT, The Rev, Henry L., BA BTh, Kenora, Ontario	2013
HILL, The Rev. Allan Massie, MA PhD BD, Verdun, Quebec	1936
HOLLINGWORTH, The Rev. W. D. Grant, BA, Vancouver, British Columbia	1969
HOWARD, The Rev. Professor O.W., BA DD, Diocesan College, Montreal	1939
HUTCHISON, The Rev. Patrick H., MA, Huntingdon, Quebec	1906
HYNDMAN. The Rev. R.B., The Presbyterian Church USA	1950
INKSTER, The Rev. J.G., BA, Toronto, Ontario	1926
ISAAC, The Rev. William James Ogsten, Truro, Nova Scotia	1985
JACK, The Rev. Hugh, BA, Sydney, Nova Scotia	1956
*JAMIESON, The Rev. W. H., MA BD PhD, Blenheim, Ontario	1897
JEANS, The Rev. C. J. St. Clair, Saint John, New Brunswick	1948
JOHNSON, The Rev. Edward Hewlett, BSc BTh, Toronto, Ontario	1956
JOHNSTON, Principal Alexandra, BA MA PhD, Toronto, Ontario	1991
JOHNSTON, The Rev. Andrew J.R., BA BTh MDiv, Ottawa, Ontario	2007
JOHNSTON, The Rev. John A., MA BD PhD, Hamilton, Ontario	1980
*JOHNSTON, The Rev. Robert, BA MA BD, London, Ontario	1899
JOHNSTON, The Rev. Robert, MA, New Glasgow, Nova Scotia	1926
KALU, Professor Ogbu, BA(Hons) MA MDiv PhD, Nigeria	1997
KAO, The Rev. Chun-Ming, Taiwan	1973
KENDALL, The Rev. Ralph, BA BD, Westhill, Ontario	1992
KENNEDY, Miss Margaret, India	1978
KENT, The Rev. Professor H. A., MA BD, Halifax, Nova Scotia	1919
*KERSWILL, The Rev. Professor W. D., MA BD, Lincoln University	1902
KIM, The Rev. Duk Sung, BD, Korean Christian Church in Japan	1986
KOUWENBERG, The Rev. J. H. (Hans), BA MDiv MA DMin, Abbotsford	2005
LANE, The Rev. David James, BA, Clinton, Ontario	1961
LAWSON, The Rev. William, Windsor, Ontario	1975
LEATHEM, The Rev. William Harvey, MA, Ottawa, Ontario	1930
LEE, The Rev. Philip J., BSc STB, Saint John, New Brunswick	1987

LEGATE, The Rev. Robert Moorhead, BD, Charlottetown	1933
LLOYD, Mr. Hugh McDonald, Toronto, Ontario	1992
LOGAN-VENCTA, The Rev. J., OBE ED MA, Ottawa, Ontario	1953
LOWERY, The Rev. Basil, BA BD, Fredericton, New Brunswick	1991
LUZZI, TheRev. Professor Giovanni, Florence, Italy	1918
MacDONALD, The Rev. Daniel, Efate, The New Hebrides	1895
MacDONALD, The Rev. Donald C., BA, Simcoe, Ontario	1970
MACDONALD, The Rev. L. George, BA BTh, Halifax, Nova Scotia	2004
MACDONALD, The Rev. Professor Murdo Ewen, MA DD, Glasgow. Scotland	1965
MacDOUGALL, The Rev. R., MA, Florence, Italy	1892
MacEACHERN, The Rev. Norman Allan, MA, Toronto, Ontario	1937
MacIVER, The Rev. Iver D., Maxville, Ontario	1973
MACKAY, The Rev. A. B., Montreal. Quebec	1889
MacKAY, The Rev. A. Lorne, BA BD, Hamilton, Ontario	1962
MACKAY, The Rev. Donald B., BA ThB, Halifax, Nova Scotia	1969
MacKAY, The Rev. James, BD, London, Ontario	1931
MACKAY, The Rev. John, BA, Principal-elect, Westminster Hall, Vancouver	1908
MACKAY, The Rev. W. A., BA BD, Woodstock, Ontario	1893
MacKENZIE, The Rev. Murdoch, Changta Ho, China	1907
MACKENZIE, Principal Emeritus F. Scott, MA BD STM ThD DCL DD	1960
MacKENZIE, The Rev. W. A., MA BD, New York, New York	1900
MacKINNON, The Rev. Archibald Donald, BA, Little Narrows, Nova Scotia	1947
MacKINNON, The Rev. Wallace, BA, Ingleside, Ontario	1978
*MacLAREN, The Rev. James F., BD, Rocklyn, Ontario	1900
MacLEAN, The Rev. Allison Osborne, BA, Halifax, Nova Scotia	1976
MacLEAN, The Rev. Charles, Victoria, British Columbia	1958
MacLEAN, The Rev. J. B., BA BD, Huntingdon, Quebec	1923
MacLELLAN, The Rev. A. D., Iroquois, Ontario	1957
MacLELLAN, The Rev. W. Lloyd, BA BD, New Glasgow, Nova Scotia	1954
MacLELLAN, The Rev. George A., BA, Westmount, Quebec	1932
MacLELLAN, The Rev. Malcolm, BA BD	1915
MacLEOD. The Rev. Norman A., PhD, Brockville, Ontario	1932
*MacLEOD, The Rev. P. A., MA BD, Attwood, Ontario	1902
MacMILLAN, The Rev. Donald N., MA BD PhD, Montreal, Quebec	1979
MacMILLAN, The Rev. William C., BA, BD, Collingwood, Ontario	1939
MacMILLAN, The Reverend Robert G., Oakville, Ontario	1971
MacMILLAN, The Rev. Alexander, MA, Toronto, Ontario	1919
*MacNAIR, The Rev. John, BA BD, Oakville, Ontario	1903
MacODRUM, The Rev. Principal M.M., MA PhD, Carleton College, Ottawa	1953
MACPHERSON, The Rev. Angus Gordon, BD, Toronto, Ontario	1947
MacRAE, The Rev. Donald, Victoria, British Columbia	1911

MacRae, The Rev. Murdock J., BA BD, North Sydney, Nova Scotia	2011
MacTAVISH, The Rev. John, Inverness, Scotland	1887
MacVICAR, The Rev. John H., BA, New Glasgow, Nova Scotia	1909
MARTIN, The Rev. J. C., BA, Aintab, Turkey	1919
MATHESON, The Rev. Gordon J., BTh BRE, Charlottetown	1996
MAWHINNEY, D. Laurence, BA BD, Lunenburg, Nova Scotia	2013
McAFEE, The Rev. Thomas Wolseley, Regina, Saskatchewan	1947
McBRIDE, The Rev. John Samuel, BA BD, Summerside, Prince Edward Island	1974
McCONNELL, The Rev. William Fishbourne, BA, Paris, Ontario	1936
McCORD, President James Iley, DD ThD LLD LittD LHD, Princeton Seminary	1975
McCORKINDALE, The Rev. Thomas Bayley, MA, Levis, Quebec	1928
McDONALD, The Rev. A. D., BA, Seaforth, Ontario	1892
McDONALD, The Rev. Donald William, BA, Dublin Shore, Nova Scotia	1951
McDONALD, The Rev. William George Sydney, BA, Halifax, Nova Scotia	2015
McIVOR, The Rev. J. G., MA BD, Okotoks, Alberta	1908
McLEAN, The Rev. William, Winnipeg, Manitoba	1961
McLELLAND, The Rev. Professor Emeritus Joseph C., BA MA BD PhD DD	2007
McNAB, The Rev. John, MA BD DD STB, Toronto, Ontario	1959
McNEILL, The Rev. James, St. John's, Newfoundland	1940
McNEILL, The Rev. WilliamTownsend, MA, Fairville, New Brunswick	1929
McPHEE, The Rev. Floyd R., BA MPS MA MDiv DMin, Cape Breton	2002
MERRILEES, The Rev. William, Westport, Ontario	1952
METZGER, The Rev. Fred W., Vancouver, British Columbia	1997
MILLAR, The Rev. Robertson, Martintown, Ontario	1960
MILLER, The Rev. Frederick A., BA BD, Owen Sound, Ontario	1981
MOIR, Professor John Sargent, MA PhD, author "Enduring Witness"	1975
MONTGOMERY, The Rev. I.A., Montreal, Quebec	1926
MORISON, The Rev. J. Archibald, MA PhD, Saint John, New Brunswick	1907
MORLEY, The Rev. Frank Selkirk, BD PhD, Calgary, Alberta	1955
MORRISON, The Rev. D., MA, Owen Sound, Ontario	1890
MORRISON, The Rev. J. P. (Ian), BA BD, Toronto, Ontario	2006
MORRISON, The Rev. Allister Evan, Truro, Nova Scotia	1963
MOWATT, The Rev. Andrew J., Montreal, Quebec	1901
MUIR, The Rev. James B., MA, Huntingdon, Quebec	1893
MULLIGAN, The Rev. William Orr, MA BD LLB, Westmount, Quebec	1938
MUNRO, The Rev. Gustavus, MA, Ridgetown, Ontario	1901
MUNRO, The Rev. Hugh, BA, Cornwall, Ontario	1927
MURRAY, The Rev Prescott W., BA, Montreal West, Quebec	1960
MURRAY, The Rev. J. L., MA, Kincardine, Ontario	1898
NAISMITH, The Rev. Dr. James, BA MD MPE, Florence, Kentucky	1939
NEIL, The Rev. Donovan Gerald, BA BD ThM, Montreal, Quebec	1984

NICHOL, Mary, BScN, MPH, Smith's Falls, Ontario	2000
NIMMO, The Rev. Alexander, Wingham, Ontario	1957
NUGENT, The Rev. William Oliver, BA, Edmonton, Alberta	1961
OGAREKPE, The Very Rev. Mba, BA MA, Calabar, Nigeria	1989
OGILVIE, Professor Margaret, BA DPhil MA LLB FRSC, Ottawa, Ontario	1998
*OSBORN, The Rev. Professor Andrew R., BD, Edmonton, Alberta	1932
PARKER, Principal Nathaniel H. Parker, BSc ThD, McMaster Divinity College	1967
PATERSON, The Rev. D., MA, Quebec City, Quebec	1892
PATH, Pastor Titus, Tangoa, New Hebrides	1975
PATTERSON, The Rev. James, Montreal, Quebec	1915
PATTERSON, The Rev. William, BA, Westboro, Ontario	1938
*PIDGEON, The Rev. George C., BD, Toronto, Ontario	1905
POLLOCK, The Rev. John, Whitechurch, Ontario	1929
PORTEOUS, The Hon. George, MBE CM BA, Lt. Governor of Saskatchewan	1977
POTTER, The Rev. James George, MA, Outremont, Quebec	1929
POULAIN, The Rev. André, BA BD STM, of Montreal, Quebec	1962
PRADERVAND, Rev. Marcel, BA STM DD, Reformed Churches Alliance	1961
REID, The Rev. Allan Stewart, BA BD, Montreal, Quebec	1931
REID, The Rev. Professor W. Stanford, BD MA ThB ThM PhD LHD, Guelph	1979
REID, The Rev. William Dunn, BA BD, Westmount, Quebec	1920
RENAULT, The Rev. Leslie Reginald, BA BD, Hamilton, Ontario	1983
RENNIE, The Rev. Professor Ian S., BA MA PhD, Toronto, Ontario	1996
ROBERTS, The Rev. Earle F., BA, Toronto, Ontario	1982
ROBERTSON, The Rev. Alexander, Venice, Italy	1894
ROBERTSON, The Rev. J. Bruce, BA BCom BD STM, Westville, Nova Scotia	1993
ROBERTSON, The Rev. James, MA, of Winnipeg, Manitoba	1888
ROCHESTER, The Rev. W. M., BA, Toronto, Ontario	1914
RODNEY, The Rev. Harry Scott, BA BD, St. Thomas, Ontario	1963
ROOSE, The Rev. John Stephens, MA	1933
ROSS, The Rev. Alexander, The Free Church of Scotland	1950
ROSS, The Rev. Professor Donald, Kingston, Ontario	1889
SAENG, The Rev. Hwang Eui, Nagoya, Japan	2000
SCOBIE, The Rev. Professor Charles H.H., MA BD STM PhD, Sackville	1981
SCOTT, The Rev. John MacPherson, BA, Toronto, Ontario	1915
SCOTT, The Rev. Paul, BA BD, Pointe Claire, Quebec	1992
SHESHADRI, The Rev. Narayan, Poona, India	1886
SIMMS, The Rev. John A., BA BD, Montreal, Quebec	1972
SMITH, The Rev. David A., BA, Vancouver, BC	1954
*SMITH, The Rev. George H., MA BD PhD, St. Catherines, Ontario	1900
SMITH, The Rev. James Cromarty, MA, Eaglesham, Scotland	1929
SMITH, The Rev. James K., MA, Galt, Ontario	1887

SMITH, The Rev. Professor Neil Gregor, MA, Montreal, Quebec	1960
SMYTH, The Rev. Principal James, LLD, Montreal, Quebec	1923
STEWART, The Rev, Rupert Gregg, BD, Toronto, Ontario	1933
STEWART, The Rev. H. Douglas, BA, Ottawa, Ontario	1967
SUTHERLAND, The Rev. G., Sydney, New South Wales, Australia	1890
SUTHERLAND, The Rev. John Campbell, BA BD, Lancaster, Ontario	1920
SZABO, The Rev. Daniel, Miskolc, Hungary	2000
TAYLOR, Margaret Jean, BA, Belleville, Ontario	1983
THOMSON, The Rev. William MacCulloch, MA BD, Sydney, NS	1930
THOMSON, The Rev. E. Archibald, BA DD, Principal Clerk of Assembly	1975
TORRANCE, The Rev. Professor Thomas F., MA BD DTheol, Edinburgh	1950
TOZER, The Rev. Vernon W., BA MDiv, Listowel, Ontario	1994
*TUFFTS, The Rev. William M., BD MA, Stellarton, Nova Scotia	1901
VAIS, The Rev. George C., BA BD, Winnipeg, Manitoba	1987
WAGONER, Dean Walter D., BA BD ThM, San Francisco, California	1967
WARDEN, The Rev. R. H., Montreal, Quebec	1888
WATSON, The Rev. Thomas J., MA ThD, Fredericton, New Brunswick	1955
WATSON, The Rev. J. Ralph, BComm BA BD, Montreal, Quebec	1988
WATSON, The Rev. James, MA, Huntingdon, Quebec	1888
WEBSTER, Margaret, BA BEd MEd, Toronto, Ontario	1971
WEBSTER, The Rev. Norman L. D., BA, Brisbane, Australia	1953
WHALE, Mary, BA, Toronto, Ontario	1982
WHITE, The Rev. Edwin J., BA, Edmonton, Alberta	1954
WILKIE, The Rev. Principal J., MA, Indore, India	1901
WILLIAMS, The Rev. Glynis Ruth, BSc (Nursing) MDiv, Pointe Claire	2009
WILLIAMS, The Rev. James Henry, BA, Toronto, Ontario	1967
WILSON, The Rev. Douglas Alfred, BA, Collingwood, Ontario	1986
WOOD, The Rev. Clarence L., BA, BD, Alirajpur, India	1953
WRIGHT, The Rev. Ernest Arthur, Prince Rupert, British Columbia	1950
WRIGHT, The Rev. P., BD, Portage la Prairie, Manitoba	1898
ZIEGLER, Jesse H., MA BD PhD, American Theological Schools	1967

*By Examination

Faculty

Principals

The Reverend Donald Harvey MacVicar, DD LLD	1873–1901
The Reverend John Scrimger, MA DD	1904–1915
The Reverend Daniel James Fraser, MA BD STB DD LLD	1916–1929
The Very Reverend F. Scott MacKenzie, ThD DD DCL	1929–1945
The Reverend Robert Lennox, MA ThB PhD DD	1948–1969
The Reverend William J. Klempa, MA BD PhD DD	1978–1998
The Reverend John A. Vissers, BA MDiv ThM ThD DD	1999–2012
The Reverend Dale S. Woods, BA MDiv MCS DMin	2014–

Acting Principals

The Very Reverend C. Ritchie Bell, BA DD DCL	1969–1973
The Reverend Donald Neil MacMillan, MA PhD DD	1973–1978
Professor Frederik Wisse, Ing BA BD PhD	1998–1999

Systematic Theology

The Reverend Professor D.H. MacVicar, DD LLD
The Reverend Professor John Scrimger, MA DD
The Very Reverend Professor F. Scott MacKenzie, ThD DD DCL
The Reverend Professor Donald N. MacMillan MA PhD
The Reverend Professor William J. Klempa, MA BD PhD DD
The Reverend Professor John A, Vissers, BA MDiv ThM ThD DD

New Testament

The Reverend John Scrimger, MA DD
The Reverend Professor D.J. Fraser, MA BD STB DD
The Reverend Professor Richard E. Mumma, BD STM
The Reverend Professor James Barr, MA BD
The Reverend Professor Charles H.H. Scobie, MA BD PhD
Professor Frederik Wisse, Ing BA BD PhD

Old Testament

The Reverend Professor John Scrimger, MA DD
The Reverend Professor Alexander R. Gordon, MA DLitt
The Reverend Professor W. R. Harvey-Jellie, MA BD DésL DLitt DD
The Reverend Professor Robert Lennox, MA ThB PhD DD
Professor Robert C. Culley, MA BD PhD DD

Church History

The Reverend Professor John Campbell, MA DD
The Reverend Professor R.E. Welch, MA
The Reverend Professor A. Scott Pearson, BD ThD DLitt
The Reverend Professor Frank W. Beare, BA BD
The Reverend Professor H. Keith Markell, BA PhD DD

French Literature and Theology

The Reverend Professor Daniel Coussirat, BA DD OIP
The Reverend Professor Charles Bieler, DD OIP

Pastoral Theology

The Reverend Professor James Ross, MA BD
The Reverend Professor Ewan A. Mackenzie, BD
The Reverend Professor G.A. Johnston Ross, MA
The Reverend Professor Thomas Eakin, MA PhD
The Very Reverend Professor C. Ritchie Bell, BA DD DCL

Christian Education

The Reverend Professor Ernest M. Best, PhD

Philosophy of Religion and Christian Ethics

The Reverend Professor Joseph C. McLelland, MA BD PhD DD

Librarians of the College

Student Colin Campbell Stewart
M.H. Scott
Professor John Scrimger, DD
Professor E.A. Mackenzie, BA
Professor A.R. Gordon, DD
The Rev. J.A. Greenlees
Students Varia
Miss Priscilla Lee, BA BLS
Mrs. Margaret Macdonnell
Miss Bessie Fraser, BLS
The Rev. Neil G. Smith, MA BLS PhD
Mrs. Karen Prevost, BLS
The Rev. Daniel J. Shute, BA MDiv MLS PhD

Directors of Studies

The Reverend Thomas Gemmell, BA BD
The Reverend Geoffrey D. Johnston, BA BD MTh DTh
The Reverend W.J. Clyde Ervine, MTheol PhD
The Reverend Stephen A. Hayes, BA BD STM DD
The Reverend Roland De Vries, MDiv
The Reverend Dale S. Woods, BA MDiv MCS DMin
The Reverend D. Ian Victor, BA BTh MDiv DD

Montreal Institute of Ministry

The Reverend Arthur Van Seters, BA BD ThD

Chaplains

Huda Kandalaft, BA MACE Dip Min
Shuling Chen, BTh MSW PhD
Lucille Marr, BA MA PhD

Sessional Lecturers

From the very beginning, there were sessional lecturers in various disciplines. The first appointments, in 1867, were the Reverends William Gregg and William Aitken. Some lecturers subsequently became professors of the College; others were from the denominational colleges of McGill (1912–1925); and still others ministers of the presbytery and beyond. In 1969, when Presbyterian College became a full partner, McGill professors provided courses for the college diploma, as well as BTh and STM degrees. Under this arrangement, McGill professors who were Presbyterian were appointed to the faculty on the recommendation of the College. Professor Gerbern Oegema was particularly valuable. For the most part, the names listed below do not include McGill divinity professors, either before or after 1969, nor faculty members previously mentioned. Lecturers were required to wear various academic hats. I have picked the subject that they are most remembered for:

Civil Duties for Ministers

A. McGoun

Christian Ethics

Professor Arthur C. Cochrane
The Rev. George L. Douglas

The Rev. W.O. Mulligan
Professor Paul Ricoeur

Christian Missions

The Rev. Thurlow Fraser
The Rev. E.A. Johnson
The Rev. D. MacGillivray
The Rev. R. Malcolm Ransom

The Rev. J. McP Scott
Dr. Glenn Smith
The Rev. J.D. Wilkie

Congregational Management

The Rev. Malcolm A. Campbell

Comparative Religions

The Rev. James Barclay

Church Architecture

The Rev, Kenneth M. Glazier
Alexander C. Hutchison

D. Norman MacVicar
A.T. Taylor, FRIBA RCA

Church History

The Rev. R.D. Dickie
Professor William Alva Gifford
The Rev. D. Barry Mack

The Rev. A.B. Mackay
The Rev. J.B. MacLean
Professor J. Clark Murray

Church Music

H.E. Key
J. McLaren
Carman H. Milligan
Phillips Motley

Charles Hopkins Ould
S.P. Robins
Bryant Robinson
W.H. Smith

Church Polity

The Rev. Wardlaw Taylor

Church Worship

The Rev. W.R. Cruikshank
The Rev. A.M. Gordon
The Rev. A.G. MacDougall

The Rev. T.B. McCorkindale
The Rev. A.R. Osborn

Elocution

John Andrew
The Rev. A. Robert George
Walter V. Holt

Principal John P. Stephen
The Rev. Alison Stewart-Patterson

Exegetics

The Rev. John M. Gibson

Field Work

The Rev. Harry A. Crawford
The Rev. Clifton J. Mackay

The Rev. Paul Scott

French

Professor Bonet-Maury

The Rev. Leon Peyric

Gaelic Language and Literature

The Rev. Neil McNish

Greek

Dr. Williamson

Hebrew and Oriental Languages

Rabbi A.A. de Sola

The Rev. W. Harold Reid

Homiletics

The Rev. E. Powell Aiken
The Rev. A.B. Cruchet
The Rev. George H. Donald

The Rev. Robert Johnston
The Rev. I.A. Montgomery
The Rev. W.D. Reid

Hymnology

The Rev. Alexander MacMillan

Natural Science

Principal J. William Dawson

New Testament

Michèle Despland

Rev. J. Charles Hay

Old Testament

Rev. Richard Davidson

Systematics

The Rev. Roland De Vries
The Rev. George L. Douglas

The Rev. Richard R. Topping
The Rev. Karla Wűbbenhorst

Religious Education

Dr. Georgine Caldwell
The Rev. Roberta Clare
The Rev. Robert C. Carter
The Rev. Charles C. Cochrane

The Rev. A.M. Hill
The Rev. W.D. Kannawin
The Rev. A.R. Osborn
Dr. Albert Rudolph Uren

Founders

Principal William Dawson
The Rev. A.F. Kemp
Warden King
Joseph Mackay

The Rev. D.H. MacVicar
Laird Paton
John Redpath
George Rogers

Benefactors

Down through the years, The Presbyterian College, Montreal, has boasted generous friends. Many scholarships and bursaries given in memory of ministers and others have come and gone. There were the Nor' Wester and the Scotch Presbyterian scholarships. The longest-lasting (beside the Calvin Gold Medal) were the McCorkils. Some of the many benefactors of the College are listed below.

L.W. Anderson
Robert Anderson
The C. Ritchie Bell Memorial Fund
Robert J. Drysdale
Ernest G.B. and Alice Foote
E.B. Greenshields
Edward, Joseph and Hugh Mackay
Senator Robert Mackay
David Morrice and Family
Cornelia Parker MacMillan
H. Keith and Eileene Markell

John and Jane Redpath
Peter Redpath
Isabella Grace Reekie
William H. and Sarah M. Robert
Lord Mount Stephen
Stewart-Patterson Family
Baron Strathcona and Mount Royal
Hon. Justice Torrance
Hugh Watson
Senator Cairine Reay Wilson

Buildings

The old Erskine Church, Peel and St. Catherine Streets	October 2, 1867
The Presbyterian College, McTavish Street	October 28, 1873
Addition of David Morrice Hall	November 26, 1882
The Presbyterian College, University and Milton Streets	April 28, 1963
Dedication of C. Ritchie Bell Chapel	November 17, 1985
Rededication of Chapel/Tracker Organ	February 17, 1993

War Memorials

1914-1919

Those who gave their lives in the Great War

Stanley M. Anderson
James Cordner
Eric A. Ford
Robert W. Keir
Cluny J. Lightbody
John Mackay

Duncan W. MacKellar
Donald Maclean
Homer L. Matheson
Harold C. Shaver
Murray C. Sutherland

and in honour of those who served

Ernest C. McCullagh
John G. Copeland
Robert Hall
John A. Jess
Cornelius K. Mathewson
J. Leslie McNaughton
Leslie C. Burgess
Donald W. MacLeod
W.H. Bagg
William A. MacDonald
William F. McConnell
Andrew T. McIntyre
Giles H. Fletcher
Wallace R. Henry
George A. Sherman
Camille A. Chazeaud
Edward J. Jamieson
Alex. D. Ledingham
Clarence R. Kneeland

Henry Cousens
Thomas J. McVittie
John L. McInnis
W.L. Hicklin
Angus S. Sutherland
Peter A.G. Clark
James Grier
Thomas E. Kennedy
William S. Taylor
James McAvoy
Charles A.E. Rochedieu
Henri E. Bourgoin
George Robertson
W.J. Walker
Thomas G. Hutton
Angus H. McLean
Douglas Woodhouse
Malcolm MacLennan

1939-1945

In grateful memory of

Niall Hope Burnett   Ian MacKenzie

Students of this College who gave their lives in the Second World War. "They died that we might live" and in honour of all students and alumni who offered themselves in the same cause.

Student Societies

Over the years, there were many, including the Celtic Society, a Hockey Club and a Dining Room Society. The earliest were the Literary and Metaphysical Society (1867) and the Student Missionary Society (1869). The Presbyterian College Students Society came later. Nor must we forget *The Presbyterian College Journal* (1881-1908) and the Alma Mater Society 1879 (renamed the Alumni Association in 1891) which have done so much for the College down through the years.

Governance

To begin with there was a Senate, usually chaired by the principal or his appointee, and a Board of Management, which was also appointed by the General Assembly. In the 1970s, governance was by a single Senate, and today it is by a Board of Governors. Those who served over the years are too numerous to list. However, it is worth recording the office-bearers.

Known Chairmen of the Board

Mr. Justice Gregor Barclay
Alexander Bissett
J. Alex Cameron
George A. Campbell, KC
Ian M. Campbell
The Rev. Malcolm Campbell, DD
John M. Cerini, QC
Thomas M. Dick
George B. Fraser
Keith V. Gardner
Professor John Hughes
A. C. Hutchison
Fraser S. Keith
Ralph Loader
Ian G. MacDonald
Lawrence G. MacDougall, QC
W.F. MacKlaier, KC
Linda Mavriplis
P. McDougall
David Morrice (1877-1912)
The Rev. Marilyn Savage
The Rev. John Simms, DD
The Rev. William Taylor (1867)
The Rev. Marc-Henri Vidal

Known Secretaries of the Board

The Rev. Lawrence Cowper
Ina Cummings
Dan De Silva
Mary Louise De Silva
Rebecca De Vries
Cheryl Doxas
The Rev. John Duff
W. Kenneth Hall (1977-1984)
John R. McCallum (1952-1977)
David McGill (1936-1951)
The Rev. W.O. Mulligan
Professor D.A. Murray
The Rev. Alan S. Reid
Donald M. Rowat (1925-1933)
John Stirling (1867-1899)
James H. Whitelaw

Known Treasurers of the Board

C.H. Alves
Willard S. Bush (1967–1982)
The Rev. W. R. Cruikshank
T. Harold Cummings
Professor Robert Curnew
Howard Davidson
F.G. Donaldson
Wm. J. Hyde

H. Douglas Lightfoot
Ian G. MacDonald
Russell R. Merifield, QC
Judith R. Mowat, CA
G. MacL. Pitts
Elspeth Smart
Donald Walcot
The Rev. R.H. Warden (1870–1905)

Though not an office-bearer, Mr. Alex Duff was a particularly valued member of the Board, who should not be forgotten for all that he did for the College.

Accountants

Earl Mundy

Sandra Steadman

Known College Secretaries

Eleanor Paul
Dale Williams
Cathy Unger McInnis

Caroline O'Connor
Jeannette Vink

Known Building Superintendants

Mario Elvé
Peter Hillenaar
Mr. Millar

Arthur G. Palmer
Stephane Richard
Arthur Turner

Food

Rolf Schroeder

Lectureships

From the very beginning, the College sponsored public lectures by distinguished scholars. The earliest was a series on Natural Science given by Principal William Dawson LLD FRCS of McGill. There were the Robinson and more recently the Alison Stewart-Patterson Lectureships. During this sesquicentennial year the College is hosting the Sola Scriptura Lecture, October 30–31, with guest Edith Humphrey, William F. Orr Professor of New Testament, Pittsburgh Theological Seminary. The best known of these public lectures was named in honour of a generous patron of the College, L. W. Anderson. Previous to the Anderson Lectures, Fall Lectures were given by Professor George E. Homrighausen of Princeton and Professor Reinhold Niebuhr of Union Theological Seminary, New York City. The interest shown in hearing internationally known theologians prompted the following series:

L. W. Anderson Lecturers

1955: Professor Emeritus Halford E. Luccock, Yale University

1956: Professor Joseph Hromadka, University of Prague

1957: The Rev. Eugene Carson Blake, Clerk, Presbyterian Church USA

1958: None

1959: The Rev. David H.C. Read, Madison Avenue Church, NYC

1960: President Emeritus John A. Mackay, Princeton Theological Seminary

1961: President James I. McCord, Princeton Theological Seminary

1962: Professor Seward Hiltner, Princeton Theological Seminary

1962: Professor J. Pelikan, Chicago University

1963: Professor H.T. Kerr, Princeton Theological Seminary

1964: Professor James Smart, Union Theological Seminary, New York City

1965: None

1966: The Reverend Donald G. Miller, Pittsburgh Theological Seminary

1967: Centennial Lectures given by

    Professor Charles Fielding, Trinity College, Toronto

    Dean Stanley B. Frost, Faculty of Divinity, McGill University

    Dean Walter D. Wagoner, Theological Graduate Union, San Francisco, California

    Dr. Jesse Ziegler, American Association of Theological Schools

1968 and 1969: None

1970: Professor Eduard Schweizer, University of Zurich
1971: Professor Thomas F. Torrance, New College, Edinburgh
1972: Professor Paul Stuart D. Currie, Austin Seminary, Texas
1973: Professor Joseph Sittler, Bryn Mawr College, Pennsylvania
1974: Professor George S. Hendry, Princeton Theological Seminary
1975: Professor James Alvin Sanders, Union Theological Seminary, NYC
1976: President C. Ellis Nelson, Louisville Theological Seminary
1977: The Rev. Dr. Ernest T. Campbell, Riverside Church, NYC
1978: Professor Emeritus Paul S. Minear, Yale University
1979: President John Dillenberger, Hartford Seminary Foundation
1980: Professor Walter Brueggemann, Eden Theological Seminary
1981: Frederick Buechner, American novelist and theologian
1982: Professor Brian A. Gerrish, University of Chicago
1983: Professor Hendrikus Berkhof, University of Leiden
1984: Professor Ramsay Cook, York University, Toronto
1985: Professor Jan Milic Lochman, University of Basel
1986: *Combined with the Birks Lectures*: Professor Jane Dempsey Douglass, Princeton Theological Seminary; and Professor Fritz Buesser, University of Zurich
1987: None
1988: Professor R. E. Brown, Union Theological Seminary, NYC
1989: Professor Geoffrey Wainwright, Duke University, North Carolina
1990: None
1991: Professor George A. Lindbeck, Yale University
1992: Professor Alister McGrath, Oxford University
1997: Professor Richard H. Hays, Duke University Divinity School
2000: Professor Douglas John Hall, McGill University
2001: Professor Ellen Charry, Princeton Theological Seminary
2005: Professor Miroslav Volf, Yale Divinity Seminary
2013: Professor Mark A. Noll, University of Notre Dame
2015: Professor Edith M. Humphrey, Pittsburgh Theological Seminary

Presbyterian College of later years has carried on an ambitious Continuing Education Program, which has been of enormous benefit to its graduates. The lecturers are too numerous to list but their service to the college is not forgotten. Continuing Education has recently been expanded into the newly launched Leadership Centre, under the directorship of the Rev. Dr. Victor Gavino.

Note

The compiler of these lists is grateful to all who have assisted, principally librarian Dan Shute. Also helpful were Ms. Jeannette Vink, Mrs. Sandra Steadman, past principals John Vissers and William Klempa, Professor Emeritus J. C. McLelland, former board chairman, the Rev. John Simms, and many others. Every effort has been made to make these lists as accurate as possible but past minutes and present memories are imperfect. Any errors and omissions are lamented by the present scribe.

J. S. S. Armour

Spring 2015

Acknowledgments

THE UNDERTAKING OF A book such as this is an effort of many hands and voices. This book has benefitted from their recommendations, some broad, some minute, all essential.

We thank the experts who contributed to our book. Early discussions were valuable with Dale Woods, Don Walcot, William Klempa, Jason Zuidema, Barry Mack, Peter McNally, Torrance Kirby, Daphne Hart, for their ideas and suggestions.

At Presbyterian College, our thanks go to the administrative support: Jeannette Vink, Jillian Wood and to Principal Dale Woods.

We thank Christopher Lyons, Osler librarian, McGill University and Gordon Burr, McGill University Archives who helped in finding archival material and photographic images. The family of Alison Stewart-Patterson provided her image. We thank David Stewart-Patterson for the right to publish his poem about his mother. We thank Bloor Street United Church and Susan Jennings for access to the portrait of George Pidgeon. Bloor Street United Church permitted the reproduction of the Rev. Dr. George Pidgeon photograph for this publication. We thank Andrew Liszewski for his photography. Every effort has been made to trace the publisher of *The Indwelling Christ* for permission to reprint Pidgeon's sermon "The Word of the Cross"; if you have information regarding who to apply to for permission, please contact Wipf & Stock. Owen Egan and Eric Klinkhoff are thanked for the image of D. H. MacVicar at Presbyterian College. The images of Andrew Grant and C. Ritchie Bell are from Bob Anger of the Archives of the Presbyterian Church in Canada. The notes for "Athletics and Religion" by James Naismith were provided by the William L. Clements Library, University of Michigan. We thank the McCord Museum for image M994.35.2 of Jane Drummond 2nd wife of John Redpath 1815–1907 by Antoine Plamondon. Jenipher. I. R. MacKenzie provided permission for the use of the sermon on Ezekiel 37 from R. Sheldon MacKenzie, *The Master's Scriptures: Sermons from the Old Testament*, 2011. Libraries and Archives Canada provided both the image of the painting and the speech by Cairine Wilson from the Cairine R.

Wilson Fonds/Reel H2301/982-984. Crucially important in the research into W. G. Brown were personal communications with Andrew Billingsley, grandnephew of Brown, and Donald Grace, MD, grandson of Brown. We thank Aleksandr (Sacha) Sverzhinsky for his help with the image of W. G. Brown. The Archives of McGill University provided the image of William Dawson: William Notman / McGill University Archives, PR009076 with the assistance of Lori Podolsky. The image of John Weir Foote is provided by Tom Hamilton with credit to the Canadian Department of National Defence. We thank Jeffrey Monseau, College Archivist, and the Springfield College, Babson Library, Archives and Special Collections for the image of James Naismith. The book was enabled by the librarianship of Dr. Dan Shute of the Presbyterian College Library.

The publication of this book is possible with the financial support of several: the Presbyterian College, the St. Andrew's Society of Montreal, and others.

Finally, we thank the fifteen contributors of the foreword, preface, and chapters in our book. We are indebted to them for their ready willingness to tell the stories of those still voices that still speak to us about the 150 years of contribution of the Presbyterian College.

Rev. J. S. S. Armour

Judith Kashul

Principal Emeritus William Klempa

Dr. Lucille Marr

Dr. Dan Shute

Montreal, Spring 2015

Made in the USA
Charleston, SC
04 November 2015